ILYA
EHRENBURG

Picasso's portrait of Ilya Ehrenburg

ILYA EHRENBURG

Writing, Politics and the Art of Survival

Anatol Goldberg

With an Introduction, Postscript, and additional material
by Erik de Mauny

Weidenfeld and Nicolson
London

First published in Great Britain by
George Weidenfeld & Nicolson Limited
91 Clapham High Street London SW4 7TA

ISBN 0 297 78383 1

Typeset by Deltatype, Ellesmere Port
Printed in Great Britain by Butler & Tanner Ltd., Frome and London

CONTENTS

ACKNOWLEDGEMENTS

The six parts of Ehrenburg's memoirs, *People, Years, Life*, are the primary source for the principal events in his life, but they are not consecutive – the narrative jumps from one decade to another as memory dictates – and they are not conclusive, since the author remains silent, either for private reasons or because of official censorship, on a number of matters. To fill these gaps, Anatol Goldberg had access to various sources, but in the case of certain people who are still alive and living in the Soviet Union, I have followed his example and refrained from naming them.

For my own part, I owe a considerable debt of gratitude to a number of people who helped me in various ways in the task of revising and completing the original draft. First and foremost, my thanks go to Mrs Elsa Goldberg, for making available to me all her late husband's archives. For additional help in research, and for a number of valuable suggestions, I would like to thank Mr Barry Holland, Mr Alexander Lieven, Miss Mary Roberts, and Mr Hartmut Schneider.

ERIK DE MAUNY

INTRODUCTION

There are many ways of approaching the life and career of Ilya Ehrenburg. It was, after all, an exceptionally long and varied career, in which he was by turns youthful revolutionary, bohemian expatriate, poet, novelist, literary journalist, war correspondent, propagandist, memorialist, and unofficial ambassador for a regime which he intellectually accepted yet often emotionally despised: so that to arrive at a balanced assessment of the man and his achievements, as this biography sets out to do, would seem at first sight an almost impossible task. Yet no one was better qualified to undertake it than Anatol Goldberg, and in following Ehrenburg's improbable trajectory through the major convulsions of his time, through two world wars, the civil war in Spain, the rise and fall of the Fascist dictatorships, and the darkest hours of Stalin's Great Terror, he has also thrown much incidental light on the nature of Russian society, both before and after the Revolution.

If one says of Ehrenburg that he was by turns a Westerner and a Slavophile, and sometimes both simultaneously, this is undoubtedly true, but it by no means explains all the complexities of his character. He was also a Jew, and as he once put it, 'As long as there is a single anti-Semite left in the world, I shall proudly call myself a Jew.' He was born into a well-to-do Jewish family in Kiev in 1891 (his father was manager of a local brewery), but fairly soon afterwards the family moved to Moscow. Years later, he was to say that there were only two cities in which he really felt at home: Moscow and Paris. In Moscow, he became friends with one of the future leaders of the October Revolution, Nikolai Bukharin, and it was Bukharin who introduced him, while he was still a schoolboy, into a Bolshevik underground organization. His activities there led to his arrest and to some months of detention in Tsarist prisons. After his release, his father managed to get him a passport, and on the grounds of pursuing further studies, he was able to leave for the West.

Arriving in Paris, he immediately fell in love with it, plunged into the life of Bohemian cafés, began to write poetry, met other poets and artists such as Picasso, Soutine, Modigliani and Cocteau, and largely forgot his earlier revolutionary sentiments. They were revived, however, by what he saw of the First World War (he was particularly incensed by the condescending attitude adopted towards Russian troops in the West), and in 1917, following the abdication of the Tsar, he returned by a roundabout route to Russia, where he witnessed many of the horrors of the civil war. This was the start of a regular see-saw movement between East and West, including periods when he lived in Belgium, and later in Berlin. But he continued to regard Paris as his second home, and it was there that he became a regular foreign correspondent for Soviet newspapers. In 1932 – ironically just as Stalin was consolidating his personal dictatorship – he finally committed himself to the Soviet regime, and travelled extensively around the Soviet Union to observe the first Five-Year Plan in action. He was soon back in the West, however, and in 1936 he began to report on the civil war in Spain, where he remained for the next two and a half years. This kept him out of the Soviet Union for most of the period of the great purge trials (the war in Spain began on 18 July 1936, and the purge trials just a month later, on 18 August); although when he did return to Moscow briefly in 1937, he was deeply shaken by what was going on.

He was equally shaken to learn, in August 1939, of the conclusion of the Nazi–Soviet Pact. By then, he was back in Paris. In the following June, he had to witness the triumphal entry of German troops into his beloved adopted city; and shortly thereafter, he had the ignominious experience of travelling back to Moscow under German safe conduct. When Hitler launched his attack on the Soviet Union in June 1941, Ehrenburg therefore greeted it with relief. He had never much liked the Germans anyway, and he now embarked upon a sustained campaign of virulent anti-Nazi propaganda, visiting the various battle zones, pouring out a stream of daily articles (in which the recurring theme was 'Kill the Germans!'), earning the gratitude of Soviet soldiers at the front, and gaining a world-wide reputation as the foremost spokesman of Russia at war. This activity also earned Stalin's approval, and may partly account for Ehrenburg's survival several years later, when so many other members of the Soviet–Jewish intelligentsia perished in Stalin's postwar anti-cosmopolitan campaign.

In the early 1950s, Ehrenburg went through a period of almost complete subservience to the *Vozhd*, the Supreme Leader; and Stalin made full use of him as an eloquent advocate of the Soviet-inspired World Peace Movement. In that role, he continued to travel frequently abroad, and if he had misgivings, he kept them to himself. But when Stalin died in 1953, Ehrenburg not only realized that a radical change was at hand, but welcomed it; and in his novel *The Thaw*, he gave voice to some of the aspirations of the Soviet people as they gradually emerged from the shadow of the Stalin era. He continued his foreign travels throughout the fifties and sixties, but still found time to write his lengthy and immensely detailed memoirs under the title of *People, Years, Life*, and from the mid-fifties until his death in August 1967, he spoke out more and more openly in favour of a fundamental liberalization of Soviet society.

I have given here only the barest outline of a career which chronologically spanned both sides of the Russian Revolution, and topographically both sides of the Iron Curtain, but it seemed to me a necessary preamble to even a brief assessment of Ehrenburg's achievements. His life was one of constant movement, and often fraught with danger: apart from his early experience of Tsarist gaols, he was at various times expelled from France, and detained during his travels as a suspected foreign agent; and in 1947, at the height of Stalin's anti-Jewish campaign, he expected at any moment the fateful knock on the door that would signal his arrest. Indeed, it is difficult now to grasp the all-pervading atmosphere of fear and foreboding which gripped virtually every section of the Soviet intelligentsia at that time. Yet in spite of all these external pressures, Ehrenburg managed to pour out a flood of books, some sixty in all, including poetry, novels, plays, short stories, translations, and some thirty volumes of collected essays and newspaper articles, to say nothing of the six-part memoirs.

Inevitably, such a huge output was bound to be uneven in quality, and this is especially noticeable in the novels. At their best, they recall some of those brilliant polychrome posters produced during and just after the Revolution. At their worst, they are either woodenly propagandist or saccharinely sentimental. Among his contemporaries, there were certainly better novelists and poets.

On the other hand, Ehrenburg knew and understood the West far better than any of his contemporaries, and he was incomparably the most brilliant journalist of his time in the Soviet Union, with the born reporter's sharp eye for tell-tale detail. Let me cite just one example. In early 1935, *Izvestia* sent him to cover the Saar Plebiscite:

I arrived in Saarbrucken in the evening. Coloured lights glimmered through the fog. In the main street, the window of a big delicatessen was adorned with a swastika made of sausages; passers-by paused to look and exchanged enraptured smiles. At my hotel, the proprietress, a stout, apoplectic woman, shouted down the corridor: 'Don't forget – I am German!' Out in the street, loudspeakers were broadcasting martial music . . . I slept badly. During the night, shots rang out. I half-opened my door. The hotel boots was collecting shoes to be cleaned. 'They probably caught another traitor . . .' he said by way of explanation.

In any survey of Ehrenburg's voluminous output, certain works stand out as landmarks. The first among these is the satirical novel which he wrote in Belgium in 1921, entitled *Julio Jurenito*. The full title takes up a further six or seven lines, but that need not detain us here: a detailed analysis of the novel will be found in the following pages. The point I want to make is that it is a fireworks display of wild inventiveness, a ferocious orgy of wit and black humour, which has lost none of its corrosive bite over the years: and although Ehrenburg subsequently directed his satiric barbs at various aspects of modern civilization, he never quite rivalled it in any of his later works.

But the sheer destructive zest that animates *Julio Jurenito* raises an interesting question. Even while still in his adolescence, Ehrenburg made an existential choice: he was to be a European first and foremost, and so he would remain to the end of his life. This did not contradict his Russianness, since he felt that Russia's rightful place was firmly within the orbit of European culture. Nor did it spring solely from his early infatuation with the life of the Paris boulevards and cafés, although that obviously counted. At a deeper level, he was drawn to the whole European cultural tradition, and as a young man he assiduously made pilgrimage to a number of its venerable sites, monuments and holy places. Indeed, the extent to which he immersed himself in that tradition may be shown by the fact that at one point, under the influence of the French Catholic poet, Francis Jammes, he even toyed with the idea of joining the Benedictine Order! That impulse turned out to be short-lived, but his interest in religion persisted for some time afterwards, and a curious streak of what one can only call religiosity crops up unexpectedly in some of his later writings.

There was, however, another side to the coin. In the First World War, visiting various sectors of the Western Front as a correspondent, he watched with revulsion the spectacle of Europe tearing itself apart in the slaughter of the trenches. But what shocked him even more, on his return to France after the war, was to witness what seemed to him a hedonistic pursuit of pleasure, in which former war profiteers revelled, and in which everyone was bent only on forgetting the lessons of 1914–18. In short, wherever he looked, he seemed to detect signs of the apparently irreversible decadence of the West; and this must go some way to explaining his decision, from the early thirties onwards, to throw his weight behind the Soviet regime.

It is at this point that one should perhaps briefly examine his attitude towards Stalin. Like much else in Ehrenburg's life, this did not follow a consistent pattern, but was shot through with ambiguities. He first saw Stalin during one of his visits to Moscow in the mid-thirties. The occasion was a ceremonial meeting of Stakhanovite shock workers in the Great Hall of the Kremlin.

Suddenly, everyone stood up and began fiercely applauding: and out of a side door which I had not noticed came Stalin, followed by the members of the Politburo . . . The applause went on for a long time, perhaps ten or fifteen minutes. Stalin was also clapping. When the applause began to die down, someone shouted, 'Hurrah for the great Stalin!' and it all burst out once more. Finally, everyone sat down, and then a woman's voice, desperately shrill, rang out: 'Glory to Stalin!' So we all sprang to our feet and started clapping all over again.

By the time it ended my hands were sore. It was the first time I had seen Stalin and I could not take my eyes off him. I had seen hundreds of portraits of him, and I recognized his double-breasted tunic and moustache, but he was less tall than I had imagined. His hair was very black, and he had a low forehead, but his eyes were lively and expressive. At times, inclining his head slightly to right or left, he laughed softly; at others, he sat motionless, surveying the hall, but still with the same animated gleam in his eyes . . .

Returning home, I had a sense of uneasiness. Of course, I thought, Stalin is a great man, but he is a Communist and a Marxist: we talk of our new culture, but we resemble worshippers bowing down before some shaman . . . Then I caught myself up: I was probably reasoning like an intellectual. How many times had I heard that we intellectuals had got things wrong, that we did not understand the demands of our age!: 'highbrow', 'fellow-traveller', 'rotten liberal' . . . But what of those incomprehensible epithets: 'All-wise Leader', 'Genius of the Peoples', 'Beloved Father', 'Mighty Helmsman', 'World Transfigurer', 'Artificer of Happiness', 'Our Sun' . . . Yet still I managed to persuade myself that I did not understand the psychology of the masses, that I judged everything merely from an intellectual standpoint . . .

This dichotomy in Ehrenburg's view of Stalin persisted for the next two decades. Having been shocked by the signing of the Nazi–Soviet Pact, he was equally dismayed by Stalin's manifest unpreparedness when the German Armies launched their assault on the Soviet Union. But then, as the Soviet Armies regained control of the situation and the tide of battle gradually turned, he seems, like so many others, to have seen Stalin in an increasingly heroic light as the chief architect of victory; and this clearly paved the way towards that period I have already mentioned in the early fifties, when for a time he showed almost complete subservience to the all-powerful ruler in the Kremlin. He could hardly disregard the brutal repressions of the postwar years, however, and he did not profess to fathom the tortuous workings of Stalin's mind.

Why did Stalin spare Pasternak, who held himself aloof, and destroy Koltsov, who had faithfully carried out every task entrusted to him? Why did he wipe out Vavilov and spare Kapitsa? Why, having eliminated almost all of Litvinov's associates, did he not eliminate the obdurate Litvinov himself? For me, all this is a great enigma . . .

Nor could Ehrenburg turn a blind eye to the fate of his fellow Jews, so many of whom perished in Stalin's postwar anti-cosmopolitan campaign, although on his visits abroad, he – the arch-cosmopolitan – pretended to be in ignorance of what was happening. This was certainly the most dubious episode in his entire career, and one which is explored in some detail in the following chapters. On the other hand, despite an allegation published in an Israeli newspaper, there is no evidence to suggest that he personally played any part in the betrayal of other Jewish intellectuals. He could, of course, have spoken out against the wave of arrests and executions, in which case he would almost certainly have joined the victims: as it was, he chose to remain silent. As he put it much later in his memoirs: 'Yes, I knew about many crimes, but it was not in my power to stop them . . . Far more influential and better informed people than I were unable to stop them . . . Silence for me was not a cult but a curse . . .' In any case, on other occasions he showed no lack of courage, notably during the period of the so-called 'Doctors' Plot', when some twenty prominent Jewish intellectuals, including Ehrenburg, were asked to sign a document acknowledging the common guilt of all Soviet Jews for the 'Plot', and agreeing to make reparation by accepting voluntary exile in Kazakhstan. Ehrenburg alone refused to sign. Instead, he wrote a letter to Stalin, suggesting that such an action would damage Soviet prestige among Communist Parties abroad.[1] In the circumstances, it was an extraordinarily bold gesture, but it produced the desired result: the document was not published, and the mad scheme for the deportation of Jews to Kazakhstan was dropped. Stalin died a month later.

It was not the only occasion on which Ehrenburg showed cool audacity. In his last years, he frequently showed himself prepared to take issue with the official line. In 1966 he joined other Moscow intellectuals in signing a protest against the trial of the writers Sinyavsky and Daniel. On various occasions, he came to the defence of people in trouble, as in his letter to Alexei Adzhubei requesting the reinstatement of a girl student expelled from the Komsomol.[2] And if, at the end, his reputation was still not entirely free from the lurking wisps of earlier suspicion, this was no doubt due to the very fact that he had survived when so many others had perished. His own explanation of his survival hinged on the element of pure chance. As he put it: 'I lived in an epoch when man's fate resembled not a game of chess but a lottery.'

Ehrenburg spent some five years writing his last major work, *People, Years, Life*, which can perhaps best be described as a sustained effort to set the record straight. It is true that on some matters, he shows a certain reticence. He says, for example, that he is not going to talk about 'affairs of the heart' (although he does sometimes refer to them obliquely, as to his relationship with Liselotte Mehr in Stockholm in the last two decades of his life); and in the case of certain political relationships and encounters (as with Bukharin, or with Trotsky in Vienna), official censorship, even after all these years, compels him either to remain silent, or to restrict himself to the merest veiled allusion. Nevertheless, he does manage to say a great deal on a multitude of themes, including many I have not had time to touch on here – such as his vigorous defence of modern art, as opposed to so many drab products of socialist realism ('like fifth-rate coloured photographs in splendid frames'). Above all, for the younger generation of Soviet readers, he opened up undreamt-of horizons: and for that reason alone, *People, Years, Life*

[1] See Appendix 2.
[2] See Appendix 3.

remains a uniquely valuable document.

* * *

At the time of his death in March 1982, Anatol Goldberg had completed the first draft of this biography, on which he had been working for several years. In Moscow, where I spent two periods as the BBC's resident correspondent in the sixties and seventies, I was able to help him with one or two useful contacts, and I therefore had some idea of the broad plan of the work. I could also well understand why he was particularly drawn to Ehrenburg as a subject. After all, they both came from much the same background: the cultivated world of the Russian Jewish professional class. Both were brilliant journalists, and shared a lifelong preoccupation with the problems of East-West relations. Both, although from very different standpoints, had devoted a great deal of thought and study to the operation of the Soviet Communist system in all its manifestations. And there is one further point of resemblance that is perhaps worth mentioning: at various points in their careers, both were the targets for sharp criticism. It must be pointed out, however, that the present study is unfinished, since Goldberg makes only the most sketchy references to the last few years of Ehrenburg's life. These were marked chiefly by acrimonious disputes with various Soviet publishers and editors over the publication of the last two sections of the six-part memoirs, and the final nine-volume edition of his collected works; and there is perhaps not much else to say. For most of those last years, Ehrenburg lived in comparative seclusion in a small village outside Moscow.

Anatol Maximovich Goldberg was born in St Petersburg in 1910. Shortly after the Revolution, in 1918, his family left Petrograd, as it had by then become, and moved to Berlin, where Goldberg was educated, and where he acquired his remarkable command of modern languages, which included German, French, English and Spanish as well as Russian. He also studied architecture for a time, and through this combination of talents, he was able to make a first visit to Moscow in the early thirties, where he was employed as interpreter while the town mansion of a former wealthy sugar merchant was being reconstructed to house the British Embassy. In later years, he talked of this episode in his life with considerable nostalgia.

In the mid-thirties, following the advent of Hitler, Goldberg left

Germany and emigrated to Britain, and in 1939, a week before the outbreak of the Second World War, he joined the BBC. It was an association that was to last until his death, and one in which, following the setting up of the BBC Russian Service in 1946, he was to win great renown for his regular broadcasts to the Soviet Union, where he gained a vast audience. I can testify to that from my own experience. I remember once standing with him in the main Leningrad railway station when the station-master, a burly figure wearing much gold braid, marched up, pumped him vigorously by the hand, and exclaimed, 'Can this really be Anatol Maximovich Goldberg? I have listened to your broadcasts for many years past. It is an honour to meet you. I do not always agree with what you say, but I have always admired your way of saying it.'

The qualities that won Anatol Goldberg his reputation as a broadcaster – those of a humane and civilized man speaking with the voice of reason spiced with a gentle irony – are those which shine through this detailed study of one of the most remarkable figures to cross our troubled and ideologically divided age. I must, however, at this point enter a double *caveat*. I do not necessarily agree with all of Goldberg's conclusions, since it seems to me that, in retracing some of the more obscure phases in Ehrenburg's career, he is sometimes too ready to give him the benefit of the doubt. Secondly, although this biography is very fully documented, it cannot be regarded as a definitive work, since there are doubtless materials still locked away in the archives in Moscow which remain inaccessible to a Western researcher. For the rest, in revising Goldberg's draft, I have made stylistic changes where these seemed necessary. I have also filled in a few obvious gaps with additional material and provided a number of footnotes and appendices; but in every other respect, this portrait of Ehrenburg, warts and all, is entirely his.

Erik de Mauny
Val Gosse
Calvados
September 1983

CHAPTER I

In the late 1920s, a small group of Soviet writers paid a visit to Berlin. They were invited to appear on a public platform with several German writers, and to read excerpts from their works. As it happened, Ilya Ehrenburg was also in Berlin at that time, and he, too, was invited to take part.

The meeting had been organized by the Association of Foreign Students, and was nominally non-political. Of the Soviet group, I remember only the poetess Vera Inber, who recited some of her poems and read a few of her children's stories. Half the audience consisted of German intellectuals, Russian *émigrés*, and foreign students like myself. The other half were Soviet Embassy staff and Soviet Trade Mission officials, who were present in large numbers in Berlin at that period.

Ehrenburg was the last to come to the rostrum, and he began by making a short speech in French. A few people got up and headed for the exit doors. I thought they were leaving because of the late hour, but the exodus continued, and by the time Ehrenburg had finished his brief address, and had started reading, in Russian, a chapter from his new novel – on the French revolutionary Gracchus Babeuf – half the audience had walked out. It was the Soviet half.

I had read all his books, and was fascinated by the man, by his voice and his masterly delivery. I was too young and too diffident to approach him, but hoped that I would see him again before too long. As it turned out, I had to wait for more than twenty years. He came to London in 1950, at the time of the Korean War, as a propagandist for the World Peace Movement, a movement which was supposed to embrace all peace-loving people (even Prime Minister Attlee was welcome, as one of its public relations officials magnanimously remarked, although that magnanimity did not extend to the Yugoslavs, whom Stalin regarded as arch-enemies, and who therefore did not qualify as peace-lovers). By that time, Ehrenburg had become a prominent figure in the Movement, and no Soviet official would have dreamt of walking out while he was making a speech. I watched him at an indoor meeting, as he stood on the platform clutching a huge bouquet of flowers with which he had been presented, looking faintly ridiculous. On that occasion, he spoke in Russian, but all that emerged was a succession of clichés. After this had gone on for a few minutes, he stopped, and the remainder of his speech was read for him in an English translation, so that one no longer had even the pleasure of listening to his voice, powerful yet soft, and beautifully modulated.

A day or so later, the same thing happened at a rally in Trafalgar Square, except that the proceedings were enlivened by a dramatic thunderstorm, and by distant shouts from some hostile faction who were holding a rival meeting somewhere in the vicinity. As far as I was concerned, however, it was not Ehrenburg who stole the show, but that eccentric warrior, Colonel Vladimir Peniakov, alias 'Colonel Popski'. Formerly commander of the small mobile force known as 'Popski's Private Army' during the Second World War, he claimed that he still liked fighting, and had associated himself with the Peace Movement only because the advent of the atom bomb had spoiled the fun. As for Ehrenburg, a writer I had long admired and whose books I had read and reread, it saddened me to find that he had now become merely a bore.

Indeed, on that day I came to the conclusion that Ehrenburg was no longer Ehrenburg: but I was wrong. Before he left London, he gave a press conference. Speaking in French, he began by saying that, not being a government minister, he would not waste time by making a formal statement; but since many Western colleagues had expressed a desire to meet and talk with him, and since he could not see each of them separately, he had decided to hold a conference instead, and was ready to answer questions. It struck me then and there that there was probably no other Soviet writer who would have dared to address a gathering of non-Communist journalists as *confrères* at such a time. The Korean War had broken out only a short time before, and the Western journalists attending the conference were mainly in a pugnacious mood, so that it undeniably demanded a good deal of courage on Ehrenburg's part to face them. For two hours, he fought a valiant rearguard action, dodging some questions and parrying others with counter-questions, seeking refuge in half-truths and veiled ambiguities, but plainly trying not to tell outright lies. In the end, however, I suppose the pressure became too much for him, since he did, finally, commit himself to several statements that proved to be deliberate lies, one of which, at least, was totally unnecessary; but he carried it off with such utter conviction that, at the time, I believed him, and only discovered the truth from something he himself wrote much later.

Then, without warning, he suddenly made another remark: 'I am not going to claim that no stupid articles ever appear in my country – it is more difficult to get rid of idiots than of capitalists.' At the time, I did not know that he had already made the same remark on earlier trips abroad, and could hardly believe my ears. Had he suddenly gone mad? For, even although he had merely stated the obvious, he had said something unthinkable by Soviet standards, especially as this was in answer to a question about the so-called anti-cosmopolitan (i.e. anti-Jewish) campaign which had been launched on the orders of Stalin. Yet he had come out with it quite calmly and unequivocally – '*Il est plus difficile de se débarrasser des idiots que des capitalistes.*' There is an old saying: 'scratch a Russian and find a Tartar'. I realized then that if one scratched Ehrenburg, one could still find Ehrenburg!

I saw him for the last time in 1960. Stalin had died seven years earlier, and by then it was not difficult to find Soviet writers, even Soviet officials, who were prepared to admit that idiots could still survive under the Soviet system. Ehrenburg had come to London to take part in a round-table conference on East–West *détente*. It was a highly respectable affair, supported by a number of distinguished members of the British Labour Party, including two former ministers, Hugh Dalton and Philip Noel-Baker. Journalists had been invited to meet some of the participants at the House of Commons, and I managed to get a seat next to Ehrenburg. He had aged considerably, but had also visibly mellowed – a process presumably not unrelated to the disappearance of Stalin. He spoke only briefly, but went out of his way to pay tribute to the then Prime Minister, Harold Macmillan. Macmillan had been to Moscow the previous year for talks with Khrushchev, and had announced on his return that 'the atmosphere of ultimatums has been superseded by that of negotiations'.

One of the moving spirits behind the conference was Konni Zilliacus M P, at that time very much the *enfant terrible* of the Labour Party (he had been expelled from it as a dangerous crypto-Communist, but taken back into the fold after being branded by Stalin as an agent of the British Secret Service!), and it was Zilliacus who introduced me to Ehrenburg when the official part of the proceedings came to an end. Ehrenburg did not appear to be particularly pleased with this encounter. Perhaps he was simply being cautious. He may well have felt that people like me, who were broadcasting to Russia, were a potential threat to the delicate and immensely complex task of liberalization on which he was engaged at home. I tried to start a conversation, but it was not easy. I sensed that he did not want to get involved in an argument, and I had somehow to convey that I had no intention of provoking one. Eventually, something I said seemed to convince him that this was the last thing I had in mind, and we were able to have a frank talk about the state of Soviet art.

A month or so later, I was covering Khrushchev's visit to France, and ran into the Soviet writer, Boris Polevoi, in a Marseilles hotel. I offered him a brandy, and quite unexpectedly, this led him to talk about Ehrenburg. 'You have only to mention brandy in his presence,' said Polevoi, 'and he will hold forth for hours on the way they make cognac in France.' He spoke of Ehrenburg with genuine affection. 'In England,' he said, 'you used to curse him . . .' I opened my mouth to protest, and he quickly corrected himself. '*You* didn't, I know you didn't. But others did, and quite wrongly – he is a very, very good man.'

Before leaving, Polevoi told me that Ehrenburg was working on a book which I would find well worth reading. A few months later, the first instalments of Ehrenburg's memoirs began appearing, under the title *People, Years, Life*, in the magazine *Novy Mir*. It was his last book and his best work for nearly forty years – since the publication of his first novel, *Julio Jurenito*.[1]

---

[1] The full title is given on p. 54.

CHAPTER II

In *Julio Jurenito*, Ehrenburg, or rather the character who bears his name, recalls how at the age of eight, he once behaved so outrageously that he was locked up in a coal shed. In a fury, he tore off all his clothes and rolled about on the ground. When he was eventually released, the family cook, seeing him naked and black from head to foot with coal dust, assumed that he had finally turned into the devil incarnate. To round matters off, the young Ilya then tried to set fire to the house by dropping an oil lamp on the sitting room floor.

Julio Jurenito is not an autobiography: it is a fantasy with a sprinkling of autobiographical elements. Yet, according to Ehrenburg's memoirs, the story of his attempted arson is basically authentic, except that he did not try to start the conflagration with a stray oil lamp, but with a bottle of paraffin acquired especially for that purpose. By comparison, most of his other escapades seem almost innocuous, such as his attempt to run away from home at the age of ten in order to join in the Boer War, needless to say on the side of the Boers, to whose leader, Oom Kruger, he had written in advance to announce his intention. His pranks at the fashionable German spa of Ems presented a more serious problem. His mother, having been unwise enough to take him with her when she went to Ems for a cure, was soon informed by the authorities that she would have to leave if Ilya did not mend his ways. In the end, it was a tutor hired by his parents to coach him in mathematics who managed to curb his extravagant outbursts. It turned out that the tutor had hypnotic powers, and – at least according to Ehrenburg's own account – literally hypnotized him into behaving like a normal human being. When I first came upon his description of this curious episode, I was inclined to take it with a large grain of salt. It is, after all, widely assumed that hypnosis cannot be induced secretly, without the subject being aware of it. Yet the experience obviously left its mark on Ehrenburg, since he continued to hark back to it on various occasions. He first mentioned it in a brief autobiographical essay in the 1920s; he turned to it again ten years later in his novel, *A Book for Grown-Ups*, which combines fiction with autobiography; and finally, he referred to it yet again, this time in somewhat greater detail, in his memoirs.

Whatever the truth of the matter, Ehrenburg's mischief-making ceased, and as time went on, he settled into a thoroughly conventional pattern of behaviour; i.e., he did all the things that most other boys, brought up in a liberal bourgeois family, would do in Russia at that time. He read avidly, pondered deeply on the meaning of life, was bored with school, and hated the Tsarist regime. He took girls out for walks along the tree-lined Moscow boulevards – so different from those of Paris or Vienna – and told one companion, to whom he was particularly close, that love must inspire a hero to fight and die for freedom. It was a pleasant enough existence, bordering on the idyllic, although he probably did not realize it at the time.

Like many other boys of his age, he recognized no authority and had doubts about everything, and in this there was nothing unusual: those who had no doubts were regarded as philistines. But when the 1905 revolution broke out, and barricades were being erected in the streets of Moscow, Ehrenburg, who was not yet fifteen, quickly joined in helping to build them. He plainly did not mind exposing himself to danger, and indeed, throughout his life, he never lacked physical courage – much later, as a war correspondent, he detested remaining in the rear, and always tried to get as near to the front as possible.

The 1905 uprising was quickly put down by the authorities, whereupon Ehrenburg decided it was time to join an illegal revolutionary organization. 'Such was the spirit of the age,' he remarks modestly in his memoirs. But if this was, indeed, the spirit of the age, not every schoolboy observed it to the letter. Vladimir Mayakovsky, the future poet, was one who did, and was arrested for the first time at the tender age of fourteen. Ehrenburg managed to escape imprisonment for a further two years, and first saw the inside of a Russian gaol shortly after his seventeenth birthday. He had been expelled from school a few months earlier.

There was one episode in his childhood which left a lasting imprint on his mind, an episode which he later described in one of his novels. His father was the manager of a brewery. Visiting the brewery one day, Ehrenburg looked in on the workers' quarters, and was appalled by their general squalor. He also looked on with revulsion as workers poured paraffin over a captive rat, set it alight, and watched the animal writhing in agony. If people could sink to such cruel diversions, he reflected, then life must seem to them utterly hopeless; and this thought was much in his mind when he began to study the programmes of the various revolutionary groups, trying to decide which one he should join. In the end, he chose to join the Bolshevik faction of the Social Democrat Party, and became a member of its so-called 'military organization'. For two years, he duplicated and distributed leaflets, disseminated propaganda among the workers, and even (which was far more dangerous) among some of the soldiers, and began to write articles for an underground newspaper.

It would have been highly improbable if, at the age of sixteen, Ehrenburg could have done all this purely on his own initiative. Half a century later, in 1966, when his memoirs were being discussed at one of those regular conferences at which Soviet authors meet and talk about their work with their readers, he was pressed to be more explicit about the influences he had come under during that early revolutionary period. One questioner was particularly insistent. 'Has not the time come', he asked, 'to name a certain friend in the Bolshevik underground organization in Moscow who led you into revolutionary action?' To which Ehrenburg replied with mock indignation: 'You insult me! I have never considered that the time was not opportune to mention one of my best friends, Nikolai Ivanovich Bukharin,[1] by name. However, I do not decide what may be printed: I only write. It was not I who decided on certain omissions, but the publishing houses . . .'

It has to be remembered that Bukharin, Ehrenburg's senior by only three years, was then, and still remains today, a 'non-person' in the official Soviet view. In an autobiographical note, Bukharin himself once recalled that in the spring of 1907, he and Ehrenburg had

[1]Nikolai Ivanovich Bukharin (1888–1938) joined the Bolshevik Party in 1907 and later played a leading role in the October Revolution. He served for nearly twenty years on the Soviet Communist Party's Central Committee, and for ten years on the ruling Politburo. From 1917 to 1929 he was in charge of the Party newspaper, *Pravda*, and was editor of *Izvestia* from 1934 to 1937. A man of principle whose writings inspired a whole generation of Soviet youth, he was close to Lenin – despite occasional disagreements – and in his final 'Testament', Lenin referred to him as 'deservedly the favourite of the Party'. Nevertheless, at Stalin's instigation, he was arrested in 1937 on charges of 'crimes against the Party', and on the night of 15 March 1938, after a lengthy trial – the last of the great Moscow purge trials – he was executed.

jointly organized a strike in a Moscow wallpaper factory; and Ehrenburg had obviously included a tribute to Bukharin in the original version of his memoirs. It was scarcely his fault if the publisher had chosen to excise that particular passage.

Clandestine operations of the kind Ehrenburg engaged in between the two revolutions presupposed stern self-discipline and singleness of purpose. It was easy to be uncompromising politically, but less easy to resist certain temptations. Fortunately, there was no taboo on falling in love, provided one took this as seriously as one was supposed to take everything else in life; and when Ehrenburg fell in love, he did it in proper Russian fashion. In Soviet novels and plays, one still comes across certain key phrases which are exchanged between lovers and those about to fall in love: 'We must clarify our relationship', or 'We must verify our feelings.' Ehrenburg and the object of his affections, a girl with a Bolshevik brother and an anti-Semitic father, did just that: they exhaustively analysed their feelings for each other. It was all very solemn and touching, and they probably thoroughly enjoyed themselves – this was not something of which a young revolutionary need feel ashamed.

There were, however, other temptations of a more insidious nature, and reading fiction was one of them: a reprehensible pastime, considering there was so much other literature – on Party tactics, on the theory of surplus value, and similar topics – to be absorbed. Yet how could one fail to be enthralled by a writer like Knut Hamsun, the Norwegian author whose novels were then all the rage? They appeared in Russia as a free supplement to a weekly magazine founded by a publisher called Adolf Marx, to whom generations of Russian readers owe a debt of gratitude: his series of supplements, which continued after his death, played an enormous part in popularizing the works of countless writers, Russian and foreign. Hamsun's novels, in particular, had an extraordinary impact. A friend of mine, reminiscing about that period, once told me that her husband, who was a difficult man, had become so enraptured by Niels Nagel, the restless and enigmatic hero of Hamsun's *Mysteries*, that he kept murmuring ecstatically, 'I *am* Niels Nagel'. No wonder then that, in the struggle for Ehrenburg's soul, Marx the publisher scored a partial victory over his more illustrious namesake, Marx the prophet of Revolution. Ehrenburg succumbed. He read Hamsun's novels by night, with a sense of sinful self-indulgence, cursing his weakness, and no doubt feeling that he was betraying the cause; not because Hamsun was a reactionary and an anti-Semite of the most primitive kind (most readers rightly attached little significance to his anti-Jewish bias or did not even notice it), but because he was a romantic. A dedicated follower of Marx (Karl) was not supposed to waste his time on such frivolity.

In *A Book for Grown-Ups*, Ehrenburg relates how he and some of his friends were arrested after having been betrayed by a member of their group who had turned informer. Later, Ehrenburg settled accounts with him in a novel: the hero, having escaped from prison, meets the informer by accident, and pushes him off a cliff into a river. But fiction has always offered lavish opportunities for revenge. What happened in real life was somewhat more prosaic. Ehrenburg did apparently have a renewed encounter with his former betrayer. It took place in a café in Paris. The erstwhile informer was sitting at a nearby table. He and Ehrenburg merely stared at each other.

It was in any case obvious that, in plunging into clandestine activities while they were still students, Ehrenburg and his companions were constantly in danger of being arrested; and when that happened, it was their families who faced the unenviable task of obtaining their release. Ehrenburg himself spent altogether five months in three different places of detention, the last being a notorious prison where he was placed in solitary confinement. In the case of Mayakovsky, the court decided that, because he was still a minor, he should be committed to the care of his parents. But the security police were not at all happy with this decision, and Mayakovsky would almost certainly have been sent into exile in Siberia for three years if his mother had not gone to St Petersburg to plead with higher authorities on his behalf. She is said to have sympathized with her son's revolutionary activities. It is doubtful whether Ehrenburg's father showed a similar understanding, but he did his best, and eventually managed to send his son abroad.

It is not clear to this day by exactly what means the youthful Ehrenburg left Russia and travelled to Paris. Initially, he was released pending trial, and placed under surveillance. He was not allowed to stay in Moscow, however, and went to his birthplace, Kiev. But he was not allowed to stay there either, so he moved on to Poltava, then revisited Kiev illegally, and finally, in a state of total desperation, returned to Moscow where he asked the police to put him back in prison! To his surprise, he found this was no longer necessary. He was informed that his father had applied for permission to send him on a short visit abroad to receive medical treatment, and had deposited 500 roubles as surety. The fact that bail had been granted meant that Ehrenburg could now stay with his parents in Moscow, but it does not explain how he actually got abroad. In his published memoirs, there is no mention of what happened to his father's application, and one cannot help wondering why, writing about it half a century later, Ehrenburg should continue to be so secretive; unless, of course, he did write about it, and the censor, for some unfathomable reason, cut it out. In the published memoirs, all he says is that when the formal indictment was issued (it took the prosecutor eighteen months to draw it up!), it was placed on record that he should never have left the country, since, not unnaturally, people released on bail were forbidden to reside abroad.

His actual departure was plainly arranged in some haste, since he stayed in Moscow for only a few days. As for the journey itself, this presented no problem, since no visas were required for travelling through Germany or entering France, and as long as they were not found to be carrying a suitcase full of bombs (Ehrenburg's was full of his favourite books), foreigners could come and go as they pleased. It was also possible, of course, to have oneself smuggled across the frontier; and in *A Book for Grown-Ups*, Ehrenburg briefly describes how this was done, but the story is told by a fictional character, and did not stem from his personal experience.

Ehrenburg's mother was opposed to the whole idea of Paris from the start. She would have preferred her son to stay in Germany to complete his education. In the mind of a good Russian-Jewish mother at that time, Germany was associated with learning, America with making money, and France with the lure of the *femme fatale*. But she need not have worried. It was not some siren of the *demimonde*, but Paris herself that became the object of Ehrenburg's ardent devotion.

CHAPTER III

In the Oxford English Dictionary, among some four full columns of definitions, a mistress is variously described as 'a woman who has command over a man's heart', and as 'a woman, a goddess, or something personified as a woman ... having dominion over a person or regarded as a protecting or guiding influence'. In the eighteenth century, when the French word *maîtresse* had already become vulgarized, some German writers still used the term *Gebieterin*. In all these senses, Paris was Ehrenburg's mistress.

He made several attempts to explain the nature of his infatuation. He wrote on one occasion:

> I don't think Paris is more unhappy than other cities. I am inclined to think that it is, in fact, happier than they are. How many starving people are there in Berlin? How many homeless people does London contain? But Paris I love even for its unhappiness, which can be worth much more than a sense of well-being anywhere else. My Paris is full of grey and viscous houses. I love Paris because everything here is fiction. Everything is fiction in this city – except its smile. Paris has a strange smile: it is a barely noticeable smile, a casual smile. A beggar who has spent the night on a bench in the street wakes up, picks up a cigarette butt, inhales and smiles. The grey houses of Paris can smile just as unexpectedly, and it is for this that I love Paris.

He wrote a good deal more in the same vein, notably about the people of Paris who, as he put it, had lived through four revolutions and fallen 400 times in love, and were now almost immune to everything. 'Paris can be joyous in grief and mournful in joy,' he wrote, 'and all this simply amounts to saying: "I love Paris." '

Ehrenburg never felt a similar emotion for any other city. He disliked Berlin, although at one time, he tried to persuade himself that there was something attractive in its dull uniformity: 'Berlin would be a suitable capital for modern Europe.' As for London, he once told me he would not want to live there, not because he thought London was ugly – on the contrary, from an aesthetic point of view he liked it well enough – but because he felt happy only in the South.

Leningrad was one of the most beautiful cities in the world, yet he had never grown fond of it, and in Russia he felt most at ease in Odessa.

These judgements need not be contested, but in themselves they do little to explain his love of Paris. For Paris is not exactly the South, even although, when he first arrived there, he was struck by the tender green of the grass in the Luxembourg Gardens, and felt hot and uncomfortable in his heavy Russian winter coat. Later, he did visit the South, and spoke of his 'beloved Italy'. But that was a different kind of love. Italy was 'a paradise and a classroom' – the country in which European culture revealed itself to him in all its magnificence. His love for Italy was serene. Paris, on the other hand, was no paradise, but a very hard school. Paris he loved fiercely and gently, rationally and irrationally. At times, he also hated it; but that kind of hatred does not banish love.

The mistress commanded, and he obeyed. He began to write verse, and ceased to be a revolutionary. Paris was the capital of Bohemia, and he became a Bohemian. Paris was the meeting place for people from a hundred different countries, and he became a cosmopolitan.

This was not at all the way he had originally planned it. His intention had been to join the other Bolsheviks in exile, to stay for a year, and then go back to Russia to resume his clandestine activities. Soon after he arrived in Paris, he had a meeting with Lenin, who invited him to his home and listened to him attentively (Lenin was always a good listener), but that seems to have been the only proper conversation they ever had, although Ehrenburg occasionally saw him again at meetings. Working in the revolutionary underground in Moscow had been in some ways like living in a monastic cell. But life among the Russian exiles in Paris was more like living in a ghetto, as is usually the case with political refugees. Only those who emigrate for good adapt to their new surroundings, while those who hope to return home resist acclimatization and suffer from a nostalgia which becomes the more acute the longer they stay. Ehrenburg was certainly not spared the pangs of nostalgia, and wrote a poem in which he voiced his yearning for the pine trees of Verzhbolovo, the railway station marking the frontier between Russia and the West. Indeed, at one point he grew so homesick that he sounded out the Russian authorities as to whether they would allow him to return, even if that meant spending a year or two in prison, only to be informed that, if he did come back, he would be sentenced to 'permanent exile' in some remote spot.

He did make one break with Paris. In July 1909, after he had been in the French capital only seven months, he journeyed to the fashionable German spa of Kissingen, to join his mother and sisters. He makes no mention of it in his memoirs, but a collection of his poems which appeared in the Soviet Union after his death contains a photograph of the family reunion. The photograph shows an elderly lady and three younger ones dressed in full Edwardian splendour, while Ehrenburg himself, in Panama hat, dark suit, buttonhole, and even sporting a small moustache, looks the epitome of bourgeois respectability, very unlike the shabbily-attired Bohemian he was to become after a further two years in Paris.

As it turned out, he did not remain in the Paris *émigré* ghetto for very long. But breaking out of it proved to be a painful experience. At first he dutifully attended political meetings, listened to debates, and met everybody who was anybody among the Russian political exiles. But then, to his dismay, he found that he was beginning to get bored. In Moscow, his underground work had involved considerable risk. In Paris, everyone indulged in orgies of speculation, but the absence of danger, the ability to talk freely without fear of arrest, merely seemed to underline the fact that it was, after all, only talk, entirely divorced from any prospect of action; and as a result, Ehrenburg felt irritated and disappointed. Yet he might still have surmounted his sense of disillusionment had it not been for Paris. It was Paris that lured him away from the ghetto into Paris proper and into the world.

Once again, he cursed himself for his weakness. But this time, his dilemma stemmed from something far more serious than his furtive reading of the novels of Knut Hamsun. A novice troubled by doubts turns to his confessor. Ehrenburg seems to have spoken of his predicament to a number of people associated with the revolutionary cause; and in a mood of revulsion from mere empty talk, he once more toyed with the idea of returning to Russia. He was dissuaded by a member of Lenin's entourage, who may well have felt that if Ehrenburg were lost to the Revolution, the Revolution could bear the loss, and who advised him to stay in France and to go on writing poetry: the Party, he said, needed such people as well. Finally, someone suggested he should go to Vienna, where he might be able to make himself useful smuggling political literature into Russia. Ehrenburg acquiesced, and set out for Vienna in the hope that, by plunging into an active role there, he might be able to resolve his doubts. These were, indeed, finally resolved, but not in the way he had expected: he left the Party.

When Ehrenburg began writing his memoirs, he confided to a friend that he had decided to tell all, because he had nothing to lose. It was only later that he realized this was impossible. There were certain things the censors would never pass, and since he could not write freely, he had to ensure that what he said should not be open to misinterpretation by Soviet readers. For this reason, he found it particularly difficult to describe what had happened in Vienna. When his memoirs first started appearing in *Novy Mir*, all the reader could gather was that he had left Vienna 'utterly devastated', as he put it, adding that he would give the full details at a later date. I remember thinking at the time that, given the problem of censorship, this seemed highly improbable. Yet he did take up the story again some three years later, more or less out of context, when the last instalment of his reminiscences appeared in *Novy Mir*, and he returned to it yet again, in slightly greater detail, when his memoirs were published as part of a collected, or rather selected, nine-volume edition of his works. In its full form, here is his account:

In Vienna, I stayed with a prominent Social Democrat, X. I have not named him because I fear that the superficial impressions of an immature youth might appear to have been coloured by later events. The work I had to do was not difficult. My task was to paste copies of the Party newspaper into cardboard rolls, then wrap the rolls in artistic reproductions, and send them off to Russia. X and his wife lived in a small, very modest apartment. One evening, X's wife told me she was unable to make tea: to light the gas in the tiny kitchen, one had to put a coin into the slot of an automatic meter. I rushed over and slid a coin into the monster's jaws.

X was kind to me, and when he heard that I was writing verse, he talked to me in the evenings about poetry and art. The opinions he voiced were not something one could argue about, but judgements that brooked no appeal. I had to listen to verdicts of a similar kind a quarter of a century later, at the First Congress of Soviet Writers. But by then, in 1934, I was forty-three, and had had time to see and understand certain things. In 1909, I was only eighteen, and did not yet know how to analyse historic events, or how to make oneself comfortable in the dock, where I was to spend nearly all my life. X regarded the poets I cherished as 'decadent', as 'products of political reaction'. He spoke of art as if it were something of secondary importance, something subsidiary. One day, I felt I could not stay there a moment longer. I did not dare say anything to X, but simply left him a silly, childish note, and went back to Paris.

At the readers' conference, already referred to in Chapter 11, at which Ehrenburg was questioned about Bukharin, he was also asked about X. Who was the 'friend', one questioner wanted to know, whom he had seen in Vienna, and who was the cause of his leaving the Party? To which Ehrenburg replied that, here, the position was reversed: the editors and publishers who had prevented him from naming Bukharin would have been only too delighted if he had revealed the identity of the mysterious X. 'However I consider it tactless, and even immoral to do so,' Ehrenburg declared, 'since my remarks concerning that incident in Vienna could be interpreted as assertions prompted by the subsequent activities of this individual and the fate that befell him.'

The 'prominent Social Democrat' with whom Ehrenburg had stayed in Vienna was Trotsky. But Ehrenburg deliberately concealed that fact. He did not want the public to think that he had criticized Trotsky in order to give pleasure to the Soviet Establishment, or that he was associating himself with the official Soviet view. While Trotsky was living in Vienna in the early 1900s, he published a paper called *Pravda*, usually now referred to as the *Viennese Pravda*, to distinguish it from its present-day namesake, which at that time did not yet exist. It was, in fact, Trotsky's own paper, not the Party's, but in referring to it as a 'Party newspaper', Ehrenburg may have wished to give his readers a clue: Trotsky was not at that period a member of either of the rival Bolshevik or Menshevik factions, but was advocating Party unity, which explains why Ehrenburg referred to his host simply as a 'Social Democrat', a term he would not normally use. Unlike Lenin, who was an attentive listener, Trotsky was prone to lecture, and in Vienna he wrote a great deal about art. He treated the subject seriously, but fiercely attacked what he called 'aesthetic nihilism', mysticism, and the 'decadent trend'. Later, in the 1920s, he adopted a much more tolerant attitude than he had shown in his conversations with the youthful Ehrenburg, arguing that literature was not a field in which the Party should lay down the law. But he continued to speak scathingly of the so-called 'decadent' poets, those whom Ehrenburg so much admired and whom he continued to defend vigorously half a century later.

For Ehrenburg, it had been a depressing experience. But it was only natural that he should rebel against authority. Something of what he felt at that time can be deduced from an article published in America in the mid-fifties by the Russian *émigré* writer, Roman Gul.

It is true that Gul is a biased witness. In the 1920s, he had been quite attached to Ehrenburg; thirty years later, this seems to have turned into intense dislike. Nevertheless, the incidental information he provides does shed some light on the behaviour of Ehrenburg as a young man who, in spite of the fact that he had already spent some time in prison, was still by no means mature. In his memoirs, Ehrenburg admits that when he first heard Lenin speak at a meeting, he produced an arrogant question, to which Lenin gave a soft answer; but adds that when he later went to see Lenin, he quickly abandoned his arrogant attitude. Yet, according to Roman Gul, Ehrenburg not only attacked but even abused Lenin in a short-lived rag which he managed to produce in Paris. In its pages he called Lenin 'a senior janitor', described the publication of one of Lenin's pamphlets as 'a premature birth', and declared sardonically that it taught one 'how to become a philosopher in seven months'.

Clearly, one should not exaggerate the importance of such youthful and rather ill-tempered outbursts. But the fact remains that Ehrenburg never rejoined the Communist Party.

CHAPTER IV

Before Ehrenburg set off for Vienna, Paris and poetry had almost engulfed him. On his return, he allowed them to engulf him completely. He spent his time at a celebrated café in Montparnasse, the Closerie des Lilas, where one could sit for hours over a cup of coffee, reading, or writing verse, or observing the French poets who gathered there every Tuesday. (Two decades later, it became Ernest Hemingway's favourite haunt in Paris, but by then it had considerably changed.) It was the kind of freedom that was bound to appeal to a nineteen-year-old aspiring poet, who was avid to absorb knowledge from every possible source. Very soon, however, Ehrenburg began to search for a new faith; and strange though it may seem, having escaped from the bondage of a political party which demanded complete, almost monastic dedication, he nearly exchanged it for a real cloister: he decided to become a Benedictine monk.

He had become a Bolshevik on perceiving how much evil there was in the world. Now, he was no longer a Bolshevik, but he found himself still tormented by the eternal question: 'Where does the root of evil lie?' In Vienna, Trotsky had made him feel that socialism was not compatible with poetry. Now, he began looking for a faith that was. He had been translating French and Spanish medieval verse into Russian. He had travelled to Italy and to Bruges, where he had learned to appreciate the great masters of the Renaissance. Paintings of the Madonna, of knights and courtiers, captured his imagination, and it seemed to him that here, at last, was a world in which ethics and beauty formed a single whole: Catholicism. He wrote a poem in praise of Pope Innocent VI, whom he portrayed clad in black velvet robes adorned with gold lace, a Pope who had been feared by princes; and yet, as Ehrenburg put it, 'it was not with the Roman sceptre but with the frail Madonna that his life had been so inextricably linked'.

That Ehrenburg should have set out on his road to Damascus from a Bohemian café was not in itself incongruous. Bohemia, as distinct from the Party, or for that matter, the Church, was a tolerant institution: it had no rules, written or unwritten. Another eminent Paris Bohemian, the poet Max Jacob, who was Jewish by origin, had become a devout Catholic, and when he was baptized and received into the Church, he had asked Picasso to be his sponsor and godfather. True, on that occasion, the old Bohemian slumbering in Max Jacob played an impish trick: he did not tell the priest that Picasso was living with a divorced woman.

It was another French poet, Francis Jammes, who aroused in Ehrenburg the urge to become a Catholic. Ehrenburg says he was attracted to Jammes because his faith was gentle and simple, because Jammes loved nature, and wanted the small donkeys of his native Pyrenees to accompany him into Paradise.[1] Since Ehrenburg was never inhibited in approaching anyone he wanted to meet, he got in touch with Jammes and went to see him at his home near the Spanish frontier. Much later, in his memoirs, he is clearly anxious to give the impression that his meeting with Jammes proved to be something of a disappointment. He quotes a few lines from a poem he wrote at the time about the cosy atmosphere in Jammes's study where they sat and talked, but claims that, while Jammes struck him as a kindly old man, he failed to impress him as a spiritual mentor. Yet there is another section of the same poem, written as an introduction to a small volume of lyrics which Ehrenburg dedicated to Jammes, but which he failed to mention in his memoirs, which does not bear this out: 'If my soul has not been destroyed in Paris, I owe that to you, Jammes, and I thank you for it. My soul still dares not name the One to Whom it turns. But you who have found in prayer the joy of an ever-running brook, say a short prayer for me, and ask that I, too, shall be able to pray.'

From the account Ehrenburg gives of this episode in his memoirs, one would hardly gather that he ever came near to being converted. He does say, in a passing sentence, that 'for a brief period', he was 'attracted by Jammes's philosophy'; which, to the uninitiated reader, provides only the flimsiest of clues. His reticence is perhaps understandable, when one considers all the other problems he had over the publication of his memoirs in the 1960s. But even in a short autobiographical sketch which he wrote in the 1920s, he chose to gloss over the matter. On that occasion, he did record that he was

[1]Francis Jammes: 'Prière pour aller au Paradis avec les ânes', in *Le Deuil des Primavères*, Mercure de France, 1901.

planning to join the Benedictine Order, but quickly added that he had no wish to dwell on the subject. At roughly the same time, the Russian critic Viktor Shklovsky described Ehrenburg as 'a former Jewish Catholic'. And among the semi-autobiographical elements in the novel *Julio Jurenito*, there is a passage which describes how all preparations had been made for Ilya to become a monk, until, at the last moment, he took fright and ran away.

At the very least, the fact that he even contemplated such a conversion is fairly remarkable, and shows how difficult he found it to live without faith; and although his active interest in Catholicism did not last, he continued to show the impact of his experience. This emerges very clearly after his return to Moscow after eight years in the West in 1917. He was struggling to grasp the significance of the Revolution. But instead of dealing with the harsh reality around him, he chose to write a play in the manner of Paul Claudel, called *The Golden Heart*. Its theme is sin committed out of pity and redeemed by a miracle, and it is full of genuine compassion, although the Church would probably not have approved of it. In later years, Ehrenburg pronounced some harsh judgements on the established churches, and poured withering scorn on those who served their church badly. But he understood the meaning of religion, and cherished the beauty and wisdom of its symbols. In one of his most revealing poems, he even chose a simile from the Gospel of St John, and compared himself to Doubting Thomas. In general, as can be seen from a conversation he had not long before his death with the Canadian scholar Paul Austin, he divided the human race into two kinds: those who had been created in God's image, and those who, as he put it, were called 'men' merely because they walked on two legs.

There is one brief mention in *Julio Jurenito* of the reason why he renounced his decision to become a monk. According to that source, it was the vision of a buxom wench bending down to plant leeks in a prelate's vegetable garden, and he certainly makes it sound as if her curved buttocks were truly irresistible. But *Julio Jurenito* is, of course, a satire, and the semi-fictional narrator called Ehrenburg is portrayed as a total cynic. In reality, there was a more romantic reason behind the decision of the author not to join the Benedictines. He fell in love.

He had often been in love before. But this time it was different, and even led to a *de facto* marriage. The girl's name was Yekaterina Schmidt – Katya for short – she was of German origin and came from

St Petersburg (there were many such families in the former Russian capital who had been resident there for generations), she had been sent to Paris to continue her studies, and Ehrenburg appeared to worship her. A daughter was born to them in 1911, and, having become a father at the age of twenty, he commemorated the event in a poem:

> O Lord, Thou has left Thy lamb in my care,
> unskilful though I am.
> What shall I do? Shall I have strength enough?

He may or may not have intended it, but 'unskilful' turned out to be the operative word; in short, he soon found himself incapable of handling the situation. Both he and Katya were receiving regular monthly allowances from their families and could have led a settled, orderly life. But Ehrenburg insisted on pursuing his Bohemian existence, whereas Katya was a much more conventional person, and refused to follow in his footsteps. After a time, she left him and married someone else. Ehrenburg's daughter, Irina, did however follow her father's example, and eventually became a writer herself.

It was while he and Katya were still together that he had his first volume of verse printed in Paris at his own expense. His poems were all written in Russian, and he sent copies of the book to various people in Russia, eliciting a favourable comment from one of the most erudite of modern Russian poets, Valery Bryusov. It was also in 1911, the year his daughter was born, that he received his first fee for a poem which appeared in a St Petersburg magazine, and as time went on, he had other poems published in various Russian magazines.

At about the same period, he abandoned the Closerie des Lilas in favour of the Rotonde, which had become the centre of international Bohemia. The Rotonde was 'so unlike an ivory tower', as he put it, and from then on it became his spiritual home. It was there that he met Picasso and Soutine, Modigliani and Diego Rivera, Guillaume Apollinaire and Jean Cocteau, and many others whose work now forms part of the European cultural heritage. They were all rebels against the established order, but each rebelled in his own fashion. In that heady and turbulent atmosphere, new challenges were arising, new forms of art were being created, and Ehrenburg was fortunate enough to witness the beginnings of the great experiment which was later to be known loosely under the title of 'abstract art'. (It is worth noting, however, that not everyone who frequented the Rotonde was a future luminary of the world of art. When Ehrenburg was arrested by the Cheka, the Soviet secret police, in Moscow in 1920, his interrogator claimed to have met him previously at the Rotonde. Perhaps he had. In his youth, the interrogator may have had literary or artistic leanings of his own; in its early days, the Cheka did sometimes recruit such people.)

The fact that some of Ehrenburg's early poems were being published in Russia was gratifying, and filled his family with pride, but it did not provide him with much in the way of an income. From his father he received 50 roubles (or 133 francs) a month, which was not unreasonable: others had to live on less. But few Bohemians know how to manage their finances, and Ehrenburg was no exception: he records that he sometimes went hungry for days on end. But although, according to his own testimony, he preferred poetry to steaks, he seems to have managed, during that period, to do most of the things he wanted to do, including travelling around Europe, even if some of the time he went on foot.

He was in Amsterdam, making his first proper acquaintance with Rembrandt, when he heard the news that Austria had declared war on Serbia. By the time he got back to Paris, the First World War had broken out.

*   *   *

To a man of Ehrenburg's temperament, war represented total horror. Yet he was also fascinated by it; and once he was back in Paris, he lost no time in volunteering for the French Army.

'It was the easiest way out', he wrote later in *Julio Jurenito*. 'At the time, it seemed much simpler to expose my belly to a bayonet, or to pierce someone else's belly with a bayonet, than to buy a newspaper and sit over a cup of coffee reading about how other people's bellies were being slit.' In his memoirs, he put it even more succinctly: 'I did it because I found it hard to watch others leave. The most difficult thing in those days was to be a mere spectator.' In the long run, however, he was forced to accept this role, since the Army doctors turned him down for active service, although Ehrenburg himself felt there was nothing wrong with his health.

So, for three years, he observed the war as a bystander, watching it as one watches a terrifying and enigmatic spectacle. In his memoirs, he frequently stresses that it left him in a state of bewilderment; he hated the war, and yet it absorbed him completely. He obviously did feel confused, but in retrospect one is impressed by the methodical way in which he tried to analyse his feelings. He may not have been aware of it himself at the time, but he instinctively rejected simple explanations, and realized that, in order to understand what was happening, he must free himself of all preconceived notions: this was a situation in which reason was powerless, and instinct a better guide. Above all, he realized that, if one was to understand that vast conflict, one must be prepared to face the grim realities. It was futile to talk of Europe's spiritual unity (as the celebrated author, Romain Rolland, was doing in Geneva) at a time when the German armies were advancing towards Paris.

But apart from absorbing all his thoughts and emotions, the war brought certain practical problems. The monthly remittances from his family ceased, and in order to live he took a job at a railway goods depot, unloading munitions. Meanwhile, the French police, who had up until then ignored his very existence, now began to show some interest in him, and he had to explain that he was not German, in spite of his German-sounding name. He still spent his afternoons at the Rotonde, but many of its *habitués* were now at the front. Among them was the painter, Fernand Léger, and whenever he returned to Paris on leave, he visited the Rotonde and talked to Ehrenburg and others about the war. They argued endlessly, but the talk went round in circles and got them nowhere.

Then one day Ehrenburg happened to see a report in a Russian newspaper on the wartime situation in France which was full of gross inaccuracies. It occurred to him that he could have provided a much better dispatch himself, and he wrote to various Russian newspapers offering his services. He soon got a reply from one of them, the widely read *Stock Exchange Gazette*, which dealt not only with financial matters but with general news as well. The editor did not seem to be worried by Ehrenburg's background, or the fact that he was a political fugitive from Russia (he probably did not trouble to check), and soon Ehrenburg was supplying the paper with regular coverage of the French scene. For a time he tried to combine this with his work on the night shift at the goods depot, but the strain proved too great, and he had a nervous breakdown. He had had a similar breakdown once before, in prison in Moscow, and on that occasion, the doctor had diagnosed 'acute neurasthenia'.

In Paris, according to the artist Marevna (Maria Vorobyova), who belonged to the inner circle of regular clients of the Rotonde, the police picked Ehrenburg up as he was wandering aimlessly and distractedly about the streets, and took him to a mental hospital, where he was not kept long, but where he was obliged to have his head shaved. Up until then, he had worn his hair extremely long, and had earned the nickname of 'Shaggy Ilya' from his friends, so that when he emerged they barely recognized him. In *A Book for Grown-Ups*, which is partly autobiographical, Ehrenburg claims that he actually enjoyed his nervous breakdown in Paris; by which he probably meant that it gave him a legitimate excuse to feel sorry for himself. Marevna recalls that, at the time, he constantly asked his friends whether he was really going mad!

In the long run, it was his new career with the *Stock Exchange Gazette* that saved him. The paper asked him to become its regular war correspondent in France, and when he finally managed to get himself accredited, the French military authorities took him, with a group of other journalists, on a conducted tour of the front. They were shown next to nothing, however, and he came back feeling thoroughly frustrated.

His next idea was to visit the sector of the front held by the British Expeditionary Force. It was not easy to get permission from BEF headquarters, but he was sure that, once it was granted, he would at last be able to do a proper job of work; and so it turned out. At that time, Ehrenburg knew nothing about England or the English, but his first contact with them fulfilled all his hopes. He admired the sang-froid of officers and men who shaved every day, even under intense bombardment, and he was immensely grateful to them for allowing him to go wherever he wanted. So, undeterred by the continual shell fire, he crawled through the mud of the trenches, heard all the deafening sounds of war, and thought he would never forget its stench.

Later he recorded his impressions in a collection of wartime sketches, which he called *The Face of War*. It is a modest narrative, and that makes it all the more impressive. Ehrenburg did not claim to have any special insight into the conflict. As he said in his preface: 'I have seen the hundred faces of war, but I do not know its true face.' He neither extolled nor denounced it, but simply put down what he had seen and heard, and what he had thought about it on each occasion. He described the symptoms, and tried to define the nature of the disease, but he did not presume to suggest a cure.

He was impressed by many aspects of the fighting, but what chiefly struck him was that this was not a contest between mere mortals, but between two mindless war machines. He wrote:

> Some people tell us that we are being ruled by all-powerful men – by the Kaiser and Lloyd George, by diplomats and arms merchants, by generals and stock exchange magnates. I wish it were so. They are, after all, only human beings. Each one has the same pulsating organ under the upper left-hand pocket of his waistcoat. When they were children they all played games, and one day each of them will die. But this war is not being waged by humans. Today, I saw our true masters: endless chains of lorries, transporting men to the front, taking the wounded to the rear, carrying bread and carcasses of meat. The soldiers are merely the slaves of that machine. They serve it and feed it with their bodies. When I first saw a tank, I was perturbed: it was majestic and loathsome, archaic and ultra-American, a combination of Noah's Ark and a twenty-first-century bus. Inside were twelve miserable pygmies, who naïvely imagined that they were controlling it.

The organization that kept the machine going appeared as repulsive to Ehrenburg as the mechanized means of warfare. An anarchist at heart, he had always tended to regard organization as an enemy of mankind. He saw supplies coming into Calais – flour from Canada, tea from Ceylon, meat from Australia, thousands of spare parts for different types of machines – all destined for Armageddon. Everything seemed to work perfectly, and the more perfectly it worked, the more it depressed him.

Yet, however mindless the machine, however soulless the organization that fed it, he felt that there was something even more evil than the front, and that was the rear. 'Poisoned by bloodlust and irresponsible hate, intoxicated by its own safety, depraved by cheap patriotism and easy money, relishing the war and yet mumbling hypocritically "When will it end?" ', the rear was the epitome of fraud and corruption. The speeches, the newspaper articles, the ladies of the smart set idling in hospitals where they arranged, 'for the benefit of the wounded', noisy social functions which disturbed the sick and stopped surgeons from getting on with their job – it was all sham, it was all one big lie. Life was out there – where death was.

At the front, caught up in the machine, were people. Ehrenburg talked to the brave and to the so-called cowards. He did not judge the latter. Anyway, what was cowardice? Was the man who had asked his NCO to let him do a job at staff headquarters, so that he could get away from the trenches for a few hours, a coward? As it happened, staff headquarters did not want him, and he was killed that same day. Was the soldier who had dropped his rifle and covered his face with his hands when he saw a German charging him with a bayonet, a coward? He, miraculously, did stay alive – the bayonet had only pierced his hand – and he kept asking Ehrenburg: 'Do you think I am a coward, Monsieur?' And what about the man who, having been twice decorated for bravery, eventually disabled himself, because all of a sudden he felt that he must spend one day in the peace and quiet of a hospital ward, even if a court martial were to sentence him to death the day after? That man said: 'I don't know whether I am a coward or not.'

Ehrenburg analysed his own reactions to danger. Once he found himself near Vimy Ridge during a heavy barrage. He was with some Anzac officers who were trying to reach a hill from which they could watch the battle. He noticed that whenever they stopped to take cover, he felt doomed; it seemed to him that a shell, or rather *the* shell that was destined to kill them, was bound to locate them, no matter how good the cover was. But as soon as they started walking, he was no longer afraid. He thought of Descartes, his favourite philosopher, and kept saying to himself, paraphrasing Descartes: 'I walk, therefore I am moving away from danger.' He wrote: 'This was wrong and silly. But fear is like that: it is naïve, whimsical and superstitious. There is everything in it – except reason.'

In due course he realized that of the war's many faces, there was another which was at least as horrifying as the struggle between mindless war machines. In a village near the front he saw a traitor about to be shot, a man who had spied for the Germans. Ehrenburg recorded in his diary:

> Hundreds of people are being killed every day. One has grown accustomed to death. But why am I so horrified, why do I feel so ashamed? My heart will not accept that this man will be killed, not in a bayonet charge, not by artillery fire, but standing against the wall of some barn, where they will shoot him calmly and without fuss. This is worse than a battle in which thousands die. It is something that cannot be.

During the war he also developed two obsessions which were to haunt him all his life. Paris had made him a Westerner. Now he became aware of the gulf between the West and Russia. He felt that the West looked down on Russia as a second-class nation: the Russians were good enough to be slaughtered, but their blood was considered less precious than that of the French, who were only too eager to put the blame on them when things went wrong. There were Russian troops in France, and although they had been welcomed as heroes when they disembarked at Marseilles, relations between them and the French soon went sour. Ehrenburg saw this as a clash between the privileged and the less fortunate, between the pseudo-civilized and the illiterate. The Russians, like the Senegalese who were fighting with the French forces, were treated as inferiors. Yet which of the two men who happened to find themselves next to each other in a hospital ward was the more valuable and the more dignified member of the human race – the French hairdresser who groaned and cried, although he was only slightly wounded, or the silent Russian peasant who lay there clenching his teeth, waiting for his leg to be amputated? It was the peasant who said to the nurse, when she explained to him about anaesthetics: 'If there isn't enough gas to go round, give it to him, he is in a bad way. I shall manage.' Who showed the more genuine charity, the Frenchwoman who had converted a Senegalese soldier and invited a crowd of her friends to a fashionable tearoom to show off her conquest, or the 'convert' himself who, anxious to reciprocate her kindness, presented her with a hideous and obscene idol, symbolizing fertility, so that she should have 'lots of men and lots of children'? According to Ehrenburg, the Russians got on well with the Africans: inferiority had created a bond between them.

Ehrenburg's other obsession was of a more primitive kind. His anti-German prejudice, which was to become notorious, stemmed from the First World War. Later, as befitted a man with a profoundly cosmopolitan outlook, he tried to suppress it, and there were periods when it was barely noticeable. During the Second World War, however, it erupted once more with full force.

Germany had never attracted him. In an essay he wrote in the early 1920s, he relates how, as a boy, he once travelled to Germany with his mother. She told him that the train would arrive in Berlin at twelve minutes past nine. He thought this was rather comical, and did not believe her. He was so used to Russian trains that he could not imagine how anyone could predict an arrival time with such precision. He goes on to say that when the train did arrive in Berlin at exactly the appointed time, it frightened him. It seems an exaggerated reaction, and perhaps the story need not be taken too literally. It does, however, illustrate an attitude which was fairly widespread in Russia, and in a number of other countries as well: German punctuality and thoroughness were by no means universally admired, and were sometimes even treated with derision. In part, this was plainly due to envy: it was convenient to equate efficiency with regimentation and to attribute it to Prussian drill. Ehrenburg's reactions, however, were not based on envy but on his general outlook on life. To him, culture was never synonymous with technological advances or superior organization. As an inveterate Bohemian, he much preferred an Italian *lazzarone* to a conscientious official who made everything function like clockwork.

As he travelled round the battlefields and saw the great hecatomb of Allied and German dead, the only hatred he felt was for death itself. He was nauseated by the bloodthirsty talk he sometimes heard in the rear about the need to massacre all Germans once victory was won; and he showed sympathy and understanding for Frenchwomen who had lived with German soldiers. But when he visited areas from which the German Army had retreated, he was shattered by the thoroughness with which the German war machine had done its work of destruction. The devastation, he noted in his diary, 'was not due to excesses committed by drunken soldiery or to the barbaric whim of some general. A plan had been carefully drawn up in advance and meticulously executed.' On one occasion, he was surprised to find an orchard in which the pear trees appeared to be still standing, until he noticed that the roots of each tree had been half sawn through. It was true that French troops might have done the same thing to an orchard in Bavaria – had he not already been depressed by the perfection of the Allied war machine? Yet from the way he described the scorched earth policy carried out by the Germans, it was plain that he associated it with the kind of efficiency that was a German national characteristic, and which he had always instinctively disliked.

It was no doubt a natural enough reaction at the time. He had not ceased to feel a deep hatred of the war; but he had come to accept the fact that Germany was the enemy to be defeated. He did not imagine that the Allies would make the world a better place to live in; but a world dominated by Germany would be a total nightmare. For that reason, he felt that, now it had started, the war had to be fought to the bitter end, even though in the process mankind was being subjected to an unimaginably terrible ordeal.

On one of his visits to the front, he met an Indian, a Hindu, who told him not to inquire, but to turn to prayer. 'I never prayed,' Ehrenburg wrote, 'and I shall probably never cease to inquire. But I often repeated Job's lament: "Why dost Thou contend with me? Thine hands have made me and fashioned me, yet Thou dost destroy me . . . . Show me why!" '

CHAPTER V

Ehrenburg did not see the end of the war in France. In March 1917 came the momentous news that the Tsar had abdicated, and he quickly joined the throng of political exiles who were besieging the Russian Embassy in Paris, singing revolutionary songs and clamouring to return home.[1]

They were told, however, that they could not be sent there all at once, and Ehrenburg had to wait several months until, with a group of other political refugees, he was able to set out on a roundabout and sometimes perilous journey: first to England, then to Stockholm on board a troop-ship escorted by two British destroyers (at one point, a German U-boat was spotted, and Ehrenburg was handed a lifebelt which he did not bother to put on), and finally through Sweden and Finland by train. He arrived in Russia in July, a few days after the Bolsheviks had clashed with the Provisional Government and Lenin had gone into hiding to escape arrest. Once the train had crossed the Russian frontier, the returning *émigrés* were placed under guard, and an officer, catching sight of Ehrenburg, pointed him out to a lady as one of the 'sealed carriage bunch' (i.e. one of those who had accompanied Lenin on his return to Russia). But the officer was wrong: Ehrenburg was anything but a Bolshevik.

He had left the Party in 1909, and in the years that followed he gave little thought to Party politics. On the outbreak of war in 1914, his only clear idea was that Germany must on no account be allowed to win. As for Lenin's attitude to the war, it impressed him as little as that of Romain Rolland.

When he heard that the Russian monarchy had fallen, he was both stunned and overjoyed. But during the following months, while he waited for transport and visas, he saw much that worried and depressed him. He went to *émigré* gatherings where all were at

---

[1]This haste to return may seem strange since, on the surface, Ehrenburg had become thoroughly Westernized. But although he was no Bolshevik, one can assume that his earlier revolutionary sentiments had never entirely disappeared, and were quickly revived by the news of the collapse of the Russian monarchy. (E de M)

daggers drawn. The main issue over which they were quarrelling and even coming to blows was whether Russia should go on fighting. He got hold of a batch of German newspapers, which were full of praise for the Russian Revolution and for those French soldiers who were protesting against the war – Germany's interest in the matter was obvious enough. Above all, he saw the effect of the Revolution on the Russian troops in France.

In these units, as in the whole of the Russian Army, committees had been set up and meetings were being held at which soldiers vented their grievances. The introduction of such revolutionary practices in a force stationed on French soil and fighting under French command, coupled with reports of a standstill on the Russian front, alarmed the French, and the French Press became increasingly hostile towards Russia. In April, the Allies launched an offensive in which the Russian brigades displayed exemplary courage and suffered heavy losses. Yet the anti-Russian campaign continued, there was talk of Russian treachery, and Russian soldiers returning from the battlefield were greeted by the French with cries of 'Boches!'. Relations with the French finally became so bad that some of the Russian officers were in favour of asking that their troops should be placed under British command.

Ehrenburg blamed the French for contributing to the disintegration of the Russian contingents. But whether or not there was any justification for this charge, the fact remained that the Russian troops were disintegrating, and their morale, as Ehrenburg himself confirms, was being undermined by people who had nothing to do with the French, namely by Bolshevik émigrés. He described their activities in his book The Face of War. 'Bolshevik agitators began to arrive from Paris. They established themselves in one of the regimental committees and set to work with their customary efficiency and skill.' He also noted the irony of their behaviour: they were internationalists and advocates of civil war, yet they did not hesitate to appeal to chauvinistic instincts, or to preach non-violence in a manner worthy of disciples of Tolstoy. They were telling the soldiers that it was madness to fight in France – if there was any fighting to be done, it should be done in Russia. But they were also saying, when they thought it suited their purpose better, that it was a crime to kill one's fellow-men, and calling upon the soldiers to throw away their rifles.

Ehrenburg met many Bolsheviks, both veterans and those newly converted, among the soldiers, and he divided them into three categories. Some were 'dreamers': Ehrenburg talked to a man who believed with equal fanaticism in peace and justice, in polygamy and Esperanto, and in doing away with handshakes, a custom which, for some reason, he regarded as pernicious. Others were fierce and embittered. One of them (like Ehrenburg) had been arrested before the war for distributing revolutionary leaflets, and had been savagely beaten by the police. Now he hated everything and everybody, supported any extremist proposal, and considered himself a Bolshevik even though he had no coherent political views. Finally, there were the ordinary Russian peasants who, having spent three terrible years at the front, had only one thought: to escape from the carnage and return to their villages. At first they were ashamed to admit it, but later, under the unremitting flow of oratory to which they were exposed, they began proudly to call themselves Bolsheviks. Ehrenburg understood their plight. But he was deeply distressed by what he saw, and from his bitter descriptions of the situation one would never have guessed that he himself had once belonged to the Bolshevik faction.

There is a passage in *Julio Jurenito* which suggests that, as Ehrenburg travelled back to Russia, he was in a sentimental mood. Perhaps he was, as most people would be on returning to the country of their birth after a ten-year absence. But his dominant emotion seems to have been one of anguish. He was convinced that civil strife in Russia would not only be a tragedy in itself, but would play straight into the hands of the German militarists. When he finally reached Petrograd (as it then was), he expounded this view to everyone he met. It was also one of the reasons why he felt unable to support the Bolshevik Revolution when it erupted a few months later.

He stayed in Russia for three and a half years, living in different parts of the country, and under several different regimes, during which time he witnessed one of the worst and most chaotic civil wars in modern history. He was in Moscow itself when the October Revolution broke out. According to *Julio Jurenito* (and he later confirmed that this passage in the book was an accurate reflection of his feelings at the time), he blamed himself bitterly for remaining inactive and, as he put it, for seeing 'thirty-three truths' without being able to grasp the one great truth that mattered. 'When it was all over', he wrote, 'people began to lament and bewail things they had not noticed in the past; and for want of anything better to do, I, too, turned to lamentation.'

He chose to express his sorrow in verse, notably in 'A Prayer for Russia':

> Let us pray for our native land,
> for the fields deserted and cold,
> for those who cannot pray,
> for those who strangle children,
> for those who march with knives and pikes . . .
> have mercy on us, O Lord!
> Do not forsake her in her last hour!
> May she return to Thee.
> And may she by her torments
> redeem these years of Hell . . .

In another poem, 'Judgement Day', he spoke of Russia's assailants. Some were young, brave and stubborn, eagerly drinking in the poisoned air; others were more like savage beasts. But there were also those who were tired, homeless and starving; and he wrote of the defenders who were ready to die for Russia while the crowd shouted: 'Crucify her!' 'Rejoice, Germany!' *'Deutschland, Deutschland über Alles!'* Russia was being buried alive: 'We crucified her in the year one thousand nine hundred and seventeen.' It seems incredible by present Soviet standards, but 'A Prayer for Russia' actually appeared in print in Moscow. A decade later, however, the *Great Soviet Encyclopaedia* noted drily that 'Ehrenburg began his poetical career as a mystic, and the attitude he adopted towards the Revolution was that of an anti-Bolshevik.'

In his memoirs, Ehrenburg does not quote from any of these poems, nor does he even mention their titles. Indeed, he seems to be deliberately turning his back on that phase of his career. What he wrote at that time, he says, was bad and false: he was bemoaning a world to which he had never belonged, and praying to a God in whom he did not believe. His explanation is that he was in a state of confusion, and he attributes this to the fact that he had grown up with a nineteenth-century concept of freedom. Since his earliest youth, he had cultivated the habit of disregarding authority; and in the critical days of the October Revolution and after, he had failed to realize that this was no longer applicable to the world of tomorrow. What he is really saying in retrospect is that, in 1917, he could not reconcile himself to the establishment of an authoritarian regime, even though that regime was being set up in the name of 'the tired, homeless and starving'.

Underlying all this, however, was his utter repugnance to violence. One can understand why he did not dwell on it in his memoirs, since to have done so would have implied that he was questioning the legitimacy of the Soviet State. But he had seen the war in France, and the effect it had on ordinary human beings. He had found it degrading, even though he had accepted the need to defeat the enemy; as for the October Revolution in Russia, and the civil conflict that followed, these appeared to him simply a continuation of the war that had already engulfed mankind.

In 1919, he wrote:

> The war has been with us now for five years. The apocalyptic scroll has been opened, the seals have been removed. Evil spirits have been released, and they cannot be exorcized by diplomats at international conferences. The war goes on. From the front, it has spread to the cities, to the villages, and into people's homes. But whether it is nation against nation, or class against class, it is the same phenomenon under different banners. Who will wrest the sword from the frenzied horseman? I do not know. But this I do know: evil cannot be conquered by evil; war cannot end war. Destruction knows no end, and we are caught in this fiery circle.

Above all, he was horrified by the fact that killing had become an everyday occurrence, that ordinarily decent and gentle people were no longer shocked by violence and cruelty. Mayakovsky had said in one of his poems: 'I love to watch children die.'[1] But this was total nonsense: Mayakovsky could not bear the sight of a horse being whipped, he could not stand the sight of blood, and he turned away merely if someone cut his finger. One wonders how he had come to write such a line. But the swift succession of events had created an atmosphere of near-hysteria. In *Hope Against Hope*, the first volume

---

[1]Vladimir Vladimirovich Mayakovsky (1893–1930) was the leading exponent of the Russian Futurist movement, and produced a vast outpouring of revolutionary poems, the best-known being 'A Cloud in Trousers' and 'My Soviet Passport'. He also wrote two plays, *The Bedbug* and *The Bathhouse* which suggest a growing disillusionment with Soviet reality. In 1930, he committed suicide. The line quoted here comes from one of his early pre-revolutionary poems. Ehrenburg saw it scrawled on a wall of the Poets' Café in the winter of 1917, together with other outrageous drawings and inscriptions, all plainly intended to shock the casual visitor.

of her marvellously vivid autobiography, Nadezhda Mandelstam[1] recaptures the atmosphere of that time, and follows with an anecdote illustrating how Ehrenburg reacted towards it:

> Why is it so easy to turn young people into killers? Why do they look on human life with such criminal frivolity? This is particularly true in those fateful periods when blood flows and murder becomes an ordinary everyday thing. We were set on our fellow men like dogs, and the whole pack of us licked the hunter's hand, squealing incomprehensibly. The head-hunting mentality spread like a plague. I even had a slight bout of it myself, but was cured in time by a wise doctor. This happened in Ekster's studio in Kiev when some visitor or another . . . read out some couplets by Mayakovsky about how officers were thrown into the Moïka Canal in Petrograd to drown. This brash verse had its effect and I burst out laughing. Ehrenburg, who was also there, at once fiercely attacked me. He gave me such a talking-to that I still respect him for it, and I am proud that, silly as I was at the time, I had the sense to listen to him and remember his words forever afterward.

Ehrenburg spent altogether about a year in Moscow, and although life was hard and often frustrating, there was another, more positive side to it. The Revolution had a number of side-effects, and one of these was to arouse much interest in the great experiment in art. Ehrenburg had followed that experiment with fascination in Paris; now he was witnessing it in Moscow. It is true that most of the older writers treated this *nouvelle vague* as a Bolshevik abomination, but the younger ones revelled in it. Ehrenburg was perturbed by some of their iconoclastic activities, which he found unbelievably childish. But he met Mayakovsky and Pasternak, and these encounters were as exciting as anything he had experienced in Paris. Cafés sprang up where poets recited their poems before bourgeois audiences, and although Ehrenburg complained that the atmosphere was not the same as at the Rotonde, he became a regular visitor and a frequent performer.

Soon after his return to Russia, he paid a visit to Valery Bryusov, the celebrated man of letters from whom he had received so much encouragement when he first began to write verse.[2] Bryusov spent

[1] Widow of the great Russian poet, Osip Mandelstam, who died on the Far Eastern fringe of the Gulag, Stalin's vast concentration camp system. She published two volumes of memoirs, *Hope Against Hope* and *Hope Abandoned*, both titles involving a play of words on her first name: in Russian, Nadezhda means hope.

[2] Valery Yakovlevich Bryusov (1873–1924) was a poet, critic and editor, and the leading theoretician of the Russian Symbolist school.

most of the time discussing the correct way to spell Theseus in Russian, and debating whether it was legitimate to assume that Theseus suffered from a sense of guilt after abandoning Ariadne on the island of Naxos, and Ehrenburg came away disappointed. He was making a great effort to understand what was happening in Russia, and the fate of the hero of Attic legend held little interest for him. Yet, before long, he was to write a play, *The Golden Heart: A Mystery*, on a theme just as far removed from Russian reality as Theseus's presumed remorse over Ariadne.

The action takes place in medieval Brittany, in a convent whose most precious possession is a statue of the Madonna holding a heart made of gold. The heart would long since have been stolen, had it not been for a superstition that anyone daring to do so would be struck blind. A blind beggar hears of this, and since he has nothing to lose, he steals the golden heart to buy himself one night of love. But a nun surprises him just as he is seizing the treasure, and he drops it into a deep well. The nun asks him to confide in her, and is so moved by his wretched tale that she spends the night with him. Her sin is discovered, and an ecclesiastical court condemns her to death. But then a miracle happens: the blind man regains his sight, the golden heart is recovered and restored to the Madonna, and the bishop bows before the saintly sinner who has shown that theft, sacrilege and fornication can all be redeemed by truly Christian compassion.

Ehrenburg wrote *The Golden Heart* in Moscow in 1918, at a time when those who frequented the Poets' Café carried revolvers in their pockets to protect themselves against the bandits who roamed the streets at night.

CHAPTER VI

In the autumn of that year Ehrenburg heard that his mother was critically ill. She was staying in Poltava, in the Ukraine, which was then under German occupation. Strange though it may seem, in spite of the generally chaotic conditions one could still travel to the Ukraine from Moscow by train, although, having boarded the train, one sometimes had to wait for days before it left, without any certainty that it would leave at all. By the time Ehrenburg reached Poltava, his mother was dead.

He was now on non-Soviet territory, in a region which would soon become one of the main theatres of the civil war. He did not return to Moscow, but stayed on in the south for two years, first in Kiev, and later in Koktebel, a small town on the Crimean coast. In Kiev, he married a young artist, Lyubov Kozintseva,[1] whose brother later became a leading Soviet film director. The marriage lasted nearly fifty years, until Ehrenburg's death in 1967.

At one point, the Red Army occupied Kiev, and he found himself once more under Soviet rule. It did not last long: six months later, the city was taken by the Whites. But during those six months, as happened each time a town passed into Soviet hands, administrative departments proliferated like mushrooms, employing everyone they could find, and frequently launching into activities which had little relevance to the more pressing needs of the moment. In this way, Ehrenburg was given a job looking after the 'aesthetic education' of difficult children, who were officially described as 'morally defective' (or 'mofective' for short): they were, in fact, simply juvenile

[1]Lyubov (or Lyuba) came from a professional family in the Ukraine – her father, M. I. Kozintsev, was a doctor, and her brother Grigory (Grisha) an aspiring artist who turned to film-making. She herself studied art under a well-known woman painter, Alexandra Alexandrovna Ekster, in Kiev, where one of her closest friends was Nadezhda Khazina, future wife of the poet Osip Mandelstam. Nadezhda Mandelstam speaks warmly of her in her memoirs, *Hope against Hope* and *Hope Abandoned*. According to one source close to Ehrenburg, his marriage to Lyubov was not a very happy one, and in his later years he developed emotional attachments elsewhere, although he made only the most oblique references to them in his memoirs. (E de M)

delinquents. Ehrenburg did not consider himself in the least qualified, but in any case, the department he worked for had been given an impossible task, and its efforts were manifestly futile. However, he still had time to write verse, and to mix with other poets and artists. In spite of the turbulence around them, nothing, it seemed, could daunt their enthusiasm. They continued to meet and to hold lengthy debates and discussions no matter which government – Red, White or Ukrainian – happened to be in power.

Ehrenburg watched the unfolding of the civil war with horror. Four different governments succeeded each other while he was in Kiev, and each time it seemed that the preceding government had been better than the one that came after it. It was in Kiev that Ehrenburg wrote: 'Evil cannot be conquered by evil.' It was a general and abstract statement. But whichever regime was temporarily in power, violence remained the common currency of the day, and he had to ask himself: to what end? In Moscow, he had held back from supporting the Bolshevik Revolution. In Kiev, he was at first hopeful when the White Army arrived; but the scenes he witnessed under the White administration were scarcely edifying, and although he tried to convince himself that things were not as bad as they seemed, his optimism soon faded. Here, too, he failed to discover the one supreme truth among the 'thirty-three truths' that had so oppressed him the year before. Ehrenburg acknowledged that some of those who had joined the White Army were idealists and romantics. At the same time, he saw crude propaganda posters being pasted up, posters which displayed the heroic image of St George, but coupled with it the image of a hook-nosed Jew being trampled to death under the hooves of the dragon-slayer's steed. One night, a vicious pogrom was unleashed in Kiev, and there were disturbing reports of other pogroms elsewhere in the Ukraine. There was a slogan going the rounds at that time: 'Kill the Jews and save Russia!' It was not an official slogan, but the fact that the authorities condoned it revealed the spiritual poverty of the White regime. Many of those who had fled south were concerned only with saving their fortunes. Watching them, Ehrenburg felt that the only thing the White regime had to offer was the restoration of a way of life against which he had rebelled while he was still at school. He did not find it any more attractive now that he was nearly thirty.

In Kiev he wrote another play in verse, which he called *The Wind: A Tragedy*. It is as little-known as *The Golden Heart*, but this time he chose a subject which had some relevance to what was happening in Russia: an episode from the Spanish civil war of the 1870s. One of the characters is a young woman, an aristocrat who is opposed to everything the rebels stand for, but finds it impossible to resist the intoxicating effect of the 'wind of rebellion'. While her friends are trying to put down the rising, she muses amid the splendour of her ancestral home: 'One can fight for one's faith, for one's country and for what one believes to be the truth. But it is useless to fight for gilded chandeliers.'

In his memoirs, Ehrenburg does not explain what made him decide to leave Kiev and go to Koktebel, where his friend, the poet Maximilian Voloshin – a lovable eccentric whom he already knew from his Paris days – was leading what appeared to be a peaceful existence.[1] It may well be that Ehrenburg did not feel safe in Kiev. He had worked for a Soviet institution and could easily be denounced by some of the local people as a former Soviet official – the fact that he had only been concerned with 'aesthetic education' was not sufficient to protect him against arbitrary arrest.

It took Ehrenburg and his wife a month to get to the Crimea, travelling by rail in cattle trucks and then by boat. By comparison, his wartime journey from France to Russia must have seemed idyllic. At that time, when he was told they might be attacked by a German U-boat, he had scorned a lifebelt. Now, travelling south, he faced the much greater danger posed by armed bands of ferocious anti-Communist irregulars, who stormed the trains in search of 'Jews, Communists and commissars'. On the last lap of the journey across the Sea of Azov, he also had to struggle with a drunken officer who tried to throw him overboard, saying he was going to 'baptize' him. He was saved by another officer, who happened to be a Jew, and threatened to shoot the assailant.

The Crimea was held by the White Army of General Wrangel. Koktebel seems to have been a relatively quiet spot, although it was visited from time to time by Wrangel's security men from the nearby port of Feodosia looking for suspects (the poet Osip Mandelstam, who, like Ehrenburg, had sought refuge in the south, was detained there for a time as a Bolshevik spy). There were other poets, artists

[1]Maximilian Alexandrovich Voloshin (1877–1932): an associate of the Symbolists, whose work is a curious amalgam of Western and Slavophile themes. After a long period in Paris, where he studied painting, he settled at Koktebel in the Crimea, where he lived from 1917 until his death.

and journalists among the refugees from the north and, as in Kiev, it seemed that nothing could thwart their enthusiasm. They founded a club called FLAK – a rather bellicose acronym if one thinks of the Second World War, but it simply meant 'Feodosian Literary and Artistic Circle' – and even managed to bring out a literary magazine, in which some of Ehrenburg's verse was published.

But although he enjoyed his contacts with fellow-writers, Ehrenburg's life in the Crimea was fairly nightmarish. For a time, he ran a kindergarten for the children of well-to-do peasants. The parents were a tightfisted lot. They disliked Ehrenburg for being a Jew, and they did not approve of his methods of education. He and his wife Lyubov starved, and Lyubov nearly died of typhus (a raging typhus epidemic was one of the by-products of the civil war, and was as terrifying as the war itself). Fortunately, among the intellectuals living in Koktebel were three doctors. Even so, it was a miracle that Ehrenburg's wife survived, considering that giving an ordinary injection presented problems which could drive one to despair. To obtain a syringe, Mandelstam's brother Alexander[1] had to ride twelve miles on horseback to Feodosia, and as there was no surgical spirit, Ehrenburg had to go from farm to farm, begging for vodka and trying in vain to convince the peasants that he needed it for medical purposes and not because he was addicted to drink. Against this background of misery and hunger, it seems strange that the small colony of intellectuals was not immune from petty feuds. They not only cared for and helped each other, but at other times they also quarrelled – sometimes so violently that they lost all sense of proportion. Mandelstam mislaid a copy of Dante's *La Divina Commedia* which he had borrowed from Voloshin, and the ensuing quarrel was such that, when Mandelstam was arrested, Voloshin was at first in no mood to plead for his release. In the end, it was Ehrenburg who persuaded Voloshin to intervene: they had not been on speaking terms either, but Ehrenburg went to see him nevertheless, and they used this opportunity to make peace.

As the White Army began to lose ground, millions of people retreated with it and eventually found themselves abroad. Some, especially those with money, were only too happy to leave Russia; those who were politically committed had no choice; others were simply carried by the tide and drifted into exile. Had this happened to Mandelstam, he would not have become a victim of Stalin's terror.

[1]Alexander Emilievich Mandelstam was the younger brother of Osip Mandelstam.

But he and Ehrenburg set out in the opposite direction. A few months before the collapse of Wrangel's Army, they both decided to return to Moscow. Separately, they made their way to Georgia, which at that time was an independent State, ruled by a Menshevik Government. It maintained diplomatic relations with Soviet Russia and Ehrenburg seems to have had no difficulty in persuading the Soviet Ambassador in Tbilisi to repatriate him. The Ambassador sent him to Moscow as a diplomatic courier; his wife and the Mandelstam brothers were permitted to go with him.

Not every Soviet official would have been so co-operative. The Ambassador could easily have presumed that, since Ehrenburg had come from Wrangel territory, he must be a spy. This kind of mentality was not confined to the Soviet side. Mandelstam was first detained by Wrangel's security men as a Bolshevik, and a second time by the Georgian police as a double agent, although, as Ehrenburg says in his memoirs, one look at him should have been sufficient to show that he could not possibly be an agent of any kind. Ehrenburg adds drily that while the author of the feeblest adventure story tries to ensure at least some degree of credibility, policemen seldom make the effort.

The Soviet Ambassador in Tbilisi was capable of thinking straight. The Cheka, by definition, was not. Shortly after Ehrenburg returned to Moscow, he was arrested and accused of being a Wrangel agent. Moreover, he was told that it was up to him to disprove the charge. He objected to this procedure but the investigator was not impressed. After three interrogations Ehrenburg came to the conclusion that he would probably be shot. However, a day later he was released.

In his memoirs Ehrenburg makes light of the whole affair. He says that the investigator was a friendly man who claimed to have met him at the Rotonde, that the Cheka officials who came to arrest him behaved courteously and talked to his wife about cubist art, and that his fellow-prisoners – a group of Red Navy officers – were exceptionally delightful people who kept up their morale by trying to improve their education. They decided that each man in turn should give a talk on a subject unconnected with his predicament, and Ehrenburg lectured about Spanish poetry and about Picasso.

There is no reason to doubt that this was so, and since all ended well, both for him and his cell-mates, he could afford to write about it in a humorous vein forty years after the event. Yet, quite apart from the fact that he cannot have found it amusing at the time, some of the things he wrote suggest that he thought a great deal about this episode after his release. He must have been struck by the irony of the situation: he had been jailed before, in Tsarist Russia, for being an active member of a Bolshevik organization; this time he had been jailed by the Bolsheviks for no reason at all. In the intervening years, a world had been smashed to pieces and was waiting to be rebuilt. Prison, however, was one of the few institutions that had been left unscathed – an indestructible bridge linking the present with the past. The stench of the latrine buckets was as loathsome as before, the food was still foul and the warders still hung about the peep-holes. 'A stick remains a stick, no matter who wields it.'

He saw only too clearly that those who had the power would never cease to wield it. Later he wrote what he called *An Improbable Story* about an honest, dedicated Bolshevik who, after the Revolution, has been given a suitably responsible post in his native town. One day he decides to visit the local prison. When he finishes his inspection, a new warder mistakes him for an inmate and keeps him inside. He spends the night in a cell in the company of a Menshevik with whom he had shared a cell in Tsarist days. Next morning, when the mistake is cleared up, he refuses to leave: he has realized that nothing has changed. He has been trying to build a house in which people would be happy; now he sees that it will have to accommodate prison warders as well. He would rather stay with the victims than be associated with those who are wielding the stick, and has to be removed by force – to a lunatic asylum.

In Moscow Ehrenburg was given a job in a department where he was supposed to look after children's theatres. For a time he worked with the great circus artist and animal tamer, Vladimir Durov, helping him to put on shows for children. But much as he admired Durov's genius, he kept thinking about something else: *Julio Jurenito*, the novel into which he intended to put everything he had seen and reflected on during the past fateful decade. He felt that it would be impossible to write the book in Russia, and in the spring of 1921, he applied for a permit to travel to France.

His request was granted only after he had been summoned to have a talk with a senior official of the State security organ, the Cheka. But there was nothing strange or sinister in the fact that the Cheka agreed to let him leave the country. It so happened that a new policy was being initiated. Ehrenburg was one of the first to travel abroad on a

Soviet passport, but he was by no means the last. Soon this became a fairly common occurrence, and in countries that were prepared to grant visas to Soviet citizens, especially in Germany after the Rapallo Treaty which marked the beginning of Soviet-German co-operation, one could see them in large numbers, private individuals as well as officials, until, in 1928, came a radical change, heralding the advent of the Stalin era, and fewer and fewer exit permits were granted.

The problem in Ehrenburg's case, however, was how to persuade the French to let him in. Paris was full of anti-Soviet Russian refugees, but the French authorities were not inclined to welcome anyone who was, and wished to remain, a Soviet citizen. France did not recognize the Soviet Government, and there was no French diplomatic mission in Moscow to whom Ehrenburg could apply for a visa. He eventually obtained one from the French Consulate in Latvia, but only with great difficulty, and after a 'semi-influential' friend in Paris had intervened on his behalf. Even so, things soon went wrong.

Ehrenburg describes what happened by saying that, when he finally got to Paris, he was 'dragged' to the Préfecture de Police and spent a long time there in its 'malodorous rooms, where I was interrogated about the date of my grandmother's birth and the profession of my aunt'. He contrasted this unfavourably with the way he had been received in Copenhagen, where he had stopped for a few days on his journey to France. In the Danish capital, no one had shown the slightest interest in his female relatives, and instead of being taken off to a police station, he had been invited to visit the municipal baths. However, once he got to Paris, he soon discovered that, in those days, worse things could happen to the holder of a Soviet passport than answering questions about one's grandmother. Barely had they arrived in France when he and his wife were expelled.

In a book he wrote shortly afterwards, Ehrenburg claims that the reason for this was that a police detective, making a routine visit to the Rotonde, had heard him praising the Russian theatre; anyway, he adds, this was the explanation given to his 'semi-influential' friend when the latter made enquiries at the Préfecture about Ehrenburg's sudden departure. It sounds a ridiculous pretext, but ridiculous things did happen. In the French police archives, in the section dealing with foreign nationals in the twenties, I found a detective's report which was equally grotesque, yet seems initially to have been taken quite seriously in high quarters, although in that instance the subject under investigation was eventually left alone. In Ehrenburg's case, whatever one may think of his own version of events, the French police probably felt that he should never have been allowed to enter France in the first place, and took steps to correct the error. He and his wife were escorted to the Belgian frontier by a police officer, and it was only thanks to Ehrenburg's persistence and a stroke of luck that they were given permission to stay in Belgium for a few months.

Even before leaving Moscow, Ehrenburg had been warned that he would have trouble with the French, but he was still determined to go. He had tried to start work on *Julio Jurenito* in Moscow, but soon had to give up the attempt. This was not because of the starvation diet of that hungry era, although that plainly did not help, but because the atmosphere was simply not conducive to writing the sort of book he had in mind. It seemed to him, says Ehrenburg, in a passage in *Julio Jurenito* that is clearly autobiographical, that if only he could sit down at a table at the Rotonde, and call to a waiter, '*Garçon, de quoi écrire!*', the book would be finished in no time. In Moscow, such a procedure was almost unthinkable, since a clean sheet of paper was as difficult to come by as a slice of bread.

But in any case, *Julio Jurenito* is essentially Western in inspiration and execution. It is a satire permeated with the spirit of the Rotonde, and one can well understand why this seemed to Ehrenburg the ideal place to write it. As it turned out, he had to write it in Belgium. But before his expulsion, he had been able to revisit the Rotonde and, what was more important, to get a whiff of the atmosphere of post-war Europe before he set to work. It is clear, of course, that his decision to leave for the West was not solely because of *Julio Jurenito*: he left Soviet Russia because he no longer wanted to live there. He had accepted the fact that the Soviet regime was there to stay, and he even sympathized with its efforts to create a new social system. But he knew that it would be a long and painful process, and could not help feeling dubious about the final result.

Paradoxically, he left Moscow at a time of intellectual and creative ferment which must strongly have appealed to him. The literary and artistic scene was dominated by the avant-garde, and full of rival schools each defending its own 'ism' with truly religious fervour, while Lunacharsky, the enlightened and cultivated Commissar for Popular Enlightenment, looked benevolently on. Mayakovsky,

Esenin and Pasternak were writing some of their finest poems, and the Russian theatre, under the leadership of men like Meyerhold, Vakhtangov and Tairov, was rapidly becoming the most advanced in the world. Indeed, when Ehrenburg arrived in the West, he described Moscow as 'the Mecca of modern art'.

Yet he had also seen something which he did not like at all: a curious chart in Valery Bryusov's study. Bryusov did not spend all his time worrying about the correct spelling of Theseus. He also co-operated with the Soviet Government in drawing up great plans for Soviet literature; and the chart indicated its future course. But as Ehrenburg stared at its intricate geometrical figures, he felt a mounting anxiety: here was 'literature transformed into an administrative office'. As long as that office was occupied by a man of Bryusov's stature, all might still be well, but Ehrenburg could not shake off the sense of foreboding. Later, in *Julio Jurenito*, he inserted a passage pouring scorn on planners who produced sinister graphs designed to regulate every aspect of human activity: work, sex and procreation, as well as aesthetic enjoyment, the latter being meted out in strictly prescribed doses so that nothing should be left to chance. Moreover, Ehrenburg, the Russian patriot, had by now developed what he described as his 'second, foreign soul', and he longed for the Paris of his earlier years.

In a volume of essays called *Zoo*, devoted to a number of his Soviet contemporaries, the literary critic, Viktor Shklovsky, once described Ehrenburg as 'a Saul who had failed to become Paul'. Ehrenburg, said Shklovsky, always remained 'Pavel Savlovich' ('Paul, son of Saul'): in other words, whenever he embraced a new creed, he could never bring himself to renounce the past completely. Ehrenburg himself acknowledged the justice of this verdict. He was drawn to various beliefs, but always dreaded and resisted total conversion. No sooner had he accepted the Soviet regime than he hurried away from it, to the West, where he remained for many years; not as an *émigré*, but as a Soviet writer living abroad. Observing his career, some people felt he wanted to have the best of both worlds; and so he did. He wanted both to be free and to belong. But for all his attachment to Russia, it was only in the West that he could be a free Soviet writer.

CHAPTER VII

Ehrenburg wrote *Julio Jurenito* in the Belgian seaside village of La Panne. He finished it in a month, which suggests that it must have largely taken shape in his mind before he put pen to paper. The book was published in Berlin in 1922, and its title took up the whole of the front cover:

> The Extraordinary Adventures of Julio Jurenito and his disciples – Monsieur Delhaie, Karl Schmidt, Mr Cool, Alexei Tishin, Ercole Bambucci, Ilya Ehrenburg, and Aysha the Negro – in days of peace, war and revolution, in Paris, Mexico, Rome and Senegal, in Kineshma, Moscow and other places, as well as various reflections by the Master on pipe smoking, death, love, freedom, chess, the tribe of Judah, construct-ivism and many other matters.

Ehrenburg's intention was to convey that this was not a novel in the traditional Russian mould, but a *roman philosophique*, the first of its kind, since Russian literature had no *Gulliver's Travels*, no *Gargantua and Pantagruel*, and no *Candide*. Some critics did, in fact, assume that *Julio Jurenito* was modelled on Voltaire's exemplary tale. Ehrenburg himself says, however, that he read *Candide* only much later. Meanwhile, *Julio Jurenito* was an instant success, not only because it was witty, inventive and written from the heart (or, as Ehrenburg put it in his memoirs, 'written from an inner necessity'), but because it came out at the right time: there was a need for a satirical novel of this kind.

In part it deals with post-revolutionary Russia, but above all it is a satire on the festering sores of Western civilization. Ehrenburg had touched on this theme in his earliest poems. Later, in a preface to his wartime sketches, he claimed that the ground for war had been well prepared by Europe's soulless and corrupt society. He recalled the crowds in prewar Paris, 'moving along the boulevards like clock-work toys', sycophants promising salvation, and a public execution outside the Santé prison – a noisy fête around the guillotine, with sweetmeat vendors, carefree girls and blasé versifiers who, having witnessed the gruesome spectacle, would recite that same evening languid poems on the beauty of Trianon. Ehrenburg had tried to take part in the fight against evil by joining the ranks of the Marxists. Afterwards, he nearly became a Catholic. Now he lashed out on his own. If evil could not be conquered, he could at least denounce it in his own terms.

The book is written in the first person singular: Ehrenburg casts himself in the modest role of a disciple who expounds the philosophy of his Master, Julio Jurenito. In deference to his friendship with the Mexican artist, Diego Rivera, Ehrenburg made Jurenito a Mexican. But Jurenito bears little resemblance to Rivera. He is, or is supposed to be, what Ehrenburg would have liked to be himself: a cynic. They meet at the Rotonde a year before the outbreak of the First World War. Ehrenburg, the romantic, is in the depths of despair, and Jurenito puts to him the simple proposition that, since everything round them is evil, everything should be destroyed. Yet to rely on an anarchist's bomb would be naïve. Jurenito has devised a more effective method: to cultivate the sores and to foment decay, thus accelerating the process by which society will destroy itself. Jurenito's mission is to be the great *agent provocateur*.

Having recruited Ehrenburg as his first disciple – the only one who knows what the Master is planning to do – Jurenito chooses six other companions of different nationalities, who are supposed to assist him in his undertaking without being aware of it. His selection is not entirely logical: three are manifestly evil men, and as such eminently qualified to act as unwitting accomplices, since everything they do fits in perfectly with Jurenito's grand design. But the other three are harmless and even endearing characters, which means that they can hardly be of much use. All of them, however (except Aysha, the Negro), represent attitudes which make up the pattern of the 'civilized' world.

One of the evil men is Mr Cool, the American. A businessman by profession and a missionary by inclination, he is confident that he can solve every problem with the help of two books: his cheque book and the Bible. His belief in the power of the former is absolute: whether it is a matter of going to bed with someone else's fiancée, or of breaking a strike (not in his own factory, but purely for the sake of maintaining the established order), or of ruining the life of an artist of whose style he happens to disapprove, it can all be arranged merely by signing a cheque and handing it to the right people. The Bible, or rather the use he makes of it, enables him to find a moral

justification for everything he does. The war adds a new dimension
to his activities, and their scope widens as the slaughter goes on. He
creates a perfect organization to feed the Allied war machine, the
kind of organization Ehrenburg had seen in Calais. He owns arms
factories and army brothels, where each visitor receives with his
admission ticket a leaflet which tells him that 'God is love'.

At one point Ehrenburg asks Jurenito: 'Master, why didn't you kill
Mr Cool?' Yet, for all his iniquity, Mr Cool is a human being. There
is nothing human, however, about Jurenito's German disciple, Karl
Schmidt, who comes close to being an automaton equipped with
what would now be called an electronic brain. Schmidt stands for
dictatorship and regimentation. He is not interested in gain or
pleasure: his only ambition is to organize the world, and he is
prepared to accept any doctrine whose declared purpose is to set up
an orderly system. He admires both the Kaiser and Karl Marx.
During the war he becomes a general in the German Army; after
Germany's collapse, he turns Communist and goes to Russia where
he hopes to put his ideas into practice. He is the man who produces
the charts that fill Ehrenburg with dismay. Ehrenburg is rather more
charitable to the Frenchman, Monsieur Delhaie, who personifies
bourgeois selfishness. He, too, is an unpleasant character, but he
appreciates good food, a quiet life and the pleasures of love, and one
can see that Ehrenburg has a sneaking admiration for his *savoir
vivre*.

Jurenito's three 'evil' disciples all belong to privileged nations. By
contrast, Alexei Spiridonovich Tishin, the idealistic, tearful and
hopelessly muddled Russian intellectual, Ehrenburg the Jew, and
Aysha the Negro all represent the underdogs, who are treated much
as Ehrenburg saw Russian soldiers being treated in France. At one
point, Jurenito and his companions, all except Schmidt, are interned
in a German camp. 'Whenever our guards were angry with the
Master, Mr Cool or Monsieur Delhaie', says the narrator, Ehrenburg, 'they would invariably punish Alexei Spiridonovich, Aysha or
myself.' The Italian member of the group, Ercole Bambucci, is of
somewhat indeterminate status: the guards chastise him for his
misdemeanours, but do not treat him as a whipping boy. As an
Italian, Ercole represents true Western culture, even though he has
never learned to read or write. Fundamentally, he is a tramp and a
joyous anarchist. He has never done a stroke of work and he despises
wealth, yet he has mastered the art of living to no lesser extent than

that plump, prosperous and respectable hedonist, Monsieur Delhaie. As for Aysha the Negro, he is the best of them all. Civilization has passed him by, and he is kind, affectionate and pure of heart. Ehrenburg presumably modelled him on the Senegalese soldiers he had met during the war on the Western Front.

Ehrenburg himself differs from the other six characters in various respects and notably in the fact that he is a Jew. Unlike his companions, he claims at one point that if he had to choose between the two most important words in the vocabulary – 'yes' and 'no' – he would choose 'no'. This is supposed to be the basis of Ehrenburg's (and Jurenito's) philosophy – a resounding 'no' to society – and as the disciples travel from country to country, everything they see confirms the Master's views on the impasse into which Western civilization has been driven. As it unfolds, the novel thus becomes a catalogue of human perversions. Religion has been destroyed by dogma. The Almighty of the Old Testament, having once unfairly put Job to the test, has ever since been playing with men's lives like a reckless gambler. The Church has devalued the currency of the Kingdom of Heaven and brought it down into the dust. Protestantism has stripped Rome of its rich vestments, without realizing how precious they were, and has found only a handful of stuffing inside. Atheists, having nothing to cling to, rant and rave in public, but privately seek refuge in cowardly superstition. As for faith, it survives only in such primitive and tender-hearted men as Aysha – who retains an inviolable and childlike trust in the beneficent power of the idols he carves out of coconut shells – while among Europeans, a genuine believer is as rare as a good-looking virgin or an upright statesman. Meanwhile, love, as a natural relationship between the sexes, has been destroyed by St Paul, whose teachings Jurenito bluntly dismisses as 'scabrous'. But since, he adds, the apostle could not castrate the entire human race, his followers have had to accept that only sex 'sanctified' by marriage is permissible; and as a result, the world has been turned into one gigantic brothel, since marriage in bourgeois society is far more corrupt than prostitution. And so on.

It is all very pungent stuff, but Ehrenburg's attempt to portray Jurenito as a total cynic does not ultimately come off. It is true that Jurenito denounces marriage as worse than prostitution and organized religion as a fraud. But if he is so cynical, why does he waste so much time denouncing these institutions? The reason is surely that, while Jurenito is not supposed to care, Ehrenburg does: so much so that, when the First World War breaks out, he makes Jurenito disappear altogether for a time, so that, as narrator, he is free to voice his own personal lament. He recalls how he felt when the wounded began to appear on the streets of Paris, 'their faces bandaged, groping, blind, or hobbling on crutches', and when he saw 'a little girl in a pale blue dress, whose legs had been torn off by a German bomb. The newsboys continued to scream: "Killed, missing, believed killed". I felt I was suffocating, unable to bear the stench of blood, of anaesthetic and printer's ink . . .'

Eventually, Jurenito reappears and the satirical narrative is resumed. Mr Cool is busy supplying guns, corned beef and whores to the Army. Monsieur Delhaie's contribution to the war effort is to denounce imaginary spies and lead-swingers to the French police. Ercole Bambucci, after a spell in the Italian Army, has managed to desert and has found refuge in the Vatican. But the underdogs, as one might imagine, have done rather less well. Aysha has been mobilized, has served in the front line, and has lost an arm. Alexei Tishín, having enlisted as a volunteer eager to save France and Russia from the common enemy, is discovered by the Master serving with the Foreign Legion in Africa, where he is subjected to every kind of humiliation (Ehrenburg seems to be suggesting that whatever a Russian intellectual tried to do, it was invariably bound to go wrong.) The Master himself decides to make a visit to the front, accompanied by his disciples, where they are captured by the Germans and given an opportunity to see their old friend, Karl Schmidt, at work. However, as soon as they hear of the Tsar's abdication, they escape to Russia.

There is a sardonic description of the standstill on the Eastern Front in the first months following the February Revolution of 1917, and of the 'fraternization' between Russian and German soldiers, about which Ehrenburg felt extremely bitter at the time. In the meantime, having arrived in Russia, Jurenito and his companions watch the orgy of freedom that sweeps the country after the collapse of the monarchy and see the chaos this creates in people's minds; the Master quickly comes to the conclusion that freedom is too heavy a yoke to bear, and that its twilight is at hand. Later, when the Soviet regime is established, he discusses the issues of freedom and power with 'the man on the captain's bridge', who is not named but is easily recognizable as Lenin. In Dostoevsky's legend of the Grand Inquisitor,[1] the latter has a lengthy debate with Christ about the nature of freedom. In *Julio Jurenito*, Ehrenburg referred to Lenin's imaginary conversation with the Master as that of 'the Grand Inquisitor beyond the Legend'.

Ehrenburg's own feelings about power, as portrayed by the narrator in this chapter, are entirely human. He has an understandable dread of those who wield it, and when he learns that he is to accompany Jurenito to the Kremlin, he is so frightened that the Master has to drag him there by main force. Jurenito, as he talks with the 'leading Communist – the captain on the bridge', mingles irony with respect. He compliments Lenin on his 'healthy' gift of singlemindedness: he fully understands, he says, that people like Lenin have to wear blinkers. 'Reflection', says Jurenito, 'is a dessert served at the last supper before death. How can anyone accomplish anything unless he is blind? The bandage round the eyes is a splendid armour against the devil of wisdom.'

Lenin listens to his views with unruffled calm. But then Jurenito mentions one inevitable by-product of this 'healthy' approach: the list he has seen in *Izvestia* of people executed the previous day. At this, Lenin at once becomes emotional and excited. He jumps to his feet and, pacing up and down the room, launches into a tirade, trying to prove – perhaps not so much to his visitor as to himself – that there is no other way, even although he finds his mission fearful and burdensome. He asserts, however, that *someone* had to put an end to chaos, and to bring under control those who had been roaming the countryside armed with pikes (cf. Ehrenburg's *A Prayer for Russia*), and drowning officers in the Moïka Canal (cf. Ehrenburg's disgust at Mayakovsky's poem); a somewhat curious explanation, nonetheless, since it makes it seem as if the sole purpose of the October Revolution was to restore order. But Lenin is adamant. Those who oppose the march towards a better future must be eliminated. And he adds: 'I am not going to pray for my sins or wash my hands clean. I am simply telling you it is hard. But it haş got to be done, do you understand?'

Lenin lacks the impassivity that Dostoevsky's Grand Inquisitor would doubtless have shown in a similar situation, but their final conclusions are much the same and equally harsh. If necessary,

[1]Based on an episode in *The Brothers Karamazov* (1880). The philosopher Vasily Rozanov later published a detailed commentary on this section of the novel, which he called *The Legend of the Grand Inquisitor* (1890).

people must be 'driven to paradise with iron whips'. This is a direct echo of what the Inquisitor says to Christ: 'Only now that we have at last suppressed freedom has it become possible for the first time to think about people's happiness. Man is a rebel by nature. Can rebels ever be happy?'

In Dostoevsky's legend, the confrontation ends with Christ implanting a gentle kiss on the Inquisitor's lips. For his part, Jurenito ends the conversation by kissing Lenin on his 'high vaulted forehead'. Out of reverence or out of pity? asks Ehrenburg. Neither, says Jurenito. It was a ritual kiss in deference to Russian tradition; a clever answer, if one recalls that Jurenito is supposed to be a cynic who has rid himself of all emotion. But Ehrenburg, when he wrote this, was surely trying to convey a certain pity for the man who, having acquired power and then become its slave, was obliged to follow in the footsteps of the Inquisitor. Meanwhile, Jurenito's German disciple, Karl Schmidt, and thousands like him, have been swinging their iron whips, only too eager to suppress freedom, and unable to comprehend the very meaning of the word 'happiness'.

It is true that not all the early Bolsheviks were like Karl Schmidt. Some of them understood perfectly well what happiness meant, and ardently desired it for others. They were selfless people, often doing dull jobs, half-starved, yet intoxicating themselves with work in the belief that what they were doing would eventually put an end to the hardships which the whole nation was suffering. Ehrenburg describes one such man, who bursts into tears when, in a moment of truth, he realizes the futility of his efforts. Such characters do not talk about freedom or even think about it: they are far too preoccupied with other matters. Ehrenburg admired their integrity, but for him, freedom remained the key issue. At a time when art and poetry are apparently flourishing in Russia, Jurenito remains firmly convinced that, in the long run, there will be no room for artistic freedom or for art itself under the Soviet regime. He predicts that art will disappear, and be replaced by what is now called industrial design, or, as it has sometimes been called in Russia, by 'technical aesthetics'. In proclaiming these views through the character of the Master, Ehrenburg turned out to be both right and wrong. He was right in that, in 1946, Stalin made an attempt, through his deputy, Andrei Zhdanov, to abolish art altogether. On the other hand, he was wrong in that Stalin was not interested in aesthetics, technical or otherwise, and simply tried to replace art by old-fashioned kitsch.

Yet Ehrenburg did have a gift for prophecy, of which he was aware and justifiably proud. He used to say that it was the writer's mission not only to see but to foresee; and in *Julio Jurenito*, he did provide one remarkable example of foresight. While the First World War is in progress, Jurenito invents a weapon of mass destruction; not in itself an original notion, since other writers had already predicted the advent of a weapon resembling the future atomic bomb. However, when Jurenito hands over his blueprint to Mr Cool, the American shows no haste to start production, not because he has a vested interest in prolonging the war, but because he feels that Germany can be finished off with French bayonets, and it is therefore preferable to keep Jurenito's deadly invention in reserve – for use against Japan!

Voltaire's *Candide* ends on a note of resignation: the hero, cured of his optimism, is content to cultivate his garden, and no longer believes in the best of all possible worlds. Gulliver ends his travels in a mood of deep pessimism: he is disillusioned with the human race, and no longer wants any further contact with it. By contrast, Ehrenburg ends his picaresque account of Jurenito's and his own adventures by sounding a note of hope. Jurenito is dead. Ehrenburg has returned to the West. He knows he himself will never see a world in which men have been set free. 'But', he adds, 'the inevitable will come in the end. I believe it, and to all who await it, to all my brothers without a god, without a programme or an ideal, to all those who are naked and despised and love only the wind and the outrage, I send my last kiss.'

A few years later, Ehrenburg came under attack from a critic writing in *Novy Mir*, who particularly objected to his fanciful portrait of Lenin. Ehrenburg, said this critic, had made the 'captain on the bridge' a pathetic and hysterical Bohemian; small wonder, then, that such a leader spoke of the masses as if they were an evil herd fated to destruction, and opened his heart so readily to a petty bourgeois interviewer who plied him with loaded questions. Such a 'captain' would indeed have deserved the kiss that Ehrenburg forced Jurenito to bestow upon him. 'Fortunately,' the writer concluded, 'in those fateful days, Russia had a very different type of man on the captain's bridge.'

This was written after Lenin's death, which made things easier from the critic's point of view. Lenin himself does not seem to have been so touchy. There is no record of what he thought of the portrait Ehrenburg had drawn of him. But when he read *Julio Jurenito*, he remembered the untidy, hirsute young exile he had met in Paris, and remarked to his wife, Nadezhda Krupskaya: 'This is by Shaggy Ilya – and it's not at all bad!' Ehrenburg only learnt of this comment some years later.

Meanwhile, *Julio Jurenito* was coming to the attention of other leading figures in Soviet political life. Shortly after its first publication in Berlin, the novel appeared in a Soviet edition, and with a preface by Ehrenburg's old friend, Nikolai Bukharin, who was by then a member of the Politburo, one of the leaders of the Comintern, and editor of *Pravda*. Bukharin made it clear that he did not agree with the author's views, but he paid *Julio Jurenito* the compliment of treating it as a piece of literature. He could, he said, have written about Ehrenburg's 'individualistic anarchism', his nihilistic 'hooliganism', his hidden scepticism, and so on. It was perfectly plain that the author was not a Communist, that he had no great faith in the coming order of things, and was not passionately keen on it either. But none of this altered the fact that the book was a fascinating satire. Ehrenburg's own particular brand of nihilism had enabled him to depict many of the ludicrous and repulsive aspects of life to be found under all regimes. Predictably, Bukharin singled out for special praise Ehrenburg's indictment of capitalism and war. 'The author', he went on, 'is a former Bolshevik . . . a man of broad vision, with a deep insight into the Western European way of life, a sharp eye and an acid tongue. He has written a lively, interesting, attractive and clever book.'

Bukharin then ended his preface in similar vein, expressing sentiments that would be strictly unimaginable on the lips of any present-day Soviet leader.

They say that there can be no arguing about tastes – *de gustibus non est disputandum*. And yet – probably because people have forgotten all about Latin gerunds and gerundives – that is all they do do: argue about taste. For our part, we hope the public will show good taste and will enjoy reading this remarkable novel, *Julio Jurenito*.[1]

[1] See Appendix 1.

CHAPTER VIII

The action of *Julio Jurenito* takes place in the not-so-distant future, i.e. sometime in the mid to late 1920s. A gentleman is spending the night in a brothel in a French provincial town, and finds a tattered book under the bed. Attached to it is a note from the madame of the brothel, informing customers that her establishment has been given high praise in this scholarly work. The brothel is one of a chain owned by the American, Mr Cool, and the book is *Julio Jurenito*. The gentleman reads it while his companion is asleep, and comes to the conclusion that Jurenito is simply a braggart, who talks of his grandiose plans, but does nothing to translate them into action, just when action is most needed.

Jurenito does indeed spend most of his time talking. And in spite of his declared intention to spur on the process of European disintegration, his activities as an *agent provocateur* do not really amount to much: he is merely an onlooker. Perhaps it was because of this, and because Europe had survived the holocaust of the First World War, that Ehrenburg decided to write another fantasy, which he called *The D.E. Trust. The Story of the Destruction of Europe*. The letters 'D.E.' stand for 'Destruction of Europe', and the hero (or, rather, anti-hero) is a man of action called Jens Boot, who finishes the task Jurenito was unable to complete.

Ehrenburg did not mean it to be a prophecy: his aim was satire. But since he set it in the future, he was obliged to have recourse to some of the more outmoded devices of science fiction. As a novel, *The D.E. Trust* is vastly inferior to *Julio Jurenito*. The tone is flippant and the humour is forced. Yet no other book among Ehrenburg's vast output reflects so clearly the dualism which played so great a part in his life – his love and hate for Europe.

When he returned to Western Europe from Russia, he was appalled and exasperated by what he saw. It was the anger of a disappointed lover who found his mistress in the arms of Monsieur Delhaie, the self-satisfied bourgeois hedonist to whom one of the greatest tragedies in the history of mankind had meant little at the time and, now that it was over, had ceased to mean anything at all. Ehrenburg found, or believed he had found, a Europe which had forgotten the war. In a postscript to a new edition of his wartime sketches, he cursed those who, 'having come back to their vomit', were intent only on banishing the memories of war from their own and other people's minds.

I look at the beach covered with refuse, and try in vain to discover some sign of a purifying tide. Those who died had a right to be blind. The duty of the survivors is to see, and all I see is a postwar Europe of profiteers – wolves gathered round conference tables, famine in Russia, millions of rickety children in Central Europe. I went to Ypres where I saw the tourists – parasites and hyenas from different lands, easing their putrid bodies out of limousines, sipping cool drinks and inspecting the tomb-stones and the rotting crosses, while invalids, blind or legless or both, moved about on crutches or crawled on the ground, selling picture postcards. I thought of a different world – the world of trenches, shells and death. Then there was hope. Now there is none. And so life goes on until there is another war. Thunderstorms, annihilation, the death of Europe: anything would be better than this disgraceful morning-after.

The death of Europe. A Europe that had forgotten her dead did not deserve to live. So, with heavy heart, Ehrenburg set out to destroy Europe through Jens Boot, the president of the D.E. Trust, the man who discovers a tattered copy of *Julio Jurenito* in a French provincial brothel founded by Mr Cool.

'But why Europe?' someone asks Boot. 'Why did you single out Europe, considering that there exist four other, equally repulsive continents?' Blushing like a girl and demurely lowering his eyes, the man who destroys Europe replies: 'Because I love her.'

Jens Boot, the illegitimate son of a Dutch peasant woman and a minor European princeling, is an adventurer who refuses to consider himself a national of any single country and proudly calls himself a European. Ehrenburg provides him with something he would dearly have liked to possess himself: a collection of passports which enable his hero to travel freely without having to beg for visas. Having tried out various professions, Jens Boot becomes a gigolo whose duties involve dancing with elderly ladies at what was then known as a '5 o'clock tea'. He accepts this occupation with equanimity, until, at one of these gatherings, he falls in love for the first time in his life. The woman's hair is like a red sunset. She is as beautiful as Europe, and though her name has no mythological associations (she is called Lucy

Flamingo), Jens Boot sees her as the Phoenician princess whom Jupiter, taking on the shape of a bull, carried away. She is Europa.

But Lucy is a society beauty and when Jens Boot asks her to dance with him, she haughtily spurns this invitation from a penniless gigolo. At that point, as he stands there shocked and humiliated, Jens Boot realizes that he has been unable to find his place in life on the continent to which he is so proud to belong. He makes one final attempt to find something in Europe worth preserving: he goes to Russia and becomes a soldier of the Revolution. But when he sees that the Communist Government is imposing State capitalism, he loses hope. He persuades three American multi-millionaires, each of whom has his own reasons for wishing to see Europe turned into a desert, to provide the necessary funds and, as president of the D.E. Trust, he initiates and supervises the process of Europe's anni-hilation, skilfully manipulating those who are ready to exterminate others, and who, eventually, perish themselves.

Most of Europe is destroyed by war – the conflict Ehrenburg predicted would come if people forgot the previous one. It is unleashed by a dictator in France, who seizes power with the help of a paramilitary organization and is wildly applauded when he announces to an obedient Chamber of Deputies: 'We have had enough of peace!' Thereafter, one country after another, including European Russia, is devastated by conventional weapons, long-range missiles, gas and germ warfare (Holland is transformed into a graveyard by poisoned rain). For those that are left, other means are devised under Jens Boot's invisible direction, in accordance with the national characteristics of the prospective victims. Scandinavia succumbs to a mysterious sleeping sickness. On Britain, the bastion of high finance, Boot inflicts economic ruin which leads to famine and cannibalism. France, the hotbed of aggression and profligacy, is unable to escape civil war and ceases to exist as a nation when her birth-rate goes down to zero, all French males having become impotent through abuse of aphrodisiacs. (Thirty-five years later, in a more sober mood, Ehrenburg wrote: 'There are many myths in this world – the myth about the French is that they are debauched.')

The whole process takes twelve years, from 1928 to 1940. Jens Boot himself leads a charmed life: rockets cannot hit him, and he is immune to all forms of bacteria. The only thing that can still make him waver is love, and at one point, having engineered the destruction of half the Continent, he is tempted to stop. The long-awaited moment has arrived – Lucy Flamingo sends for him. They meet in Venice, and in that beautiful and sea-girt city, Jens Boot enters a realm 'in which gods become bulls and bulls assume divine shape'. He decides to spare what remains of Europe, and to spend the rest of his life with the beautiful Phoenician. But his dream is soon shattered. Lucy tells him:

> *Mon petit Jean*, I love you so much. I shall always dance with you, and with you alone. I have waited for you so long, although I didn't realize it myself. They say such extraordinary things about you – they call you the King of Europe. And now, I want to ask you to do something for us – [Lucy, needless to say, has a husband who, on this occasion, has tactfully stayed out of the way] – please, do arrange for the Italian lire to rise. We need it so badly – we are ruined.

So Boot finds himself the victim of a monumental fraud. Lucy is no exalted Phoenician princess, but merely a vulgar and grasping woman; she could be a tart from Genoa or Marseilles, a woman with flabby breasts, a greasy skin, and small, covetous eyes buried in layers of fat. His earlier vision of a glorious head of hair like a red sunset has vanished: now he sees in it only tarnished streaks of verdigris (caused, as she does not fail to point out, by the inferior brand of peroxide she has been reduced to using). With revulsion, Boot jumps out of the bed and pulls up the blind. Beyond it, Venice lies stretched out before him. But he is impervious to its beauty. Instead, he sees only a dead city which smells of carrion, while on the bed, a blowzy creature in lace underwear keeps repeating monotonously, 'Please arrange it, *mon petit Jean*, please do arrange it.' So this is what Europe has come to! Jens Boot must return to his work of destruction. He unfolds a map and draws a line through Italy.

But to remain indifferent to the disappearance of Italy (Ehrenburg's 'beloved Italy') is as impossible as to banish the image of the unforgettable Phoenician, and Jens Boot is plunged into the torments of hell. He takes a train to Rome, and on the train meets an eminent man of letters, who launches into a strange, allusive phantasmagoria, summing up the splendours and miseries of Europe's past: a drop of melted wax on the statue of Eros; Christians in the catacombs; devout thieves carousing with the hangman in a dingy tavern; the rose of roses and the pearl of pearls; Leonardo's wild bird; Candide's courteous vapidity and tedious adventures (a passing dig at those critics who had accused Ehrenburg of imitating Voltaire); the revolutionary strains of the 'Carmagnole'; the clouds of yellow gun smoke and other theatrical effects cherished by the Little Corsican. Then comes a final spasm: the shooting of the Communards – '*c'est la lutte finale . . .*'

As he listens to the venerable and wise man of letters, who, like himself, is in love with Europe, Jens Boot longs for death. But he has devised a different finale. Rome is two thousand years of memories turned into stone. The punishment that is now meted out to Italy takes the subtle form of a deadly disease, the first symptom of which is loss of memory. This is transmitted by fleas brought back by soldiers from a punitive expedition to Africa, but the fleas carrying the germ do not find Boot's flesh to their taste. He would give anything to lose his own memory. He envies a man who stops him in the street and asks, 'Could you please tell me who I am and where I live?' But Boot is doomed to remember. In the ruins of a temple in the Roman Campagna, where legionaries about to embark for service in Africa or the East had once worshipped Europa, he passionately embraces a slab of marble, and curses fate for not allowing him to succumb to the disease which would have brought him oblivion.

But his task is done: Jens Boot has finally destroyed Europe. The D.E. Trust is dissolved, and in New York, at a final board meeting, the three Americans who have financed the whole operation pass a vote of thanks to the president, and offer to reward him handsomely for his services. But Jens Boot does not want any reward. He flies back across the Atlantic, and lands on a continent from which all trace of human habitation has vanished. In ecstasy, he venerates each tree and each blade of grass. He can walk without harm among the beasts of the field: a she-wolf even gives this strange two-legged creature a friendly lick. Europe has become Paradise. 'Europa! Europa!' cries the last man in Europe as he gazes at the red splendours of the sunset; and then, kissing the earth, he dies.

Ehrenburg provided his own explanation of this strange tale. He wrote:

> Jens Boot killed Europe because he was a typical European of that particular period. From the end of the nineteenth century onwards, there had developed in Europe a new kind of patriotism. People of different nations – the French, the Dutch, the Germans – had begun to think of themselves as belonging to one great country: they saw Europe as a garden which was their common heritage. The garden might be withering away, but it was still the finest in the world. Unfortunately, this did not prevent members of the European confraternity from exterminating each other.

All Europe was in the grip of a suicidal mania, and all Jens Boot did was to make the grand gesture of a suicide.

Love does sometimes make people blind, and in many respects Ehrenburg seems to have been blinded by his love for Europe. Wars are usually suicidal, and although it was on a vast and devastating scale, the European war was no more suicidal than those which had ravaged other equally 'repulsive' continents. A kind of pan-European patriotism certainly did exist among the intellectual élite and among the poets and artists of the Rotonde, but it was neither that élite nor the *habitués* of the Rotonde who had started the 1914–18 war. What did exist, on a much wider scale, was what one can only call European snobbery: a European superiority complex which manifested itself in a diversity of ways. When the Kaiser Wilhelm II of Germany appealed to the nations of Europe to 'protect their most sacred values', he may have thought he was speaking as a European patriot; but in fact, he was merely coining a useful slogan for keeping Asians in their place, and for combating what was known at the time as 'The Yellow Peril'. Pseudo-intellectuals constantly vaunted the lofty superiority of Europeans and the European ideal, but genuine intellectuals were not immune from European snobbery either.

In Ehrenburg's case, it took an anti-American bias, as clearly emerges from a tragi-comic chapter of *The D.E. Trust*. This relates how, at an interim stage in the operation of destruction, one of its American sponsors decides to take his honeymoon in the devastated region of Central Europe. Unhappily for him, his virgin bride promptly cuckolds him: she cannot resist the attractions of one of the surviving savages, whose only item of dress is a pince-nez. She finds him irresistible precisely because he is a European, and thus a romantic lover, of a kind (according to Ehrenburg, at least) not to be found on the other side of the Atlantic. Her distressed husband tries to force her to go back to America, but she prefers to commit suicide on European soil.

Ehrenburg was certainly not free from European snobbery, especially when directed against the Americans. On the other hand, he was infuriated by its anti-Russian variety. He deeply resented any suggestion that the Russians were not really Europeans and could therefore be treated as *Untermenschen* (as he felt the Russian soldiers had been treated in France); and it was because of this that he made Jens Boot include the European part of Russia in his scheme. But since Ehrenburg considered himself a Soviet writer, his attitude, on any dispassionate reckoning, was both unpatriotic and illogical: unpatriotic because, if the Soviet State was deserving of survival east of the Urals, it ought to have been allowed to survive west of the Urals as well; and illogical because, his anger being directed primarily against Western Europe, he had every reason to leave European Russia intact. In fact, he was caught in a dilemma. He could have allowed Jens Boot to spare Moscow, Petrograd and Kiev. But this would have been tantamount to an admission that Russia did not belong to Europe; and that, especially in the face of other manifestations of so-called Western European superiority, was something Ehrenburg would never concede.

It is interesting to speculate why Ehrenburg chose to make his dictator a Frenchman, with his demagogic slogan: 'We have had enough of peace!' In other respects, his vision was certainly prophetic. On 1 August 1939, Hitler appeared before a jubilant Reichstag to make a speech amounting to just that. But Ehrenburg had written *The D.E. Trust* in Berlin nearly two decades earlier. All around him he saw the misery of a defeated country, and although he was surprised to find portraits of the Kaiser still decorating the walls of German middle-class homes, like so many other people he could not imagine that Germany would ever find the strength to emerge once more as the aggressive Power he had so deeply hated during the First World War. On the other hand, France, as he saw her, was not only victorious and rich, but arrogant and chauvinistic.

Besides, she had expelled Ehrenburg, which was an unforgivable thing to do.

CHAPTER IX

In the autumn of 1921, having finished *Julio Jurenito*, Ehrenburg moved to Berlin, where he was to stay for the next two years. This was the longest period he ever spent in exile, if by exile one understands enforced absence from the country where one would prefer to be, which is not necessarily the same thing as the country of one's birth.

Ehrenburg could have returned to Russia whenever he liked. The critic, Viktor Shklovsky, who at that time was living as an *émigré* in Berlin, remarked in his book *Zoo*: 'Nature has given Ehrenburg a lavish endowment – he has a passport! He lives abroad with this passport and thousands of visas.' Shklovsky himself was desperately homesick and longing to go back to Moscow, which was why he envied Ehrenburg his Soviet passport. But he need not have envied him the 'thousands of visas'. Most of these were no more than souvenirs which Ehrenburg had acquired during the various stages of his tortuous journey to the West, before he eventually landed up in Berlin. There was only one visa which he really cared for – the visa he had obtained at the French Consulate in Riga – and this had been rendered null and void by his expulsion from France. Ehrenburg was not a refugee from Russia: he was an exile from Paris.

He had no cause to complain about his life in Berlin, however. *Julio Jurenito* had first been published there, and had brought him fame, and enough money to live on. Berlin was, in fact, something of a Russian literary capital, second only to Moscow and Petrograd. It had a large number of Russian publishing houses, some of which specialized in works by authors with Soviet connections, and Ehrenburg had no difficulty in getting his work into print. He managed to produce one book after another with a speed and apparent ease that were truly astonishing. Moreover, as soon as he arrived in Berlin he started writing for a Russian literary magazine called *Russkaya Kniga* (later renamed *Novaya Russkaya Kniga*), which was in many ways a remarkable publication. Its editor was a certain Professor Alexander Yashchenko, who had set himself the task of collecting and publishing every scrap of information he could find about the fate of Russian writers during the chaotic years of the civil war. Yashchenko wanted to know what had happened to all of them, regardless of whether they were still in Russia or living abroad, and he was passionately interested in all Russian books wherever they appeared, whether in Moscow or Berlin, Sofia, Paris or Petrograd. Because of this, not unpredictably, he found himself facing accusations of being a Soviet agent – a charge that has always been bandied about freely in Russian *émigré* circles.

In the Professor's case, it was alleged that he was trying to blur the distinction between Communist and non-Communist Russia, in order to undermine *émigré* morale. Yet his approach seemed natural enough at the time. Altogether, some 300,000 Russians had converged on Berlin, and there were inevitably wide differences of view among them. Some were viscerally anti-Soviet; others, having reached the conclusion that the Soviet regime had come to stay, had begun to show some sympathy for it; and there were still others who were in a state of indecision, not knowing whether to remain abroad or to go back. It is significant, however, that, far from shunning each other, all these people (with the exception of a few die-hards) frequently met and sought each other's company. The writers among them got together in various cafés, which they turned into clubs, and there they debated, lectured, recited poetry, read excerpts from their work, and argued furiously; often before audiences consisting largely of young people who, after the turbulence and confusion of the civil war, were at last able to listen to various celebrities, either well-known or beginning to make a reputation, in the comforting knowledge that no shots would be fired outside.

One of the best-known of these establishments was called The House of the Arts, a haunt much frequented by Mayakovsky and Esenin whenever they came to Berlin. Sometimes there were noisy demonstrations. On one occasion, Esenin, arriving there with Isadora Duncan, was greeted with catcalls and whistles. When the clamour subsided, Esenin remarked scornfully, 'You're no good at it. Let me show you how it's done!' Whereupon he put two fingers in his mouth and emitted a whistle of ear-splitting shrillness. Esenin often liked to pose as a street tough, and plainly welcomed any opportunity to demonstrate that, when he portrayed himself in that guise in his poems, it was based on real-life experience. In his memoirs, Ehrenburg says The House of the Arts resembled Noah's Ark where the 'clean' and the 'unclean' happily rubbed shoulders, and he marvels at the fact that the writer Chirikov, who had worked for the Propaganda Department of the White Army during the civil war in the Ukraine, could sit down at the same table as Mayakovsky. But by the same token, Ehrenburg could, of course, have marvelled at Mayakovsky sitting down with Chirikov; and perhaps this was exactly what he meant to convey. In any case, in those days it was taken for granted that Russian intellectuals of all shades – Soviet and pro-Soviet, liberal and anti-Soviet – could meet and mingle freely; and certainly no one could have predicted that only a few years later, Soviet students and officials would meekly get up and leave a Berlin concert hall because they were about to be addressed, not by some implacable enemy of the regime, but by Ilya Ehrenburg, who ranked as a Soviet writer, even though he was under heavy fire from Soviet literary critics.

Russkaya Kniga reviewed every Russian book worth reviewing among those which appeared in Russia or abroad. It also published autobiographical sketches by Soviet and *émigré* authors, regardless of their political persuasion, and a multitude of documents, such as a letter from a group of Russian writers to the Commissar for Popular Enlightenment, Lunacharsky, complaining that, while the Soviet authorities were using thousands of tons of paper for publishing government decrees, there was hardly any paper left for printing books. Ehrenburg's first article for the magazine was called '*Au-dessus de la Mêlée*' and dealt with a particularly vital problem: that of political pressures on literature. It is worth recalling that, at that time, Russian *émigrés* of a certain type (although by no means all) flatly refused to acknowledge that anyone in the Soviet Union could possess the smallest spark of literary or artistic talent. To such people, Mayakovsky was merely a 'rowdy'; Esenin, because of his disorderly private life, was decried as 'a second Rasputin'; and the celebrated Russian literary critic, Kornei Chukovsky, dismissed as 'a Soviet lickspittle'. Ehrenburg protested against such judgements, which he described as 'monstrous'. Instead, he proposed to make a calm analysis of the situation, remaining *au-dessus de la mêlée*, and 'without the hate that is so laboriously cultivated nowadays'. He then propounded the view ('the heretical view' as he termed it) that, as poets, Balmont, who reviled Communism, and Bryusov, who sang its praises, both deserved to be treated with respect. 'Personally,' he added, 'I do not like the poems of either Balmont or Bryusov, and politically I am remote from both of them; but this does not give me the right to abuse them, or to speak of them with contempt.' On the other hand, there were a large number of Russians living abroad, 'whose attitude ... towards those writers who have remained in Russia is determined solely by the continuing political struggle'. Ehrenburg then recalled how Alexander Blok, the greatest poet of his generation, had been hounded by those who objected to his poem, 'The Twelve', because it expressed his acceptance of the Revolution. Such persecution was sacrilegious, he said, 'since art must remain sacred to us all'; and he insisted that writers and poets should be treated fairly while they were still alive, not merely after their death in 'magnificent obituaries'. Blok had died a year earlier, and Ehrenburg obviously had him in mind. But his remark also turned out to be prophetic. In the years that followed, both Mayakovsky and Esenin committed suicide. Once they were safely out of the way, they, too, became the subjects of 'magnificent obituaries' and other elaborate tributes.

Ehrenburg wrote several articles in a similar vein. He also reviewed much of the poetry that was being published in Russia and abroad, and in one review attacked 'those over-confident and ill-informed *émigré* critics who make the mistake of calling Pasternak "an insignificant novice" '. As for his own writings, these were regularly reviewed by other contributors to *Russkaya Kniga*. At that time, it was Roman Gul who spoke most warmly of his work, even though the same Gul was to say so many disparaging things about Ehrenburg thirty years later. It was Professor Yashchenko himself, the magazine's editor, who reviewed *Julio Jurenito*; and it is plain from his comments that, in this instance, Ehrenburg succeeded in projecting the image of himself that he had tried so hard to create: that of the complete cynic. Ehrenburg's novel, said Yashchenko, amounted to a hymn in praise of everything that was 'hypocritical, shabby and paradoxical in our, admittedly, still imperfect civilization'. He acknowledged that Ehrenburg's satire had an irresistible bite when it was directed against war: those passages, he said, had a genuine bitterness. But for the rest, the book was a denial of everything on which human society was based: it was imbued with a kind of scepticism which made parts of it quite unacceptable. A satirist must have ideals: Ehrenburg had none. He had held so many different beliefs that he had ended up in a void, which was why he was the only one of Jurenito's disciples who had said 'No' to mankind. Admittedly, his laughter was not that of Satan. But it was the laughter of 'a man with a burnt-out heart'. He had made the novel's central character, Jurenito, say before his death that his soul had been ravaged, not by hate, but by profound dislike. 'Dislike of all things', concluded Professor Yashchenko, 'could well be the motto of this book.'

Another critic, writing in the same journal, took an even harsher line in reviewing a collection of Ehrenburg's short stories called *Thirteen Pipes*, in which each pipe serves as a peg for a new episode.

> It is a strange book. One cannot put it down, which means that one must be enjoying it. But when one has put the book aside, one finds that it has left a bitter taste in the mouth. For Ehrenburg, there are no human beings. He sees only miserable automata dressed in suits, hats and shoes, and in each of the stories in *Thirteen Pipes* he strips his arrogant heroes of their garments, leaving them naked. He seems incapable of tenderness or affection, and one wonders whether he even has any respect for himself. It would seem not, because after pouring venom on his readers and his characters, he even brushes his own work scornfully aside. But in that case what is there left to live for? What is the point of such a book, even if it is the work of a gifted writer? In the old days, a Russian girl student would have killed herself after reading it, and left behind a note saying the book had convinced her of life's futility and hopelessness. But those girls are now grown-up. And besides, in view of the way we live nowadays, committing suicide has become an idle pastime. Ehrenburg gazes at mankind through a telescope from Mars: he sees the contours, but is unable to discern the expression on a person's face.

This assessment makes curious reading today, since, in fact, several of the stories in *Thirteen Pipes* are crudely sentimental. Ehrenburg was himself aware of the fact. As he said in the final story: 'People may laugh at me, but it cannot be helped: I am exceedingly sentimental, and I am not in the least ashamed to admit it. I love melodrama . . . I know that the icy blue glance of a demigod and the tearful stare of an old dog waiting to be kicked can both mean love.' A Russian girl student, however sensitive, would hardly have committed suicide after reading *Thirteen Pipes*, although she might well have shed a tear over one or two of the stories: over one in which the small son of a French Communard is shot by the government troops from Versailles; or another, in which a ne'er-do-well actor, crazed by poverty and blinded by jealousy, kills his wife's wealthy lover. The critics thought Ehrenburg was being ironical. In fact, he was portraying the truth as he saw it.

At the time, however, nothing could have suited him better than to be branded a cynic. How flattering, at the age of thirty-one, to be called 'a man with a burnt-out heart'! As he noted later in *A Book for Grown-Ups*, 'They called me a cynic, and I did not object.' In fact, it was an image he carefully cultivated. In the words of Viktor Shklovsky, Ehrenburg had several professions: smoking a pipe, being a sceptic, and writing *Julio Jurenito* – by which Shklovsky meant that, although the novel had been finished before Ehrenburg arrived in Berlin, he continued to behave as if still immersed in writing it, making a deliberate effort to identify himself with his hero. Pipe smoking was an essential part of the act. In homage to the memory of Jurenito, there is a dedication in Spanish following the title page of *Thirteen Pipes*, in which Ehrenburg recalls his first meeting with the Master at the Rotonde, when, as a callow and unhappy youth, he had complained that everything seemed to him unreal and insubstantial, and the Master gave him a pipe as one tangible proof of reality. But apart from being Julio Jurenito's favourite object, a pipe had other virtues: it suggested philosophical detachment, being *au-dessus de la mêlée*, or, as the *émigré* critic had put it, looking down on mankind through a telescope from Mars.

To be effective, an image needs to be cultivated in public, and Ehrenburg, who was the least domesticated of men, spent most of his time in Berlin in a bar called the Prager Diele (at that time, *diele* was the fashionable German word for a bar). The Prager Diele had no Bohemian associations of any kind, and took its name solely from the fact that it was located on the Prager Platz, a West Berlin square not far from the pension where Ehrenburg had his lodgings. In short, it was an unremarkable establishment, but one which Ehrenburg tried hard to turn into a minor replica of the Rotonde. Anyone who wished to see him was almost certain to find him there, sitting at his favourite table, working on a book, or holding court. Some of his visitors found him arrogant. In fact, he had considerable charm when he chose to exert it; but he also had a mordant wit, he did not suffer fools gladly, and he could be highly disagreeable to anyone whom he disliked. If he did not consider someone worthy of his attention, he simply sat there in silence, refusing to speak. Patience had never been one of his virtues, but this kind of behaviour also fitted in well with the world-weary pose he had adopted. In retrospect, some of the attitudes he took pleasure in now seem petty and even puerile; but perhaps he indulged in them because he had been deprived of such pleasures in earlier days, when he had submitted himself to the austere discipline of underground revolutionary activity.

CHAPTER X

The table reserved for Ehrenburg at the Prager Diele was a small, self-contained world, far removed from the city in which he now found himself living. The two years he spent in Berlin were productive in literary terms, and brought him fame. But Berlin itself never appealed to him, and he never ceased yearning for Paris.

Before coming to rest at the Prager Diele, he had cast about in other quarters, trying to find a substitute for the Rotonde. The nearest equivalent in Berlin was the Romanisches Café, which had the reputation of being the favourite meeting place for German and foreign writers, artists and journalists. Ehrenburg was not impressed, however, and vented his disappointment in a sharply critical essay:

> This is the headquarters of fanatics and tramps, of universal fixers and crooks, unhampered by the shackles of narrow nationalism. It is difficult to determine the professions of the people who come here. The shapeless soft hats, the stained flamboyant ties and unshaven jowls are all equally characteristic of the Dadaist poet and the currency speculator who is trying to do a deal in single dollar bills. A seedy-looking Italian is proclaiming in a stage whisper that by June or July at the latest, an international workers' march on Rome must be organized. A Dutchman, who seems to have something to do with literature, is declaiming against the visit of the Moscow Kamerny Theatre, which he describes as retrograde. Just imagine: at home in Holland, he and his friends have issued a manifesto doing away with authors and actors altogether, and now they find that a theatre from Moscow is daring to play Racine! Next to him, someone of indefinable nationality is expatiating indignantly on quite a different theme: yesterday, he acquired some Danish kroner, and now the exchange rate has dropped . . .

There is more in the same sour vein. Perhaps Ehrenburg had momentarily succumbed to an illusion often cherished by those living in exile: that what annoys them abroad cannot possibly exist at home. At that period, it is true, when Germany was in the throes of the worst inflation in its history and currency speculation was rife, the Romanisches Café had been invaded by a great many peculiar and shady characters, an international scum brought to the surface by war and revolution. Yet it was out of keeping for someone like Ehrenburg, who had always prided himself on being a cosmopolitan, to speak contemptuously of 'seedy-looking' Italians, provincial Dutchmen, or people of 'indefinable nationality'. As for shapeless hats, flamboyant ties, and wild chatter about politics, or art, or the future of the theatre, all these could equally well be found at the Rotonde.

To be fair to Ehrenburg, he did make an effort to understand Berlin, even though he spoke of it as 'a shabby barracks with broken windows'. He even tried to persuade himself that he was developing some kind of affection for the city. Berlin did have a special magic, a charm of its own; but to appreciate it, one had to enjoy living there, and Ehrenburg longed to be elsewhere. He tried to look at the city through the eyes of an artist. Most of the houses were ugly, built at the worst possible period, and decorated with heavy and unattractive ornaments. But at least they were all grey, and that made the ornaments less conspicuous. They were all five storeys high, the streets were straight, and the general effect was one of monolithic uniformity, or harmony, depending on the way one chose to see it. This, in the artist's eye, made Berlin a true *Grosstadt*, as distinct from *grosse Stadt* – the urban symbol of the machine age.

Ehrenburg wrote in a fictional *Letter to a Friend*:

> Some say Berlin is faceless and, in a way, they are right. Berlin is depressing, dull and devoid of local colour. But that is its 'face' and I have grown fond of it. Berlin is the only modern city in Europe. True, London has more motor-cars. But in London, apart from cars, there are cosy-looking little houses, speakers in Hyde Park, Christmas turkeys and other bucolic joys. London is not a city at all: it is a combination of 'Paradise' and 'Hell' – of the kind one sees in picture books. Paris is just 'Paradise', and when I was thrown out of there, I smiled self-consciously, like Adam. Think of the *midinettes* under the chestnut trees, of the secondhand bookstalls along the Seine, of the thrushes and the symbolist poets in the Luxemburg Gardens. Is it not a grandiose provincial place inhabited by the happiest of men? Paris has a face and so has London. Berlin is just a metropolis and could be the capital of Europe.

While Ehrenburg stayed in Berlin, his anti-German feelings were held in check. He felt in duty bound to sympathize with an impoverished nation, all the more as it was being ruined by those who were in power in France and whom he, the exile from Paris, hated as much as the average Russian refugee hated the Soviet regime. He made an effort to analyse what was happening in Germany, but he was no political analyst and did not have enough contact with Germans to gain a proper insight into the situation. He was puzzled by the fact that, in spite of the overthrow of the monarchy, photographs of the Kaiser and his family could still be bought at the stationer's, and that none of the street names had been altered (in Russia, changing and restoring street names had been one of the main preoccupations of the various regimes during the civil war); but he did not seem to realize to what extent the incipient democracy of the Weimar Republic was being sabotaged by large sections of German officialdom and the German middle class. What shocked him was not the political scene but vice. He had developed a puritanical streak and was appalled by the cafés and bars where homosexual prostitutes, male and female, assembled to meet their customers. 'By comparison,' he wrote, 'the ordinary modest street-walker who makes tactful advances to the passer-by seems a paragon of virtue. And how can anyone bring himself to ask the nice-looking blonde girl at the newspaper kiosk for a homosexual magazine, even if it is discreetly called *Freundschaft*?' There is no reason to suppose that vice was more rampant in postwar Berlin than it was in postwar Paris, and Ehrenburg must have known it. But Paris was far away, and Ehrenburg felt that in Berlin vice was being paraded, which made it look as if Germany was taking a pride in her moral decline.

He detected something even more morbid in contemporary German art. One of its exponents was the expressionist *Sturm* group. Ehrenburg disliked it intensely. 'Expressionism is hysteria,' he wrote:

> In the *Sturm* gallery, I saw a large canvas sprinkled with lots of red paint. It was called *Symphony in Blood*. The man responsible for it clearly had no intention of producing a work of art: all he wanted to do was to scream and to rebel, and it so happened that he got hold of a tube of paint. Had he got hold of a gun instead, it would have been worse. Poets also come to the *Sturm* gallery and make an unbearable noise, as they shriek about 'blood' and 'mystery'. This is no joke. A young girl who is having a fit of hysterics can still be attractive. But when I see a healthy, hard-working man affected with convulsions, I feel deeply depressed.

This is hardly a fair description of German art and poetry in the early 1920s. For whatever one may think of *Sturm* – or may have thought of it then – it was not the only modern trend or even the dominant one. As for individual artists, there was George Grosz, whom Ehrenburg admired; he was an artist who saw all that was evil in German bourgeois society with the percipient and voluptuous eye of a genius, and expressed in his masterly drawings what Ehrenburg, much less successfully, was trying to put into words.

Yet, in spite of his highly subjective approach, Ehrenburg did recognize some of the more important signs of the times. He appreciated the significance of the fact that, in spite of misery and economic ruin, Germany had not collapsed into revolution or disarray. Work had not stopped, and to someone who had lived through the civil war in Russia, when production had almost come to a standstill, this was the most striking thing of all. 'The Germans,' he observed, 'cannot live without work in the same way as the Neapolitans cannot live without songs.' He compared Berlin, and Germany itself, to a gigantic railway station which continued to function simply through the law of inertia. The trains were all leaving on time, but neither the station-master nor the engine-drivers knew where they were going: beyond the station lay only un-certainty. It was a vision worthy of Kafka. No one could tell where Germany was going, least of all Germany herself. This had its alarming aspects, but to Ehrenburg as a writer, it also conveyed a strange sense of exhilaration: this 'wonderful uncertainty', as he put it, seemed to him characteristic of the whole of postwar Europe. London and Paris did not know where they were going either, even though this might not initially be apparent to the casual observer. These were prosperous cities which concealed their disquiet beneath their wealth; in Ehrenburg's phrase, they were 'ostriches of stone'. But Berlin was different. Berlin was without pretence: and he liked and admired it for its frankness. He wrote in his *Letter to a Friend*:

> True, London is still a bulwark of morality, and lovely English girls with their angelic Pre-Raphaelite looks do not sell such journals as *Freundschaft*. True, Picasso is still painting superb pictures, which have nothing in common with the ravings of the expressionists. But it is only in Berlin that one feels the pulse of Europe. That is why you must learn to love Berlin. I want you to love this city as you love Europe, that unhappy, deranged woman who flounders in dried blood and liquid mud. For her unwitting envoy – the messenger she has dispatched into the wonderful uncertainty of the future – is this city of hideous monuments and anguished faces: Berlin.

Ehrenburg revisited Germany a few years later, during the brief period of her economic recovery. Again, he did not probe very deeply into the political situation, but again he seized on some of the things that mattered. The uncertainty was still there, but now it was no longer exhilarating or wonderful. He wrote with foreboding:

> Someone will have to pay for the energy that is being poured into erecting this huge and sumptuous edifice called the German Reich. Germany has everything to make life comfortable: modern amenities, industry, books and pastry shops. But she has no ideals or sense of purpose. Even an umbrella should know why it must open to protect its owner against the rain: otherwise, even an umbrella will go mad.

But at last he had been given permission to return to France. As he sat in the train carrying him back to Paris, he thought: 'At least this is one train that still remembers its destination − it won't go off the rails. But who knows what may happen in the future?'

CHAPTER XI

In the early 1920s, *épater le bourgeois* was an ambition that was easier to satisfy than it is nowadays, when the bourgeoisie has become used to being outraged. At the start of that decade, I was not yet old enough to attend some of the more spectacular manifestations at which this art was practised. But I did get a whiff of it in 1925, at a poetry reading given by the Russian poet Anatoly Marienhof, while he was on a visit to Berlin. Marienhof was not a very good poet. His chief claim to fame was his friendship with Esenin – they were co-founders of the so-called 'imaginist' school – and not having much to offer, Marienhof was all the more anxious to shock. On that occasion, having advanced on to the stage, he stood there for a good two minutes, arms akimbo, surveying the audience with an air that was meant to convey supreme contempt. Finally, he condescended to speak, and launched into a brief talk on the literary scene in Russia, devoted largely to a defence of the use of obscene words by the imaginist poets. In particular, he quoted some verse by Esenin, which contained the word *blyad* – a vulgar expression for 'whore'. The audience duly gasped. They might use the word often enough in private, but were accustomed to seeing it in print only as a 'b' followed by four discreet dots, and they certainly did not expect to hear it pronounced, loudly and clearly, on a public platform. Marienhof then went on to explain that their squeamishness was due to their ignorance of Russian etymology. 'One ought to know the origins of one's own language', he proclaimed pedantically, and proceeded to argue that the word *blyad* had perfectly respectable roots: according to him, it was derived from the verb *obladat* – to possess – and from *Lado* – the old Slav god of love. This was, in fact, arrant nonsense: the word has nothing to do either with possession, or with gods or goddesses of love, but comes from the verb 'to err' (in Russian *bluzhdat* or *zabluzhdatsya*). Marienhof then read one of his own poems which, as it happened, was devoid of obscenities and contained one impressive line. When he had finished, he quickly turned his back on the audience and walked off-stage, ignoring the applause. It was all very embarrassing. Fortunately, his studied exit was followed by the appearance of his wife, a charming and talented actress, who recited some well-known poems by Mayakovsky and Esenin. She was no doubt less advanced than her husband: I noted that, in reciting one of Esenin's poems, she omitted a stanza in which the poet spoke of an urge to urinate on the moon.

One might have thought that by that time, Ehrenburg had no need to ape the mannerisms of a Marienhof. He was, after all, over thirty, and already a mature writer. Yet shortly after he finished *Julio Jurenito* in the autumn of 1921, he produced another book which was clearly intended to shock the reader. It was a study of modern art, in which Ehrenburg, writing in a mood of almost schoolboyish defiance, closely identified himself with one of the current 'isms': constructivism.

He called the book *And Yet the World Goes Round* (the title was printed in ten languages, including English), after Galileo's legendary pronouncement *eppur si muove*. A note by the publishers said that they did not agree with the author's views. The author, for his part, had protested against the use of the old Russian spelling which had been abolished after the Revolution but which most of the Russian publishing houses in Berlin refused to give up. But while the publishers must have been adamant on this point, they did satisfy quite a number of the author's whims. Each page looked like a propaganda leaflet, with some words set in capital letters and others in bold type four times the normal size; and on each page Ehrenburg was toppling old idols and proclaiming a new creed.

All the old forms of art were dead, declared Ehrenburg with crushing finality. Those who still clung to the past – the *passéistes*, as he called them – the people who were trying to imitate Joshua, the son of Nun, in the hope that they could stop the earth from moving, as Joshua had stopped the sun, would never succeed. Art for art's sake would vanish, there was no room for it in the future. Industry had given birth to a new style: constructivism, based on the recognition of the beauty of the machine and of any rationally designed object or installation that was of use to mankind. Ehrenburg claimed that on his journey to Western Europe, having left Soviet Russia behind, he had been impressed, not by art exhibitions, but by the new cranes in Copenhagen harbour and by London's *pissoirs* (actually, the latter were not all that impressive but they did compare favourably with the antediluvian French *vespasiennes*, and with the virtual absence of such conveniences in Moscow). At present, Ehrenburg went on, the artist was still working for the collector or dreaming of finding a place in a museum. But collectors were jailers and museums were graveyards. Now, thousands of madonnas were being kept behind bars to be stared at by people on Sundays. Their future equivalents would be counted in millions. Even a spittoon could be as beautiful as a madonna (if, indeed, there were any spittoons left, considering that spitting was a noxious habit). The triumph of constructivism would ultimately lead to the total disappearance of art, and through this supreme act of *hara-kiri* a new perception would be born, in which art and life would merge into a single whole.

The *passéistes* despised machines because they derived more pleasure from extolling their own 'divine ego'. They looked down on America, the land of industry and technical progress. But America's star would rise. Artists were beginning to look toward the Far West; and even if most Americans were as yet unaware of the beauty of their country's achievements, and American aesthetes still preferred elegiac vomit to the magnificent bridges built by their own compatriots, America, the ugly duckling, would soon reveal itself as a swan. (This was, I think, the only book in which Ehrenburg openly praised America, despite the villainous behaviour of Mr Cool.) Constructivism, proclaimed Ehrenburg, would transform each man's life into an organized creative process. The new art was a faith with its own Trinity: Work, Clarity and Organization.

Organization! Not just with a capital 'O' but set in capital letters each time it was mentioned! It was a strange metamorphosis. Up till then, Ehrenburg had always regarded organization as a monster, to be dreaded and shunned. It was the evil he had pilloried in *Julio Jurenito*, in the nightmarish personage of Karl Schmidt, the inveterate meddler, who begins by regimenting his own life, then, as a general in the German Army, organizes death for others, and finally, having travelled to Russia and become a Communist, organizes plans to regulate the lives of millions of ordinary Soviet citizens. Indeed, as he later revealed in his memoirs, Ehrenburg's original flight from Russia had been largely provoked by his horror of Valery Bryusov's charts, which he saw as an attempt to squeeze literature into a strait-jacket.

At the same time, it was not at all clear from Ehrenburg's exposition how constructivism was supposed to change literature.

The development of industrial design, the building of houses fit to live in, the improvement of sanitation and the installation of modern dockside cranes: all this could conceivably come under the heading of 'the new art'. But what was constructivist writing? Since a prophet cannot afford to evade any issue, however difficult, Ehrenburg tried to provide an answer. There were two modern inventions, he said, which would influence the use of the written word in the new age: the newspaper and the telegraph. Although the Press was largely corrupt, working for a newspaper did at least teach one to be succinct, and in sending a telegram, one had to remember that each word cost money. Thus, telegraphese could in future serve as a model for writing verse.

Unfortunately, the examples Ehrenburg chose to illustrate this theme were not very convincing. He took a good poem by Pasternak and set it against an inferior one by the popular symbolist poet, Balmont. Balmont was verbose, whereas Pasternak used words sparingly and to the point. Ehrenburg ignored the point however, that a good poet always avoids the use of superfluous language. Instead, he claimed to have proved that Pasternak was a true exponent of the present, while Balmont, although still alive, was a ghost from the past. (It was only forty years later, in writing his memoirs, that Ehrenburg admitted that Balmont had written some good verse which might one day regain its appeal for poetry-lovers.)

At the time, however, Ehrenburg abjured his past errors with all the fervour of a true convert. His recantation took the form of a conversation with Janus, portrayed, on this occasion, not as the two-faced Roman god, but as the spirit of Bohemia with a divided heart: in other words, he embarked on an argument between his two divided selves. He wrote:

> As a boy I fell in love with science and with the State that was yet to be built. I loved the MICROSCOPE and the REVOLUTION. But when I was eighteen, I landed on the magnificent CAMPO SANTO of Europe and the ensuing temptation proved too strong for me. Like those of my ancestors who betrayed Jehovah for the sake of Alexandria and its splendours, I renounced justice, reason and organization for A BOTTLE OF SCENT IN THE SLAUGHTERHOUSE: for a type of art that was fraudulent and dead . . . I spent many years in Paris without perceiving its greatness. I knew every one of the churches devoted to Notre Dame, but scarcely spared a glance for the Eiffel Tower . . . I travelled all over Italy, and explored the treasures of its churches, yet never once saw the iron works of Lombardy or Piedmont . . .

Then came the war, and rising from the first spilling of blood, justice called beauty to account. My eyes were not opened all at once. For five years I vacillated . . . Then, early in 1920, I began to see the light, and I KILLED MYSELF in order to live. I rebelled, not in the name of freedom, but AGAINST FREEDOM, in order to struggle for organization, justice and clarity. And now, I say to my self of yesterday: it is a terrifying road that lies ahead. I have lost everything on the way. I am naked. But I would not exchange this deserted mountain pass even for the Promised Land. If you can come with me, COME!

It is not clear why Ehrenburg was terrified of the road that lay ahead of him, or at least pretended to be, unless he felt that he might stray from it: as, indeed, he was to do before long. Viktor Shklovsky commented that, from being a Jewish Catholic and a former Slavophile, Ehrenburg had now transformed himself into a European constructivist. At the time, he was certainly enjoying his new faith, and he ended his book on a rousing note of uplift, by quoting a conversation between the eminent French artist, Albert Gleizes, and a workman who was installing radiators for an exhibition at the Paris Salon. Gleizes asked the workman which of the exhibits he liked best. The latter pointed to a 'construction' by the sculptor Lifshitz and said: '*Ça, c'est un objet!*' 'You may laugh at him,' commented Ehrenburg, addressing himself to the older generation, 'but we need no higher praise. While you laugh, we proudly assert *And yet the world goes round!*'

A few months later, Ehrenburg and his friend, the artist El Lissitsky,[1] decided to found a new art journal, and in honour of the workman who had so neatly defined the essence of constructivism, they named it *Object* (*Veshch* in Russian), with the subtitle in German *Gegenstand*, and in French *Objet*.

A statement by the editors, which appeared in the first issue, followed roughly the lines of Ehrenburg's book. But the style of *Object* was different. It did not set out to shock the middle classes, although some of its contributors certainly tried to use it for that purpose, nor did it limit itself to propagating the constructivist creed. In fact, it did very little preaching of any kind. Its main purpose was to provide a forum for a serious debate on modern art and poetry,

[1]El Lissitsky (1890–1941). Born in Russia but spent many years abroad in Germany and Switzerland. An architect by training, he became a leading exponent of the Russian Constructivist movement, working on large-scale propaganda montages extolling the Soviet Union and making lavish use of photographs and elaborate typographical effects.

and it dealt with all the current trends. It was not a glossy publication, since the editors were financially restricted in their choice of printing facilities, but it had a formidable list of contributors. Ehrenburg's contacts and personal friendships dating from the years he had spent at the Rotonde proved invaluable, and Lissitsky, too, was well connected. There were contributions by Le Corbusier and Gleizes, by Arkhipenko and Tairov, and many other prominent figures. Fernand Leger, in a brief article, gave a far more convincing explanation of constructivism than Ehrenburg had done in his rather long-winded book, by drawing a distinction between industrial design and what was supposed to be a new form of artistic expression, inspired by the beauty of the machine; a beauty which he himself had discovered in brutal circumstances, namely, at the front, where he watched, horrified but with the eye of a professional artist, the new mechanical means of destruction. Few of those who wrote for *Object* agreed with each other, and their widely differing views were, as a rule, published without comment, though on one occasion the editors did point out tactfully that they regarded as debatable the claim put forward by the Russian poet, Alexander Kussikov (another member of Esenin's entourage and unquestionably a very poor imitation of the master), that 'there is no art but imaginism and imaginism is its prophet'.

Object attached great significance to the fact that it was not merely a Russian but an international review. While the greater part of the material was in Russian, some contributions appeared in the original German or French, and one of the journal's declared aims was to act as a link between Russian and Western art. The editors emphasized that the seven years of enforced separation, counting from the outbreak of the First World War, had demonstrated the need for joint action against philistinism which was still rampant everywhere. 'Everywhere' meant in the East as well as in the West, and it seems clear that it was the East which was uppermost in Ehrenburg's mind.

There were good reasons for this. Some Russian *émigrés* (and this applied both to those abroad and to the 'internal *émigrés*' at home) regarded the upsurge of modern art in Russia as part of a diabolical Communist plot, a deliberate attempt by the Soviet regime to destroy Russia's cultural heritage. Those who were sympathetic to the regime praised it for promoting new trends. Both groups, though violently opposed to each other, connected the emergence of new forms of art in Russia with the revolutionary attitudes of the men in power.

Ehrenburg knew better. He realized that although modern artists and poets had benefited from Lunacharsky's patronage, most Soviet leaders intrinsically disapproved of modern art; and he dwelt on this in some detail in his book. He pointed out that Russian political revolutionaries, whether they were Bolsheviks, Mensheviks or anarchists, had always been people of 'obtusely conservative tastes' and that their views had not changed after the Revolution. While they set out to destroy the old political, economic and social structures, in art they still preferred the old-fashioned lyre to any other symbol. At first they had not interfered with Lunacharsky's efforts. But now, said Ehrenburg, the political revolutionaries (in other words the Communist Party) were acting as a reactionary force and obstructing the development of new art, so that the role of those who were trying to revolutionize art was being reduced to nought. Artists were being admonished to paint portraits of Comintern leaders rather than evolve a style that would accord with a new way of life. Ehrenburg even felt that in some respects the situation was better in the West. Western governments, however reactionary, did not care what kind of pictures were being painted, while the political left-wing generally took it for granted that modern art was inseparable from a new social order. Unfortunately, said Ehrenburg, left-wing intellectuals in Western Europe still assumed, quite wrongly, that the Soviet regime supported the cultural avant-garde, and pilgrimages by Western Communists to Moscow did nothing to dispel this illusion, since the pilgrims were usually less interested in art than in being received by Trotsky. One of the tasks *Object* had set itself was to draw attention to the fact that philistine attitudes persisted and were gaining ground in Russia. It published reports from Moscow, which showed how strongly modern trends were being discouraged there, and Ehrenburg claimed that protagonists of modern art were being treated by Soviet officialdom 'like members of a semi-illegal sect'.

In 1960, when I talked to Ehrenburg in London, I reminded him of *And Yet the World Goes Round*. He seemed surprised and rather pleased to hear that someone still remembered it. Later, in his memoirs, he said that, in retrospect, it was a silly book to have written. To me he said: 'We were all young and rather irresponsible in those days, and we have a lot to answer for. We amused ourselves with all sorts of "isms". It was all very enjoyable, but what we failed to see was that, by behaving as we did, we were only hastening the arrival of that cursed photography that was to plague us for twenty-five years.'

He was referring, of course, to the Stalin period, and by 'cursed photography' he meant the doctrine of socialist realism, under which artists were forced to paint in a manner which suited Stalin's taste, or rather, lack of it. Ehrenburg had, however, foreseen the advent of 'cursed photography' long before there was any question of Stalin assuming absolute rule. And he had also clearly foreseen that if the official Soviet approach to art were to triumph, this would lead to Russia's cultural isolation.

CHAPTER XII

In order to keep himself in the public eye, Ehrenburg had to start writing serious novels. He produced one with his usual speed and facility. It was called *The Life and Downfall of Nikolai Kurbov. A Novel*, and in contrast to the pervasive cynicism of *Julio Jurenito*, it frequently exploited a sentimental vein, especially in its opening sequence, which might be described as a variation on the time-honoured theme of 'she was poor but she was honest'. In this instance, the heroine earns her daily bread by making artificial flowers, until, like so many others, she falls victim to a rich man's crime. The story has an original twist, however. The rich man happens to be impotent, and the child she bears is not by him, but by a vulgar lecher to whom her semi-platonic lover sells her virginity, being temporarily short of money after losing heavily at baccarat. After a while, everyone deserts her, and when the child is born she is forced to go on the streets. She is determined her son should become a gentleman, however, and manages to send him to school. He is an affectionate lad: in the mornings, when she is out shopping, he kisses the mattress on which her body is used by men at night. He is also exceptionally bright, and when his mother dies of pneumonia, having been dragged out naked into the cold by one of her drunken customers, a kindly schoolmaster obtains a grant for him so that he can complete his education.

The grant is provided by a wealthy merchant of the old school, barbaric and illiterate, and each time the boy goes to collect his allowance he has to humiliate himself before his benefactor. He manages to finish his studies, however, and is then employed as private tutor to the son of a millionaire, whose family condescendingly treat him like a servant. Like Ehrenburg himself in his youth, he becomes enraptured by Marxism and biology, and his most precious possession is a microscope on which he has spent all his savings. But his ungrateful pupil, a small monster of depravity, steals the microscope and buries it in the garden; while his equally depraved older brother, who needs money to seduce some woman of easy virtue, filches some securities from his father's desk. Inevitably, suspicion falls on the penniless tutor, who refuses to allow his room to be searched because he has hidden a pile of revolutionary leaflets under the bed. The millionaire is finally magnanimous enough not to have him arrested as a thief, but he does have him thrown out of the house (rather as Baron Thunder-ten-tronckh, although for different reasons, evicted Candide from his baronial castle with a series of powerful kicks in the backside).

The young man has by now become a Bolshevik. He works for the cause, is betrayed to the police, is put on trial and sentenced to exile in Siberia, but manages to escape. Then comes the October Revolution, and he throws all his energies into helping the Party to build a new and better world. In recognition of his efforts, he earns the dubious recompense of being appointed to the Cheka, where he is put in charge of a special section, with orders to hunt down enemies of the new Soviet State. He is strong and handsome, ascetic and virtuous, and remains uncorrupted by power. When he signs a death warrant, he is never assailed by even a moment's doubt.

The cover for *The Life and Downfall of Nikolai Kurbov* was designed by Ehrenburg's wife, the artist Lyubov Kozintseva, and carried two cryptic sub-headings. One was a quadratic equation:

$$x = \sqrt{\frac{p^2}{2} \pm \frac{p^2}{4} - q}$$

and the other was a line from a Russian ditty popular at the time: 'The chickens also want to live'. The formula for solving the quadratic equation sums up Nikolai Kurbov's mentality and his approach to life: for him, there is only one Truth, simple and unchallengeable. Complications are man-made and are not supposed to arise, while emotions are automatically excluded. But the popular song about the chickens, which virtually everyone in Russia knew by heart, showed what he was up against. It had a catchy tune (Kurt Weill later used it, in a modified form, for one of the songs in *The Threepenny Opera*) and the words expressed what millions of people felt in the first years after the Revolution. It was, in effect, the timorous lament of dull ordinary citizens, leading dull ordinary lives, who could not, or would not, grasp the magnitude of the events that had overtaken them or their historic significance, but found them a heavy burden to bear, and consequently felt as helpless as chickens. Yet surely a chicken also had the right to live? So the plaintive voice of the little man recounted the misfortunes of the wretched chicken as it was dragged around the various departments of the Cheka: a chicken doomed to extinction, by boiling or frying, but still stubbornly insisting that it wanted to live.

To a pure revolutionary like Nikolai Kurbov, however, it is precisely the chickens that are anathema. Enemies present no problem: they can always be removed. One can even make use of crooks. Kurbov is not much enamoured of many of his colleagues in the Cheka. There are some unsavoury characters among them. Yet they have a role in helping to clear away the accumulated garbage and to get rid of the stench of corruption. But what is one to do with chickens? Kurbov sees them, not as pathetic, but as noxious creatures. They can no longer, it is true, inflict on others what he himself had to endure when he was at the mercy of his merchant benefactor or his millionaire employer, but they still embody selfishness and greed, and by their very existence undermine everything that is being done to create a new society. Individually, each of them may feel helpless, but their strength lies in numbers: they are as powerful as vermin. Some of the more despicable specimens hide in dark corners, and in the course of investigating a terrorist plot, which turns out to be directed against himself, Kurbov visits one such haunt: a reeking den in which pimps and thieves swill home-brewed spirits, stuff themselves with such delicacies as smoked dogmeat, and then retire with prostitutes to dingy rooms which are let by the hour, without beds for those who are content to use the floor, with beds for those who are prepared to pay.

As Kurbov sits there, fighting off feelings of nausea, a girl enters this insalubrious establishment, and they become aware of each other's presence. The girl, too, is poor and honest, but her background is aristocratic, and she has fallen victim, not to a rich man's whim, but to her own romantic fantasies. Her widowed mother has sent her to an exclusive school for daughters of the gentry; and there she has gone through the kind of experiences that are bound to befall a well-bred young Russian woman intent on dreams of self-sacrifice. She has shown her nobility of character in a number of ways. When her best friend steals a medallion from some princess or other and is on the point of being found out, she gladly takes the blame upon herself and is nearly expelled. A young guards officer, with whom she dances a mazurka at the graduation ball, asks her to marry him, but she high-mindedly refuses, because she knows her best friend has eyes on him as well. But now, the Revolution has swept away officers and mazurkas, and with them, old-style romanticism and old-style self-sacrifice as well. As a result, she looks upon the Revolution with deep hatred; and when an anti-Soviet conspirator[1] approaches her and suggests she should assassinate Nikolai Kurbov, as a leading Cheka agent and a monster in human form, she joyfully accepts this chance to play the avenging angel. The fact that she has to meet her fellow-plotters in a low thieves' den does not trouble her in the least. This is all part of the game. Besides, unlike Kurbov, she is capable of rising above her surroundings.

So it is in this sordid setting that they first see each other. Their eyes meet, and in that moment it is as if the two halves of one soul, which had been cruelly torn apart and condemned to a ceaseless search, have at last come together again (this brief passage is one of the most touching in the book, and helps to redeem much of the rest). Gradually, they find out all about each other. The girl has never really grown-up, so she takes it all lightly: she hands him the weapon with which she had intended to shoot him, and vows repentance, rather like a child promising not to be naughty again. But for Kurbov, who has had no proper childhood, who has been grown-up all his life, their love spells catastrophe: not because of the normal difficulties that might arise from their coming together, but because the quadratic equation has not worked. The wretched song about the chickens has triumphed over Truth. Kurbov discovers he is no different from the others. He, too, wants to live: he, too, is a chicken.

He is plunged into even deeper gloom when he thinks of what is happening elsewhere. He has been to a meeting at the Kremlin, a place he has always hated. Others may rave about its glittering splendours, but to Kurbov, this surface glitter is no more than the iridescence of decay and putrefaction. To him, the Kremlin exemplifies all that is worst in Russian history: the bestial cruelty, the shameless bigotry, heavy boots trampling on suffering humanity, tongues licking heavy boots, loud yawns signifying complacency, indifference and boredom. In short, it seems to him a thoroughly

---

[1]This character was modelled on the famous Russian terrorist, Boris Savinkov, whom Ehrenburg had known at the Rotonde in Paris.

undesirable residence for the men who are now guiding the destinies of the new Soviet State, and whose way of thinking is so clear and precise that Kurbov likens them to geometrical symbols. Lenin is a sphere, the most harmonious of all forms, Trotsky a triangle, and Bukharin an 'ideal straight line'. But now, at the meeting which Kurbov has reluctantly been forced to attend, a new offspring has appeared with an ugly, prematurely aged countenance: the NEP, or New Economic Policy, which is to restore private enterprise. So here, too, at the highest levels of Soviet power, the quadratic equation has failed to work. Here, too, it is the chicken that has emerged triumphant. The voracious bird is visibly gaining weight, and being no respecter of persons, will soon have ingested all of them, including the sphere, the triangle and the straight line, in its capacious crop.

For Kurbov, there is only one way out of this intolerable dilemma. He arranges a rendezvous with the girl in the sordid den where they first met, and asks the oily proprietor for a room with an iron bedstead; and there, where the two halves of one divided soul have rediscovered each other, their two virgin bodies unite between filthy sheets. Then Kurbov shoots himself with the gun with which the girl was supposed to kill him.

The novel evoked a mixed response both inside and outside Russia. Reviewing it in *Novaya Russkaya Kniga* in Berlin, Roman Gul predicted that it would spark off a fierce controversy, although one based on political rather than literary considerations. Gul wrote:

> One already knows what both the White and the Red Press think of it. To the first, it is an attempt to 'whitewash the Cheka', while to the second, it is a 'slander' on that institution: two opposing views but both imbued with the same spirit. In Russia, Glavlit [i.e. the chief censorship organization] would like to see the book banned, and if there were an *émigré* Glavlit somewhere on the banks of the Seine, it would no doubt pass an equally severe sentence.

The Life and Downfall of Nikolai Kurbov did appear in Russia, but Soviet critics in general gave it a cool reception. Outside Russia, there was a good deal of indignation among Russian *émigrés*, who viewed the novel as setting the seal on Ehrenburg's reputation as a Soviet sympathizer. Some others, who up till then had regarded him as an independent writer, felt – prematurely as it soon transpired – that he was beginning to conform. The sentimentality of the novel was largely ignored. But some critics commented on its mannered style, and such comments were indeed pertinent. In reality, the novel was not a political but a literary experiment. As a convert to European constructivism, Ehrenburg had not only repudiated his former Slavophile leanings, by comparing the Kremlin to a relic from the evil past, but had attempted to handle his prose narrative in accordance with the constructivist doctrine he himself had elaborated, and to that end, he made copious use of 'poetic' telegraphese. He was not the only one at that period to resort to such artificial techniques, and he did it quite skilfully; but one could see that he was not likely to restrict himself to this kind of experiment in future. Indeed, in *The Love of Jeanne Ney: A Novel* he explored a sentimental theme without trying to be either striking or original, and with much greater success.

The Love of Jeanne Ney is a novel about fiends and angels. Jeanne Ney, its French heroine, falls in love with a Russian Communist who is plunged into a mood of restlessness after the civil war, and contrives to get himself sent to France on a subversive mission. Through a fortuitous combination of circumstances, he is arrested on a murder charge, and the only way to prove his innocence is to disclose the real reason why he has come to France. But he chooses to remain heroically silent, and is sentenced to death for a crime he has not committed. The fiends are Jeanne's lecherous uncle, a kind of 'super-chicken' of the French variety, and a Russian *émigré*, the principal villain, who is the real murderer. The angels are Jeanne herself, who agrees to sleep with the villainous *émigré* in a vain attempt to save her lover, and the lecherous uncle's blind and ethereal daughter, Gabrielle. The story moves backwards and forwards between France and Russia, and cherubs and minor fiends enliven the scene by conducting the struggle between good and evil at various levels.

Ehrenburg said later that he had been influenced by Dickens. This passed unnoticed by the critics, however, some of whom compared him mockingly to a Russian writer of a very different calibre: Anastasia Verbitskaya. At the beginning of the century, there were two Russian woman novelists who specialized in trashy sentimental novels. One was Lydia Charskaya, whose stories, designed for children, were mainly about life in schools for young gentlewomen, or about orphans who were maltreated by their wicked employers or relations. The other was Anastasia Verbitskaya, who produced equally tear-jerking novels for adults. She appealed mainly to women readers, but even most of them read her surreptitiously, since to be known to have a weakness for Verbitskaya would have compromised them in the eyes of their intellectual friends.

To Ehrenburg, this was a cruel blow. First, the critics had said that he was not as good as Voltaire. Now, they were saying that he was not much better than Verbitskaya. Yet, whatever its faults, *The Love of Jeanne Ney* was an eminently readable book. Girls in Russia shed tears over it, and the celebrated German film director, Georg Pabst, made it into a film. This must have been some consolation to Ehrenburg, at least initially, although he was much depressed by the final result, especially as the UFA film company insisted on a happy ending, and Pabst was forced to agree. None of Ehrenburg's other novels ever reached the screen. A Hollywood producer did once think of making a film of *The Life and Downfall of Nikolai Kurbov*, and persuaded Ehrenburg to write the script for it, but the idea was eventually abandoned.

There is no doubt that Ehrenburg felt a deep affection for his heroine, Jeanne Ney, and to that extent, the book was a sincere reflection of his feelings. As for the fate of Nikolai Kurbov, a stern yet romantic Communist whose world is finally smashed to pieces, that, too, reflected some of Ehrenburg's own feelings. To those who disagreed with Communist practice but had retained some faith in Communist ideals, the NEP, was a horrifying measure: if a Communist regime ceased to be Communist, its very reason for existence was removed. It was unfair to compare anything Ehrenburg had written to the outpourings of Anastasia Verbitskaya. Yet the fact was that the man who sat in the Prager Diele in Berlin, enveloped in clouds of pipe smoke, posing as an arch-cynic and churning out sentimental tales, was a gifted writer, but no more. In short, he was not a genius. But he often appeared to be furious with himself for not being one.

CHAPTER XIII

The Love of Jeanne Ney was the last book Ehrenburg wrote in Berlin. At the end of 1923 he left Germany, and after a short stay in Prague, returned to Moscow early in 1924. He had not been back to Russia for three and a half years; and he had not been back long before he came under critical fire from a new quarter. Both Lenin and Bukharin had liked *Julio Jurenito*. But in those days, rank and file Party members could challenge even the most authoritative pronouncements from on high; and when a group of Communist literary critics decided to bring out a new magazine, *Na Postu (On Guard)*, the first thing to appear in its pages was an article which accused Ehrenburg of slandering the Soviet State.

It was an article dealing with *The Life and Downfall of Nikolai Kurbov*, and the prediction of the *émigré* critic, Roman Gul, that the novel would be badly received in the Communist Press proved to be accurate: the reviewer fairly fumed with indignation. Ehrenburg, whom he described as a Paris Bohemian and a Catholic mystic, had had the temerity to behave as if he knew exactly what went on in the Party Central Committee and was on intimate terms with the Soviet leaders. 'If you have never talked to Lenin, Trotsky or Bukharin, if you have never met them face to face,' wrote the *Na Postu* critic with heavy irony, 'you have only to read Ehrenburg: he is, after all, a revolutionary writer who has decided to adopt a benevolent attitude towards the leaders of our Party!' He then proceeded to excoriate Ehrenburg for ridiculing the Bolshevik underground. He had described it as a collection of grim, unattractive or foolish men, and of women who were either oversexed or completely sexless: there was not one normal human being among them. (The reviewer entirely disregarded the fact that Ehrenburg himself had once been a member of that same underground.) But what could one expect from a person who, in the fateful years before the Revolution, had led an idle and vapid existence, dressed up like a marquis (this must have been meant figuratively, since Ehrenburg in his Paris days looked more like a tramp), hobnobbing with mystics and Catholic monks?

Moreover, in writing of the Cheka, Ehrenburg had had the impudence to question the integrity of some of its members. The reviewer went on:

> Have patience with us, comrade reader, and do not blame us if you feel sick when you read the passages we are going to quote. This kind of literature does make one vomit, but it has to be studied in order to show what kind of people are receiving money from our publishers. Ehrenburg does not give a damn for the heroic role played by the Cheka in unmasking the conspiracies of the White Guard. He is not at all interested in the doings of such people as Bruce Lockhart or Boris Savinkov. Like most counter-revolutionary petty bourgeois, Ehrenburg probably does not believe that such things as anti-Soviet conspiracies ever existed, and prefers to treat them as Bolshevik fabrications. But the Revolution was forced to resort to terror only in the face of mortal danger. It was a temporary measure, and it imposed a painful duty on those working for the Cheka. But all that is of no concern to Ehrenburg. All he is concerned with is settling accounts with the Cheka, in deference to the wishes of the NEP people who are his backers.

The reviewer wound up his list of grievances by calling Ehrenburg a pornographer (he took particular exception to a passage in which a prostitute's breasts are compared to a pair of melons offered for sale), and then explained why he had dealt with the novel in such great detail:

> Our proletarian youth must be told the truth about people like Ehrenburg. Now that the civil war and the Red terror are over, they are making up for lost time and slandering the history of our Party, its institutions and its leaders. And yet, every scrap of paper covered with anything they choose to write is at once snapped up and paid for as if it were worth its weight in gold. Our Press reports their every move, and our publishers, who are good Communists, but far too soft and kind-hearted, are so reluctant to hurt their feelings that they dare not utter a word of criticism.

The declared aim of the *Na Postu* group was to promote proletarian literature and to unmask the so-called 'fellow-travellers', of whom Ehrenburg was one. The phrase had been coined by Trotsky in his essay 'Literature and Revolution', which appeared a few months after the first issue of *Na Postu*. There was nothing pejorative in the term 'fellow-traveller', which later acquired an entirely different meaning in the West, where it was applied to crypto-Communists and sometimes indiscriminately to all left-wingers. Trotsky was referring to Russian writers who had accepted the Revolution and were travelling with it, even though, as he put it, no one could predict at what point they might get off the train. He recognized, furthermore, that the majority of talented writers came into this category. If one were to ignore them, said Trotsky, little would remain except a few 'promissory notes' signed by those who believed in proletarian literature, but still to be redeemed, since no such literature had yet come into existence. He then listed those fellow-travellers whom he considered the most important, and discussed their work. Ehrenburg's name was not among them.

The men who were in power were thus anxious to ensure that art and literature should continue to exist; and in that respect their attitude differed radically from the policy adopted a quarter of a century later by Stalin, who felt that the Soviet State could not afford such luxuries and instructed his deputy, Andrei Zhdanov, to ban all creative writing. Acceptance of the necessity for art and literature naturally leads to a considerable degree of artistic freedom; this made it possible for Bukharin to recommend a book like *Julio Jurenito* to Soviet readers. There was, it is true, an important proviso, namely, that no writer must advocate, directly or implicitly, the overthrow of the regime. Everything else, however, was a matter of taste – *de gustibus non est disputandum*, as Bukharin said. Trotsky, while accepting the need for a vigilant censorship, emphasized that art must make its own way by its own methods. It was not a field of human activity where the Party was called upon to command. Where art was concerned, the Party's function was to protect and to help, said Trostky; it could 'lead' only indirectly.

There was at that time a spate of literary and artistic organizations in Russia, each claiming the monopoly of revolutionary wisdom. Mostly, they were at each other's throats; sometimes they formed alliances and concluded treaties as solemnly as if they were sovereign States. *Na Postu* was, from the Communist point of view, the most radical and, from the literary point of view, the most reactionary. It deplored the stand taken by Trotsky. It poured abuse on Lunacharsky when a Moscow theatre produced a play of his, which one of the *Na Postu* zealots found wanting in revolutionary spirit. It rebuked Bukharin for showering praise on Ehrenburg in his preface to *Julio Jurenito*. The group did not call itself *On Guard* for nothing: when an *émigré* paper accused it of being a literary Cheka, *Na Postu* replied that it took this as a compliment. Fortunately, it did not have the powers of the Cheka. All it could do was lament, protest and swear. Why did the Soviet leadership support the follow-travellers? Why were their books brought out by State enterprises? (There were at that time many private publishing firms which were prospering under the New Economic Policy.) Why were the fellow-travellers making so much money? The least a State publishing enterprise could do, declared *Na Postu*, was to use the preface as 'a powerful weapon of Marxist criticism': in other words, no unorthodox book should be allowed into print without an introduction warning ᵗhe reader of its harmful effects.[1] It so happened, however, that *Na Postu* was printed by the same publishing house that had brought out *The Life and Downfall of Nikolai Kurbov*, which simply added insult to injury.

The magazine did not wait long before launching another broadside against Ehrenburg. It was not just that he appealed to the petty bourgeois reader, it said; he had also found favour with the 'less stable section of proletarian youth'. He had achieved a popularity not unlike that once enjoyed by Verbitskaya and Artsybashev. (Artsybashev, who wrote mainly about sex, was not greatly respected in Russia, although his supposedly 'advanced' views on the subject earned him a reputation as a serious writer in the West.) Ehrenburg understood that bourgeois civilization was doomed, said *Na Postu*, yet he was himself a petty bourgeois, selfish and incapable of understanding the Revolution. He was predicting the final collapse of all civilization, but secretly the prospect terrified him, so that he resorted to general derision to conceal his panic fear. Behind the sardonic smile of this modern Petronius it was not difficult to detect the bourgeois intellectual clinging to the old world. In *The D.E. Trust*, he had portrayed the downfall of Europe in a spirit of Mephistophelean mirth, but this had not prevented him shedding bitter tears over the corpse of the Phoenician princess. Ehrenburg knew the old world, he was flesh of its flesh, and some comrades were impressed by his satirical barbs at capitalism. But they were quite mistaken if they thought this kind of cynical display had any useful role to fulfil. It was permeated with hopelessness,

[1]Some years later, a publisher in Italy, under the Fascist regime, brought out one of Ehrenburg's novels, then apologized to him for adding a preface, without which, he said, the book would not have been allowed to appear. The preface denounced Ehrenburg's 'erroneous views', adding that Italian readers would not mistake 'red chaff for wheat'.

disenchantment and a spirit of *fin de siècle* decadence. 'Ehrenburg', the magazine thundered, 'is one of the most poisonous products of a decaying bourgeoisie.'

Na Postu was the mouthpiece of a frustrated clique, animated mainly by jealousy of others who were more successful, and in the following year the Party closed it down. Its outbursts were significant, however, in that they marked the beginning of a long struggle, which was to go on for many decades: a struggle between those who had genuine talent, and the mediocrities who sought to reduce all writing to their own dull and unimaginative level. Another literary journal of a very different stamp, as could be seen from the fact that one of its co-editors was Lunacharsky, was *Novy Mir* (later to win fame as the most progressive Soviet periodical of its kind). Yet, when *Novy Mir* reviewed all four of Ehrenburg's major novels that had appeared in the Soviet Union by 1925 – *Julio Jurenito, The D.E. Trust, The Life and Downfall of Nikolai Kurbov* and *The Love of Jeanne Ney* – some of the conclusions it reached were not all that different from those of *Na Postu*, although the article was more dignified in tone and its analysis a good deal more profound.

One of the characters in *The Love of Jeanne Ney* is an aged French author called Jules Lebeau (he is, in fact, only sixty-two, but to Ehrenburg, who at that time was only just over thirty, he must have seemed the right age for someone who was supposed to be ancient and decrepit). Jules Lebeau is a famous satirist and sceptic who, because of his left-wing views, is regarded in French conservative circles as a rabid Bolshevik. In reality, he is nothing of the kind. Jules Lebeau loves no one and has no love for Communism either: he feels that Communists are a crude and preposterous lot. But he and the Communists do share a hatred of the same things, and on these grounds, the *Novy Mir* critic claimed that Ehrenburg had drawn a self-portrait: Jules Lebeau was what he himself would like to be in old age.

This was plausible, but only up to a point. In fact, Jules Lebeau was clearly modelled on Anatole France. It is interesting to note that Anatole France is mentioned only briefly in Ehrenburg's writings. Ehrenburg does not appear ever to have met him, although he did catch an occasional glimpse of him by the bookstalls along the Seine. Yet from the sparse references that do occur, Ehrenburg seems to have been much attracted by the smiling philosopher, whose wit was equalled by his *savoir vivre*, and who could have been, and probably was, one of the spiritual progenitors of *Julio Jurenito*. Thus, one can well imagine that Ehrenburg, in contemplating what he might become when he grew old, would not have been at all reluctant to see himself as another Anatole France, admired by many, reviled by some, and surveying the evils of this world with supreme detachment from a vantage point on the Left Bank. Moreover, Ehrenburg was similar to Jules Lebeau in another respect: without being a Communist, he shared the Communists' hatred of certain things, and this determined his attitude towards the Soviet regime. There was also, however, an essential difference between Ehrenburg and Lebeau, which the *Novy Mir* critic failed to note. Ehrenburg was a sentimentalist and in love with his heroine, Jeanne Ney. Lebeau, on the other hand, as portrayed by Ehrenburg, is an unhappy man who dies in despair because he has never understood the meaning of love. The critic chose to ignore this, and claimed that Ehrenburg, like Lebeau, was an apostle of what could be termed the 'cult of dislike'.

Novy Mir acknowledged that Ehrenburg had talent: he was a gifted epigone and a skilful satirist. Yet what was the essence of his satire? It was directed against capitalism but its purpose was not to prepare the way for a brighter future, since Ehrenburg satirized the future just as mercilessly as the present. His 'cult of dislike' was tantamount to a cult of decadence and death. He saw the Revolution as a scourge for those who were making it, whether it was Lenin, 'the captain on the bridge', as portrayed in *Julio Jurenito*, or Nikolai Kurbov, the virtuous agent of the Cheka. This was not due to any refusal to support the Revolution on ideological grounds. Unlike his opposite number of *Na Postu*, the *Novy Mir* critic did not accuse Ehrenburg of being a disguised counter-revolutionary, backed by the anti-social elements who were profiting from the NEP. But he did describe him as a decadent individualist and a Bohemian, one of the last representatives of a vanishing race. His heroes, whether they were involved in the Revolution or not, invariably came to a bad end. Revolution, countries and continents, millennial cultures and ordinary human happiness: all were doomed to destruction. Slowly but surely, the world was drifting towards extinction. Soon there would be nothing left except non-existence, and Ehrenburg was its prophet.

In short, a nihilist. The word began to creep in nearly every time Ehrenburg's name was mentioned in print. It was the term Gorky used when another writer, Fyodor Gladkov, one of the future luminaries of the *Na Postu* camp, complained to him about the 'vomit' that Ehrenburg and other fellow-travellers were producing. A certain critic called Tereshchenko even devoted a lengthy essay to the subject under the title 'Ehrenburg the Nihilist'. Bukharin, in his preface to *Julio Jurenito*, had brushed aside references to Ehrenburg's 'individualistic anarchism' and 'nihilistic hooliganism', because he felt them to be infinitely less important than the pleasure an intelligent reader would derive from the book. But now these phrases began to be heard on all sides. Some called Ehrenburg a nihilist because they believed it; others did so because it was the safest and simplest way to pigeon-hole him. It was left to Lunacharsky to point out that there was a good deal more to Ehrenburg than that.

The fact that Lunacharsky's views did not tally with the opinion expressed in *Novy Mir*, although he was responsible for that journal, need cause no surprise: things were not as well organized then as they were to be later. In a lecture on Western literature, Lunacharsky spoke about Heinrich Heine, and in this context said:

> We have one author who, though he is a small man beside Heine, is similar to him in many ways. It is Ehrenburg. In his books there is a certain amount of sentimentality, at times there is sadness. He feels sad because of his lack of principles. But he does not completely lack principles. At first he was with the Whites, then he went over to the Reds, but intrinsically, he adopts a sardonic attitude towards both. Both are merely targets for the shafts of his brilliant satire. He is an extremely gifted writer, though far from being of Heine's calibre. He is a sceptic who would like to reduce everything to ashes and would leave nothing intact. He is sceptical about the values of the old world, and from this point of view he is in some respects our ally.

It was a cautious statement. Yet to be compared to Heine, even with the obvious qualifying remark that he was not of the same calibre, was not only high praise but must have given Ehrenburg particular satisfaction; he says in his memoirs that Heine was the poet to whom he had always felt closest. Heine combined venom with sadness, and Lunacharsky was one of the few to observe that this was also true of Ehrenburg. It does not really matter that he attributed Ehrenburg's sadness to his 'lack of principles', by which he must have meant absence of commitment or lack of faith; besides, he immediately toned this down by saying that Ehrenburg did not completely lack principles. What matters is that a writer who is sad is neither a cynic nor a professional hater, and consequently not a nihilist in the vulgar sense of the term. He is someone who cares.

As for the public, whether it was petty bourgeois or insufficiently stable, as *Na Postu* suggested, it did not seem to be in the least disturbed by what the critics were saying. Ehrenburg's books were exceedingly popular, even though highbrow readers found his occasional mannerisms irritating and his style slipshod. Some were deeply moved by the sufferings inflicted by his all-too-fiendish fiends on his all-too-angelic angels. Others did not take his writings seriously but enjoyed them all the same. It was a matter of taste.

CHAPTER XIV

Ehrenburg remained in Moscow for only a few months, until May 1924, but he returned there again two years later. In the interval, he achieved his most cherished ambition of being allowed back into France, and was once more able to take up residence in his beloved Paris.

In Moscow, on both occasions, he saw the NEP in operation. He had left Russia a short time before it was introduced in 1921, and he found the changes staggering. The NEP meant different things to different people. To the peasants, who had always been a separate nation in Russia (Ehrenburg's fictional account of his conversations with them in *Julio Jurenito* suggests that they had about as much in common with the urban population as with men from Mars), the NEP was a development of vast importance, since, after the period of compulsory requisitioning, it meant that it was once more worth their while to provide the towns with food. As a result, for millions of citizens, the NEP brought a return to normal life. It was once more possible to walk into a shop and buy whatever one wanted, legally, in unrationed quantities, and in an orderly manner, simply by handing money over the counter. Moreover, those who were able to afford it could have a good meal in a restaurant, or even get drunk in a nightclub to the strains of the latest Western dance music, something that was especially appreciated by the new *jeunesse dorée*.

And for the business class, the NEP meant making money. Some businessmen returned to their former occupations, set up new enterprises and supplied whatever was in demand. Others preferred to make money the easy way, trying, as Ehrenburg points out in his memoirs, to enrich themselves with feverish haste, since no one could tell how long this state of affairs would last. The most farsighted soon went abroad, making use of the fact that foreign travel was relatively easy. Others stayed because of a natural reluctance to face the hazards of *émigré* life and to give up the prosperity they were enjoying at home, even if the future was uncertain. Others told themselves that they would leave in a few months' or a year's time, but not now, since it would be a pity to leave when things were going well, and kept postponing departure until everything was lost and it was no longer possible to escape.

Corruption was rampant. Those who handed out bribes and the officials who took them often managed to get away with it, if they lived unostentatiously and were content to spend only a small fraction of the proceeds. Those who threw money about were watched, discovered, and gaoled or shot. Punishment was meted out freely, and to stress its educational and ideological value, the authorities described it as 'taking the scum off the NEP'. Side by side with new wealth there was appalling poverty, of the kind that existed in any capitalist country, but aggravated beyond measure by the indescribable misery resulting from the civil war with its many gruesome legacies. Worst of all were the swarms of abandoned children, the *besprizornye*, whom the well-to-do and the police regarded as a pest.

Ehrenburg says in his memoirs: 'People in Moscow had gained weight and grown more cheerful. As for me, I was both pleased and sad.' Not to be pleased would have been monstrous. How could anyone, least of all Ehrenburg, who had spent nearly three years in the West where he could eat as much as he liked, begrudge people in Russia the fact that they could now have a square meal? He was sad because, as he put it, 'the heart has its own logic'. He knew that, in spite of the NEP, there were people who were interested in other things than making money. During a lecture tour he undertook while in Russia, he was asked not only about Paris fashions, and which of the new ballroom dances was most popular in Berlin, but also about matters on which he could speak with greater authority, such as the relative merits of Voltaire and Anatole France. But the new order, with its dismal social contrasts, filled him with revulsion, and he castigated it as furiously as he had castigated capitalism in the West. When he was attacked for giving prominence in his writings to the sordid aspects of Soviet reality, his answer was that he had a gift for satire and that, being aware of his limitations as a writer, he chose to do what he thought he could do best, rather than depict the virtuous behaviour of the many young veterans of the civil war, who were now studying at universities and technical colleges, living several to a room on beggarly stipends, and working day and night to acquire knowledge. As an excuse, this sounded plausible. Yet it did not quite explain the bitterness with which he wrote about what he saw in

Russia at that time. The NEP was a necessity, said the official Press. What made Ehrenburg sad and angry was precisely the fact that it had proved to be a necessity. It meant that everything that had happened before, during the period of so-called 'War Communism' and civil strife – 'the years of heroism and madness, cruelty and infamy', as he called them – had been in vain. Capitalism had been restored and the one great ideal of Communism, social justice, had been abandoned.

He looked back on the years which had preceded the NEP and wrote, half in scorn, but with great feeling:

It was a wonderful time. No author of science fiction, not even H. G. Wells, could have thought up anything as unreal as the way people lived in a Russian city – let us say, Kharkov – during that period. Women wore army greatcoats, and their hats, which looked like suprematist contraptions, were made of green baize taken off card-tables. Tea was made from dried carrots or beans. When one ate bread, one behaved as if one were eating fish: there seemed to be bones in it and the bread often got stuck in one's throat, causing acute discomfort. When one went to see a friend, one brought a few lumps of sugar as a contribution to the feast. But if the friend had a lavatory that was in working order, one rushed there first of all: the opportunity was too precious to miss. Everyone went to the theatre to see plays by Shakespeare, Calderón or Carlo Gozzi. Everyone wrote poetry, mostly about the universe and mostly without metre. At night the streets remained unlit, and this helped lovers. Outside a derelict house, which was so fouled by human excrement that it took one's breath away, a poster proclaimed, 'We are electrifying the globe!'; and no one laughed, because it was true. Money was being printed in fabulous quantities, with inscriptions in many different languages, but people had long forgotten what money meant. They lived without money in a blissful utopia, relying on rations (provided by the authorities and usually microscopic) and their own resilience. Letters could be posted free of charge, but as there was no paper (all of it went to the administrative departments), postmen lost interest and no longer bothered to empty the letter boxes. In the Cheka, people were being shot, but when they were arrested they were addressed as 'comrade'. Everyone starved and struggled, but everyone knew that they were all in the same boat. They also knew that their ordeal was not in vain. Social revolution was not just a slogan but something that was bound to happen tomorrow. The earth shook and there was no point in getting excited when the authorities requisitioned a couch. No one was surprised at anything. I repeat: it was a wonderful time.

A wonderful time indeed. Ehrenburg had no illusions about the hardships of that earlier period, but that was how he felt as he looked at the kind of society the NEP had produced. The ordeal had been in vain, and he pitied its countless victims. He even pitied the harmless *ci-devants*, those who had never believed that a great social revolution was just round the corner and would not have cared if it were, since they expected nothing from it. Their trials and sufferings, too, had proved to be pointless and could no longer be justified by bland commonplaces about the impossibility of making an omelette without breaking eggs, or its Russian equivalent which says that 'chips must fly when the trees are felled', since the omelette had failed to materialize and it seemed that the trees had been felled to no purpose. Ehrenburg wrote in one of his novels of the period:

> While we salute the flag that flies so proudly from the skyscraper of the Revolution we cannot ignore what goes on in another part of that majestic building: namely, the basement, which houses the victims of the great historic upheaval. Not those fortunate victims whose memory people honour when they walk past the Kremlin wall,[1] but those who are revered by no one. No scrap merchant will stop to pick up their wrecked lives. While the Revolution was in progress, most of them felt nothing but fear, but that they tasted to the full. They knew fear in all its aspects. They panicked at the mere sight of a leather jacket or an official's briefcase. Then came tears, denunciations, and sometimes madness. In a different epoch, they would have led dull but contented lives. Now, these people have been crushed by events, and are doubly unhappy because they cannot understand why history has placed such a heavy burden on their shoulders, which were not made to sustain anything heavier than the weight of a jacket. Nor do we ourselves know the answer. All we can feel is pity.

This passage occurs in a novel called *The Go-Getter* in which the principal character, a Communist corrupted by the NEP, amuses himself by telling an old lady, one of those who have long since ceased to be surprised by anything, that he will denounce her to the secret police for trading in home-made sweets. As the old lady does not know that this is now a perfectly legal occupation, she hangs herself.

Then there were the *besprizornye*, the homeless waifs and strays. As Ehrenburg looked at them, he recalled his own activities in Kiev

---

[1] The Kremlin wall behind the Lenin Mausoleum contains memorial tablets to many people who gained prominence in the Revolution and after, including one commemorating John Reed, author of *Ten Days that Shook the World*.

during the civil war, when he had had to deal with the 'aesthetic education' of so-called 'mofective' children. The word 'mofective' was as ludicrous in itself as the task to which he had been assigned. Now he found himself regretting that the truckloads of documents setting out the innumerable projects which had accumulated in the Education Department had not been preserved for posterity. But they had all been burned, either because people were afraid to keep them when the city was occupied by the White Army, or because they had used them as fuel to heat their rooms. He wrote with bitter irony:

All these projects were lofty and vastly intriguing. The kind of life that was being planned had all the alluring aspects of Paradise Regained. There were to be Palaces of Labour and Palaces of Art. A multitude of unintelligible schemes had been drawn up, containing astronomical figures to indicate the number of roof gardens and electric fans destined for some wretched little town where plumbing was unknown and where there was not a single house fit for habitation. Then there were Children's Palaces (they had to be palaces – the pedagogues would never settle for less), in which the children were supposed to be gaily romping about. Officials argued endlessly about the kind of wallpaper needed to decorate the rest rooms, considering that children were sensitive creatures, and the wrong colour scheme might have a harmful effect on their nervous systems. So the Department pursued its labours, while in the reformatories for juvenile delinquents and teenaged prostitutes, the boys were beaten with the strap and the girls' arms were pinched until they were black and blue with bruises. Elaborate circulars were sent to the reformatory supervisors, explaining that pinching was not the kind of punishment which accorded with modern educational principles. The circulars were duly read, and subsequently used for purposes for which they had not been intended. Inside the reformatories, everything was lacking: no food, no proper clothes. At night, the girls would climb out of the windows and run to find the nearest Red Army men, shouting 'Dyadya, we know how to do it!' The dyadya ('uncle') appreciated their services, and rewarded them with slices of sausage, cabbage soup, and syphilis.

In a railway buffet, Ehrenburg saw a little girl begging for food. An overfed customer handed her the remains of his meal on a plate, but as the child showed her joy in anticipation, a waiter seized the plate and literally threw the leftovers into her face. She was another of those, thought Ehrenburg, for whom they had failed to build a palace.

He had often felt sceptical about the future shape of things in the Soviet State. At a very early stage, he had realized that it was incapable of providing freedom, and he feared that it would turn into an epitome of soulless efficiency which would paralyse all independent thought. The one thing he had not expected was that, under a Communist leadership, human beings would once more be treated like dirt simply because they were poor; that minor officials would again cringe before the rich; or that it would once more be possible for a railway guard to take pleasure in bullying a peasant woman because she had inadvertently tried to enter a first-class carriage (in deference to the ideological myth of a classless society, these were discreetly called 'soft-seat' carriages). Moreover, as Ehrenburg watched such lamentable developments, he seems to have felt that they had a specifically Russian character. In the past, he had been incensed by Western assumptions of superiority, and had defended Russian soldiers against the arrogance of the French. Now, he began to find Russia itself repellent, and attributed a number of the iniquities he observed to a purely Russian origin. There had already been evidence of this attitude in *The Life and Downfall of Nikolai Kurbov*: to Kurbov, the Kremlin is not a symbol of Russian pride, but an abscess, the relic of an evil past. Similarly, in a passage in *The Go-Getter*, the novel he wrote after his visit to Moscow in 1924, Ehrenburg dwelt on the specific nature of Russian cruelty:

> Volumes have been written about the atrocities committed during the civil war: about the disembowelling of both Jews and Gentiles; about officers' insignia being carved with penknives on some people's shoulders and five-pointed stars on the foreheads of others; and about many other devices invented by a resourceful, self-taught nation. Bestiality is common to all. Other nations, too, are not exactly soft-hearted: it is enough to recall the fate of certain heroic insurgents who were tied to wooden stakes in the malaria-infested swamps of Cayenne. But there is something about cruelty in our country which makes it quite specific, something which exists only within our frontiers. Nowhere, except in this long-suffering country, is cruelty so inextricably linked with boredom. Nowhere is the shedding of blood accompanied by such abysmal wolfish yawns, where, in the intervals between applying the most refined forms of torture, the sleepy tormentor keeps scratching his head and spitting on the floor, as men do when they are bored to death. O, that cursed Russian boredom!

Boredom is what Nikolai Kurbov hates most about the Kremlin, the boredom that makes people indifferent both to other human beings and to their own actions; and boredom was what Ehrenburg hated about the selfish Russian middle class, which had again come into its own during the NEP. In the same novel, *The Go-Getter*, he describes a tram ride in Moscow on a winter's night, during which, for want of anything better to do, the hero surveys his fellow-passengers, watching their synchronized yawns. Their brains are slowly digesting the contents of that day's *Izvestia*, while the cabbage soup is slowly being digested in their stomachs. Everything moves as slowly as the tram. The go-getter suddenly becomes acutely aware of the horror of the Russian climate. If only he had been born in Italy, or even Germany! Climate is more important than ideas or political systems. 'He realized then that he hated Russia. He hated her with a dull and vicious hatred. What a pleasure it would be to slap her in the face, to break her nose, to trample on her breasts, to humiliate her in every possible way!'

The character who expresses these thoughts is a thoroughly despicable creature, a frustrated careerist and a crook, and it would obviously be quite wrong to identify his spleenful meditations with Ehrenburg's own feelings. Ehrenburg points out, however, that such base reflections about Russia are part of the Russian national tradition. He goes on:

In describing them we are being strictly objective. Which of our compatriots has not at least once in his life felt similar despair? Which of them has been able to resist similar attacks of malicious fury? These fits of anger have been represented as a political protest against various regimes, or as a revulsion against the spiritual poverty of our history, with its lascivious, fat-bottomed empresses and drunken uprisings. All sorts of theories have been advanced, yet, in the final analysis, these fits of rage invariably stem from self-accusation.

These are dark reflections, but whatever one may think of them, Ehrenburg plainly intended to convey that his anger with Russia was of the traditional Russian kind, and had nothing in common with the moods of a Western intellectual, who might be suspected of treating Russia with contempt.

When he made a further visit to Moscow in 1926, he stayed with friends in a slum quarter of the city, and there he heard of a hair-raising case. A group of abandoned children had stolen a ham from a wealthy shopkeeper, and in revenge he had blocked up the exit from a dark and airless cellar in which they were sheltering from the cold. Ehrenburg does not say how the matter ended in real life. But he used this episode in his novel *In Potochny Lane* (published in England under the title *A Street in Moscow*), and there the children are saved from suffocation by the shopkeeper's small son, who warns them of what his father is planning to do. On this occasion, Ehrenburg kept his anger under control, and the result was a moving book about real people. Most of the people who live in the wretched slum are desperately unhappy, not knowing what to do with their lives. The abandoned children, having escaped death, try to make their way south in search of warmth. They travel hobo-fashion. One of the boys is killed. 'I don't know what happened to the others,' wrote Ehrenburg. 'They may have been run over, or beaten to death, or they may have died of exhaustion.' He compared them to Russia herself, 'our own Russia, orphaned and young, dreamy and embittered, with no one to look after her – a child that has experienced everything, moving along a forsaken road. Will she ever reach her goal? Will she ever reach it?'

Russia orphaned, with no one to look after her! By present-day standards, it seems a miracle that this ever got into print at all. It did, but with predictable results, since Ehrenburg now seemed to have perpetrated the unforgivable. Anticipating what was to come, the publishers adopted the method recommended by *Na Postu*, and prefaced the book with a statement setting out their reservations. From the ideological point of view, they said, the book was undoubtedly a failure; and they went on to quote, out of context, Bukharin's remark that Ehrenburg had no great faith in the coming order, or any enthusiasm for it. Ehrenburg's tendency to glorify everything that was rotten and corrupt could not go unchallenged. But since they needed to justify themselves for the actual publication, the publishers paid tribute to his literary skill, and added, paraphrasing Bukharin, that, like *Julio Jurenito*, this was an interesting and intelligent novel.

It was no use. The critics pounced on the book like vultures and tore it to shreds. Pity for Russia was worse than anger with Russia. All Ehrenburg had succeeded in doing was to make a multitude of new enemies. The episode I happened to witness in a Berlin concert hall, when the Soviet half of the audience promptly walked out as soon as Ehrenburg was called upon to speak, occurred shortly after the publication of *A Street in Moscow*. To Soviet officials at that time his name was mud.

CHAPTER XV

Ehrenburg had returned to Paris in the summer of 1924 with a sigh of relief, but a certain disillusionment soon set in. His re-entry into France had been made possible by the electoral victory of the French left-wing groups – the Cartel des Gauches – which was, in fact, a coalition of moderate parties. It was expected that diplomatic relations would soon be established with the Soviet Union, and it was no longer automatically assumed that any Soviet citizen who applied for an entry permit must be an agent of the Comintern. In Ehrenburg's case, however, there was a problem: he had already been expelled from the country once, and the deportation order was still in force. From Moscow, he and his wife travelled first to Italy, where the French Consul in Rome, who knew nothing of the earlier business, issued them with visas. Once they reached Paris, a liberal politician was persuaded to use his influence with the French police, and they were allowed to stay. They stayed for sixteen years.

To return to one's first love is often an unsettling experience, and at first Ehrenburg felt only disappointment. He hardly recognized the city for which he had once had such a deep affection, although in actual fact Paris had preserved much of its former atmosphere and way of life. Berlin had changed radically in the postwar years, but Paris had not. In many respects, it was still delightfully old-fashioned. The boulevards were still crowded, most of the cafés still had the nostalgic false glamour of the *belle époque*, and the bearded academic-looking gentlemen strolling past the second-hand book-stalls on the left bank of the Seine seemed to perpetuate the image of Anatole France, and to confirm by their serene presence that Paris was still as Ehrenburg had once described it: an overgrown provincial city inhabited by the happiest of mortals. When he came to look back on it forty years later, he admitted that in the middle of the 1920s, Paris must still have been an idyllic place. But in 1924 he was hankering after the Paris of his youth, the Paris of 1912. He did not see the similarities, but only the changes; and these were not at all to his liking.

The plain reason was, of course, that Ehrenburg himself had changed. It was true that some of his former friends had disappeared. Modigliani was dead, Diego Rivera had gone back to Mexico, and Picasso had departed from Montparnasse. But many old friends were still there. Even if Picasso had moved to the Right Bank, he was not exactly out of reach. Yet Ehrenburg felt lonely and nostalgic. Now that it was possible to travel to France on a Soviet passport, Russian poets and artists made frequent visits to Paris, where they continued to argue, as in the old days, about poetry and art. But Ehrenburg no longer found such discussions exhilarating. He had lost his naïve faith in constructivism. His recent visit to Italy had made him realize, as he later confessed, that there was no such thing as 'progress' in art, that true art never became obsolete, and that 'isms' were of little or no importance. (One might argue that he should have realized all this much sooner, but rebels often fail to see the obvious – and where would the world be without rebels?)

An International Exhibition of Decorative Art was being held in Paris, and people raved about the Soviet pavilion, which many took to be the last word in constructivist design. Three years earlier, Ehrenburg would have hailed them as converts. Now he dismissed them as mere slaves to contemporary fashion. He noted that the stairs inside the pavilion were difficult to climb, and that when the weather was bad, the roof let the rain through. Once he had loudly proclaimed that in the modern world art and industry would become one. Now he saw that as a theory this did not make sense, and that in practice many of those who proudly called themselves 'constructors' did not care whether their constructions were suited to human needs or not. The former co-editor of *Object* now began to resent the intrusion of man-made objects into people's lives, especially of objects that moved and made a noise, such as motor-cars, and neon lights, which not only did not add to the beauty of the urban scene, but struck him as garish and oppressive. Formerly he had thought that America would point the way to the art of the future. Now he no longer believed in such an art, and his brief infatuation with America gave way to a violent dislike of everything America stood for, both in reality and in his imagination. He was dismayed at the growing popularity of the American way of life, he felt that Paris was being Americanized (in that view, he was not alone), and he was irritated at the invasion by American tourists of Montparnasse, where dozens of night-clubs had sprung up for the benefit of transatlantic visitors. In a vein both elegiac and ironical, he proclaimed his gratitude to Montparnasse: 'O Montparnasse, my second home: district of eternal glory and furnished rooms; the brothel which welcomes 40,000 impotent men every year; the alms house where madness proliferates; the lice-infested paradise where my despair grew.' But although this also contained a valedictory note, it was not intended to be a farewell. Montparnasse no longer meant to him what it once had, but he still spent much of his time at the Rotonde, and later at the Dôme across the road. (He claimed that he had been forced to transfer to the Dôme because the Americans were monopolizing the Rotonde. It does not sound like too great a hardship, but Bohemians are notoriously conservative in their habits and hate having to move.)

Some people, when they feel lonely in a big city, gradually shut themselves up and cease to notice what is going on around them. But others begin to see too much. Their minds lose their protective coating and are exposed to the full impact of horrors against which they had previously immunized themselves. Ehrenburg summed up his feelings in a novel which he wrote shortly after his return to France. He called it *Summer 1925*, it is written in the first person, and is full of violent and sometimes grotesque contrasts, as in this description of the Paris working-class district of Belleville:

> Old women were fighting over scraps of offal which a butcher had thrown out into the street. They tore each other's hair, their shrieks frightened away the cats, their hands were smeared with blood. Infants lustily demanded their share. They were given half-chewed bread and pieces of rag to suck. One baby, with the face of an angel from a country chapel, had calvados poured down its throat. A nervous canary, clearly a casual visitor from distant parts, was trying to sing, perched on a window-sill above three rickety children who were merrily spitting at each other, their sole distraction. Apart from children and cats there were women, a pitiful collection of shabby goods such as one sees in an old-clothes shop, who tried to tempt the passers-by with bursts of sullen laughter. Neither the dark night nor thick layers of powder could hide the dirt and wrinkles of their rash-reddened necks. What happened next I do not know. Did one of the hags manage to seize a piece of offal and consume it in peace? Did the infant, after being given its drink of calvados, survive to become an enfranchised citizen of the Republic, or did it renounce that privilege, writhing in agony? And what did it matter anyway?

I made my way to the Champs-Élysées. Here, the air is the product of the best scent factories in Europe, but all I felt was physical disgust. The odours, the sounds, the bright colours were throttling me. I had only one desire: that everything should vanish, that these incompatible worlds, the rickety children of Belleville and the ladies riding side-saddle to the Bois de Boulogne, the smell of bread, the fragrance of flowers and the stench of vomit, all should cease to exist. Above all I wanted to banish the sun, that shameless symbol of equality, which shone with professional indifference on the *pavé* of the great avenue and on the dingy courtyards of Belleville, where at night the moon wallowed in puddles of dirty water . . .

Belleville, with its narrow streets and crowded housing, was one of the more insalubrious quarters of the city. But as Ehrenburg's footsteps – or rather those of his first-person narrator – took him to various parts of Paris, he seemed to see everything through the prism of an apocalyptic vision.

I wandered through the cursed labyrinth of the Paris streets and found myself in an enormous building. Escalators dragged me upward. I floundered through a mass of sticky human bodies; everywhere there were ribbons and enigmatic signs: 'Salamander burns six months', 'Remnants – *crêpe de Chine*'. In vain did I look for the exit: hundreds of mirrors reflected hundreds of doors. An elderly wax doll sprayed me with scent which smelled of chemicals and cost the equivalent of a month's pay. A zealous ghost offered me a choice of braces at 7 francs 95 centimes a pair. He distended their snake-like bodies and their vertebrae cracked. Somehow I managed to get away. Outside there were too many streets: it seemed to me that here, too, there must be mirrors which multiplied them. Electric stars, in perpetual motion, directed one to shorthand classes and promised to supply one with dentures. They moved chaotically, like snow-flakes in a snow-storm, and the fury of the storm never abated. I kept closing my eyes, but then I heard the sounds: the hooting of cars, the noise of the radio, the whispers of touts and whores.

Someone who sees and hears too much should be careful to avoid so-called places of entertainment, since these are particularly apt to bring on apocalyptic visions. If he does not, if he rushes from bar to bar and from night-club to night-club, he will find that everything conspires against him.

Coloured doormen laughed at me. They were pushing the doors too quickly, and I could not get out of the revolving cage. Inside, people were dancing. I was knocked off my feet, pelted with paper balls and got entangled in paper streamers. The jazz band stamped and roared. Somewhere in the State of Mississippi a Negro had been lynched and his soul, as frail and tender as a young tropical plant, whined through the saxophone. The Chinese barman had purple eyelids and the girlish hands of a professional executioner. It occurred to me that he knew the meaning of nirvana and would also know how to impale a man. He measured with great care the required quantities of the varicoloured liquids – gifts of monasteries and the mountain flora. Green mint struggled angrily with St Benedict's gold. The philtres were being shaken, warmed up or iced in preparation for dance and crime. When the barman was not mixing drinks, he stared at the empty glasses or gazed at the ceiling. He was indifferent to the fate of men. Confucian wisdom and cocktail recipes provided him with a solid barrier against the outside world.

There was a dark and slimy leech – an Argentinian pimp or something – trying to extract from a middle-aged woman a dose of motherly affection and a cheque made out to the bearer. There was a cattle-dealer from Chicago, eagerly testing the piece of goods he was about to buy: in this case, some Mademoiselle Fifi or Babette, with a bust from the Louvre and a soul from the fashion house of Poiret. Needless to say, there was also a Russian 'prince', whose grand gestures accorded with the size of his former estates, and who kept smashing glasses on credit. There was a youngster who, before going out for the evening, had stolen a kiss from *maman* and a packet of contraceptives from *papa*. There were card-sharpers, homosexual poets, private detectives, professional gigolos, an assortment of ghosts, each ready to receive from the Chinese barman a death potion in exchange for 10 francs. A tiresome swarm attracted by the nightly glow of the Place Pigalle. By day these non-persons do not exist; they hide, like bedbugs, in hotel rooms that are let at varying rates.

Then the narrator is once again out in the streets, escaping from the thicket of lights, champagne corks and shallow kisses, fleeing from unknown persecutors.

I reached the stone steps that led up the hill. There was no one about, and I thought I was safe. But then I heard sounds as sharp as the clatter of typewriter keys. Someone on crutches was walking up the steps, trying to catch up with me. I ran. When I got to the top of the hill, I was out of breath. Stray dogs were licking the sugar-loaf walls of the Sacré Coeur. The dogs were howling. Down below lay the unreal city, orange-coloured, delirious with gold, lights and blood. I was suffocating. The crutches were now quite near me. 'I am a war hero . . . gassed . . . please . . . thirty-two positions for only 4 francs . . .' As I ran down, I heard the wood knocking against the stone and could not bear the misery of it. The thirty-two positions were bulging out of the brightly-lit windows. It took me some time to get to the Seine, where idyllic-looking barges and the moon rocked peacefully on the water.

And, finally, the narrator is bound to stop and stare at a building which he wishes to see least of all, and which he would never have noticed but for feeling so helpless and abandoned.

I found myself outside a police station, with its red lamp that looked as if it was filled with the blood of those who had been beaten up inside. All police stations are alike, no matter where they are. They are like tears and ink: latitudes and political upheavals do not affect them. The bloodshot eye, which burns in the night, tells everyone: this is the place where they will certify your signature and where they destroy your soul. Try to remember what a police station smells like. What is it? Boot polish? Musty paper? Blood? Sweat? Vomit? Yes, it smells of all these, and of many other things besides. In fact, it smells of life: not the kind of life that is portrayed by writers of fiction, who lavishly employ scented words to disguise their heroes' bad breath, but life as it really smells when one is awake.

There is nothing more terrifying than to be awake when this means shedding that outer skin which most human beings need in order to survive. But there is no reason to assume that Ehrenburg shared the feelings of his narrator in every detail. It is true that he was not the kind of man who enjoys strolling through a department store, and he disliked night-clubs because to him they symbolized a tawdry, false glamour and sex without affection. Neon lights got on his nerves, and he had good reason to look with repugnance on police stations, both in Russia, where he had spent time in the cells under arrest, and in France, where, like many other foreigners, he felt that the police had subjected him to various humiliations. But was he really so sensitive that the clamorous, brightly-lit streets appeared to him to be inhabited by ghosts or wax dolls, leading him into the depths of despair? He did not lay claim to any such morbid excess of feeling; he had, after all, been writing a work of fiction. The plot, as he himself admitted, was somewhat far-fetched, but that was unimportant: his intention had been to show how hopelessly alone a man could feel in a great city like Paris.

Some critics took the book to be purely autobiographical, which, as far as the events described in it were concerned, it was not. Nevertheless, as in *Julio Jurenito*, the character who tells the story bears Ehrenburg's name, and also mentions that he is the author of *The D.E. Trust* and *The Love of Jeanne Ney*. As narrator, he complains that scepticism has been the bane of his existence. This was the cause of his expulsion from school; and later, for the same reason, all the critics, publishers and censors of his 'virtuous homeland' turned against him. So it is clear that the fictional narrator does have a good deal in common with the author. Ehrenburg's feelings about Paris – 'the true capital of the world that determines the spirit of our age as well as the latest fashion in garters' – must have been not unlike those of his hero, although presumably somewhat less intense.

In his memoirs, he refers to *Summer 1925* as the saddest book he ever wrote. Later, after he had surmounted the emotional crisis that led to it, all his old affection for Paris flooded back. But he never lost a sense of impending doom. He had predicted that there would be a new war if people ever forgot the tragedy of 1914–18. Now, as he saw it, people were once more leading shallow lives, with greed and vice everywhere triumphant. They seemed, indeed, to have banished the last war from their memories; and he awaited the day of reckoning.

CHAPTER XVI

Shortly before the outbreak of the First World War, Julio Jurenito, in the course of his rather sluggish efforts to accelerate the collapse of civilization, drafts the text of an announcement in which he predicts the destruction of the tribe of Judah. This is to be carried out both in the traditional manner, that is to say by burning and burying Jews alive, and by more modern methods, such as 'evacuation' and 'removal of doubtful elements'. This is the starting point for Ehrenburg's own analysis of the Jewish question that was to torment Europe over the coming decades. When Jurenito's Russian disciple, the kindly but muddle-headed Alexei Tishin, protests that nothing so monstrous can possibly happen in the twentieth century, Jurenito retorts that this is going to be 'a very jolly century without the least moral scruples'. (Ehrenburg was writing with the benefit of hindsight, having seen the pogroms in Russia during the civil war, but he also had forebodings of what was still to come: 'evacuation', being synonymous with deportation, was an uncannily accurate prophecy.) The dreamy Alexei Tishin still refuses to believe it. 'Surely', he says, 'Jews are people just like us.' To which Jurenito replies firmly, 'Certainly not'; and to prove his point, he asks his companions which word they would retain if the rest of the vocabulary were to be abolished – 'yes' or 'no'. Six of them, including Tishin, choose 'yes'. The only one who says he would rather keep 'no' is Ehrenburg, the Jew. He confesses that he cannot help feeling pleased when things go wrong. As the saying goes, 'There is a time for gathering stones and a time for casting them.' Both activities are equally legitimate. Ehrenburg prefers to cast stones. While he is speaking, the other disciples move uncomfortably away. Then Jurenito, who is supposed to be wiser and more profound than any of his companions, including the character who bears Ehrenburg's name, explains the real meaning of the Jewish 'no'.

The fundamental difference between the Jews and the others, says Jurenito, is that the others accept the world as it is, whereas the Jews keep asking: 'Why must it be like this?' They constantly question the established order and try to undermine it by inventing subversive religions – of which Christianity is the most striking example. The trouble is that such a religion soon ceases to be subversive. It becomes a pillar of the established order, whereupon it repudiates the Jews and is repudiated by them. This does not cure the Jews of their fatal weakness, however, since they go on banging their heads against the wall and paying for it with their lives. Israel, says Jurenito, has now given birth to a new child (he is referring to Communism); it has wild eyes and its tiny hands are strong as steel. But in due course it, too, will substitute expediency for justice. The Jews will again bang their heads against the wall, moaning 'How long?', and the earth will be drenched with their blood. Their blood, says Jurenito, is 'the world's great medicine'. In his self-appointed role as the great subverter of civilization, he cannot help loving the spade that turns over the soil; and he goes up to his lonely Jewish disciple and kisses him on the forehead.

The paradoxical effect of Julio Jurenito's discourse was to please both anti-Semites and Zionists alike, because they each saw his argument in a different light. A race of conspirators bent on fomenting unrest: was this not what the Jew-baiters had been saying all along? A people that would never escape persecution because it could not rid itself of its urge to change the world: was this not the chief point in the Zionists' argument? But surely, to pursue that argument, should not the Jews stop worrying about the fate of the world, and start concentrating instead on what they could do to help themselves? Ehrenburg, who was no Zionist, did not think they should. He was one of those who continued to bang their heads against the wall, and he was proud of it. He did not feel that the Jews should exchange their tragic and unique destiny for a settled life within narrow national boundaries, and in an essay he wrote a few years later, he contemptuously dismissed as 'naïve Jewish patriots' those who claimed that the Jews should have their own university, their own country, and 'even their own police'.

The essay was a disjointed piece of writing with a good title – 'A Spoonful of Tar'. There is a Russian proverb which says that a spoonful of tar will spoil a whole barrel of mead. Ehrenburg claimed that the opposite was true: that a spoonful of tar, in the figurative sense, improved the quality of the mead. Pure mead meant conformity. Tar stood for scepticism and dissent. The Jews were born sceptics and dissenters. Ehrenburg preferred mead with tar.

He quoted a poem written in Spanish by a Sephardic rabbi:

> Which is the better of the two,
> Andalusian wine or a thirsting mouth?
> The taste of the most wonderful wine is soon forgotten.
> Unquenched thirst stays on.

The Jews, said Ehrenburg, made good wine. They had been hard at work for over two thousand years, and had discovered many religious, philosophical and social potions. But they made no use of them: they left it to others to taste the wine. Their own lips remained dry because, like the Sephardic rabbi, they had chosen thirst. In every Jew there was something of the Wandering Jew. Paradise, from which they had been so recklessly expelled, no longer appealed to them as a domicile, and what others saw as Jewish inconstancy could be called by another name: Freedom.

By and large, this was the attitude of a cosmopolitan, but it contained a number of inconsistencies. Ehrenburg was wedded to the cosmopolitan ideal (he often quoted a remark by the German poet Ernst Toller: 'To say "I am proud of being a Jew" is as ridiculous as saying "I am proud of having brown eyes." '), but like many people, he found it difficult to apply in practice, and at times contradicted himself. From a true cosmopolitan viewpoint, some of the ideas expressed in 'A Spoonful of Tar' might pass muster, but most of Julio Jurenito's oratory is racialist nonsense. 'Our Jew is left alone', says Jurenito to his other disciples, pointing at Ehrenburg. 'You can destroy the ghettoes, you can wipe out all boundaries, yet nothing will remove the gulf that separates you from him.' But a genuine cosmopolitan would surely have said: 'The gulf has nothing to do with Ehrenburg being a Jew. If there is a gulf, it is between the young, embittered romantic, who is anything but a 'no'-sayer, and the American shark who manufactures weapons and runs a chain of brothels, between Ehrenburg the Bohemian and the German maniac who is infatuated with organization.'

Did Ehrenburg ever feel there was a gulf between himself and the others at the Rotonde? His chapter on the Jewish question in *Julio Jurenito* shows all the signs of having been written in a moment of spleen and bad temper, since it contains too many sweeping generalizations about the alleged Jewish propensity to foment unrest, and is often confused and self-contradictory. But for much of the time, Ehrenburg did not allow the question to weigh upon him.

Indeed, in several of his novels, he went out of his way to demonstrate that, for him, there was neither Greek nor Jew. For example, he painstakingly introduced the requisite number of Jewish fiends and Jewish angels to match their Gentile counterparts. His Jewish villains, it is true, are not quite as fiendish as the others. In *The Love of Jeanne Ney*, the Russian villain is not only a crook but a murderer; his Jewish associate is merely a crook. In *United Front*, a novel on the evils of capitalism, the Jewish financier is as ruthless as the others, yet he does have a sense of humour, he has become a shark simply because he is bored with life, and he thus compares favourably with the other sharks who have shed almost all vestiges of humanity. But these were minor lapses. In general, Ehrenburg tried hard to view the world from a genuinely cosmopolitan standpoint.

It was when he started reflecting on the past that his cosmopolitan ideals were most put to the test. In particular, he recalled what had happened on his first day at school in Moscow. One of the boys had recited an anti-Semitic jest that was then going the rounds: 'A Jewboy is sitting on a bench, let's impale him on a pin.' In his memoirs, Ehrenburg makes light of the episode. He says he slapped the offender in the face and they later became friends. But when he referred to the same episode in an earlier autobiographical sketch written in 1926 he omitted to mention the mitigating sequel. It was a brief and condensed account of his life up until then, and was supposed to contain only the things that had mattered to him most. Obviously, this particular incident mattered.

In 'A Spoonful of Tar' Ehrenburg described the Jews as a people who had given the world many romantics, madmen, and a few geniuses. In *A Street in Moscow*, he drew the portrait of one such Jewish romantic, a hunchbacked violinist, who is not mad but is considered mad by others. He feels sick at heart as he watches the misery and frustration all around him, but is overjoyed when he learns that the abandoned children immured in an airless cellar by the vengeful shopkeeper have not perished, as was thought, but are still alive. 'Rejoice with me, dance, go mad!' he shouts, and as he plays his violin, the squalid street begins to blossom. Having begun by asserting that 'no' was the only appropriate response to life, Ehrenburg now proclaimed that he had abandoned this in favour of a resounding, all-embracing Jewish 'yes'. Shortly afterwards, he wrote *Lazik Roitshvanets* (published in England under the title *The Stormy Life of Lazik Roitshvantz*), his only full-length novel about a

Jew. Among all his books, it is also the only one that was never published in the Soviet Union.

Lazik is a Jewish tailor from the Belorussian town of Gomel, and although he is not a hunchback, he has plenty of other burdens to bear. To begin with, he is of diminutive stature, which is especially unfortunate in view of his propensity for falling in love with women who do not regard intellect as nature's most precious gift. He also has a talent for putting his foot in it, a fundamental inability to see through the foibles of false friends, and an outrageous family name which causes much merriment among the many people who speak Yiddish in his native town. He bears these burdens stoically, and even with pride. He is enough of a realist to know that one must adapt to one's surroundings in order to survive, but he is not prepared to go beyond certain limits. When he is put on trial on a false charge of having shouted anti-Soviet slogans, he refuses to confess to an action he did not commit. When he is told his prison sentence will be reduced if he recants, he says that he sees no point in recanting. When he is employed as a buffoon, he slips into the role up to a certain point, but draws the line at ultimate degradation. In general, he takes his troubles philosophically, and is not surprised when he falls into various traps that are laid for him, since he knows that people like himself are always being trapped.

Lazik's wanderings take him to many cities, and in and out of a succession of gaols, both in Russia and the West. He is no angel, and there are occasions when he behaves like a charlatan. In Moscow, he poses as an eminent literary critic, greatly respected by the *Na Postu* crowd; it is easy to master clichés, and he quickly learns how to write an orthodox Marxist preface to a rubbishy book (this was Ehrenburg's sly revenge on his *Na Postu* detractors). In Frankfurt, he pretends to be a wise rabbi, and delights the wealthier Jewish citizens by explaining why they need not observe some of the more tiresome religious injunctions. In Paris, he passes himself off at the Rotonde as a modern artist whose works are so original that he dares not show them to anyone, for fear that others will imitate his style. But although, on such occasions, he abuses other people's trust and hospitality, he never does anyone any real harm.

On the other hand, he is often the victim of other people's malice. He is shamelessly exploited, cheated and persecuted, and is frequently arrested and beaten up. He has studied the Talmud, and knows many moving stories of wise and just men. He tells these to his fellow-sufferers, who do not understand them, and to his tormentors, who do not listen. His peregrinations end in Palestine under the British mandate. The British are as unkind to him as are the local Jews, and he feels his strength failing. He is thrown into prison once more, this time by the British, and after yet another beating up, administered by the local Jews, he dies – with a beatific smile on his face. Once before, when he was in love, he had the same blissful smile, but then came the rude awakening. Now he can truly sleep in peace. 'Poor Roitshvanets! No more shall you dream of injustice or a modest slice of smoked sausage!'

Lazik is not one of those who are trying to change the world. But he knows the meaning of the word 'justice', and although he claims to be an agnostic, he also knows the meaning of the word 'God'. There is a god invented by men, a god whom they have created in their own image. But this man-made deity has nothing in common with the true God of the just, and this is the God to whom Lazik pays reverence in his stories. In one of them, a crowd of heartless sinners, fearing divine vengeance, gather in a synagogue and beat their breasts, swearing that they will renounce their wicked ways. God is not impressed – He knows what their repentance is worth – but He smiles and forgives them when a little boy, growing bored with the service, blows a tin whistle. In another story, a rabbi goes up to heaven on the Day of Atonement to plead for an evil-doer. Having succeeded in his mission, he argues with God, in an effort to persuade Him to send a messiah who will put an end to mankind's sufferings. But although he seems to be making headway, he suddenly interrupts his own argument and hurries back to earth, because he knows that the Jews in his synagogue will go on fasting until he returns, and that if he does not return immediately, one of them, an old man, will die. At such times, God rejoices, but most of the time He is sad. In yet another story, a Jew, a poor tailor like Lazik, is ordered to race round Rome naked, for the entertainment of the Pope and his distinguished guests. When he is on the point of collapsing from exhaustion, another naked Jew appears to take his place. The rescuer's name is Jesus. The saved man has nothing to live for, but Jesus promises him he will find peace after death. Jesus himself, however, can never find peace. Crimes are being committed in His name, and He must rush hither and thither to help the victims.

The Stormy Life of Lazik Roitshvantz was an instant success with Ehrenburg's Jewish readers. Anti-Soviet Jewish *émigrés*, who had formerly disliked him for being a Soviet writer, and had branded him a cynic or at best dismissed him with a shrug, now succumbed to Lazik's charm. Ehrenburg had at last revealed himself as a Jewish writer, and that was what mattered. They did not seem to notice that other Jews in the book are less attractive than Lazik himself; most of the false friends who cheat and exploit him are Jews. They ignored the fact that the blissful smile on Lazik's lips at the time of his death had nothing to do with his dying in the Promised Land, and everything to do with his release from hell, a region covering all lands, the Promised one included. The essential point was that Ehrenburg had extolled the wisdom of the ghetto. At that time, the ghetto was still very close to Jewish hearts.

The book was published, in Russian, first in Paris, and a year later, in Berlin, but it did not appear in the Soviet Union. The first part of it is a biting satire on Soviet society, which is depicted as a society infested with sycophants, petty intriguers and lying bureaucrats. Ehrenburg had said similar things before, and Soviet publishers had actually published them. But they had not been forgiven, and by now he had become so unpopular with the Soviet authorities that some people wondered how he was allowed to publish anything at all.

But these were not the only reasons for the book's non-appearance in the Soviet Union. In 1934, when the first Soviet Writers' Congress was being held in Moscow, Ehrenburg was invited to a reception, where he met all the members of the Politburo except Stalin. Some of them, notably Kalinin, Voroshilov and Kaganovich, talked to him about *The Stormy Life of Lazik Roitshvantz*. They all said they liked the book, but regretted that it contained hints of the existence of anti-Semitism in Russia. Kaganovich also criticized the novel for having what he described as a Jewish nationalist flavour. He was by then the only Jew left in the Politburo, and was presumably anxious to demonstrate that he was opposed to nationalism in all its guises, including the Jewish variety. Ehrenburg expressed polite surprise, but since there was really nothing in Kaganovich's attitude to be surprised at, this must have been feigned.

CHAPTER XVII

In his private life, Ehrenburg appears to have gone through a grave emotional crisis in the late 1920s, but this is barely touched on in his memoirs. 'Certain things were happening to me at that time, but I prefer not to talk about them,' he remarks laconically. The fact was that he had fallen in love. Not only that, it seems to have been one of those encounters which happen only once in a man's lifetime, if at all, in which the two participants discover a perfect affinity of heart and soul. In a later section of the memoirs, Ehrenburg refers briefly to a young French actress called Denise, the grand-daughter of the authoress Severine, who wrote with much passion of social injustice and towards the end of her life joined, first the Socialist and then the Communist Party. Ehrenburg eventually paid tribute to Denise by making her the beautiful, courageous, self-sacrificing heroine of one of his best-known novels: she was the model for Mado in *The Fall of Paris*.

But even before this encounter took place, Ehrenburg's life was in a state of some confusion. After the publication of *A Street in Moscow*, and the non-appearance in the Soviet Union of *The Stormy Life of Lazik Roitshvantz*, there were rumours that he had either broken with the Soviet regime or that a breach was imminent. The rumours were unfounded. Officially, Ehrenburg remained a Soviet writer. But he did not renounce his unorthodox views, and this did not endear him to Soviet critics. 'He has seen and meditated a great deal, this spiritual nomad who has been running away from his own country but still feels an alien wherever he goes,' said the Soviet newspaper *Literary Gazette* in an article published in 1931. 'As he wanders from place to place,' the article went on, 'he tries to find a way of travelling through time, either into the past or the future, because he is afraid of the present. But there is no getting away from the present. H. G. Wells's Time Machine does not yet exist.'

Literary Gazette was commenting on Ehrenburg's *The Visa of Time*, in which he had recorded his impressions of the many countries he had visited. His life may have been going through a confused phase, but he did enjoy one great advantage: he was able to travel. With the signing of the Treaty of Locarno in October 1925, the atmosphere in Western Europe had become sufficiently relaxed to allow greater freedom of movement, even to the holder of a Soviet passport. There were still some places where such a document was scarcely an asset, and where visas were not readily granted to Soviet citizens; but in spite of the difficulties ('life is short and consular officials are heartless'), Ehrenburg usually managed to get to his chosen destination. He had always been interested in national characteristics (hence the multinational origins of Julio Jurenito's disciples), and whenever he went to a new country, he made an effort to 'understand its soul', as the Russians say. In other words, he tried hard to be objective. All the same, his judgement tended to vary according to his prevailing mood. After a visit to Poland, where he was attacked by an anti-Semitic section of the Press, he was harsh in his remarks both about anti-Semites and Jewish religious fanatics. At the same time, he noted similarities between Poland and Russia, and came to the conclusion that Russia's traditional anti-Polish bias was due mainly to Poland's geographical proximity. 'Russians never get excited over the Portuguese or the French,' he wrote, 'but the Poles are near and yet they are foreigners: therefore, they are regarded as being worse than foreigners, which accounts for Dostoevsky's powerful but unfair description of them.' As a Russian and a Bohemian who had spent his formative years at the Rotonde, Ehrenburg disliked the ostentatious efficiency of the Czechs, but was attracted by the simpler ways of the Slovaks. In Ruthenia, or Subcarpathian Russia (the region has had a variety of names, depending on who ruled it at any given period) Ehrenburg's Russian patriotism was aroused by hearing Russian spoken, and he felt that this obscure segment of Central Europe should really be part of Russia. In Scandinavia, he preferred the Norwegians to the Swedes because 'the Norwegians are poor, and poverty, even when it is relative, seems more human than an abundance of bathrooms' (a typically Russian sentiment). In Denmark, he admired the integrity of the well-known writer, Karin Michaelis, but whereas a few years earlier he had praised the Danes' friendly attitude towards him in contrast to the official hostility he had encountered in France, he now found them disappointing as a nation. They were, he said, 'only interested in breeding pigs and making money'. In 1926, he visited Spain for the first time, crossing the frontier without a visa; a feat made possible by his 'indomitable zeal as a traveller, and the total absence of any zeal on the part of the Spanish frontier officials'. Years later, he fell in love with Spain. But on that first occasion, he saw only one or two provincial towns, including Seo de Urgel, and noted only apathy, obscurantism, and the presence of a great many army officers wearing uniforms that 'would have delighted the wardrobe mistress of the local opera house in Minsk'. In *The Visa of Time*, he does not mention the English, but in his memoirs he says that he looked upon them at first as men from another planet. It was an attitude that was fairly widespread on the Continent at that time. For example, the eminent Dutch scholar, G. J. Renier, who lived in England, once wrote an amusing book called *The English – Are They Human?*. Ehrenburg, too, must initially have had doubts on this score. Only later did he discover that the English were human enough, and that he could talk to them because they loved Chekhov and were moved to tears by his plays.

Meanwhile, *Literary Gazette*'s attack on Ehrenburg concentrated largely on his approach to nationalism. It was, of course, a good thing if, as Ehrenburg claimed, the Ruthenian peasants of the Subcarpathian region were looking with nostalgia towards Russia. On the other hand, the paper regretted that, instead of explaining this in Marxist terms, Ehrenburg attributed it to the feeling of 'kinship', since this meant that the Ruthenians were attracted by Russia rather than by the Soviet socialist system. Some years later, in 1939, when Stalin ordered his troops to march into Poland, he would speak of the 'kindred' peoples of Western Belorussia and the Western Ukraine, to whose fate the Soviet Union could not remain indifferent. But *Literary Gazette* could scarcely have foreseen that development. In 1931, when the article appeared, 'kinship' was still regarded by orthodox Communists as a dirty word, and the paper claimed that by attributing to the Ruthenian peasants the wrong motives (what they really felt did not seem to interest *Literary Gazette*), Ehrenburg had shown that he was a racialist, a Slavophile, and an advocate of Great Power politics. The charge of racialism was nonsense, but the rest was not entirely devoid of truth. Although at times he voiced his anger at Russia, he still retained much of the Russian patriotism he had acquired during the war, and there were even times when he behaved almost like an old-fashioned chauvinist, referring to other nations with barely disguised contempt.

It was not true, as *Literary Gazette* had claimed, that Ehrenburg constantly sought to escape into the past or the future, but the paper was correct in noting the significance he attached to time in the title of his book. *The Visa of Time*, apart from reflecting his constant preoccupation with pursuing visas that were difficult to obtain, was also supposed to mean 'the stamp of the epoch'. It was true that he had come to detest the epoch in which he lived: the 1920s were indeed a period of acute frustration for those who were not ideologically committed but could not help seeing that postwar Western society lacked moral and intellectual stamina. Yet, far from trying to escape from the present, Ehrenburg was fascinated by it; and in his writings he did his best to catch its mood. Jens Boot, of *The D.E. Trust*, destroys Europe but breaks his heart in the process, and eventually returns to Europe to die. Ehrenburg once remarked that one could have a feeling for the period in which one lived not unlike that which one has for one's country or continent. There was, as he put it, a 'patriotism in time' as well as a 'patriotism in space', and although he regarded both as rather fatuous, he was not immune from either.

Those who reflect on such matters generally agree that, whatever the calendar may say, the twentieth century really began, not in 1900, but either at some point during the war (such as the Battle of the Somme) or in its immediate aftermath. In the West, one of the characteristics of the postwar period was a never-ending quest for pleasure. The types of pleasure varied, and Ehrenburg was not alone in finding many of them superficial and corrupting, including the dancing and jazz craze, the passionate interest in boxing, the record-breaking mania in other fields of sport, most films (although people on the Left generally made an exception for the films of Charlie Chaplin and a select few others), and the worship of the motor-car (unless one happened to own one – but very few European intellectuals did). This attitude now seems absurdly puritanical, but at the time it did reflect a genuine concern over the ability of the postwar generation to prevent another global catastrophe; and in the long run the puritans were proved right.

Ehrenburg enjoyed writing about the vulgar excesses of the twentieth century. He was good at it. It was not only vice in Berlin or the crush in a Paris department store that inspired some of his more forceful descriptions. He conceived an especially violent dislike of the cinema, so that the mere sight of people leaving some picture palace at the end of a showing was enough to induce an apocalyptic mood.

The last performance is over. Huge crowds pour out of a thousand picture houses. They disperse, stunned and half-dead. They run and vanish into dark, narrow lanes, leaving abuse, cigarette ends and tears behind them. They feel that someone is chasing them, that someone is still projecting patterns of light on the wall. Someone – a woman's voice – is still singing 'Harry, I shall love you forever' – and they hear it outside the window, in the chimney, in their bathroom taps. The dreams will not leave them, those beautiful dreams manufactured by Paramount or the UFA studios. They will follow them into their stuffy bedrooms, they will sink into the heat of their pillows, they will turn into chaotic visions – until the alarm clock rings in the cruel, grey morning. And then . . . Keep pounding the typewriter keys. Ramon Navarro may yet fall in love with you. Or, perhaps, it will be your boss. He will grab you, give you an unpleasant disease, and drop you. Then you will die and policemen will conduct you to paradise. Angels and worms will keep you company. This is the magic box that rules the world. A great invention. An invention which spells boredom, blinding, all-consuming boredom. Such is the cinema.

But apart from being vulgar and corrupt, the twentieth century, as Ehrenburg now saw it, was also absurd. It represented the final absurdity born of a marriage of capitalism and technical progress, and this became the theme of several of his books, which were meant to demonstrate the workings of a crazy system and its impact on mankind. He called these books documentaries, and claimed that a good deal of research went into writing them. But the actual result was a highly impressionistic and often crude picture of how he thought the system operated. In one of these 'documentaries', the least-known of the series, he attacked the Czech shoe manufacturer, Tomas Bata, whereupon Bata sued him for libel. This may have persuaded Ehrenburg that he was working on the right lines; but as an indictment of capitalism these studies never attained the power of similar works by Upton Sinclair, and were soon forgotten. What he did manage to convey, as he described the struggles between rival industrial concerns, their internecine battles on the international stage, and the lengths to which they were prepared to go in order to impose their products on the public, was a sense of the futility of it all. There had been a time, he observed, when capitalism, ruthless and immoral though it was, had had a definite function; but now, in the twentieth century, it had outlived its usefulness. Business tycoons still went through the motions, but they no longer had any real sense of purpose. They were both the originators and the victims of a general feeling of boredom, and their pointless activities merely demoralized the world.

In the best-known of this series, Ehrenburg dealt with the more glaring symbols of the modern age: with the cinema (in *The Dream Factory. A Chronicle of our Time*) and the motor-car (in *Ten Horse-Power. A Chronicle of our Time*). In each case, he compiled a detailed catalogue of the alleged iniquities of the capitalist system as they manifested themselves at each stage of the industrial process, whether in the rubber plantations of Malaya, on the shop floor and in the boardroom of an automobile plant, or in the motion picture studios of Hollywood. But he also made it clear that, irrespective of the way these two inventions had been exploited by capitalism, he personally did not regard either of them as a boon to mankind. It was a strange about-turn and a highly un-Marxist view. Ehrenburg, the eternal rebel and former constructivist, had now become a kind of Luddite. In short, he deplored technological progress. He even seemed to have developed a most unlikely yearning for the quiet life of a nineteenth-century Russian squire. He had been visiting the country home of the deeply conservative Russian writer Aksakov, and wrote about it in terms of regretful nostalgia: 'Easy chairs and maple trees . . . Aksakov had time to meditate. In his letters to Gogol, he depicted in leisurely fashion the period in which he lived and what he thought of it. But as for ourselves, we have no easy chairs and no maple trees. The only rest we get is in a railway carriage when we travel by train.'

Above all, Ehrenburg had come to hate speed. 'The film runs quickly: sixteen frames a second. One can't tell it to slow down. One can't tell it to stop. If only it would stop! Our eyes hurt. Our heads are swimming. We can't stand it any more. But the film runs on . . .' Similarly, 'One can't say to a motor-car in full motion, "Stop – I want to have a proper look at you." One can only catch a fleeting glimpse of its headlights. Or – and this, of course, is always a possible solution – one can find oneself crushed under its wheels.'

In *Ten Horse-Power* he recounted with morbid delectation a number of stories, mainly culled from the newspapers, in which the motor-car had played a sinister role. He happened to be in Italy when Fascist thugs assassinated the socialist deputy Matteotti. How was it done? Matteotti was kidnapped and killed in a car. A French jeweller had robbed and murdered a man to save himself from bankruptcy. What did he do next? He put the body in a car, the car was traced, and the jeweller was guillotined. It was the car that had made him think he could dispose of the body; without a car, he would probably not have dared to commit the crime. Then there was the case of a learned eccentric in Leipzig, who was so engrossed in the study of ancient Indian folklore that he was entirely unaware of what was going on around him: predictably, he was run over by a car. A respectable French bourgeois had often indulged in armchair day-dreams of travelling round the world, until the fateful day when he decided to buy a car: the car crashed and the wretched man was killed. But, in Ehrenburg's eyes, the baneful influence of the motor-car was not confined to the capitalist world. And to make this unequivocally clear, he related the sad tale of a young Soviet woman, who had been driven to such despair by her unromantic lover that she threw herself under the wheels of his car. And why was the lover so unromantic? Because he held a senior post in the Soviet administration, was perpetually in a tearing hurry, and used his official car whenever he went to call on the girl. If there had been no car, he would have stuck to his desk, and would probably never have started the affair in the first place.

Literary Gazette admitted that Ehrenburg showed a healthy detestation of capitalism, but added: 'He does not really expose the contradictions inherent in the system; in fact, he covers them up.' Ehrenburg was concerned about the fate of the individual under capitalism, and the paper agreed that 'capitalist conveyor belts and capitalist mechanization' did not leave much room for individuality. On the other hand, he had failed to point out that socialist conveyor belts and socialist mechanization would have quite a different effect, and this omission, said *Literary Gazette*, could hardly be accidental. The paper was correct in its assumption. Ehrenburg did *not* believe that individuality could flourish under the Soviet system, and while he equated capitalism with boredom, he did not think that Soviet Communism would add to the gaiety of nations.

The *Literary Gazette* article was entitled 'A False Visa', and was specifically cited in an entry on Ehrenburg in the *Great Soviet Encyclopaedia*, thus conferring on it the stamp of authority. *Literary Gazette* declared that Ehrenburg was too pessimistic to understand the greatness of the epoch in which he was privileged to live. He had said that one 'possible solution' was to find oneself crushed under the wheels of a car. Yet there were a number of alternatives: one was to take a job at the Nizhny Novgorod car factory, and another was actually to drive a car: such actions would have been more in keeping with the spirit of the age. Unfortunately, said the paper, Ehrenburg did not see it that way. Moreover, like Pasternak and certain other writers, he seemed to feel that the emergence of socialist art would mean the end of art altogether. This was precisely what Ehrenburg did feel.

CHAPTER XVIII

In a comment on Ehrenburg's mercurial temperament and frequent changes of attitude, the critic Viktor Shklovsky had once described him as 'Pavel Savlovich', or Paul, son of Saul, a remark neither of them ever forgot. Forty years after the event, Ehrenburg quoted it in his memoirs, and Shklovsky returned to it even later. In 1973, some six years after Ehrenburg's death, he came to England on a visit, and when he was asked what he thought of Ehrenburg, replied simply: 'I called him Pavel Savlovich.'

There came a time, however, when Ehrenburg decided to shake off this name and patronymic, suggesting as they did too many hesitations on his personal road to Damascus, and to identify himself completely with the Soviet regime. In 1932, he became the Paris correspondent of *Izvestia*, and in this way accepted the total commitment he had previously avoided for so many years. In his memoirs, he says that he accepted the post with some misgivings because, as a freelance writer, he was not sure whether he would be able to cope with an exacting journalistic routine. But this scarcely sounds very convincing. He had always had a capacity for hard work, and although he must have enjoyed the freedom to organize his writing as he pleased, the thought of losing this freedom must have been considerably less alarming than the prospect of having to write what pleased *Izvestia*, as he would obviously have to do from now on. As it happened, however, his *Izvestia* appointment merely clinched a decision he had reached in the course of the previous year; and when the paper approached him, his mind was already made up. He had come to the conclusion that he must cease being the son of Saul.

In his memoirs, he describes it as an agonizing decision, and one can well believe him. The irony of it was that, for years, while Russia was governed by a group of ruthless but imaginative men who realized that artists must have some degree of creative freedom, Ehrenburg had remained a fellow-traveller and refused to commit himself, largely because he felt that the Soviet system would lead to the suppression of the individual. Yet now that this was about to happen, as Stalin began to impose his despotic rule, he gave the regime his full support. Moreover, he did it with his eyes open. 'I had not renounced any of the things that were dear to me,' he wrote later in his memoirs. 'But I knew that I would have to clench my teeth and try to master the most difficult art of all – the art of remaining silent.'

From the practical point of view the issue was clear-cut. Either he must accept the regime, or become relegated to the status of an *émigré*. At least, that was how the Soviet Government would regard him, even if he did not join in the anti-Soviet chorus. Stalin had no use for fellow-travellers who disagreed with the engine-driver, and sometimes even went so far as to claim (as Ehrenburg had done in *A Street in Moscow*) that the driver had lost his head and no longer knew where he was going. Ehrenburg thus had every reason to fear that, unless he changed his position, his books would soon cease to appear in the Soviet Union. Nor could he be certain how long they would continue to be published abroad. His documentary series on capitalism was no substitute for *The Stormy Life of Lazik Roitshvantz*, let alone for *Julio Jurenito*. His popularity was on the wane. In a few more years he might fade away from the literary scene altogether, which was the last thing he wanted.

Yet it would surely be doing Ehrenburg an injustice to attribute his decision solely to practical motives. However much he may have been concerned about his future as a writer, there had to be a moral justification for the step he was about to take. It has been said that it was the rise of Fascism in Europe that proved to be the decisive factor in his case. This would make more sense if Ehrenburg's change of heart had occurred in 1933, after Hitler had triumphed in Germany. At that time, it was argued by many people who saw Hitler as the precursor of a new world war that the only Power able and willing to fight the Nazi regime was the Soviet Union, and quite a few people who had never had any fondness for Communism felt it was their duty to support the Soviet State for that reason. But Ehrenburg had come to his decision in 1931, when it was still widely assumed that a civilized country like Germany could not possibly be ruled by a vulgar Jew-baiter. Moreover, although he had often forecast that Europe was heading for a new catastrophe, he had not specifically connected this with Hitler.

In *A Book for Grown-Ups*, which Ehrenburg wrote in the mid-thirties, there is a passage which was intended to be read as a confession (although not a full confession, as he prudently observed), in which he explained why he had decided to break with the past. He claimed that he had grown tired of saying 'no'. He had been saying 'no' ever since the famous debate on 'yes' and 'no' in *Julio Jurenito*. He had been saying 'no' to the West because he held it responsible for millions of wrecked lives, and also because the West had failed to resolve his doubts. But although he had accepted the Soviet regime because he and the Communists hated the same things, he had not been able to bring himself to love it. In Russia he had seen hypocrisy, servility and obtuseness. 'It seemed to me that the great ideals, like ill-fitting clothes, had been left hanging on the rack . . . I was saying "no" to myself and to my chance of happiness. It is terrifying to live by negation alone.'

Now, Ehrenburg finally brought himself to say 'yes'. It was the era of the first Five-Year Plan, which in theory was certainly more acceptable than the NEP. Moreover, having been away from Russia for a long time, he could not know exactly what the new era was like in practice. But the great ideals still existed, whereas the West had no ideals at all, not even hanging on the rack. Whatever the Soviet regime might be in real life, its ideology was unassailable.

There is a tendency, especially among the pragmatic Anglo-Saxons, to dismiss ideology as something of no great significance. Yet throughout history theory has always been more important than practice and ideals have mattered more than results. If a doctrine rests on a solid ethical foundation, and its ideals are presented in a sufficiently inspiring way, there is no need to practise what is being preached: if there are lapses, excuses can readily be found. In this way, ideals can be trampled underfoot, and every crime committed in their name is condoned and forgiven by the faithful. Had it been otherwise, not one of the great religions and not one of the established churches would have survived. To believers, the only unforgivable sin is loss of faith.

In the early fourteenth century the Order of Templars was put on trial in Paris. The motives were political. The King of France was anxious to destroy a rival establishment which had become a state within a state, and to seize the Order's riches in the process. The Knights Templar were accused of a variety of sacrilegious, obscene and idolatrous practices. It was alleged, for example, that at the initiation ceremony new members had to kiss their seniors on the behind, that they were told they could resort to homosexual intercourse if they found celibacy too difficult, and – by far the most serious allegation – that they were ordered to spit on a crucifix and deny Christ. Confessions revealing these supposed practices were obtained in the customary way, i.e. under torture, and were later withdrawn; notwithstanding which more than fifty Knights, including the Grand Master, were burned at the stake, and the Order was suppressed. Historians have been arguing ever since about the truth or falsity of these charges. A French scholar, Raymond Oursel, dismissed most of them as ridiculous, but admitted that the ritual of denying Christ could have been part of the initiation ceremony.[1] Oursel sympathized with the Templars, and offered various explanations, quoting different sources: it could have been a test of blind obedience; or a symbolic reminder of what might be demanded of the Knights in Saracen captivity, implying a warning against apostasy; or (the most sophisticated explanation and one preferred by many historians) it could have been a reconstruction of what had happened to the Apostle Peter, and thus designed to impress upon new members that, as humble Christians, they must never be too certain of their ability to fulfil the commitment they were about to accept.

It may well be that this particular charge was false. But since some experts believe that such a ritual may have existed, it is worth asking oneself why it never occurred to them to offer the simplest explanation of all: that the initiation ceremony was a moment of truth. The crusades, after all, were not exactly an exercise in Christian charity, and one could hardly be a Knight Templar, or any other kind of warrior knight, without breaking the commandment 'Thou shalt not kill.' Is it not therefore possible that, having sinned many times by their actions, the Templars decided to admit this in the intimacy of their own closed circle, and to let the new members see what they were letting themselves in for? Unfortunately, this simple explanation is also the most improbable. The Knights would hardly have dared to bring their ideology into line with their record of violence and killing. The Order had emerged intact from the crusades, and so had the Church which had given the crusades its blessing. The fact that it continued to preach the Christian faith and Christian ethics made its position invulnerable. Its demonstrable failure to practise what it preached had, as usual, been ignored.

[1] *Le Procès des Templiers*, traduit, présenté et annoté par Raymond Oursel, Denoël, Paris, 1959.

So it was with that new church of the twentieth century – Communism. Like other churches which had gone before it, it derived its strength from ethical principles, and it did not hesitate to trample those principles into the dust. But here again, the power of ideology was such that the faithful were willing to forgive all things. How else can one explain the fact that able and intelligent people in the West remained blind to Stalin's crimes? Why else should they have refused to believe he was committing them? Or, if they were not quite blind, why should they have dismissed those crimes as historical necessities, or at least as the kind of excesses that were regrettably bound to occur in an imperfect world? It was not a question of material advantage: some Western Communists and sympathizers sacrificed promising careers for their belief. Nor was it a question of asserting one's superiority by being different from the rest: some were eminent scientists enjoying universal respect. It was ideology, and ideology alone, that impelled them to remain Communists *in spite of* Stalin. And this is no doubt the reason why, in the long run, Khrushchev's denunciation of Stalin did such relatively little damage to Communist Parties in the West. Of course, there were people in the West who, after Khrushchev's revelations, severed their connection with the Communist Party; but the Party soon made good those losses. So one is forced to ask why many more people did not leave the ranks of the Party at that time, and why so many chose to stay? To which there is surely only one answer: because they dreaded the prospect of having to live without faith.

In Ehrenburg's case, too, it was ideology that provided the moral justification (or, as some would say, the excuse) for his change of heart. He had spent his youth in search of a faith. This had been followed by a period, lasting several years, in which he ostentatiously paraded his lack of faith, and frequently adopted the pose of a cynic. Now, at the age of forty, he at last entered into the embrace of the Communist Church, even though he did not resume his membership of the Party. But whatever he says in his memoirs, he cannot have been fully aware of the price he would have to pay. That he would have to clench his teeth and remain silent about a number of things was obvious enough. But he can hardly have realized that, in the course of time, the silence would become well-nigh absolute. He did see that there was a growing threat to art and literature under the Soviet regime. But no one, not even Ehrenburg with his remarkable prophetic flair, could have predicted that fifteen years later, Stalin would instruct his deputy and cultural hatchet-man, Andrei Zhdanov, to impose a virtual ban on all forms of art and on all creative writing.

In 1932, a month before he accepted the post of Paris correspondent for *Izvestia*, Ehrenburg finished a novel called *Moscow Does Not Believe In Tears*, in which, for the nth time, he expressed his disgust with Western capitalist society. He compared it to a lavatory in a fifth-rate Paris hotel: 'It was as ancient and as cruel as human conscience. Here, life stank, frankly and without embarrassment.' But there is a character in the book, a Soviet artist who lives in Paris and who has been attacked by a critic at home on the ground that his work can appeal only to ten or twenty 'degenerate bourgeois Bohemians'. The artist reflects:

Let's assume that man is right – such people are usually good at arithmetic. Let's also assume that what others produce appeals to tens of thousands of people. Does this mean that I have to pander to their bad taste? Art is intended to give joy and that has nothing to do with statistics. I don't insist on being an artist. If you've calculated that my pictures are of no use to anybody, I can be a house-painter – I shan't mind that at all. But then, don't say that you want art. As long as I stay at my easel, I don't give a damn for your figures.

Ehrenburg was challenging those in power: if they felt there was no need for art, they should say so. He obviously assumed that they would never dare to say it openly; consequently, the artist was in a strong position and there was no need for him to surrender. Twenty-eight years later, in London, he said to me that there could be no 'aesthetic dictatorship'. Political and economic dictatorship, certainly; but aesthetic dictatorship was impossible. I pointed out that a dictator could solve the problem by abolishing art and literature altogether. I did not specify that I was referring to the Zhdanov period but Ehrenburg understood without being told, and immediately agreed that this was certainly theoretically possible. 'But if one wants art to go on, it will always remain a field where no dictatorship can be established.' Whether he really believed this in 1960 is not certain. In 1931 he seemed to take it for granted. Politically, everyone in Russia would have to submit; yet art would go on, the artist would still be able to fight, and Ehrenburg intended to take part in the struggle.

Having decided to set out on a new course, he paid an extended visit to the Soviet Union where he did much travelling and saw the

Five-Year Plan in operation. A year earlier, *Literary Gazette* had attacked his pessimism and suggested as a possible remedy a job at the new motor-car factory in Nizhny Novgorod. This was meant metaphorically: instead of bemoaning the machine age, Ehrenburg should associate himself with Soviet industrialization. Now, on his return to Paris, he wrote a novel about the construction of the gigantic iron and steel works at Kuznetsk in Siberia. He called it *The Second Day*, meaning the Second Day of Creation when the world began to take shape. To choose a biblical title (more easily recognizable as such in Russian than it is in English) was not a very orthodox thing to do. But even less orthodox was the content. It was not at all what the rank and file priests of the Communist Church expected from an eminent convert, and the publisher to whom the manuscript was offered rejected it out of hand.

To force the issue, Ehrenburg took a most unusual step (in his memoirs he calls it an act of despair): he had a limited edition printed in Paris at his own expense and sent copies to members of the Politburo and other influential persons who might be able to help. It was a luxury edition: folio volumes bound in thick grey cloth with the title printed on the binding. It was a costly venture but the scheme worked. *The Second Day* duly appeared in the Soviet Union. Stalin, in a lucid moment, must have realized that unorthodox propaganda could be good propaganda. He was to maintain this attitude towards Ehrenburg for a long time to come.

In his assessment of what he had seen at Kuznetsk, Ehrenburg tried to be as truthful and sincere as he thought he could afford. This went far beyond the limits of what the publisher had originally considered feasible, but even so, Ehrenburg's frankness was tempered with caution. What was likely to shock the authorities was balanced by remarks that were intended to appease them. He gave a graphic description of the living conditions at the construction site, which were so appalling that even the rats had moved out, being unable to bear them. But the workers did bear them, and Ehrenburg paid tribute to their 'iron will'. At the same time, he did not fail to point out that not all of them were enthusiasts: some had come to Kuznetsk only because they had heard that they would be supplied with overalls, which were unobtainable elsewhere; others were peasants deported to Siberia as kulaks. The deportees were sad and angry. 'Not one of them was guilty of anything; but they belonged to a class that was guilty of everything.' Ehrenburg also mentioned a case where the official agitator, having assured the peasants that collectivization was voluntary and that they did not have to join the collective if they did not want to, told them in the same breath that they would have their guts cut out if they refused to join. At that time there was much talk of sabotage, and some 'wreckers' trials' had already been held. Ehrenburg hinted that he did not believe the official version, according to which industrial equipment was being damaged at the instigation of foreign agents. But he did introduce a character who deliberately wrecks a piece of machinery, not for any political or ideological reason, but in a fit of bad temper after a drunken orgy during which a neurotic intellectual unwittingly puts him in a destructive mood.

The neurotic intellectual, a student called Volodya Safonov, is the hero of the novel, although Ehrenburg claimed that it had no hero. He personifies the feelings which had haunted Ehrenburg for a long time, and from which he was now trying to free himself. Safonov is an outsider who sees too much. He does not believe that a furnace is more beautiful than Venus. He knows that lilac came into the world before Marx and that spring existed before the October Revolution; therefore, as he puts it, he knows nothing at all. He is revolted by the absurdities and the pettiness of Soviet life, and feels that the regime's main concern is to stop people from thinking. He believes that poetry in Russia is dead. There had been two corpses at the beginning (Pushkin and Lermontov) and two corpses at the end (Mayakovsky and Esenin), and if a poet of genius were to emerge now, he would either fall silent or go mad within five years. The new industrial State is being built by ants and he, Safonov, does not fit into the communal ant-heap.

At the same time he is convinced that things are no better in the West. He has seen a film in which people are dancing that decadent Western dance, the foxtrot (Ehrenburg's dislike of the foxtrot seems to have been pathological), and has come to the conclusion that in the West, as in the East, people behave like clockwork automata so as to avoid the burden of thought. But when a French journalist, in search of anti-Soviet material, bombards Safonov with loaded questions, he is so incensed that at a meeting a short time later, instead of denouncing the state of affairs in Russia as he had originally intended, he cries, 'The future is ours! We shall conquer!' 'Curiously enough, I spoke sincerely,' he notes. 'But I was not saying what I thought. Or, rather, I was and I wasn't. We are all double-dealers, fakes and hypocrites. But we dissimulate with relish, our cant comes from the bottom of our hearts, and our hypocritical devotion is such that we develop genuine stigmata.' Unable to find a way out of his predicament, Safonov finally hangs himself.

One is inclined to feel that in making his hero commit suicide, Ehrenburg was killing off that part of himself which he could no longer reconcile with the path he had now taken. In talking with Paul Austin, a Canadian scholar who visited him a short time before his death, Ehrenburg said that Safonov had to die because the 1930s afforded little latitude for the individual. Fortunately, he added, there were now many more people like Safonov, who would eventually show the way to the future. In his memoirs, Ehrenburg speaks of Safonov in detached tones, almost as if he had been a real person, and disclaims all responsibility for his tragic fate. Safonov, he says, was simply a victim of his own over-sensitive conscience. He would have survived if he had had fewer scruples and a little more tenacity; and Ehrenburg might have added – 'like myself'. In fact, in the years that followed he was going to need more than a little tenacity. He was going to need all he could muster.

CHAPTER XIX

At the beginning of 1934, Nikolai Bukharin, who had been ousted from power, vilified and, after his recantation, relegated to minor posts, made a reappearance. He was no longer quite at the top of the Party hierarchy, but still in its upper echelons, and he was subsequently appointed editor-in-chief of *Izvestia*. So Ehrenburg's old friend became his boss. Ehrenburg himself had by now become a respected member of the Soviet Establishment. Yet even as he began to slide down the slope towards full conformity, he still made desperate efforts to remain true to himself.

A few months later, the first Soviet Writers' Congress was held in Moscow, and Bukharin was the main speaker. The Congress was a memorable event in many ways. It aroused a number of false hopes before it began, and many more after Bukharin had delivered his address. In fact, however, it was meant to be the beginning of the end, although at the time this was clear only to the initiated. Ehrenburg was present and took the chair at two of the meetings. But seated together with him and with Pasternak on the platform was the future liquidator of Soviet art and literature, Andrei Zhdanov. The Congress took a number of practical steps. It formally set up the Soviet Writers' Union, the organization which was subsequently to help Zhdanov in his task, and approved its charter. It also officially proclaimed the principles of socialist realism, under whose banner the liquidation was later carried out.

Yet, on the surface, things did not seem all that bad. Zhdanov made only a few brief and boring remarks. There were a number of intelligent speeches and, within certain limits, a lively debate. Bukharin praised Pasternak as one of the greatest living Russian poets, and took a swing at some of the minor hacks who were present. When the said hacks protested, he demolished them with such vigour that he later apologized for having been rude; but he did not retract anything that he had said in essence. An amendment to the charter of the Writers' Union was proposed and accepted, stressing that socialist realism must include the greatest possible variety of style. In his memoirs, Ehrenburg says that the atmosphere was euphoric, and confesses that he was naïve. Perhaps this need not be taken literally. But he did seem to think that Soviet literature could still be saved, and this determined the tone of his speech when he was asked to address the Congress.

He was aware of the significance of Zhdanov's presence. Zhdanov, who had just been made a Secretary of the Party's Central Committee, was there as the representative of Stalin; and Ehrenburg began by saying what a tremendous advantage it was for Soviet writers to be able to discuss their problems with the 'men on the bridge', as he put it, recalling the simile he had used in *Julio Jurenito*. He made no attempt to challenge what had already been decided before the Congress began and did not question the principles of socialist realism. But he did emphasize that if the purpose of Soviet literature was to inspire people and help them to build a socialist State, then authors should write about human beings rather than about machines. 'We must tell our readers the truth,' he said, 'the truth which is felt by all, and yet is as difficult to define as the blue of a colourless sky, or the sounds of a silent noon in August.'

In effect, he was saying that literature should be literature, and not merely indifferent advertising copy for the Five-Year Plan. He went on:

> In our novels workers often appear to be divorced from life. Yet workers are human beings. They struggle, they love and kiss, they read and dream, they are jealous husbands and lovers, sometimes they do silly things. Occasionally attempts are made to enliven a story about shock workers or a machine tractor station by inserting tidy little love scenes. But two or three kisses and a few rationed tears do not make dummies human. Our people have as little in common with what has now become the classic image of a shock worker as their oppressed ancestors had with the amorous shepherds of pastoral poetry. Some of our authors follow the line of least resistance. They find it safer to repeat monosyllabic declarations than to write about life as it really is. There are those who prefer skilful manoeuvring to the agony of creation. They avoid difficult subjects, they keep saying: 'One cannot possibly write about such things now!' Some, who are fond of their craft, seek refuge in exotic or historical themes. Others make it look as if they were dealing with issues that matter, but emasculate them beyond recognition. They brush aside the difficulties against which our nation has to fight, and ignore the complex process that goes on in many people's minds, where new ideas struggle with obsolete prejudices.

Ehrenburg then spoke out against literary critics who, he said, were at least partly to blame for this state of affairs, and recalled the insults that had been hurled upon him from that quarter. Authors, he said, were either praised or pilloried. There was no serious literary criticism, and he marvelled at the 'fabulous ease' with which the critics altered their approach to an author's work, switching abruptly from adulation to abuse. He protested against the practice of putting an author on a pedestal one day merely to topple him the next. It was also intolerable, he said, that literary criticism should have an immediate impact on a writer's social standing or his financial position. 'One must not regard the artist's failures and setbacks as a crime, and his successes as a rehabilitation.'

This bold statement of principle clearly touched a responsive chord in his audience, and when he said that he had nearly finished, there were cries of 'Please, go on!' According to the shorthand record of the proceedings, he wound up his speech to an outburst of 'tempestuous applause'. (There is a fixed Soviet scale – a kind of ideological Richter scale – on which applause is measured. It can be simply applause, or it can be 'prolonged' or 'tempestuous', and sometimes both. The highest accolade at that time – the phrase 'tempestuous and prolonged applause developing into an ovation: all stand up' – was reserved either for Stalin personally, or for a speaker paying tribute to Stalin.)

In short, Ehrenburg did rather well. But whatever benefits he might have expected his fellow-writers to gain from his advice, he himself did not manage to profit by it. His next book on the Five-Year Plan was dull and lifeless, even though he made his characters fall in love, kiss, have fits of jealousy, and do quite a number of silly and even mildly reprehensible things. Nor was his journalism at that time much better. Bukharin's appointment had, almost overnight, turned *Izvestia* into the liveliest of Soviet newspapers, and some of this even rubbed off on its competitor, *Pravda*. People were heard to remark that '*Pravda* has become much better since Bukharin became editor of *Izvestia*.' Yet compared with the kind of journalism he had produced before joining *Izvestia*, the articles Ehrenburg was now writing for the paper were generally dull and pedestrian.

There was, however, one notable exception, and one which must have given him unadulterated pleasure. He published a scathing attack on the official Soviet travel agency, Intourist. Sixteen years later when he came to London, having by then become a pillar of conformity, he faced a crowd of mainly hostile journalists at a press conference. But one of them, perhaps feeling more charitable than the rest, reminded him of the Intourist article; whereupon Ehrenburg beamed with satisfaction. 'Yes, I did write it,' he said, 'and the result was that for a good many years afterwards, I found it impossible to get a room in any Intourist hotel.'

The article would probably never have been published if Bukharin had not been the paper's editor-in-chief. It all arose from an incident in which Ehrenburg was personally involved. When he returned to Moscow for the Writers' Congress (he actually arrived two months before it was due to open), he managed to get a small but expensive room in the National Hotel. At first, everything went smoothly. But one evening a waiter informed him that he would no longer be served tea or, for that matter, anything else. Ehrenburg went to see the manager, and was told he must leave the hotel immediately because a large party of foreign tourists had arrived.

It was an unpleasant shock, and not one that Ehrenburg was prepared to take lying down. Abandoning caution, he wrote about the incident for *Izvestia*, calling his article 'Frank Talk'. He had never been favourably disposed towards tourists. In his younger days, he had sometimes taken Russian visitors round Paris, and he did not enjoy it. Later, he came to dislike tourists as a species, and conceived an even more violent aversion to the organizers of guided tours. And what he now saw in Moscow appalled him. Everything Intourist was doing was false and in the worst possible taste. The picture that was being presented to foreign visitors was that of a Russia which not only had nothing to do with Soviet reality but had never existed except in bad comic operas in the West and in the imagination of chauvinistic maniacs in Russia itself. Ehrenburg was sickened by the sight of waiters in bright green Russian blouses, by the orchestra playing hackneyed tunes which had nothing in common with the real Russian folksongs, by the salt-cellars in pseudo-Russian style. And, on top of this, he had been ordered to vacate his room.

In his article he conducted an imaginary conversation with three foreigners – 'Mr Davis of Liverpool, M. Durand of Perpignan, and Herr Schulz of Zurich' – and begged them not to judge the Soviet Union by the hotel, as it was being managed by people who did not know the difference between hospitality and obsequiousness. What the tourists were being shown was 'a bad fairy tale'. Ehrenburg went on:

If I were your guide I would not tell you to look at an old church on your right merely because there is a queue in front of a shop on your left. I would not be afraid to show you the queue as well. Our people want to have everything but we are still short of everything, we are short of leather and meat and textiles and cigarettes and newsprint. We are only beginning to live. I have written about the Second Day. The Seventh Day, when one can rest and enjoy the fruits of one's labour, has still to come.

Having decided to speak frankly, he then lashed out at everything that had infuriated him in Russia, and went on to tell many more 'sad tales'. There were bureaucrats who were capable of driving one mad because of a scrap of paper. In Gorky, there were huts where entire workers' families – old men, young married couples, and children, all slept together without partitions – 'a cruel tale, and I am not keeping it from you'. At Voronezh, he had seen houses built for industrial workers which looked more like gloomy barracks. He had watched obtuse officials turn people out of a railway station into the pouring rain. He had visited canteens where the stench was unbearable.

He balanced all this by telling some 'wonderful tales' about rest homes for peasants in the Crimea and the high standard of education among Soviet workers. He had heard them discuss French literature with André Malraux. They had talked to him about Balzac and Stendhal. One of them had even mentioned Paul Valéry. 'And what do *you* know about Paul Valéry, Monsieur Durand?' he asked his imaginary French tourist. He did not spare the West. In Paris, tourists were taken to Montmartre, without ever seeing Belleville, the shops were full of goods but empty of buyers (which was true of some shops during the economic crisis of the early thirties). He forecast that in a few years' time the material difficulties in Russia would be overcome and young people would find the sad tales he was relating as difficult to believe as the stories they heard now about 'that wonderful and unbearable year 1920'. The time would come when foreigners would seek refuge in the Soviet Union from the chaos that prevailed in a world ruled solely by money. He said all this, and a good deal more. Needless to say, there was trouble, and Bukharin had to come to his defence. The Riga correspondent of *The Times* of London picked up the article, and published a report which seemed to suggest that, according to Ehrenburg, foreign tourists in Russia were being cheated and fleeced in the most barefaced way. Although this was a legitimate deduction from what

Ehrenburg had written, it was not, strictly speaking, accurate: Ehrenburg had not used those words; and he wrote an angry letter to *The Times*, rebuking its correspondent for attributing to him ideas he had not expressed.

But the occasions when Ehrenburg could show that he was still Ehrenburg were few and far between. Most of the articles he was writing for *Izvestia* were designed to show the lamentable state of affairs in France. In general, he deplored the decay of the West, and hailed the new life that was being built in the East. 'They used to compare us with abandoned children', he wrote. 'But now it is their world that is sick, and confined to bed, wheezing and gasping. We shall have to take over its legacy.'

Actually, it was he himself who had once likened Russia to her abandoned children, and what he wrote now looked rather like a tactful recantation. In fact, the method of oblique or implied recantation was one which Ehrenburg used quite frequently at that period. From the Soviet point of view, some of the things he had said in the past, notably about the cinema and the motor-car, were plainly heretical. But now he criticized the French writer, Georges Duhamel, for condemning these two modern inventions. It was not the camera's fault, he declared, if it was used for making bad films, and the role of the car depended exclusively on the person at the wheel. Broadly speaking, Ehrenburg attacked those French authors who did not sympathize with the Soviet Union, and glorified those who did, especially André Gide (the greater was his disappointment when Gide turned away from the Soviet regime, but that came later). Some of the things Ehrenburg wrote about France were true – the atmosphere there *was* unhealthy – but he kept writing them week after week, and although he had managed to preserve his distinctive style, the overall effect was monotonous.

In the end this would probably have demoralized him completely, had it not been for Hitler's victory in Germany. To people like Ehrenburg this terrifying event was in some ways a source of inspiration. Here was something to fight against. Right in the centre of Europe, in one of the best organized and reputedly one of the most civilized countries in the world, evil had emerged triumphant: evil in its purest, distilled form, staring one in the face, boasting of being evil, appealing to man's beastly instincts, proudly telling its worshippers that their aim in life was to humiliate and enslave other men. By comparison, some of the things Ehrenburg disliked about

Russia paled almost into insignificance. The Soviet Union might be technically backward, the Russian individual might be losing the last vestiges of freedom, Soviet bureaucrats might be heartless and obtuse, some of them might even have the arrogance to tell writers what they should write and the power to prevent books from being published; but at least they did not burn books, as was done in Germany at a solemn ceremony arranged by the Nazis.

In 1914 Maurice Paléologue, the last French Ambassador to Imperial Russia, noted in his diary that no event of the war had made such a striking impression on the Russian imagination as the German bombardment of Rheims and the destruction of the Cathedral. He attributed this to the Russians being excessively emotional, hungering after melodrama, and being indifferent to reality except when it appeared 'in the form of picturesque and theatrical happenings'. But here, Paléologue was being unfair. Not only the Russians but most people, wherever they are, tend to be impressed by a theatrical manifestation of evil. Ehrenburg noted that the book-burning ceremony in Berlin, broadcast over the German radio with a gleeful running commentary, had acted as an eye-opener to many French writers who until then had been unable to grasp what Nazism meant. Copies of his own books, which had appeared in German translation, were among those burned, together with the works of Heine, and Ehrenburg was proud of it. When he contrasted Russia with Nazi Germany, he nearly always made the point: 'We do not make a bonfire of books. We read them.'

Unfortunately, he could not write about Nazism all that often. Apart from the fact that Stalin had initially adopted a cautious attitude towards the new German regime, Germany was not Ehrenburg's territory, and he could not even travel through it. But he did travel fairly widely elsewhere for *Izvestia*. Early in 1934 he was sent to Vienna after the right-wing Government of Chancellor Dolfuss sent in troops to crush the Austrian Social Democrats; although, according to experts, his account of that affair was inaccurate. He travelled to the Saar to cover the Plebiscite which resulted in another triumph for Hitler, to Alsace, and to the town of Eupen, which Germany had ceded to Belgium after the First World War. In all these places he saw Nazi propaganda in action, and from time to time in his articles he attacked the theories of Nazism. He did it eloquently, but the opportunities were limited, and hardly sufficient to satisfy him. He understood very well the growing menace of Fascism, he knew it had to be fought, and he wanted to be in the thick of the fight.

On returning to France from Moscow after the Writers' Congress, he had an idea. During the Congress, Karl Radek,[1] who had not yet fallen victim to the Great Purge and at that time still represented the Soviet Establishment, had chided the French left-wing writer, Jean-Richard Bloch for being, as he put it, 'a *franc tireur* of the Revolution' and an individualist unwilling to submit to Party discipline. Bloch, who had identified himself with the Communist cause only after a great deal of soul-searching, took this very much amiss. In a spirited reply he stressed that the Communists were not the only ones who were opposed to Fascism; and he cited the example of the mayor of Grenoble, a moderate Republican, who earlier that year, when France was threatened with a right-wing coup, had rallied the people of his city in defence of the Republic. If people like Karl Radek persisted in their narrow dogmatic approach, said Bloch (and by implication his warning was addressed to the whole Soviet leadership), it was Fascism that would reap the benefit.

Back in Paris, Bloch and Ehrenburg agreed that it was essential to unite all anti-Fascist writers, and discussed at length how this could be done. They worked out certain proposals, which Ehrenburg put on paper and sent off to Moscow. In his memoirs, he does not say to whom the letter was addressed. It may have been Bukharin: as editor of *Izvestia*, he would have been the proper channel. In any case, the letter was passed on to Stalin, who expressed a wish to see Ehrenburg. Ehrenburg was immediately summoned back to the Soviet Union.

Stalin's interest in the letter was understandable. A few months earlier he had agreed, after some delay, to a proposition that the French Communist Party should make a pact with the Social Democrats, and similar proposals had been put forward by the Communist Parties in other Western European countries. Thus, almost overnight, the Social Democrats ceased to be labelled 'Social Fascists' and became allies in the struggle against Fascism itself. This policy of a united front was, in fact, the prelude to the formation of the Popular Front, which was to embrace not only Marxists, but all who shared an anti-Fascist viewpoint. Ehrenburg's letter was thus

[1]One of the early Bolshevik leaders, of Polish-Jewish origin. In January 1937, he was accused, together with sixteen others, of carrying out orders from the exiled Trotsky to wreck the Soviet regime, and was later executed.

well-timed. But it also had one important result for him personally. Stalin realized how useful Ehrenburg could be; so useful, in fact, that his talk about freedom for the artist, and the other liberties he had taken, including his attack on Intourist and the frankness with which he had spoken about Soviet conditions, could be disregarded. Dictators do have their clear-sighted moments, and this in the end saved Ehrenburg's life.

As it happened, the projected audience with Stalin did not take place. While Ehrenburg was waiting to be called to the Kremlin, Kirov was assassinated and this event absorbed all of Stalin's attention. Ehrenburg was told to return to France. But the plan he had drawn up with Jean-Richard Bloch had been approved, and he began to prepare a Congress of Anti-Fascist Writers with a view to setting up an International Anti-Fascist Writers' Association.

It was his first political venture. The Congress was not easy to organize: a number of Western authors suspected that it was purely a Soviet propaganda exercise, which was indeed what Stalin meant it to be. In fact, it was the prototype of all those future international congresses which the Soviet-dominated 'Peace Movement' arranged after the Second World War, although it compared favourably with what came later. There was an impressive array of participants both from the West and from Russia, the latter including such men as Pasternak and Isaac Babel.[1] Less reassuring was the fact that, on the official side, the Soviet Union was represented by Shcherbakov, a Party bureaucrat who had been made Secretary of the Soviet Writers' Union, and whose job was to keep the Soviet delegation in order. Although Ehrenburg later described the Congress as a great occasion, he admitted that at the time he exaggerated its political significance; in other words, as a weapon against Fascism, it did not amount to much. His own speech to the Congress was that of a Soviet propagandist and showed little of the broad outlook of a cosmopolitan, but this was clearly deliberate. The dispatches he sent to *Izvestia* (he covered the Congress himself) also make dull reading. But in reporting the proceedings, he was clearly trying to help Babel and Pasternak, whose position in Russia was shaky, and he therefore

---

[1]Isaac Emmanuilovich Babel (1894–1941?). Outstanding Ukrainian-Jewish writer of short stories, notably the collection entitled *Red Cavalry* (1923). He was arrested in 1939 and disappeared; he is thought to have died in 1941, but the date is uncertain. In his memoirs, Ehrenburg describes their first meeting in Moscow in 1926, and refers to Babel not only as a 'superlative craftsman', but as his 'dearest and most loyal friend'.

repeatedly stressed the impact of their speeches on a sophisticated international audience. It was a well-meant, but ultimately futile attempt to sway things in their favour. For when it came to deciding how Soviet authors should be treated at home, Stalin was not about to let himself be influenced by people like Ehrenburg. He preferred to trust to his own hunches. Pasternak survived. Babel vanished in a concentration camp.

Ehrenburg still imagined, however, that he could do something positive to help Soviet literature, and when he visited Moscow again in the autumn of 1935 he wrote a couple of articles in which he defended the artist's right to be more than just a hack at the Party's bidding. The articles duly appeared in *Izvestia*, but within two months it became abundantly clear that Ehrenburg's hopes had been as vain as the 'tempestuously' applauded speech he had made the year before. The pogrom against the arts was now under way, the Party zealots were pouring abuse on Shostakovich, Meyerhold, Tairov, Eisenstein and Pasternak, and some even launched into renewed attacks on Ehrenburg himself. He seems to have been more upset than frightened. The fact that Stalin had expressed a wish to see him must have made him feel that his position in Paris was relatively strong. In the midst of the general gloom, he even managed to write *A Book for Grown-Ups*, in which he cleverly blended a not very exciting plot with autobiography. It is a good piece of writing, but a shock awaits the reader in the closing pages. During his latest visit to Moscow, Ehrenburg had attended a gala meeting of Stakhanovite shock workers, and there for the first time he saw Stalin in the flesh, and witnessed the interminable ovations and other manifestations of the 'cult of personality', as it later came to be known. In his memoirs, he says that he was deeply disturbed by this spectacle. But in *A Book for Grown-Ups* he wrote in a somewhat different vein: 'I went to the Kremlin Palace and saw the man whose name reverberates all over the world . . . I saw Stalin as he talked to textile workers and miners about their work.'

No Soviet writer could afford not to pay tribute to Stalin, and Ehrenburg accepted this as a fact of life. *A Book for Grown-Ups* was duly published in a literary magazine, but it took much longer for it to appear in hard covers. The purges had started, their victims were steadily on the increase, and since Ehrenburg had mentioned some of the people concerned, their names had to be removed from the galley proofs. By then, however, Ehrenburg had found a new focus for his energies. With the outbreak of the Spanish Civil War, he had gone to Spain. Here, the struggle against Fascism had burst into the open, and at long last Ehrenburg was in the thick of it.

CHAPTER XX

When Ehrenburg decided that he must cover the course of the civil war in Spain, where he was to remain for the greater part of the next two and a half years, he could not know that in this way he was escaping from another, even more terrible reality. The Spanish conflict coincided almost exactly with the period of the Great Purge in the Soviet Union. The fighting in Spain began on 18 July 1936. The first of the spectacular 'treason trials', which ended with the former Soviet leaders, Zinoviev and Kamenev, being sentenced to death, opened in Moscow just a month later, on 18 August. So, for Ehrenburg, Spain became a kind of refuge. It was not a question of physical escape. In the midst of his 'Spanish period', he even revisited Moscow, which was, to say the least, unwise, and it was only by a miracle that he was allowed to go abroad again. But by covering the war in Spain, becoming totally absorbed by it, and fully identifying himself with the Spanish Republican cause, he was able to avoid too many uncomfortable reflections on the alarming turn of events in Russia.

He had been fascinated by Spain ever since, as a young man, he had tried to translate into Russian the poems of the Archpriest Juan Ruiz, a devout and bawdy genius who, if he had not existed, might well have been invented six centuries later by Anatole France. In the 1920s, out of curiosity, he had made one brief foray into Spain without a visa, but came back disappointed. His second visit, in 1931, was much more rewarding. Spain had become a republic, and he fell in love with it; with every rock, with every mountain path, as he put it, and with the 20,000,000 Spanish poor, each of whom seemed to him a Don Quixote in rags. Russians respect poverty; it creates an automatic bond between them and other nations. In Spain, Ehrenburg saw a poor but proud people whose love of freedom surpassed anything he had witnessed before, and later he recalled the words of Cervantes's hero: 'Freedom, Sancho, is one of the most precious gifts bestowed by Heaven: none of the treasures hidden in the bowels of the earth or at the bottom of the sea can compare with it. Servitude, on the other hand, is the worst misfortune that can befall a man.'

It was during his visit to Spain in 1931 that, for the first time, Ehrenburg met genuine anarchists, who were a rare species in such countries as Germany or France. True, there were Bohemians at the Rotonde who called themselves anarchists, and some could even be found at the Romanisches Café in Berlin. But they were mostly people who, as Ehrenburg put it, confounded freedom with licence, and equated the great Russian anarchist Bakunin with Stirner, the apostle of extreme individualism; such people knew nothing either about the peasants or the working class. In Russia itself, anarchists had played a certain role in the chaotic years following the Revolution, but they had later acquired a bad reputation. Few Russians now regarded the chief anarchist leader, Nestor Makhno, who had controlled a sizeable territory during the civil war, as a faithful disciple of Bakunin, or even as a kind of modern Robin Hood.

But in Spain it was different, as emerges from Ehrenburg's description of a meeting he had with an anarchist, an agricultural labourer, at Fernan Nunez, a small town not far from Cordoba, in a café which had been turned into a local socialist club.

> He worked from sunrise till sunset; then he read, talked to people, and pondered deeply. At the café, he had to face many awkward questions. He answered them politely but firmly; nothing could induce him to change his views. When the socialists began arguing about the relative merits of the Second and Third Internationals, he replied simply: 'I am for the First International. Our teacher is Bakunin.'

The First International had been dissolved in the 1880s, Bakunin had been dead for over half a century, but the anarchist of Fernan Nunez still spoke of 'Compañero Bakunin', as if he were still alive. He clung to the belief that compulsion must never be used, and that everything could be achieved by persuasion. Ehrenburg continued his account of their meeting:

> He was a man of flesh and blood, not a ghost from the past, and yet he was saying quite distinctly: 'I am for freedom'. Nor is he the only disciple of Bakunin's in Spain. There are many of them in Fernan Nunez, Jerez and Seville. It is easy to prove that their theories are confused and their tactics ineffective: guerrilla warfare and random strikes are bound to lead to defeat. You may call this labourer from Fernan Nunez a crank, yet he is

brave, poor and uncompromising. His political views are naïve; yet who will dare to assert that his vision of a free Commune is just a mad fantasy, or something taken from an outmoded pamphlet? He may not fit into our epoch; yet his calm and tenacity have made me think of man's inevitable triumph and of the new epoch that will surely come.

Some bitter irony may be discerned in this passage, in which Ehrenburg seems to envy the freedom of the brave, uncompromising, semi-literate Spanish labourer, since he wrote it in January 1932, only a few months before he finally gave up his own freedom. But he had other revealing encounters during that visit to Spain, and one of them was with the anarchist leader Buenaventura Durruti. Durruti had already been condemned to death on three occasions, and had been expelled from something like eighteen countries, which was bound to endear him to the author of *Julio Jurenito*. 'Durruti could have built himself a home only in no-man's land,' commented Ehrenburg, 'but unfortunately, there is no provision for any such territory in the Treaty of Versailles.' He described Durruti as 'one of those people whose biographies do not fit into history'. This was something that often happened to poets, and could lead to a fatal encounter with the muzzle of a gun (he was doubtless thinking of Esenin and Mayakovsky). It could also happen to those who were dreaming of a new social order, but could not bring themselves either to recant while there was still time, or to keep their mouths shut. (This one may perhaps take as a reference by Ehrenburg to his own predicament, and an indirect explanation of why he was about to fit his own biography into history, preferably without recanting, but knowing full well that from now on he would have to keep quiet, even when he felt like shouting at the top of his voice.) As for Durruti, after the overthrow of the monarchy, he returned to Spain and found a job in a factory. Ehrenburg noted that, although nothing could shake Durruti's faith in anarchism, as a factory worker he recognized the need for order, because he knew that there could be no production without discipline and organization. It was a pertinent observation on Ehrenburg's part.

But one did not have to be Ehrenburg to side with the Spanish Republic when Franco rose to overthrow it. Later, the civil war was to prove a traumatic experience for many ardent anti-Fascists who had rallied to the Republican cause, and many emerged from it sadly disillusioned. But when the war began, to thousands of intellectuals and to millions of ordinary Europeans, it meant only one thing: that there would be no surrender to Fascism, no meek acceptance of a *fait accompli*. Henceforth, battle had been joined with a malign force allied to Hitler and Mussolini. So, for Ehrenburg, 18 July 1936 was, indeed, an historic date, and he was impatient to leave for Spain immediately. *Izvestia*, however, decided otherwise. It was in no hurry to send him there, and for the first few weeks he reported the war from Paris, quoting from the French Press, and occasionally obtaining fresh material by telephone from friends in Madrid. He published an indignant open letter to the famous Spanish writer, Miguel de Unamuno, who had been a refugee in France and a frequent visitor to the Rotonde, but had now declared his support for General Franco. 'You may look like Don Quixote,' wrote Ehrenburg with biting sarcasm, 'but in reality you are merely one of those egotistical old men who stood by and watched as their servants maltreated the unhappy hidalgo.'

After a time, Ehrenburg grew tired of waiting, and set off for Spain without informing his editor. In the second half of August his articles were still appearing in the paper with a Paris dateline, but his descriptions of the Spanish scene were so vivid that the word 'Paris' tucked away at the bottom looked incongruous. Later, he began referring to episodes he had witnessed in Spain 'last August'. It was not until the end of September, however, that his presence in Spain was acknowledged in print; and it was only after a hiatus during which there were no reports from him at all that there appeared in *Izvestia* a special 'Letter from Spain', the first of a series that was to continue for many months.

From these reports, it is clear that Ehrenburg was constantly on the move, and was more or less free to go wherever he pleased in the various battle areas. The subjects he wrote about were varied and were clearly of his own choice. As a life-long satirist, who had made a profession of castigating evil, he seemed almost at ease in reporting his conversations with captured Italian soldiers and Nazi airmen. In the past, the author of *The Love of Jeanne Ney* had succumbed only too often to sentimentality. But now, in Spain, as he tried to convey the impact of carnage and destruction, he did not need to feel ashamed of revealing his sentiments. His style was direct, and his sentences brief, each radiating a passionate commitment. The picture he painted of the war was an idealized one, without any pretence at objectivity. The pieces he wrote were meant to inspire. They were, in short, very like the impassioned dispatches he was to write a few years later, after the Soviet Union became engulfed in the Second World War, and which earned him tremendous popularity among Russian soldiers at the front.

One of his early Spanish articles dealt with a visit he paid to the Aragon front, where Durruti was in command of an anarchist division. It is clear that Ehrenburg wrote it not only as a tribute to a man he liked and admired, but with a special purpose in mind. He wanted to convince the Soviet Government that, although the Spanish anarchists remained faithful to Bakunin (whose ideas were considered pernicious by Soviet theoreticians), although they continued to preach and even tried to practise a form of *comunismo libertario*, or 'free Communism', and although they had covered the walls of Barcelona with posters extolling 'the organization of anti-discipline', they were gradually mending their ways and becoming more realistic, and were therefore worth supporting, especially as they were strong in Catalonia, and Catalonia's help was essential to winning the war. Ehrenburg then recalled some of the arguments he had had with Durruti in 1931, and mentioned that they had discussed a number of topics that must now be regarded as 'past history'. The important thing, he said, was that Durruti was now building up a proper fighting force; he showed no mercy towards bandits and deserters, and when people started arguing in his presence about principles, he banged the desk with his gun and shouted: 'This is not the place to talk about political programmes! There's a war on!' 'They have learned a great deal,' wrote Ehrenburg. 'Here, at the front, they no longer speak of organizing anti-discipline, but of the need for discipline. They used to talk a lot about respecting the principles of guerrilla warfare. Now they say: "If necessary we shall decree conscription. We are prepared to renounce everything except victory!"'

There was one colourful detail, however, on which Ehrenburg remained coyly silent: when he turned up at Durruti's headquarters, Durruti wanted to shoot him, all because of an article he had published two years earlier, in which he had criticized anarchist tactics. The reference to 'past history' in Ehrenburg's later article indicated that he had tried to persuade Durruti to let bygones be bygones, but he revealed this only a quarter of a century later in his memoirs. At the time, he managed to escape summary execution only by firmly pointing out that this was no way to treat a guest; whereupon Durruti relented and they soon became friends. A few weeks later, Durruti moved to the Madrid front, and was killed in action.

Ehrenburg did complain, however, that in spite of Durruti, and even while the latter was still alive, the anarchists were only too prone to argue about principles and political programmes to the detriment of the war effort itself. On one occasion, their commanders held a council of war to plan the capture of Huesca, a nationalist stronghold on the Aragon front, but instead of deciding on operational details, they became immersed in a discussion of Marx and Bakunin. In the same sector, a front-line anarchist newspaper produced a detailed analysis of the tactics and philosophy of Nestor Makhno, whom the paper portrayed as the most outstanding hero of the civil war in Russia. Most Russians, however, did not associate Makhno with any philosophy except that of the loaded gun. 'Whatever one may think of his philosophical concepts,' observed Ehrenburg sardonically, 'Makhno would have been quite incapable of defeating Franco's superbly equipped army, or for that matter, of taking Huesca, which had been fortified by German experts.'

Ehrenburg was also critical of the social reforms which the anarchists were hastening to introduce in the areas under their control, such as the abolition of money, and the nationalization of practically everything, including chickens. As for Barcelona, which was partly anarchist and partly bourgeois, in Ehrenburg's view it was not taking the war at all seriously, at least not in that first year. He was shocked by the easy-going ways of that 'carefree' city:

> Restaurants, modishly trying to look austere, were serving 'wartime luncheons' of four courses. In the night-clubs, semi-naked girls regaled the customers with songs about military virtues. Posters advertised anarchist literature, and appealed to parents, in the name of human dignity, not to give their children toy soldiers to play with – all this at a time when German airmen were bombing Madrid and swarms of Blackshirts were pushing on from Malaga towards Almeria.

As a result, when Barcelona was shelled from the sea by an enemy warship, Ehrenburg was positively delighted. 'The city has at last been made to realize that there is a war on', he wrote primly. 'The era of multicoloured flags, high-sounding slogans and reckless optimism is over.'

Ehrenburg did his best not to portray the anarchists through rose-tinted spectacles. He knew that, for a time at least, it was easy for any ne'er-do-well to join their ranks with no questions asked. Yet he was also plainly fascinated by them, as he had been in 1931. As the author of *Julio Jurenito*, he warmed to them because they were dedicated, idealistic and naïve, and because 'without such magnificent lunacy there would be no struggle, no life and no history'. In one of his dispatches, Ehrenburg mentioned a name which awoke an echo in my own mind – the name of a man I had met in Berlin seven years earlier. He was a young Spanish artist, an anarchist, who looked like Rudolph Valentino, and who used to express his contempt for Berlin's Bohemia by announcing solemnly: '*J'ai fait l'amour avec toutes les femmes du Romanisches Café – elles n'ont pas de vie intellectuelle!*' At that time, he seemed to belong to the category of those who 'confused Bakunin with Stirner'. Now, in Spain, according to Ehrenburg, he had accomplished feats of almost superhuman heroism, and this was reputed to be typical of the anarchists, who on occasion acted with utter disregard for personal safety. The fact that Ehrenburg understood their mentality was duly appreciated by senior Soviet emissaries to Spain, and they appointed him their liaison man with the anarchists, having come to the conclusion that he was one of the few people who knew how to talk to such eccentrics.

There were a number of Soviet officials with whom Ehrenburg was in close contact during his first year in Spain, among them the Ambassador, Marcel Rosenberg, the *Pravda* correspondent, Mikhail Koltsov, whose political functions made him a far more important figure than the Ambassador, and a veteran revolutionary called Antonov-Ovseyenko, who had played a leading part in the storming of the Winter Palace in October 1917, and was now Soviet Consul-General in Barcelona.[1] All three were doomed men: they perished during the Purges and were rehabilitated posthumously

---

[1] Marcel Israilovich Rosenberg. Soviet career diplomat, he arrived in Madrid as Soviet Ambassador in August 1936, where he loyally carried out Stalin's directives – which did not prevent his subsequent liquidation.

Mikhail Koltsov. The leading foreign correspondent of *Pravda*, he arrived in Spain in September 1936 as Stalin's special envoy, and played a military and political role far transcending that of journalism, including the organization of support for a Communist-led *junta* during the siege of Madrid.

Vladimir Alexeyevich Antonov-Ovseyenko. A veteran revolutionary and a member of the first Bolshevik Government, he was appointed Soviet Consul-General in Barcelona in August 1936, where he later took a leading part in the suppression of the POUM, the semi-Trotskyist organization in Catalonia.

under Khrushchev. Koltsov disappeared at the end of 1938, and Ehrenburg, to judge by his memoirs, was certain that he had been shot at that time. But in a recent edition of the *Great Soviet Encyclopaedia*, the date of Koltsov's death is given as 1942, which suggests that he died in some place of detention. While he was in Spain, he and Ehrenburg were among a group of Soviet participants in the civil war who were awarded the Order of the Red Banner.

The Soviet Union was the only European Power that was giving military aid to the Spanish Republic, and as a Soviet journalist Ehrenburg was in a privileged position. This was something new to him (he was more accustomed to being treated off-handedly and even bullied by the authorities), and although he may inwardly have felt humble about the services he was rendering to the cause, some of those who met him in Spain found him arrogant and overbearing. He had always found it difficult to deal with people who did not particularly interest him. In Spain he seems to have behaved with a kind of aristocratic disdain: he would talk to his betters and to the common people, but he despised the middle classes. He was always ready to speak to Spanish soldiers and peasants, he enjoyed the company of the more prominent members of the International Brigade, some of whom he knew from Russia, and he sought the friendship of such men as Ernest Hemingway and leading Spanish writers on the Republican side. But he would cut ordinary foreign journalists dead, even if they were Communists, or treat them so patronizingly that they could not help but take offence, and contrasted his supercilious attitude unfavourably with the courtesy and warm-hearted manner of Mikhail Koltsov.

But even more important than the privileges he enjoyed in his dealings with the Spanish authorities was Ehrenburg's special position within the Soviet Establishment in Spain. He had no political influence (which, in the long run, was fortunate for him), but as a journalist he was allowed an extraordinary degree of freedom. Moreover, he exploited that freedom not so much in what he wrote, as in what he did *not* write. In other words, he managed persistently to avoid certain subjects which others could not afford to ignore. At the show trials in Moscow, everything that displeased the Soviet Government was being ascribed to the devilish intrigues of Trotsky. But Ehrenburg seemed determined not to write a single phrase about so-called 'Trotskyite Fascists'. Admittedly, it was easier to stick to such a resolve from the relative distance of Spain – but only for a time. In May 1937, fighting broke out in Barcelona between Catalan Government troops and some of the militia units controlled by the anarchists and the POUM,[1] a Party which was regarded in the West as semi-Trotskyite with anarchist leanings, but in Soviet quarters as purely Trotskyite, although it had no direct affiliation with Trotsky's political movement. After the orthodox Spanish Communist leadership had branded the 'rebels' as 'Fascist provocateurs', the Soviet Press poured liberal showers of abuse on the POUM. Antonov-Ovseyenko, who sometimes stood in for Ehrenburg as *Izvestia* correspondent in Barcelona, went out of his way to condemn 'Trotskyite treachery' in Catalonia (as a former follower of Trotsky, Antonov-Ovseyenko was making a strenuous, although as it later turned out, an entirely fruitless effort to demonstrate his loyalty to Stalin). But in his own dispatches, Ehrenburg said nothing at all about the events in Barcelona. He was not there when the fighting began, but was visiting the southern front; and there he stayed, writing about what he saw. Yet, although he could not have reported the Barcelona street battles on a day-to-day basis, one would have expected a Soviet journalist of Ehrenburg's calibre to compose, at some later date, a powerful and indignant piece about the way the Spanish Trotskyites were disrupting the Republican war effort; it would have been natural for Stalin to order it, and for *Izvestia* to insist on having it. Yet no such article by Ehrenburg ever appeared.

In July, on the first anniversary of the war, the 'Trotskyite bandits' in Barcelona were once more dealt with in *Izvestia* by Antonov-Ovseyenko. As Soviet representative in Catalonia, he was now pressing for the liquidation of the POUM, whose troops on the Aragon front he accused of refusing to fight, and of passing military information to the enemy. Meanwhile, in the same issue of *Izvestia*, Ehrenburg was paying tribute to the steadfastness of the Spanish girls who stood at the factory lathes in their fashionable shoes, working hard to provide the country with all it needed. George Orwell, who had joined a POUM unit, said of the British and French Communists who heaped abuse on the POUM: 'It is not a nice thing to see a Spanish boy of fifteen being carried down the line on a stretcher, with a dazed white face looking out from among the blankets, and to think of the sleek persons in London and Paris who

[1] Partido Obrero de Unificación Marxista (Workers' Party of Marxist Unification).

are writing pamphlets to prove that this boy is a Fascist in disguise.' Ehrenburg clearly shared Orwell's view. A quarter of a century later, he wrote in his memoirs that it was 'naïve' to attribute what had happened in Barcelona only to provocation. 'Naïve' was an understatement, like Orwell's 'not a nice thing', although Orwell's understatement was deliberately chosen, whereas Ehrenburg, even twenty-five years after the event, was still not free to speak his mind.

He was, admittedly, sometimes forced to mention Trotskyites, on those rare occasions when he was acting as a reporter and summarizing other people's speeches. But even then he referred to them as little as possible. Two months before the clashes in Barcelona, he covered a Spanish Communist Party conference, and noted in one dispatch that a delegate had referred to 'the subversive activities of the Trotskyites'. He pointed out that the Party's General Secretary, José Diaz, had spoken frankly about 'the danger in the rear' and about 'demagogues who promise everything but are leading the people towards defeat'. But he did not include Diaz's categorical statement: 'Who are the enemies of the people? They are the Fascists, the Trotskyites, the irresponsible elements!' It was left to *Izvestia* to reproduce this remark on the same page, in a dispatch from the official Soviet news agency, TASS. Even more striking was Ehrenburg's reporting of the Second International Anti-Fascist Writers' Congress, which he had helped to organize, and which was held in Spain in 1937 as a demonstration of support for the Republic. It opened in Valencia less than a month after the execution of Marshal Tukhachevsky and other top Soviet military commanders, and to the dismay of Ehrenburg, who felt that this was scarcely a morale-booster for the embattled participants in the Spanish Civil War, the Soviet delegates, instead of concentrating on the struggle in Spain, spoke at great length about 'treason' at home. Alexei Tolstoy, who had attended the main show trials in Moscow and was probably the most talented Soviet author of that period, excelled himself in particular. He told the congress:

> Trotskyism must be mercilessly stamped out all over the world. It must be unmasked and extirpated as has already been done in the USSR . . . Trotsky's pseudo-internationalism amounts to a denial of nationality . . . Trotsky despises the people of Russia . . . His agents – I heard it with my own ears! – have confessed that they committed murder, engaged in espionage, and were preparing to destroy our country . . . They allied themselves with Fascism in order to gain power at any price . . .

It was quite a lengthy tirade, but Ehrenburg summarized it all in one sentence: 'He [Tolstoy] indignantly denounced the treacherous role of the Trotskyites as accomplices of Fascism.' *Izvestia* was not to be fobbed off, however, and printed the full text of Tolstoy's speech two days later. After that Ehrenburg stopped reporting the speeches of the Soviet delegates altogether. *Izvestia* reproduced the speeches verbatim, but without reference to its correspondent on the spot, and without even a Spanish dateline. So Ehrenburg was left free to exercise his skill as a reporter on material that he found more congenial, such as his own address to the Congress, in which he spoke of the Archpriest and poet Juan Ruiz, and contrasted Spain's ancient culture with the destructive activities of the German airmen and Mussolini's 'Fascist marauders'.

To Western observers, the way Ehrenburg was able to operate during that period presents something of an enigma. After the troubles in Barcelona, he seems to have made no further reference to the POUM. But as a Western Communist who spent the civil war in Spain once remarked: how did he get away with it? This was, indeed, the crucial question, and one that kept recurring both then and later, on all those occasions when Ehrenburg emerged unscathed while others around him perished. In December 1937, he returned to the Soviet Union in response to an invitation to attend a writers' congress in the Georgian capital, Tbilisi. He must have seen accounts in the Soviet Press of the various trials that were then in progress, but he does not seem to have grasped the scale on which people were being arrested right and left, and not just at the summit but at every level, including his own. On his arrival in Moscow, he found that many of his friends had disappeared. At the congress in Tbilisi, he had particularly wanted to see two Georgian poets; but one was in prison and the other had committed suicide. Wherever he went, people talked in whispers about those who had been seized by the police, and when he expressed a desire to return to Spain, he was told by *Izvestia* that he would have to wait: the matter would have to be considered. In March 1938 he was given an admission ticket to the court room where what he refers to in his memoirs as the trial of 'Maxim Gorky's assassins' was being held. In his memoirs, he gave no further details of what happened, but promised that he would one day return to the subject. He never did. The event that he refers to was, in fact, the trial of Bukharin. Ehrenburg had been invited to watch his old friend being sentenced to death.

To have been on friendly terms with Bukharin was by then practically a criminal offence in itself – people were being jailed for far less. But no one troubled Ehrenburg. One of the defendants in the same trial was Christian Rakovsky, an old Bolshevik and a prominent Soviet diplomat, who was sentenced to twenty years imprisonment. In his book, *United Front*, Ehrenburg had written about Rakovsky with admiration and affection, which, again, could easily have sealed his fate. But once more he remained unharmed. At one point, it is true, it did look as if something unpleasant might be about to happen. The question of his return to Spain was still unresolved. *Izvestia* was unable to give him any positive guidance. So he decided on a bold move. He wrote to Stalin with a personal request. Stalin turned him down. He then did something which, to his friends, smacked of sheer madness. He wrote to Stalin a second time, asking him to reconsider his decision. As Ehrenburg's daughter, Irina, once put it, he even dared to complain to Stalin about Stalin; and on the second occasion, Stalin said 'yes'. His immunity seemed more bizarre than ever.

There were rumours at the time (there are always rumours about survivors) that Ehrenburg had been protected by Yezhov, who is generally regarded as having been the most bloodthirsty of all the former heads of the Soviet secret police. Ehrenburg may well have been aware of the rumours. He mentions Yezhov briefly in his memoirs, perhaps in order to show that, in fact, they had never had any real contact. Ehrenburg had merely been told by his friend, Isaac Babel, who knew Yezhov's wife and had talked to her about the Great Purge, that it was not Yezhov but Stalin himself who was responsible. In any case, Yezhov was executed shortly afterwards, while Ehrenburg survived for many more turbulent years. Clearly, he must have had a different protector, one who could afford to make exceptions. This can only have been Stalin himself.

For all their paranoid obsessions while in power, dictators do sometimes yield to an uncharacteristic impulse, and this is what seems to have happened in Ehrenburg's case. Stalin had authorized the publication of his unorthodox novel *The Second Day*, and at that point he must have decided that Ehrenburg had a certain usefulness. Moreover, he might be all the more useful if, like a medieval court jester, he was allowed a degree of liberty. To be sure, that liberty must not go beyond well-defined limits. But as time went on, Ehrenburg developed an extraordinary flair for gauging just how far he could go and no further.

Meanwhile, he had spent four months of nightmarish suspense in the Soviet Union, waiting for permission to return to the West. Towards the end of that period, his nerves were strained almost to breaking point, so that he could scarcely eat. And during all that time, he wrote only one article. Its subject was Spain, and its central theme was: 'Fascism = Death'. Ehrenburg related how, at the start of the civil war, one of Franco's generals had proclaimed at a public meeting: 'Down with reason! Long live death!' To which Ehrenburg's reply was: 'Death shall not pass!'

He called his article 'To Life!' It appeared in *Izvestia* just two weeks after the execution of Bukharin.

CHAPTER XXI

Ehrenburg had been lucky and he knew it. But his stay in Moscow had been a harrowing experience, and he returned to the West shaken and depressed. 'There were days,' he says in his memoirs, 'when I lost all desire to go on living.' His only recourse was to plunge once more into the Spanish conflict and to drug himself with hatred of Fascism in order to forget.

It was the spring of 1938, a year which Dr Goebbels rapturously described as 'the happiest year in the history of the German people'. But if it was a happy time for the Nazis, it was a sad year for others. Ehrenburg received his exit permit from the Soviet Union at the end of April, but before he left Moscow he published a May Day tribute to Spain in *Izvestia*. In one respect, it was an unusual and unorthodox tribute. He saw Republican Spain not merely as a bastion of popular resistance to Fascism, but as a nation defending Western values generally. Without the Spanish people, said Ehrenburg, what would have become of the West which, contrary to what certain textbooks might say, was once a source of light for mankind? But to extol the West in this demonstrative fashion was not at all a proper function for a Soviet writer. Stalin would hardly care for it, and it was doubtless no mere coincidence that, a week later, *Izvestia* published another article entitled 'The Revolution Came from the East', which made the point that, although Marxism had originated in the West, Communist Russia was the only true source of light by virtue of her historic achievement.

Ehrenburg himself had often been irritated by Western pretensions, and was not usually given to praising the West in such unqualified terms. But his motives were understandable. Since the East appeared to have gone mad, and developments there did not bear thinking about, he instinctively concentrated his thoughts on Western Europe. His love for Europe remained strong, even if it had been overshadowed by his systematic reporting of European misdeeds, and it was a horrifying thought that what he had predicted fifteen years earlier in *The D.E. Trust* no longer seemed totally implausible. So this was an appropriate moment to recall, in the form of a tribute to the Spanish Republic, what Europe had meant to humanity.

On his return to the West, he divided his time between Spain and France. By then, as he recognized later in his memoirs, the issue in Spain had in effect already been decided: the Republicans could no longer win. He probably did not realize this at the time, however, or if he did would not admit it to himself, and his dispatches followed the same pattern as before. His first piece from Barcelona, when he arrived there in June, was called 'Seven Hundred Days of War'. Next came a description of yet another meeting with captured Germans and Italians. 'The Italians', he wrote, 'are frivolous, talkative and good-humoured, but the Germans have been so thoroughly in-doctrinated that even their guts, their fingernails and the corns on their feet are impregnated with propaganda.' He railed at the French frontier officials who made life difficult for him, while doing their best, or so he believed, to help foreign correspondents travelling to the Franco side. As before, he continued to visit as many sectors of the front as possible. But the events which made 1938 such a happy year for Dr Goebbels began to multiply and weigh heavily. Ehrenburg was in Spain when the Czechoslovak crisis came to a head, and on the day of the Munich Agreement, he described in a dispatch to *Izvestia* the recent German and Italian bombing of Barcelona. But important though this was, a journalist of his calibre obviously needed to be elsewhere, and he hurried back to France to observe the aftermath of Munich. If there was anything that could make him forget all he had seen and heard during his uncomfortably prolonged stay in Moscow, this was it. 'A Second Sedan for France' and 'The Story of a Betrayal' ran the headlines, and there was an image of Western prime ministers 'grovelling like minor princelings before the Tartar Khan at his Bavarian headquarters'. Most people in the anti-appeasement camp regarded Chamberlain as the chief villain, but Ehrenburg felt Daladier was worse. Daladier, he claimed, had been particularly eager to capitulate. Ehrenburg cared deeply about France, and it was perhaps natural that he should vent his anger more on the French Premier than on his British colleague. But he also felt there was a difference between Britain and France in their approach to Munich. The British Government had acted selfishly, which was what Ehrenburg had expected it to do, but at least there were people in the British Establishment who did not approve of

Chamberlain's actions. France, on the other hand, was not only selfish but demoralized, and lacked the stamina to resist Hitler.

His despair over France turned into an obsession. From this perspective, wherever he looked he saw the moral fibre of the nation being destroyed. No one in France had followed the example of Duff Cooper, who had resigned from the British Government in protest against the Munich Agreement. Six weeks later, when Germany was swept by a wave of pogroms and the synagogues began to blaze, he bitterly noted the absence of any strong French reaction, which he saw as yet another sign of moral decay. (It must be remarked, however, that from the Soviet viewpoint this was good propaganda, since the *Izvestia* reader was bound to contrast the indifference of the French with the protest meetings that were being held on Stalin's orders in Moscow, Leningrad, Kiev and Tbilisi, at which people like Shostakovich, Alexei Tolstoy and other celebrities inveighed against the barbaric persecution of the Jews in Germany.)

So Ehrenburg thundered on against the various species of appeasers: the pacifists, the traitors, the would-be Fascists, and certain young supporters of the French Radical Party whom he portrayed as turning a deaf ear to the humanitarian voice of Edouard Herriot, preferring Nazi-style parades to clear thinking. As he did so, he also began using the term 'Trotskyite', which he had been at pains to avoid up until then. It was an epithet he applied to the French newspaper *La Flèche*, whose leading articles, he remarked sardonically, seemed to have been hastily translated direct from the German. The paper had indeed welcomed the Munich Agreement, but there was no evidence of any connection between its editor, Gaston Bergery, and Trotsky or any Trotskyite organization. Bergery had been a Radical deputy. He then became one of the most vociferous advocates of a 'common' (i.e. popular) front, and was now a left-wing appeaser. Two years later (history always has some surprises up its sleeve), the Vichy regime sent him to Moscow as its Ambassador. To call *La Flèche* a Trotskyite publication was unwarranted. But the four nail-biting months Ehrenburg had spent in Moscow had left their mark. Since the term 'Social Fascist' had been ruled out by the advent of the Popular Front policy, Stalin now demanded that any left-wingers who disagreed with the Soviet Union should be branded as 'Trotskyites', and Ehrenburg, who had previously resisted this, now conformed. It was yet another step on his part towards complete surrender.

Spain was never far from his thoughts, however, and in the last days of 1938, he was able to visit it once more. He did so with a feeling of relief. Spain was doing what France had failed to do: resisting the enemy. 'A half-forgotten people on the outskirts of Europe has been the only one to accept battle', he wrote. 'Others have bargained with death, pawned their freedom, and sold their honour. This people alone said "No", and what became a year of shame for others has been a proud year for Spain.'

This was the substance of his dispatch from Barcelona which appeared in *Izvestia* on New Year's Day 1939. By that time it was not easy to cling to the illusion that the war could still be won, and as he gave Spain New Year greetings, he added: 'This must not sound like mockery, I know that this is the nine hundredth night of the war. I know that many families in Madrid are living on potato peelings, and have no fuel for heating. I know all that and much else besides. And yet I feel that, here in Spain, one need not be afraid of the New Year.' It is the job of the propagandist to keep up morale, even when everything seems on the point of collapse, and even two months later, as he watched the last act of the Spanish tragedy at an emergency session of the Cortes in the small Catalan town of Figueras, Ehrenburg still kept repeating with an almost religious fervour: 'They will fight to the end! Spain cannot die! Spain will conquer!' It was only when he saw the sad exodus of Spanish refugees streaming out of Catalonia into France, there to be interned in camps by the French authorities, that he conceded defeat. 'Woe to the victors!' he exclaimed.

It was over. Ehrenburg's 'Spanish period', a crucial period in his life, had come to an end. He had seen an embattled people resist Fascism, and had gained an insight into what this meant. He had not himself achieved anything especially historic. The war in Spain had done more for him than he had been able to do for the cause: it had saved his soul, and taken his mind off the terrifying events taking place inside Russia. During his visit to Moscow, he had passed his first major test of survival. Most of the prominent people Stalin had sent to Spain were later imprisoned and shot on Stalin's orders. Ehrenburg, who had travelled to Spain on his own initiative, without even waiting for his editor's permission, was spared.

He wrote one more impassioned piece under his own name about the fate that had befallen the Spanish refugees in France. 'I always loved France', he wrote. 'Now, I am ashamed for her.' After that, he continued his reporting of Spanish affairs, but under the *nom de plume* of 'Paul Jocelyn'. This was a name he had invented a few months earlier, when *Izvestia* had asked him to send more straight news stories. From that point on, he reserved his own name for serious political comment. 'Paul Jocelyn' supplied the routine stuff *Izvestia* was demanding, although from force of habit he did occasionally deal with it in the Ehrenburg manner. For example, when it was learned that France was planning to recognize Franco's Spain, 'Paul Jocelyn' commented: 'Madrid is still holding out; Paris is not.' When Marshal Pétain was appointed French Ambassador to General Franco's headquarters at Burgos, 'Paul Jocelyn' wrote that France was 'advancing from Verdun towards a second Munich'. Nevertheless, as Ehrenburg's *alter ego*, he was quite respectful towards the aged Marshal. He refrained from recalling that the Spanish Republican slogan '*No pasaran!*' (which had cropped up frequently in Ehrenburg's 'Letters from Spain') had its origin in Pétain's famous Order of the Day to the French troops at Verdun in 1916: '*Ils ne passeront pas!*' It was left to 'Paul Jocelyn' to describe the final drama in Madrid, where a Defence Council had been set up to negotiate surrender, but immediately became engaged in a battle with the Communists, who had been instructed by Stalin to continue the war. 'Paul Jocelyn' did what was expected of him. He accused the Socialist members of the Defence Council of being Trotskyites and friends of the POUM, and called his article 'Yet Another Betrayal'. In his memoirs, however, Ehrenburg admits that what happened in Madrid in March 1939 had no bearing on the outcome of the civil war in Spain.

Izvestia continued to publish brief news reports from 'Paul Jocelyn', generally taken from French newspapers and Western news agencies, almost every day. But Ehrenburg's name did not reappear in the paper until the beginning of April, when he wrote a dull piece about an impending general election in Belgium. It seemed strange that he should be dealing with such an uninspiring subject when infinitely more important events had been taking place elsewhere in Europe. Hitler had swallowed up Bohemia and Moravia, Czechoslovakia had ceased to exist, and people in Britain, even former appeasers, were now comparing the German Führer to Attila the Hun. One would have expected at least one or two passionate and wrathful articles from Ehrenburg, denouncing the aggressor and pointing out the evil fruits of appeasement. Instead, 'Paul Jocelyn'

published a few insipid lines about the situation in the Carpatho –
Ukraine after the dismemberment of Czechoslovakia, and later a few
more lines about independent Slovakia; stories that could have been
written by anyone. In his own name, Ehrenburg remained strangely
silent. True, 'Paul Jocelyn' became slightly more eloquent when Italy
invaded Albania, but that was still nothing compared with what
Ehrenburg had written at the time of Munich.

In fact, the rather indifferent piece on Belgian internal politics was
to be the last article signed Ilya Ehrenburg to appear in *Izvestia* for a
long time to come. 'Paul Jocelyn' lasted a little longer. On 12 April
1939 he published two brief reports: one on the Greek Government's
reaction to the Italian conquest of Albania, and the other on the
alleged suicide of forty-seven Spanish Republican commanders
whom the Italians had been holding captive in Alicante. This was his
swan song. At least it ended on a Spanish note.

In the mid-sixties, a Barcelona publishing house brought out
several of Ehrenburg's works, including the first two volumes of his
memoirs, as part of a popular series. I wonder whether he ever learnt
that he had actually been published in Franco's Spain? He was still
alive at the time.

CHAPTER XXII

Ehrenburg's disappearance from the pages of *Izvestia* was the result of a high-level decision in Moscow, and he must have found it highly frustrating. At a time when Nazi blackmail was reaching its peak, he was obliged to suspend his activities as a leading anti-Fascist propagandist.

A month earlier, in his address to the Eighteenth Soviet Party Congress in March 1939, Stalin had dropped the first hint that he might have to reconsider his tactics. He was speaking about the appeasement policy of the Western Powers, whose aims he defined as follows: to allow Germany and Japan to become embroiled in a war with the USSR; to wait until each side had been bled white; then to intervene and impose the West's own terms on the exhausted belligerents. This would, of course, be 'cheap and nice' for the appeasers, said Stalin, but they would find that it was a dangerous game to play.

'Cheap and nice' was a phrase taken from a mildly bawdy Russian popular song, the refrain being 'Come with me to the brothel, it's so cheap and nice', and Stalin doubtless knew that his listeners would have no problem in identifying the allusion. But this touch of crude jocularity did not make his pronouncement any less momentous. He was telling the world at large that he would not be a pawn in what he took to be the appeasers' game. Moreover, although this was not immediately apparent, he was also giving notice that he intended to try and play a similar game himself, and if necessary to produce his own version of appeasement. He could not be certain of success – Hitler might not respond to such overtures – but the matter was worth exploring.

At first, no one paid much attention to this passage. In London, *The Times* did not even include it in its summary of Stalin's speech. Yet gradually the notion began to filter through that Stalin did not regard war with Germany as inevitable, and would make a major effort to avoid it. There were further straws in the wind. At the beginning of May, the Soviet Foreign Minister, Maxim Litvinov, was dismissed, and this caused a far greater stir in international circles than any of Stalin's cryptic utterances. Litvinov had become closely identified with the Soviet demand for a collective security system in Europe, which in effect meant a defensive alliance of the non-Fascist nations. His dismissal therefore seemed to suggest a major change in direction. *The Times*, it was true, still thought it 'not prudent' to assume that it would lead to a switch in policy, and government spokesmen in various capitals, when asked for comment, preferred to remain non-committal. But a correspondent in Berlin described official German opinion as 'half-mistrustful and half-pleased', while from Tokyo came a report which clearly suggested that the sacking of Litvinov heralded a Soviet-German *rapprochement*.

It was only then that Ehrenburg, biding his time in Paris, was finally informed of *Izvestia*'s decision. No one had bothered to tell him about it any sooner. He had continued to send reports to the paper, which had simply failed to appear. Becoming more and more perturbed, he had asked for an explanation. He was now told that he should send no more dispatches. He would remain on the paper's staff, however, and continue to draw his full salary. From the financial point of view this was gratifying, but from every other aspect the situation was both puzzling and alarming. Ehrenburg turned to the Soviet Ambassador in Paris for advice. The Ambassador was an experienced diplomat called Yakov Surits, with whom Ehrenburg was on close and friendly terms. To go by Ehrenburg's memoirs, Surits reacted to his visitor's anxious enquiries much as a doctor might to the babble of an overwrought patient who complains of slight indigestion in the midst of a cholera epidemic. In other words, he rather peremptorily told Ehrenburg to stop worrying. Then, having produced this lenitive diagnosis of Ehrenburg's problem, he added reflectively: 'It's true that Maxim Maximovich [i.e. Litvinov] has been removed. But that's by the way, it has nothing to do with your case.' It was still too early at that point to see the connection clearly. Yet Surits must instinctively have sensed that there was some link between the two cases, and his diplomatic instinct did not let him down. Stalin was indeed clearing the decks in preparation for possible talks with Nazi Germany. But if such negotiations were to be held, they could hardly be conducted by Litvinov, the Jew, whom the German radio usually referred to as 'Litvinov-Finkelstein', and who ranked as the foremost advocate of the anti-Nazi collective security policy. As for Ehrenburg, another

Jew, whose books had been ceremoniously burned in Berlin and whose articles attacking Fascism were well-informed and well-known, it was better to silence him as a precautionary measure until his services were needed again. By removing Ehrenburg from the public eye (and more particularly from the eye of the Nazis), Stalin was in fact paying him a great compliment: he was acknowledging Ehrenburg's effectiveness as a leading anti-Nazi propagandist. But the Soviet leader was also observing a rule he had followed in all his dealings with Ehrenburg: to let him do only those jobs for which he was best equipped. And at that juncture, no such job existed. A eulogy by Ehrenburg of the Nazi-Soviet Pact, if such a pact could be negotiated, might not make very convincing reading.

In the circumstances, the decision to publish no more articles by Ehrenburg was a blessing in disguise. But that was something Ehrenburg himself could only appreciate with the benefit of hindsight. At the time, the blessing was well concealed, and he fell into a state of acute depression. The news coming out of Russia was still terrifying, even though the purges had slackened off. On the international front, Ehrenburg had been lashing out for nearly two decades at those who were preparing for war, or who accepted it as a legitimate instrument of policy. But now, having been silenced by his paper, he could only watch the approaching catastrophe as a casual bystander. This was demoralizing enough, but it was nothing compared with what was still to come.

On 22 August 1939, it became known that the Nazi–Soviet Pact had been successfully negotiated and would be signed the next day. Learning of this development, I could not help thinking of Ehrenburg, and even wondered whether he would commit suicide. He refrained from that final gesture, but in his memoirs he relates how the news brought him to the verge of a total collapse. As a youth, he had had one nervous breakdown in a Russian prison, and he suffered another in Paris during the First World War. Now he suddenly found that he was unable to eat. It was as if the Nazi-Soviet Pact had literally stuck in his throat. For months, he was hardly able to swallow anything at all, and it was not until another shock had been administered, with the news of Hitler's offensive in the West, that he overcame his nervous disorder.

Some years later, when the war was over, Ehrenburg inserted a passage into his novel *The Storm*, in which he attempted to vindicate the Pact. The hero of the novel, who is attached to a Soviet trade delegation in France, explains to a well-disposed but bewildered enquirer: 'It's really quite simple. An attempt had been made to trick us, and we refused to let ourselves be tricked.' It might have been possible to think of other explanations, but Stalin himself preferred the one which stemmed from his speech to the Eighteenth Party Congress, and Ehrenburg simply reproduced the logic of the supposedly infallible leader. This was legitimate in a novel, and it was plainly a wise move on Ehrenburg's part. His hero's explanation was precisely the one a Soviet official in France would have given to a friendly questioner. It was probably what Ehrenburg himself had been told by the Soviet Ambassador, who must have tried to convince him that the Pact was a political necessity. Ehrenburg even says he was convinced, but only in his head, not in his heart. This was, after all, a very human reaction, and typical of the way many people felt during that nightmarish summer. I remember an experienced international observer using almost exactly the same words about the coming war only five days before it began: 'In my head I know there will be war, but in my heart I simply can't believe it.'

But whatever intellectual justifications might be produced for the Pact, to Ehrenburg it meant that the authority of the Soviet Union as an anti-Fascist Power had been shattered. The Soviet Union had been anti-Fascist by definition, and to Ehrenburg and those like him, this had been its most valuable asset. That such an asset was fast disappearing was alarming enough in itself. Even worse, however, was the fact that the Soviet Government seemed positively anxious to discard it. It was demonstratively signalling to the world, and in the first place to Nazi Germany, that it no longer wished to be regarded as an anti-Fascist Power. A week after the Pact was signed, the Soviet Prime Minister, Molotov, addressed the Supreme Soviet on its significance, and in doing so, pointed out the true meaning of Stalin's speech to the Eighteenth Party Congress and praised Stalin's wisdom. Stalin, he said, had correctly assumed that Germany would respond to his peaceful overtures. He had foreseen that certain countries, acting as *provocateurs*, had been trying to involve the Soviet Union in a war with Germany, and had stepped in to prevent them carrying out their sinister designs. But then Molotov went somewhat further. 'One has to admit', he said, 'that there were some short-sighted people in our own country who were so carried away by oversimplified anti-Fascist agitation that they ignored the activities of the *provocateurs*.' To Ehrenburg's ears, as he says in his memoirs, this remark by Molotov produced the most jarring effect of all. He had, after all, been in the forefront of the struggle to warn people of the menace of Fascism. Now he had to stand by and watch the Soviet Government solemnly renounce its anti-Fascist stand.

On that occasion, speaking to the Supreme Soviet, the Soviet Prime Minister still actually used the word 'Fascist'. 'The German Fascists, our enemies of yesterday, are no longer our enemies today', he declared. But that was the last time the term 'Fascist' was heard in public for nearly two years. For Ehrenburg, Fascism was still the main enemy, and he knew enough about human nature to gauge the probable effect of eliminating that word from the official Soviet vocabulary. Even if one disregarded the sycophants, who would automatically follow the lead of their superiors, once the term was outlawed ordinary people would soon forget that the thing itself existed. Once Hitler was no longer associated in their minds with Fascism, which for so long had been synonymous with evil, they would begin to look upon Germany with respect, and some of them even with admiration. Ehrenburg knew that there were some aspects of Fascism which were likely to appeal to a certain class of people in Russia, and that this tendency might spread now that Fascism was officially non-existent and Hitler's Germany had been hailed as a friendly country. In his postwar novel, *The Storm*, he refers specifically to those who, at the time of the Pact, admired Nazi Germany, either because this was the done thing, or because they cared little about what happened to the rest of mankind. His hero, having returned to Moscow from France, listens with his family to a Soviet news broadcast reporting the heavy losses inflicted by German U-boats on Allied shipping. 'They're sinking them good and proper!' laughs one of those present exultantly. The hero, who has remained uncorrupted by the current fashion, retorts in disgust: 'I don't see why we should rejoice over Fascist successes!' Eyebrows are immediately raised. 'Fascist? Your terminology is a bit out of date, isn't it?'

The Soviet Government was doing a good deal to encourage this kind of attitude – Stalin seemed to think it would impress Hitler. In November Molotov once more addressed the Supreme Soviet, and announced that the terms 'aggressor' and 'aggression' had acquired different meanings in the past few months, and could no longer be used as they had been formerly. Germany, Molotov declared, was now interested in making peace, whereas the Western Powers were eager to continue the war. It was an 'imperialist' war, and Molotov rejected the claim of the Allies that they were fighting for the destruction of Hitlerism. Ideological wars, said the Soviet Prime Minister, belonged to the Middle Ages, the epoch of savagery, superstition and religious strife. Hitlerism was an ideology which one could either accept or reject: what mattered was that an ideology could never be destroyed by force.

There is no record of how Ehrenburg reacted to this statement, but it is reasonable to assume that he was sickened by it. As a doctrine, Hitlerism did not even pay lip service to ethical principles, but merely proclaimed that some people had the right to trample with impunity on others. To place it on a par with other ideologies was a very strange aberration for the head of an allegedly Marxist Government. A few weeks later, Hitler and Ribbentrop sent a message of congratulations to Stalin on his sixtieth birthday. In his reply to Ribbentrop, who had mentioned Soviet-German friendship, Stalin said that that friendship had been 'cemented by blood', thus implying an equal respect for the losses the Germans had suffered in invading Poland, and those suffered by the Red Army, which had encountered some resistance during its own thrust into Poland from the East. Ehrenburg's reaction, when he read the text of this message in the Soviet Press, can be imagined. At first he could scarcely believe his eyes. Then he lost his temper, and roundly told Surits what he thought of it. The Ambassador merely pointed out that there were worse things than replies to congratulatory telegrams. However, Surits himself clearly feared a strengthening of Soviet-German friendship.

Meanwhile, Ehrenburg's position in France was as paradoxical as the behaviour of the Soviet Government, although in a different way, and also profoundly humiliating. In the past, the French police had regarded him with mistrust because he represented a foreign Communist newspaper and had published a good many disagreeable things about France, accusing the French Government of betraying Republican Spain, of capitulating to Hitler at Munich, and so on. Now, he was placed under surveillance as a potential Nazi spy. In his memoirs, he tries to suggest that the police were simply paying off old scores. This may have been partly true, but it was also perfectly natural for the security people to keep an eye on him, now that France was at war with Germany and the Soviet Union was not. In

any case, whatever the French police may have thought of Ehrenburg's record as an anti-Fascist, that record no longer held good. It
had been invalidated by the fact that the Soviet Union and Nazi
Germany had become partners, and that he had been consorting
with Communists who were now faithfully obeying Stalin's instructions and opposing the war. This was something that must have
weighed heavily on Ehrenburg, but it was an issue that he never faced
squarely or honestly in his writings. The nearest he came to dealing
with it was in his novel *The Fall of Paris* (1947), which was published
when it was no longer necessary to avoid saying anything that might
hurt Hitler's feelings. In that novel, a French Communist explains to
his fellow-workers that without the Nazi-Soviet Pact the Soviet
Union would be lost, and that without the Soviet Union the
international working class would be lost. On the other hand, if
France decided to fight in earnest, the Soviet Union would doubtless
help her. This line of argument was calculated to satisfy Stalin. But
whether Ehrenburg really believed what he had made his French
worker say no longer mattered by the time the book appeared. The
attitude of the Western Communist Parties towards the war with
Germany at the time of the Nazi–Soviet Pact could not, of course, be
explained away that easily.

For the time being, Ehrenburg continued to be harassed by the
French police, the French papers occasionally attacked him, and a
number of his old friends avoided his company. If the West had been
inflicting crushing defeats on Nazi Germany, he would obviously
have rejoiced. But the West did not seem to be fighting the war with
much conviction. He found this reprehensible, but in another way it
was a source of comfort. In Spain, he had drugged himself with
hatred of Fascism, in order to avoid thinking about what was
happening in the Soviet Union. Now, in order to surmount his feeling
of humiliation, he drugged himself with the notion that the conflict in
the West was a 'phoney' war (as it was indeed popularly called), and
that France was merely pretending to be anti-Fascist, preferring to
arrest French Communists rather than fight the Nazis. He never
admitted, then or later, that there had been a valid reason for
arresting Communists. On the other hand, it was true that little was
being done to prosecute the war.

He tried to leave France, but was unable to do so. He claimed that
this was due to a bureaucratic imbroglio. The French police would
have been glad to see the last of him, but he could not obtain an exit

permit because of some ridiculous misunderstanding over income tax. Then, on 10 May, Hitler's armies launched their blitzkrieg in the West, and the war abruptly lost its phoney character. Since Ehrenburg still could not leave, the police decided to treat him as a spy. He was arrested, but released almost immediately, thanks to the intervention of the Minister of the Interior, Georges Mandel. Then came the fall of France, and with it the collapse of Stalin's policy of appeasing Hitler. It had worked well enough to begin with, but now all the earlier calculations had been confounded. The two major Continental Powers, France and Germany, could no longer bleed each other white in combat. One had been knocked out of the fight altogether. The other was victorious, and growing stronger day by day: so much so that, less than a year later, Hitler attacked the Soviet Union.

CHAPTER XXIII

In mid-June, Ehrenburg watched the German Armies enter his beloved Paris. Never had he dreamt he would witness such a calamity – and witness it without danger to himself! Everything had been turned upside down, and nothing made sense any more. In Republican Spain he had enjoyed certain privileges as a Soviet journalist. Now, he was under the protection of the Nazi-Soviet Pact. In peacetime, he had not been allowed to set foot in Nazi Germany, and had to follow a roundabout route to reach Moscow from Paris. Now, when he finally left France at the end of July 1940, he travelled through wartime Germany unmolested, and even spent two nights in a hotel in Berlin to which Jews were not admitted. He and his wife were being evacuated from Paris together with a party of officials from the Soviet Embassy, and the Germans were not supposed to know who he was. But even if they had known, it is unlikely that they would have made any trouble.

After the fall of France, he remained in occupied Paris for nearly six weeks, during which time he paid a brief visit to Vichy. In Paris, at the suggestion of the Soviet chargé d'affaires, he stayed at the Soviet Embassy, and in his memoirs he describes his feelings of shock when a staff car flying a swastika flag stopped outside the building, and he realized that German officers had come to pay a courtesy call. It was the first time he had seen the Nazi-Soviet Pact in operation, and it filled him with a feeling of deep shame.

After he had moved into the Embassy, it would have been prudent to have remained indoors, at least for the first few days, but curiosity drove him out on to the streets. The swift succession of events had a kind of gruesome fascination, and he absorbed them with avidity. He had already watched the great exodus from the city, as thousands of cars headed off for the south and the west, while many thousands of people camped out near the railway stations, although they had been told that no more trains would be running. He wrote:

> On 10 June, towards evening, Paris became enveloped in a black fog: oil storage tanks had been set on fire, and it was quite dark. On the 11th,

Paris Soir appeared for the last time. The paper carried a photograph of dogs being bathed in the Seine, with the caption: *Paris reste toujours Paris.* Meanwhile, the whole of fashionable Paris – *le Tout Paris* – was abandoning the French capital. When nearly everyone had departed, posters appeared in the streets announcing (for whose benefit? for lonely old women? for the birds? for the dogs that had been left behind?) that Paris had been declared an open city. On the evening of 13 June, more oil tanks were set on fire. It was raining, and the rain was black.

Finally, on 14 June 1940, Ehrenburg saw a squad of German soldiers marching towards the Arc de Triomphe. After that, he could only survey the deserted city with a feeling of desolation. Paris without people was a contradiction in terms.

All the shutters are closed, and the houses look as if they had gone blind. There are streets in which one does not meet a single soul. In the poorer quarters, one sees only the old, the hunchbacked and the lame: all those who failed to get away. In the Tuileries, there is no one to cut the grass any more, and it has grown quite high around the forgotten statues. In the Rue de Rivoli, where the arcades used to be thronged with people at all hours, all is still and quiet, except for the occasional tramp of jackboots. One of the theatres is showing a revue called *Immer Paris*, its theme song being that old refrain of Maurice Chevalier's, *Paris reste toujours Paris.* Yes, everything is still there: the Eiffel Tower, the Place de la Concorde, and the Café de la Paix. Only one thing is missing: Paris itself.

This sombre sketch of the city formed part of one of Ehrenburg's articles on the fall of France which appeared in the Soviet Union a month after his return. He had been silent for over a year. But in the previous few months he had seen and heard things which no other Soviet writer had seen or heard, and he was determined to tell as much of it as he could. He had seen France collapse because the nation was psychologically unprepared for war. He could not bear the thought that this might happen to Russia also, when Hitler attacked her; and he was absolutely convinced that Hitler would do so before long. Both the Soviet Government and the ordinary man in the street, all those self-deluded people who had welcomed the pact with Nazi Germany as a propitious event, must be given some warning of what was coming. But it was easier said than done. A few friends who thought as he did were eager enough to listen to him; but that was preaching to the converted. Those in influential positions showed much less interest. He talked, among others, to the Deputy Foreign Minister, Lozovsky. Lozovsky had a genuinely international outlook, and he probably did not doubt Ehrenburg's words for a moment; but he only remarked sadly that the Government was 'pursuing a different policy', which meant that what Ehrenburg was saying was not what Stalin and Molotov wanted to hear. Besides, Lozovsky had a special reason for showing caution: he was a Jew. To Ehrenburg himself it was made clear by certain people, whom he tactfully refrains from naming in his memoirs, that while it was natural enough for a Jew to dislike the Nazi-Soviet Pact, the Government – thank God – was not allowing the Jews to shape Soviet foreign policy, and they had better not try to interfere. In the circumstances, it was something of a miracle that Ehrenburg found anyone prepared to publish his pieces on the fall of France. *Izvestia* refused to touch anything he had written, and eventually it was *Trud*, the organ of the State-controlled trades unions, which accepted his articles. It also seemed miraculous that they appeared so quickly, since a battle had to be fought with the censor beforehand.

Censorship in any shape or form is undoubtedly an oppressive, crippling and soul-destroying phenomenon. Yet it is not always wholly negative. For if, instead of a flat rejection, the censor utters a cautious 'yes . . . but', it can even have a stimulating effect on the author. Once the author knows he is not up against a brick wall, he uses all his literary skill to circumvent the censorship, and this can sometimes result in a disciplined and highly concentrated piece of writing, which may even turn out to be more impressive than what the writer would have produced if given an entirely free hand. Ehrenburg fought a stubborn battle. He was defeated on some points, but on balance he won. His first-hand account of the fall of France was later reprinted, with some additional material, in a Soviet magazine, a copy of which reached England while the Nazi-Soviet Pact was still in force; and reading it, I remember being amazed at how much Ehrenburg had managed to say in spite of the censor.

To begin with, he assumed, correctly, that no one in the Soviet Union had the faintest idea what a Nazi occupation was like. He had been warned that he must not say anything offensive about the Germans, although he was free to pour abuse on the French. He therefore referred to the Germans only in passing, but he did describe some of the effects of their presence in France. He had to give careful thought to the impact of each sentence on different types of Soviet reader. For those who had always had an idealized image of Paris, he wrote: 'In the Place de la Concorde (the square to which Mayakovsky dedicated one of his poems) there are concerts of martial music, conducted by a Professor Schmidt.' In another passage, he jolted the memories of those who might have forgotten the Nazis' deep-rooted anti-Semitism, or had never believed it (there were such people in Russia, incredible though it may seem, among those who naïvely put their faith in Western civilization): 'Some cafés and restaurants have put up notices: *Purely Aryan establishment – no Jews admitted.*' And for the same kind of people, he also produced a quotation from one of the new French newspapers, *La France au Travail*: 'In each of us there is something Jewish. Each of us needs an inner pogrom.' Meanwhile, for those whose infatuation with the Pact had blinded them to the fact that the Nazis were no friends of the Communists, he cited another editorial comment from the same paper: 'It is time everyone realized that there are no more Communists. We do not need a civil war. The murderers of the people should note that there will not be another Commune.'

To criticize former French leaders like Daladier and Reynaud, whom he had always attacked, was not difficult. He felt that France had been betrayed. Until the country was invaded, there had been only 'a token war'. He would have liked to call some of the French politicians and generals 'Fascists', but was told emphatically that under no circumstances could he use that word. He got round it by comparing certain French politicians to crusaders who, having proclaimed a crusade, had immediately turned round and embraced Islam, i.e. the faith of the enemy. He managed to insert a brief passage about General de Gaulle, the one French military leader who understood modern warfare, but whose advice had been ignored by his superiors. Strictly speaking, de Gaulle was not supposed to be praised. He was by then in London, organizing the Free French forces, and a tribute to him from a Soviet source was not exactly in keeping with Soviet neutrality, but the censor let it pass. Ehrenburg even gave a mention to Churchill, which was favourable by implication, but the implication was so well camouflaged that the censor let that pass as well. In a critical reference to the behaviour of the French Prime Minister, Paul Reynaud, Ehrenburg said that, while Reynaud was on friendly terms with Churchill, he entrusted the conduct of foreign affairs to Baudouin, who openly boasted of being pro-Italian; from which a very sophisticated reader might deduce that Ehrenburg was contrasting Churchill's implacable resolution with Reynaud's weakness and indecision. There was also a hidden but implied tribute to Britain in one of Ehrenburg's remarks about Marshal Pétain. He recalled Pétain's dislike of 'one of France's allies' during the 'first imperialist war' (a clear reference to the Marshal's well-known anglophobia), and thus implicitly contrasted Pétain's capitulation to the Nazis with Britain's determination to fight on. In fact, it was the fall of France that induced Ehrenburg, for the first time in his life, to look towards Britain with some sympathy. In the Soviet Embassy in German-occupied Paris he had started listening to the BBC in French; it was his only source of hard news. He continued listening when he returned to Russia, and when he heard that London was being bombed he wrote a poem in which he tried to express his feelings. It was something he never forgot. There was an occasion in 1947, for example, when he addressed a postwar rally in Warsaw. He fully understood what Warsaw had been through, he told his audience, and added: 'I could not speak like this to people anywhere else – *not even in London.*' (My italics.)

To keep on the right side of Stalin and Molotov, and to ensure against trouble with the editorial board of *Trud*, with the censors, or with anyone else who might be concerned, Ehrenburg did make one concession. In one of his articles there is a sentence in which he refers to the war in Europe as 'the second imperialist war', which was, of course, how Molotov had defined it in the late autumn of 1939. But to anyone who read Ehrenburg's series as a whole, the message was clear. He had ignored Molotov's condemnation of the war against Germany, and far from believing that the Western Allies should not have entered into the war at all, he felt very strongly that it should have been fought with the utmost vigour, and clearly regarded it as a tragedy that France had failed to do so. In the slightly amended version which appeared later in a Soviet magazine, Ehrenburg touched briefly on his homeward journey through Germany, and mentioned that soon after the train crossed the German frontier, he heard the wail of sirens. (This was not in itself surprising, since the Soviet Press had been factually reporting the British air raids on German cities.) But he ended this passage on a solemn note. 'Sirens sound the same in no matter what country', he wrote. It was his way of echoing Homer's line, 'The day will come . . .' or the cautiously implicit equivalent of what he had already noted at the end of the Spanish war: 'Woe to the victors!'

He had been allowed to give the Soviet public at least some idea of what was happening, and he desperately wanted to tell more. One of the State publishing houses was persuaded to bring out a volume of his poems. In this he was helped by the writer Vsevolod Vishnevsky, who had some influence in high quarters. But the principle by which he had already been constrained remained the same: it was permissible to criticize the French, but he must not say anything against the Germans. Thus, the poem in which he had paid tribute to bomb-scarred London could not even be considered. Vishnevsky offered the explanation that 'Stalin knows best', which simply meant that certain things were better not discussed, even among friends. Finally, agreement was reached on a selection which included poems about both France and Spain. Spain was a subject on which the attitude of the Soviet authorities was somewhat vague. Ehrenburg had produced an earlier book on Spain, and it had been accepted for publication, but was then scrapped because of the Nazi-Soviet Pact. This time it was apparently considered that a few poems would do no harm. Besides, Spanish propaganda occasionally attacked the Soviet Union, and the Soviet radio replied in kind, commiserating with the sufferings of the Spanish people 'under the yoke of dictatorship'. The selection also included one poem on a French theme which must have provoked a lengthy and fascinating discussion. It was Ehrenburg's lament for enslaved Paris, and it would have had no chance of being published at such a time, but for the fact that the word 'Paris' did not occur in it once. For poetic, or politico-poetic reasons, Ehrenburg simply referred to 'The City', although from the context it was perfectly plain which city he had in mind. It was the city of Balzac, the city in which the writer of the poem had spent his youth; and now that city had been defiled by 'alien brass' and 'alien arrogance'. To give the poem an air of respectability, Ehrenburg was persuaded to entitle it 'The Eighteenth of March' – the day of the Paris Commune. Moreover, it was placed in the book next to a poem dealing with Spain, so that at first sight it might look as if the author had a Spanish city in mind, perhaps Madrid (resistance in Madrid had collapsed in March 1939). As it happened, however, neither the censors, the publishers, nor Ehrenburg and his influential friends need have worried. By the time the volume appeared in print in 1941 the moment was fast approaching when the Soviet Press would start referring to Hitler as a monster, a cannibal, a reptile, and similar suitably-chosen epithets. In a subsequent edition, the poem was given its proper title: 'Paris 1940'.

It is doubtful whether anyone was really taken in by such

disingenuous tricks. Their purpose was simply to provide Soviet publishers with a formal excuse for publishing such material. Subterfuges of this kind would certainly not have fooled Stalin, if he had bothered to take an interest in the matter. The Soviet leader may or may not have read Ehrenburg's series of articles on the fall of France. If he did, he must have seen immediately that they were anything but neutral. The fact that their publication went ahead must therefore have been due to a change of climate at the top. Either Stalin read them and gave his agreement, or some of his close advisers sensed that he would not object if Ehrenburg were permitted to tell the public some of the things he had witnessed, provided this was not done too conspicuously (there was no question of such material appearing in *Pravda* or *Izvestia*), and the necessary proprieties were observed.

All the same, observing the proprieties was a complex and delicate business. It was particularly difficult to know what was proper and what was not, and the editors and censors generally preferred to err on the side of caution. Ehrenburg kept on writing, but much of what he wrote was rejected, or an editor would sit on one of his articles for weeks on end, pondering whether it was not 'too strong'. Some members of the Soviet literary bureaucracy even felt it more prudent to avoid his company altogether. But then something happened which drastically changed the situation, and filled his compatriots with awe.

He had been working hard on his novel, *The Fall of Paris*. The first part dealt only with the prewar years and made no mention of the Germans, so it was passed for publication, although with some cuts. The second part, however, was held up, although here too Ehrenburg had avoided all reference to the Germans, and he was plunged into perplexity, having reached the stage at which he would have to describe the German invasion. Suddenly, at the end of April 1941, came a totally unexpected message. He was told to telephone Stalin.

It was the only conversation they ever had. Ehrenburg had never spoken to Stalin before (it will be recalled that a meeting had been arranged in 1934, but this was cancelled because of the assassination of Kirov), and he was never to speak to him again. But it was a remarkable encounter in more ways than one. Stalin said that he had read the first part of *The Fall of Paris*, and had enjoyed it. Did Ehrenburg intend to write about the Germans in France? Ehrenburg replied that this had indeed been his intention, in a projected third section of the novel, but he feared that he would never be allowed to publish it. To which Stalin replied quietly: 'You carry on writing. Together, we may be able to push the third part through.'

From Ehrenburg's personal point of view it was a gratifying conversation, and from the political point of view, a momentous one. Stalin had, in effect, signalled to him that there would be war with Nazi Germany. Ehrenburg had been trying to tell everyone this for months, but the people who mattered had refused to listen, had tried to fob him off with threadbare excuses, and had even muttered ominous warnings. Now, it looked as if Stalin was on his side. In his memoirs, he relates that instead of feeling triumphant, however, or even relieved, he felt utterly depressed. Obviously, like many other people back in 1939, he had never really believed that there would be war. He had known it in his head, perhaps, but in his heart he had refused to accept it. But now, he had to accept that a conflict with Germany was fast approaching. Stalin had not asked him to keep their conversation secret, which meant that he was at liberty to convey the gist of it to his friends, and to those who, learning of his interview with Stalin, would seek to ingratiate themselves. All this plainly enhanced his prestige, but it did not make him happy.

'And yet,' Ehrenburg notes in his memoirs, 'when the war came, it did take Stalin by surprise, in spite of the fact that he had been worried as early as April.' It appeared that by June, when the blow came, Stalin had managed to persuade himself that his apprehensions were groundless. But even earlier, in April, he seems to have done little to forestall the impending conflict, except to refer to it obliquely and enigmatically in his conversation with Ehrenburg.

CHAPTER XXIV

The period which began on 22 June 1941, when the German Armies finally invaded the Soviet Union, was the most fruitful of Ehrenburg's entire career. Never before had his writings been so effective, and never before had he enjoyed such popularity. He acquired fame as a Russian, as a European, and as a Jew.

For more than two years, he had had to stand by almost in silence as the European tragedy unfolded. It was only to be expected that after so much pent-up frustration, he would erupt into a fury of activity, and he did. In hundreds of broadcasts and articles he denounced the evil force which had subjugated most of Europe. One could expect the author of *The Stormy Life of Lazik Roitshvantz* to speak out as a Jew, at a time when his earlier prediction about the approaching martyrdom of the tribe of Judah was becoming an appalling reality. 'I grew up in a Russian city. Russian is my native tongue', he declared in an address to the Anti-Fascist Jewish Congress in August 1941. 'I am a Russian writer. But the Nazis made me remember something else. My mother's name was Hannah. I am a Jew.' When he spoke of the fate of the Jews under the Nazi regime, he thundered like an angry Jewish God, and even thousands of miles away from Moscow, people wept as they listened to his words. But all this was only natural. What was less predictable was the immense impact his words had when he spoke as a Russian. It was true that he had spent his childhood and youth in Moscow, that he wrote in Russian, and was entitled to call himself a Russian author. But in other respects there was little outward resemblance between this cosmopolitan intellectual, who had spent most of his adult life in the West, and the ordinary Russian peasant in uniform who was now told he must repel the full might of Hitler's formidable military machine. Yet somehow Ehrenburg managed to find words that went straight to the Russian soldier's heart. He became the soldiers' favourite writer, and when they opened their copies of the Red Army newspaper, *Red Star*, the first things they looked for were the articles of Ilya Ehrenburg.

It came about more by accident than design. On the first day of the war, when Soviet editors, like everyone else, were completely taken by surprise and were desperately looking around for competent people, Ehrenburg was invited to the offices of *Red Star*. He had previously done a certain amount of lecturing to the armed forces, and his association with the army newspaper was to last throughout the war. Meanwhile, the wartime Soviet propaganda department, known as the Informbureau, which issued the celebrated daily communiqués on which the world waited with bated breath, wanted him to undertake a different task. He was to make propaganda for the Soviet Union in the West, to popularize the Soviet position in the Allied countries, to arouse whatever sympathy he could among the neutrals, and to encourage resistance in occupied Europe. Ehrenburg was the obvious man for the job, and he had already caught the eye of Stalin. The head of Informbureau, the redoubtable bureaucrat, Shcherbakov, instructed him to write an article each day for Western consumption, and Ehrenburg did his best. He wrote articles for Allied newspapers, and whenever possible, for neutral ones as well, he broadcast to Western Europe, and he addressed himself to Hitler's victims as a fellow-European who understood their plight. He particularly wanted the French to know how he had felt when he was stranded in Paris, and had watched the German troops enter the city. It was all brilliantly done, in spite of the Soviet censorship, which queried everything that was not a paraphrase of the official clichés, and in spite of Shcherbakov, who rebuked him for 'trying to be original'. It was clear, however, that Ehrenburg himself attached a good deal more importance to the work he was doing for *Red Star*.

He knew that every word that appeared in *Red Star* mattered. It would be read by those who were doing the actual fighting, and they were badly in need of encouragement. The country, as Ehrenburg had feared, was psychologically unprepared for war, and at the outset Russia had no Winston Churchill, no magic voice to spur her on. On the day the Germans crossed the frontier, Stalin remained silent. Molotov spoke, but failed to rise to the occasion. It was not until ten days later, after Stalin had pulled himself together sufficiently to make his first wartime broadcast, that the Russian people heard the voice of their leader. It sounded like the voice of an old man in a panic. The Germans continued to advance, and Ehrenburg knew that they could only be stopped if the will to resist took precedence over everything else. He himself could think of nothing but the war, and in his *Red Star* pieces he poured all his energy, all his skill, all his emotions, into instilling the notion of resistance into the minds of his soldier readers.

He was well-equipped for the task. Probably no one in the Soviet Union knew the enemy better than he did. He understood the very essence of Fascism. To many Russians at that time, Fascism was merely a dogmatic term of abuse which had been banned for nearly two years, a ban they had accepted unquestioningly on the grounds that 'Stalin knew best'. Now it was once more legitimate to use the word, but few had bothered to try and discover the real meaning of Fascism. It was even doubtful whether the leaders themselves knew. Ehrenburg was shocked when he heard Stalin and Molotov speak of Hitler's 'breach of faith' after the Nazi invasion of Russia – as if anyone could put his faith in a man like Hitler! Moreover, most Soviet intellectuals did not seem to have any clearer idea of what Hitler was really like. They still preserved their traditional attitude towards Germany, which was one of respect. Ehrenburg knew that Germany had succumbed to barbarism, but they did not. To them, Germany was still a 'Western' nation, technically advanced and consequently civilized, whatever people might say. In May 1942, at a time when things were going reasonably well for the Soviet Union and Ehrenburg felt that such an admission could no longer do any harm, he put this on record in one of his articles. 'At the beginning of this extraordinary war', he wrote, 'many of us failed to grasp what kind of people were defiling our land. Some of us were too trusting [i.e. had always respected the Germans], some were too mistrustful [i.e. they automatically disbelieved anything the Soviet Government said], and thought that Hitler's Army was the Army of a hostile but cultured country, consisting of well-mannered officers and disciplined men.' As for the ordinary Russian soldier, Ehrenburg added, he, too, was easily overawed; if he found a German cigarette lighter, he would exclaim admiringly: 'That's what I call culture!'

Much later, in his memoirs, Ehrenburg advanced an argument which sounds much less plausible. According to him, in the early days of the war many Soviet soldiers were convinced that the German lower ranks would throw away their rifles and fraternize if only someone on the Soviet side would explain to them the true meaning of working-class solidarity. Stalin, in his first wartime broadcast, did indeed say that the ordinary German people must be regarded as potential allies, and the Soviet troops must have heard a good deal about working-class solidarity from their political instructors. But it is hard to imagine that they believed it, or even remembered what they had been told, when they found themselves under enemy fire. Ehrenburg's claim that such illusions existed, and that he regarded it as his duty to dispel them, looks more like a retrospective attempt to vindicate his own style of anti-German propaganda, which had not been immune from criticism. But there was another factor which Ehrenburg must have recognized, although he did not mention it publicly, either then or later: that in the opening phase of the war, morale was low because the Soviet leadership was not as popular as it pretended to be (to put it mildly), and quite a few retreating Russian soldiers were not sufficiently dismayed at the prospect of finding themselves in German captivity.

All this drove Ehrenburg to the simple conclusion that the war would be lost unless the soldiers learned to hate the enemy. His task, as he saw it, was to teach the Russians to hate. 'War without hatred is amoral', he said later, during a debate on his writings. 'It is like sex without love.' He knew that hatred was a precious commodity: it must not be frittered away, but directed against the enemy in its most concentrated form. No one could hate Fascism more than he did. Besides, he had always disliked the Germans. While he was living in Germany, this had even sometimes embarrassed him, and he had tried to rid himself of his anti-German bias. But now that there was a war on he turned his old prejudice into an asset. His first wartime article, written on the very day of the German invasion, was somewhat weak and inhibited; he was still stunned by what had happened, even though he had seen it coming. But it did not take him long to find his feet, or to fashion a vocabulary suitable to his task. Soon he was lashing out at 'the swarms of brown lice' which were crawling over the body of Russia, trying to devour her. As for Hitler, Goering, Goebbels, Himmler, and the rest of the criminal Nazi rabble, 'posing as Napoleons and pretending to be Caesars', they would be annihilated like pestilential rats. He searched for an appropriate epithet for Hitler, one which would combine contempt with abuse, and was soon writing about the 'Tyrolean mountebank', the 'Tyrolean house-painter', the 'Tyrolean police spy', or simply the 'Tyrolean crook'. A letter found on a dead German soldier at the start of the Russian campaign had said: 'We shall soon be in Moscow.' 'They did not get to Moscow then,' wrote Ehrenburg in August, 'and they will not get there now. Nor will they get there in

January; in fact, they will never get there. They will soon be longing to get back to Berlin, but they won't get there either. We shall find graves for them here'. Each s s man had been promised 100 hectares of Soviet land; instead, he would get 2 metres – just enough to bury him in. The women of Germany had expected to see trains arriving from Russia full of meat and other foodstuffs; all they got were trains loaded with crippled Germans. And Ehrenburg's fury redoubled: 'We shall pay them back in full, they will not be spared one jot of what they deserve. They will curse the day Hitler sent them here. The war will find them out, no matter where they try to hide. They started it, but we shall end it.'

Like many people during those wartime years, he seemed to be living in a trance, seeking refuge in overwork and in the irrational belief that this would help to avert defeat. As the Germans continued to advance, he kept repeating the same incantatory phrases: 'Hitler will not reach Moscow . . . The dead will arise, the forests will rebel, the rivers will swallow up the enemy. In the mornings we say, "We have gained another night!" In the evenings we say, "We have gained another day!" ' 'I do not want to make things look better than they are', he wrote in an article called 'Stand Firm'. 'The Russian people have never been as methodical as the Germans. But Russia has always grown strong in adversity.'

On 7 November 1941, the first wartime anniversary of the Russian Revolution, Stalin, having recovered his nerve, took the traditional military parade on Red Square, despite the fact that the Germans were almost on the outskirts of Moscow, and Ehrenburg greeted this spectacle with a lyrical outburst:

> Moscow is no longer just a city – it has become the hope of the world. We bare our heads in homage before the graves of others. The defenders of Moscow have not forgotten London's powers of endurance. 'Glory to Britain!' say the Russians. It was not the Channel that stopped the Germans, but the determination of the British people. We salute the British airmen. They were the first to say to the enemy, 'We shall pay you back in kind!' and they struck at the beast's lair.

It was not the first tribute Ehrenburg paid to Britain. As soon as Stalin, in his first wartime broadcast, had acknowledged Churchill's offer of help to Russia, Ehrenburg held up Britain's decision to fight on after the fall of France as a shining example; and all through the terrible summer of 1941 he kept on stressing that the Soviet Union was not alone. He wrote:

The courage shown by London was the first victory over Fascist barbarity. That huge wonderful city had been subjected to terrifying bombardments from the air. After the French Fascists betrayed their country, Britain stood alone. But she did not capitulate. Historians will describe those long winter nights in London. Whole districts of the city were on fire. Yet the English calmly said 'no'. It was not just the Channel that saved Britain from the Nazi cannibals, but the British will to resist. It was summed up in that phrase which the people of those islands learn as children . . . 'Britons never shall be slaves!'

War certainly does do strange things to people. How otherwise can one explain the extraordinary phenomenon of Ehrenburg quoting from 'Rule Britannia' with evident admiration!

At the beginning of December 1941, the Germans were forced to abandon Rostov. It was their first setback on the Eastern Front, and the German communiqué gave the palpably absurd explanation that the troops had been withdrawn so that the Luftwaffe could destroy the city as a reprisal against the civilian population. Ehrenburg wrote:

This is no time for laughter, but let us have a laugh just this once. When the Germans want to kill the inhabitants of Belgrade, they do not go to Zagreb. When they want to torture the people of Paris, they do not move on Lille. If they have withdrawn from Rostov, it is because they have been kicked out of Rostov. Their official claim is that they have left Rostov in order to punish it. Well done, men of the ss! You will soon be forced to punish the whole of Russia in the same way. Rostov, the first of our liberated cities, says to the defenders of Moscow: 'Stand firm! Don't retreat an inch! The Russians have shown that they can beat the Germans.'

During the following months, after the German offensive against Moscow had failed, this became Ehrenburg's constant refrain: 'We have learned how to beat them. We now know how to deal with the German rabble. We have matured by a hundred years. Victory has not just been handed to us as a gift from Heaven. We have had to pay for it.' In another article, he pointed out, with some justification, that there was no true parallel between the battle for Moscow and the 'miracle of the Marne' in 1914, since the French victory in the First World War had been at least partly made possible by the Russian offensive in the East. But now there was no Second Front in the West to relieve the pressure while the Germans were advancing on Moscow. 'We have had to bear the full weight of the blow,' wrote

Ehrenburg. And at that stage it still sounded like a simple statement of fact, set down without rancour. It was not long, however, before Soviet propaganda was complaining bitterly against the delay of the Western Allies in opening a Second Front, and soon, authoritative voices in Russia were proclaiming that she was fighting the war 'single-handed'.

Ehrenburg had been hammering away at the theme of national resistance. He had urged the men at the front to stand firm at a time when the German war machine seemed in danger of crushing them completely. He had promised the world on their behalf that they would stand firm, and after the first Soviet victories in the winter of 1941–2, he addressed himself to the young men who were then entering the Red Army, telling them to defend the honour of their regiments, to look the enemy straight in the face, and thus to overcome the fear of death. He even had special words of praise for General Vlasov, whom he had met and whom he regarded as a fine and patriotic commander (he was not to know that General Vlasov would later switch to the German side). 'General Vlasov says: "It is not a question of feeling sorry for people. Our duty is to protect them." If you, the new recruits, feel sorry for yourselves under enemy fire, the enemy will simply wipe you out. He who does not protect his comrades is worthless as a soldier. But if you protect your comrades you protect yourselves.'

'Stand firm!' – 'Don't retreat an inch!' – 'Don't feel sorry for yourselves!' – 'Protect your comrades!' – Ehrenburg's articles were studded with such injunctions, because he knew they were what the men at the front wanted to hear. He also knew that if anything he wrote rang falsely or sounded presumptuous he would never be forgiven. In *Julio Jurenito*, he had described how, during the First World War, that pleasure-loving Frenchman, Monsieur Delhaie, pays his one and only visit to the front to admonish the *poilus*: to which one of them replies with a speech full of elaborate obscenities, while another decorates Monsieur Delhaie by putting a dead rat in his buttonhole. To his great distress, Ehrenburg was not allowed to visit the front until the winter of 1941–2, when the Germans began their first retreat. Even more humiliating, during the dangerous autumn of 1941, Shcherbakov, who felt that Ehrenburg's first duty was to write for the West, had him evacuated from Moscow to Kuibyshev, together with foreign diplomats and the staff of the Informbureau. In Moscow, there had at least been the danger of bombing. But when Ehrenburg wrote his articles in Kuibyshev, he was addressing the Russian soldiers from a place of safety miles behind the front line, and he was well aware that a single false note could destroy his credibility. The editor of *Red Star* assured him that the front-line troops eagerly devoured his pieces. 'Perhaps this was because what I wrote did not sound like a leading article', Ehrenburg says in his memoirs. There may be something in this, but it would hardly have sufficed alone. The men of the Red Army must have become convinced that they and Ehrenburg had one thing in common: like them, he was totally absorbed by the war. Many of the soldiers might have preferred to find it less absorbing; but being at the front, they had no choice. Ehrenburg could have avoided the war, but chose not to do so; and in this way he became part of their lives.

In due course the Soviet successes of the first wartime winter and the stalemate of the following spring were succeeded by another near-disaster in the summer, as the German armies renewed their offensive into the Russian heartland and far beyond it, into the Caucasus.

The danger continued to grow, and Ehrenburg tried to convey all he had felt since the day the war began:

> There are no more books, or love, or stars. We shall fight like fanatics, we shall fight like those possessed . . . There is so much hate in each of us that it is difficult to live with it. It burns like fire. It makes us gasp. It does not let us sleep. Hate loads our rifles for us, hate drives us into the attack. We never knew it was possible to hate so much.

The Russian soldier, said Ehrenburg, had only one supreme duty: to kill Germans. He wrote:

> We know all about them, we remember everything, and there is something we have come to understand: the Germans are not human beings. Don't let us waste time on talking, or on feeling indignant. Let us kill! If you haven't killed a German in the course of the day, your day has been wasted. If you don't kill the German, he will kill you. If you can't kill a German with a bullet, kill him with your bayonet! If you have killed one German, kill another: nothing gives us so much joy as German corpses. Your mothers say to you: kill the German! Your children beg of you: kill the German! Your country groans and whispers: kill the German! Don't miss him! Don't let him escape! Kill!

In wartime, it is true, there is a primary duty to kill the enemy. But Ehrenburg had his own way of hammering this lesson home, and in the long run it did him a good deal of harm.

CHAPTER XXV

In Bernard Shaw's *Caesar and Cleopatra*, there is a scene in which a Roman officer explains to Caesar why he has cut the throat of Cleopatra's vicious nurse. He did not do it to punish her, he says (although she deserved to be punished), or as an act of revenge. He did it without malice, as he would have killed a hungry lion that would otherwise have devoured him; and Caesar says: 'It was well done.' One could hardly expect Shaw's (or Caesar's) cool detachment from a deeply-committed Soviet writer in the fraught summer of 1942. The Nazis were a unique phenomenon, and the war against them, if not unique, was at least something exceedingly rare: a truly just war. One can therefore well understand Ehrenburg's sentiments in 1942, when it looked as if nothing could stop the German Armies. 'We shall stop saying "good morning" or "good night" ', he wrote. 'In the mornings, we shall say "Kill the Germans", and at night we shall repeat the same words. There must be only one thought in our minds: how to kill them, how to smash them, how to bury them . . . After that, we shall be able to sleep.'

Then came Stalingrad, and although no one could yet sleep in peace, the tide began to turn. In the following months, Soviet victories vastly outnumbered Soviet setbacks. Yet long after Stalingrad, in late 1943, Ehrenburg still pursued the same line in writing about a real or imaginary German soldier called Karl Peters:

> Let me reiterate what I said in the most nerve-racking days of last summer: Kill the German. He must not stay alive. The earth recoils from harbouring such evil-doers. Kill the German before he sets fire to a hundred more villages . . . kill him for all the things he has done and for all the things he is planning to do. Kill him if your son has been killed, or even if your son is still alive – the German wants his life. If Karl Peters has failed to kill your son, remember this: he will have a son himself, and that son will be an assassin. No son must be born to Karl Peters . . .

A year earlier, it had been permissible to employ all and every means to help stave off disaster. But this was the end of 1943, and as Ehrenburg was to record a few weeks later, Russia had now safely crossed the line that divided catastrophe from ultimate triumph. Of the final outcome of the war, there could now be no doubt. The enemy was being steadily pushed back, although at no small cost to the Soviet Army, a cost which Soviet tactics sometimes made heavier than it need have been. But to hear that no son must be born to Karl Peters was bound to stiffen German resistance. Ehrenburg's wartime writings had not escaped the notice of Nazi propagandists, who now began using them for their own ends. They began to build up the image of Ehrenburg as a sinister Jew who, in league with the Soviet Power, was bent on utterly destroying the German nation. In short, a demoniacal figure who personified the very menace against which Hitler had been warning the world. But Ehrenburg went on undeterred: 'Kill Karl Peters now. Tomorrow he will be gone. He will try to hide, he will disguise himself, he will bleat like a lamb, and shed floods of tears. So kill him now, while he still has a gun in his hand. Your conscience demands it . . .'

As the Germans retreated, Ehrenburg was able to witness the destruction they had wrought and learn of the atrocities they had committed, and to his obsession with final victory was now added another: 'The Germans must be made to pay for what they have done. Justice demands it. They must not get away with it.' His fear that they might indeed get away with it, and his conviction that they probably would, only grew stronger as the end of the war ceased to be a distant dream and could be visualized as a reality. Naturally, there was no danger that Stalin would be moved by any 'bleating' or floods of tears on the part of Karl Peters. But the West might respond. Some soft-hearted people might be impressed by German pleas for mercy, while others, who were already jealous of Soviet achievements, would exploit that sentiment.

At home, Ehrenburg had begun to receive lavish recognition for his work. On May Day 1943 he was awarded the Order of Lenin, the highest Soviet decoration. The year before, he had received the Stalin prize for his novel *The Fall of Paris*, a work that pleased Stalin, but one which in fact was much inferior to the earlier sketches on the fall of France which he had managed to get past the censor on his return to Russia. Apart from that, the war helped him, as it did others, in a number of ways. It is true that Shcherbakov, the propaganda chief, was something of a thorn in his side. But as he says in his memoirs, Soviet writers at that time enjoyed a greater degree of freedom than ever before, if only because the war had compelled Stalin to shelve his plans to put a curb on all creative writing. In 1941, Ehrenburg had been shocked by one of Stalin's remarks. Addressing the troops at the 7 November parade on Red Square, Stalin had said that the enemy was not as strong as 'certain frightened little intellectuals' imagined. Of course, it had demanded courage to hold such a parade in Moscow while the Germans were advancing on the capital. But to hear the Supreme Leader speak so contemptuously of the intelligentsia was somewhat hard to take, when he himself had failed to prepare the country for war and had initially lost his head when it actually started.

Gradually, however, Ehrenburg came to accept what most people accepted: that it was Stalin who was holding everything together. Like many others, as the situation improved, he ascribed this, first, to Stalin's energy, then to his wisdom, and finally, as the tally of Soviet victories mounted, to Stalin's genius. Obligatory praise of Stalin began to creep into his prose pieces, although it did not become a dominant theme. In reality, Ehrenburg may well have believed, or more than half-believed, what he was saying about Stalin: in wartime, faith in the leadership is necessary to ward off thoughts of defeat. So one cannot really blame Ehrenburg for proclaiming, after the battle of Stalingrad, that there was 'an organic link between the name of the city which has become sacred to Russia and the man who has helped our people to carry out its historic mission'. Similar sentiments were being expressed outside the Soviet Union, by people who were under no compulsion to express them, and not even Ehrenburg, for all his prophetic gifts, could foresee that in less than twenty years, the 'sacred' city would be renamed, for reasons of which he would wholeheartedly approve.

Abroad, he had by now achieved international fame. His articles and the texts of his broadcasts circulated widely throughout the countries of the Grand Alliance. In Moscow, he was regularly invited to foreign embassies, where he was treated with due respect, if not with any great degree of warmth. Western diplomats, looking back on their wartime experiences in Moscow, referred to him with little affection: to some, he had even seemed an unpleasant character. It was one thing for him to praise the steadfastness of the British people, but it was another to get on to a friendly footing with Anglo-Saxon embassy officials. There was a further factor which made for a chilly relationship. Right up until June 1944, the Soviet Union conducted a relentless campaign for the opening of a Second Front in

Europe, and it was part of Ehrenburg's duty to further that campaign whenever and wherever he could. In 1942, when the situation in Russia was critical, he had written a reproachful article in the left-wing British newspaper *Reynolds News*: ' "Where is the Seçond Front?" ask the Red Army men. Our men are waiting, mutely and grimly, for the Second Front to open.' There was nothing more hazardous, he warned the Western Allies, than marking time. Earlier, he had welcomed the British air attacks on German cities, but now he said: 'Bombs dropped on Düsseldorf will not change the course of hostilities in the East. Friendship is not sealed in wax but in blood. My fatherland is in danger. It is my duty to tell our Western friends that Britain and America are no less in danger. Neither the Channel nor the Atlantic can replace the Red Army.' He dwelt on this theme at great length whenever he met anyone sufficiently important from the West. In the past his manner had often been arrogant, and one can easily imagine that his behaviour on such occasions was positively aggressive, with a calculated desire to give offence.

Those who resented his manner probably did not realize, however, just how strongly he did feel about the absence of a Second Front. All they saw was the former Bohemian from Montparnasse, now clothed in Soviet respectability, who was rather clumsily obeying orders to plug a certain line. There is no doubt that he was doing what he had been told to do; but that was not the point. The point was that he did not have to be told. To the Soviet Government, and to the Soviet people as a whole, the Second Front was a matter of vital necessity. But to Ehrenburg personally it also meant something else. The delay in starting up operations in the West conjured up too many traumatic memories – memories of all that he had witnessed in France during the First World War, when Russian soldiers had been humiliated without having in any way deserved such treatment. They had fought with exemplary courage, they had shown truly remarkable powers of endurance, and yet they were looked upon by the French with contempt simply because they were Russians – a second-class nation.

It was true that now, in the midst of the Second World War, the Russian soldiers were being praised to the skies by their Western Allies. But had things really changed? Russia was bleeding from multiple wounds, while the West was still training its forces, resting, preparing for battle, carrying out useful but small-scale military operations; doing everything, in fact, except fighting on a scale to match the Soviet effort. Did this not mean that Russian lives were still considered less precious than British and American lives? That Russia was still regarded as a second-class nation? Even the Nazis were not behaving in the West in the way they behaved in the East. In Russia, they had perpetrated horrors that they had not dared to perpetrate in France. Why? Why were the Nazis so much more gentlemanly in France? Was it not a case, even in this unique war, of Western solidarity once more manifesting itself, that nauseating solidarity of the technically advanced and prosperous against the technically backward and poor? Ehrenburg had written about it in *Julio Jurenito*, in the episode in which Jurenito's disciples are captured by the Germans and interned. The American capitalist, Mr Cool, and the smug French bourgeois, Monsieur Delhaie, automatically enjoy certain privileges (they are even allowed to board with the camp commandant's wife), but Alexei Tishin the Russian, Aysha the Negro, and Ehrenburg the Jew nearly starve to death, and are kicked in the stomach whenever the guards are dissatisfied with the behaviour of Mr Cool or Monsieur Delhaie. Ehrenburg was haunted by the idea that this time, too, Western solidarity would triumph and would protect the Germans, who would go unpunished merely because they were a Western nation.

There were times, it is true, when he shook off these gloomy forebodings, and conjured up a different, more radiant vision of the future. He still felt a passionate love for Europe, still looked upon her as the princess that had once been carried off by a god masquerading as a bull. In the grim war years, Europe had suffered another kind of rape, by a beast that put itself forward as a demi-god. But the hour of liberation would come, and now that Russia's decisive role in defeating the Germans had been acknowledged in the West, would she not at long last be able to join Europe as an equal? Ehrenburg certainly longed for that moment, when Russian culture would be recognized as an integral part of European culture. In the past, he said, there had been much prejudice and blindness. But now, prejudice and blindness would be swept away. Mistrust might still extend to words, but not to the blood that had been shed. If, among Russian or English schoolboys, there happened to be at that moment a budding Tolstoy or Shakespeare, it was due to Russia's sacrifices that they would be able to fulfil their destiny.

When the Allied forces entered Rome, Ehrenburg greeted their victory with a rapturously enthusiastic article. Of course, the Italian campaign still did not amount to the opening of a proper Second Front (nor did the Allies make any such claim), so that the fall of Rome could only be regarded as a prelude to more important operations. Nevertheless, wrote Ehrenburg, 'Rome is the first European capital to be freed, and today our hearts are full of joy.' And he went on to recall everything that made Rome dear to him: the ancient Roman virtues, the greatness of the early Christians who had secured the triumph of ideals over brute force, the brilliance and clarity of the Renaissance.

Then came the Allied landings in Normandy, and Ehrenburg's comment reflected his heartfelt relief:

It has begun! How often have we said 'if only . . .' How often have we been told of the *coming* decisive battle. How wonderful that the waiting is over, that the decisive battle has started, that we no longer need to use the conditional or the future tense. In the autumn of 1941, I said that Carthage must be destroyed; at that time, it sounded like tempting fate. Now, even the dullest German knows that Carthage *will* be destroyed.

At such a moment, it even seemed possible to believe in a postwar world of peace and lasting East-West harmony.

But however optimistic Ehrenburg may momentarily have felt, he still could not banish that other, gloomy vision of the Germans being forgiven by the West and saved from the punishment they deserved. For that reason, he said, it was vital that the Red Army should take Berlin. As this happened to coincide exactly with Stalin's own plans, he was able to express his sentiments freely, and by 1944, his old slogan of 'Kill the Germans!' had been superseded by the cry: 'To Berlin!' Once the Red Army reached Berlin, the Germans would no longer be able to escape the consequences of a lost war. On the contrary, they would be made to feel the full humiliation of defeat. Retribution would be exacted, and the Soviet Union would reap the full fruits of victory. The vital need was to get to Berlin as quickly as possible.

In the summer of 1944 the Soviet Armies launched a fresh offensive. 'The Germans know we are moving westwards, that we are on our way to Berlin', wrote Ehrenburg. 'We have a few matters to discuss with them, and there is no way they can dodge the encounter.' He drew a picture of the men of the Red Army – the peasants from Siberia, the miners from the Donbass, the factory workers from Leningrad and Moscow – marching 'along the silent streets of Berlin (it sounded very much like Brecht's line – *Und an jenem Tag wird es still sein am Hafen*), past the ugly statues of the conquerors in the Siegesallee, past the Prussian eagles and the spidery swastikas'. Earlier, he had rejoiced over the liberation of Rome. Now he declared: 'There is a saying that all roads lead to Rome. But today I prefer to say: all roads lead *away* from Rome, they all lead *to* Berlin.' 'The last thing I want to do is to belittle the achievements of our Allies,' he wrote on 22 June 1944. 'Nevertheless, I think it is only fair to say that the battles we fought made the landings in Normandy easier. Some people keep asking: what is the aim of our present offensive? Is it Minsk, or Brest, or Latvia? No, we are advancing on Berlin – and we shall get there!' The same theme recurred a week or so later. 'We are advancing at top speed because we have had our fill of the Germans. We are pushing forward because we are nearing the German frontier. We are hurrying because we have a rendezvous with the most beautiful of all maidens – Justice! We must get to Berlin by hook or by crook, and we shall get there!'

Meanwhile, his articles took on a steadily more threatening note. 'People are asking: what is to be done about the Germans? The answer is simple. The time has come to free the world of this army of the living dead. The world must be cleansed: let the world know this!' And again:

> We have reached the German frontier. It is now the dead – all those who were asphyxiated in the gas chambers and the children of Babi Yar – who are knocking at the gates of Prussia. Woe to this land of evil-doers! Woe to Germany! She will not surrender immediately . . . because she wants to save her filthy skin. But virtue demands that there be no mercy for the German executioners. No just man can forget what the Germans have done. Stalin will not forget. Russia will not forget. We say this as we stand on Germany's threshold – woe to Germany!

At last the great day came when Soviet troops entered East Prussia. 'We are on German soil', wrote Ehrenburg. 'There is pain in our hearts, a pain that has grown steadily over forty months. We have waited for this day and it has come. Now the trial begins. It is not revenge we want. All we want is justice. They will not escape retribution.' By then, Ehrenburg was indeed so obsessed by the idea of retribution that he even found it possible to condone what had reportedly happened to France's most popular singer, Maurice Chevalier, who was said to have been executed by the French

Resistance because he had entertained the Germans during the war. Fortunately, the report turned out to be false. (Maurice Chevalier lived for nearly three more decades, and in 1974, a Soviet magazine published an abridged version of his memoirs, accompanied by a glowing tribute to the 'great artist from the Paris working-class suburb of Menilmontant'.)

Ehrenburg regularly insisted that it was not vengeance he was seeking. 'We do not want to set fire to Goethe's house, nor do we want to burn the lips of German children with prussic acid,' he wrote, 'but we do want to put Germany into a strait-jacket. One can forgive human beings, but not robots. One can forgive what has been done to oneself, but not what has been done to one's children.' By then, the Red Army had reached Maidanek, the first of the major Nazi extermination camps to be discovered (the Western Allies had not yet seen the horrors of Belsen). Ehrenburg's outbursts began to jar on many Western ears, and one English reader, Lady Gibb, rebuked him in a letter for 'instilling something very evil, a desire for revenge after victory is won' in the minds of the Russian people. She urged him instead to use his great talents in the service of Russia for a just and lasting peace, which could never be founded on self-righteousness and feelings of vengeance. Ehrenburg quoted her remarks and repudiated them in a lengthy reply, in which he said that the only way to overcome evil was to fight it. He spoke witheringly of what he called misplaced humanitarianism, and denounced those (although he did not include Lady Gibb among them) who, he claimed, were using it to create a climate of opinion unfavourable to Russia. But whatever lay behind it, whether it was humanitarian sentiment or anti-Soviet intrigue, it was an attitude of mind that drove him to fury. After all, what did these Westerners know of Russia's ordeal? The Americans had loudly condemned the German destruction of the Czech village of Lidice; yet there were thousands of villages in Russia which had suffered a similar fate. There were no Maidaneks in the West; the Nazis were too cautious for that. 'And so the dawn of victory is already being darkened by uncertainty: will these murderers of our children go unpunished?' he asked. 'I respect American honesty and British justice', he went on. 'But when I think of justice, I do not associate it with a judge's wig or a diplomat's dress suit, but with the discoloured shirt and parched lips of the Russian soldier; and it is with our men that justice is marching westwards.'

In the autumn of 1944, a Soviet publishing house brought out a three-volume collection of Ehrenburg's wartime pieces, *The War*, and they were warmly praised by *Red Star*, where most of the articles had first appeared. 'The fourth volume is being written now,' said the paper, 'and Ehrenburg will finish it in Berlin when the city is captured by the Allied forces.' This would indeed have been a fitting apotheosis to his wartime career. Ehrenburg had followed the Red Army on a number of battle-fronts, sometimes while the shooting was still in progress. He had gone with it into East Prussia, and it seemed reasonable to suppose that, having heralded the final conquest of Berlin in such stirring and eloquent terms, he would follow the Army there as well, to be in at the kill, and to wind up the whole gruesome saga with an even more powerful piece than any he had yet written. It turned out, however, that *Red Star* was wrong. Ehrenburg was, in fact, in the process of over-reaching himself; and he did not get to Berlin.

CHAPTER XXVI

After the Soviet troops had entered East Prussia in the autumn of 1944, they found a document in which Ehrenburg's name figured prominently. It was an order-of-the-day issued to the German troops by the commander of German Army Group North. In it, he claimed to have seen a Soviet leaflet in which, as a spur to action, Ehrenburg had told the Russian soldiers that they could regard any German women as their rightful booty. The general's response to this was that German soldiers had a duty to defend their womenfolk, and that any retreat in such circumstances would be a cowardly dereliction of that duty. The matter was reported to Ehrenburg, who quickly produced a riposte in *Red Star*. 'Only a German could invent such filth', he wrote. Soviet soldiers had not fought their way into Germany in search of blondes. It was Germany herself they were after, and 'that blonde hag', said Ehrenburg, '*is* in for a bad time'.

In January 1945, he was given permission to travel to the East Prussian front, and visited a number of places where fighting was still in progress. The Soviet forces had just taken the small town of Bartenstein, and the Soviet commander asked Ehrenburg to assure the staff of the local hospital that they and their patients had nothing to fear. Ehrenburg duly passed on this reassurance to the doctor in charge of the hospital. 'That's all very well,' said the doctor, 'but what about Ilya Ehrenburg?' To which Ehrenburg replied: 'Don't worry, Ehrenburg is not here. He's in Moscow.' In relating what happened in his memoirs, he calls the episode 'ridiculous and disgusting'.

It was indeed ridiculous, and he may have been disgusted by it, but he did not seem to realize that it reflected a harsh reality, and one for which he himself was responsible. Through his wartime articles he had been supplying the Nazi propaganda machine with just the ammunition it needed, and it was now being used inside Germany to considerable effect. Ehrenburg had never written a leaflet of the kind mentioned in the German general's order to his troops. If such a leaflet did exist, it had in all probability been composed by someone in Dr Goebbels's Propaganda Department, perhaps even by Goebbels himself. But the damage had been done. Nearly twenty years later, German right-wing extremists brought up the matter once again, as a protest against the publication of Ehrenburg's memoirs in the Federal Republic. No one had been able to produce a copy of the alleged leaflet, but that did not prevent the protesters from issuing a 'reconstructed text' from memory; from which it was all too easy to see what a valuable propaganda gift Ehrenburg had virtually handed to the enemy on a plate. The 'reconstruction' began and ended with the words 'Kill, kill, kill!' It also had Ehrenburg allegedly proclaiming that *all* Germans were guilty, 'not only the living but those not yet born'. Ehrenburg had not, in fact, put it in those terms. But he had said that Karl Peters's son would be an assassin, and that therefore he must not be allowed to be born. He had denounced German racial arrogance, and had laid the blame partly on German women. In the 'reconstruction', this became a positive injunction: 'Use violence to break the racial arrogance of German women!' And then, between a few of Ehrenburg's genuine utterances, and others which merely sounded moderately plausible, was embedded the phrase: 'Take the German women as your booty!' Ehrenburg could not have issued such an order. On the other hand, he had provided the Nazis with so much other ammunition that it was not difficult to persuade people in Germany that he was quite capable of saying it. And so the harassed German doctor in Bartenstein had asked: 'What about Ilya Ehrenburg?'

It was a warning which Ehrenburg should have taken seriously. He should have realized, from the doctor's anguished question, that he had used the word 'kill!' a few hundred times too often, and that his call for justice sounded more like a wild clamour for revenge. He should also have realized that, at that stage of the war, when Germany's defeat was certain, the only thing that really mattered was to save Russian lives. In short, it was plain that from the moment the Red Army reached the German frontier, and the Germans saw that war was about to be carried on to their own territory, the Soviet side had every interest in inducing German soldiers to surrender. But Ehrenburg continued producing his dark refrain, 'Woe to Germany!', thus encouraging the Germans to resist to the bitter end. At the beginning of the war, he had justifiably ridiculed the idea of trying to undermine German morale by dropping Communist leaflets on the German positions to remind the German soldiers of international working-class solidarity. Some of them might once have believed in it. But Ehrenburg was certain that not even the most persuasive leaflets would stop an army that was scoring major victories and entirely confident of its own strength. No doubt he was right at the time. But now, everything had changed. Now, the Germans were being beaten, and the new situation clearly demanded a new approach. Yet for all his skill as a propagandist, he failed to see it, and went on as before, thus making it that much easier for the German commanders to persuade their troops that nothing could be worse than surrender, that their only hope lay in resistance.

In East Prussia, for the first time since the start of the war, he came face to face with German civilians. Some of them he found pathetic, and others repulsive, but he did not gloat. There is an episode in his memoirs concerning a Soviet major, a Jew, who had been made military commandant of a small East Prussian town. The major's family had been destroyed by the Nazis, and as Ehrenburg puts it, he must have dreamt of vengeance innumerable times. Yet, as town commandant, he soon came to realize that such dreams were far removed from reality, and he did his best to protect the local population. Ehrenburg appears to have had similar feelings himself. But they were in no way reflected in his writings. In *Red Star*, and in *Pravda*, he went on vociferating all the old threats: 'The process of retribution has begun. It will be followed through to the end.' It was as if he were still trying to drive the Russian soldiers onwards towards Berlin almost by a process of hypnosis. 'We think of Berlin as we fall asleep, we think of Berlin as we wake. We think of it when we are silent and we think of it in our sleep. Some people ask: "Haven't you had enough?" Yes, we have had enough . . . and that is precisely why we are in a hurry to get to Berlin. We want to be finished with the Germans.'

Meanwhile, the debate that had begun in the West on the best way to deal with Germany once the war was over filled him with feelings of outrage. A number of people were advocating humane treatment for a variety of different reasons. Some did it because they foresaw the Cold War and the coming East-West struggle over Germany. Others were motivated in a different way, a way which Ehrenburg, having been to East Prussia and having seen that vengeance was not a practical proposition, ought to have understood. Yet he appeared not to take account of this variety of approaches, and scattered his anathemata at many widely different targets. For example, he attacked the Roman Catholic Archbishop of Münster (which was by then in British-occupied territory), but he was no less vehement in his criticisms of the distinguished American left-wing journalist, Dorothy Thompson. To him, every plea for a humane settlement was a further manifestation of the detested solidarity of the 'haves' against the 'have-nots'; and he thought he saw further proof of this when, shortly before the end of the war, German resistance in the West began to collapse. He noted sardonically in *Pravda* that the city of Mannheim had surrendered to the Western Allies by telephone; that a group of German officers had driven in a Red Cross car from Heidelberg to meet the advancing Allies and 'to offer them their services as guides'; and that, according to the BBC, one American unit had advanced fifty kilometres without firing a shot. All this while the Red Army was still battling against fierce German resistance in the East. To Ehrenburg, it was all part of the same old story. In the East, the great blood-letting continued, while in the West, it appeared that the Allies were enjoying a walkover. Ehrenburg wrote:

> I have great admiration for the military prowess of our Allies. I know that they had to break through strong enemy defences, and I am overjoyed that they are achieving great victories at little cost. This is no time for jealousy. But even as we rejoice at this wonderful harvest, it is as well to remember those who planted the seeds of victory. Our British friends who survived Dunkirk must know what kind of an army it was that invaded Russia in 1941.

Then, having paid this slightly sour tribute to Russia's Western partners, he rounded on those in the West who had criticized his own attitude. There were some people, he said, who were already founding societies for the protection of the Nazi hangmen. Such people accused the Russians of planning to sentence all Germans to slave labour. But this was a lie. He wrote:

> All we demand is that those guilty of arson should rebuild what they have burned. One cannot change them by sermons or gifts of tinned food ... The Germans have plenty of lawyers to defend them. But prosecutors and judges will be needed as well. Soviet fighting men are still shedding their blood. On the Eastern Front, cities do not surrender by telephone, and the world still needs the Red Army.

A week later, on 11 April 1945, he published an article in *Red Star* under the heading: 'Enough'. It proved to be an ill-omened title. The article itself was not all that different from much he had written before, except that it was rather more bad-tempered than usual, as the title suggested, and that it also spelt out certain matters in greater detail. 'For a whole year,' wrote Ehrenburg, 'the Press abroad has been discussing the term "unconditional surrender". Yet the real question is not whether Germany will be willing to capitulate. There is no one to capitulate – there is no Germany. There is only a gigantic gang, which dissolves as soon as responsibility is mentioned.' He then turned to the easy victories the Allies were winning in the West, and quoted from a German newspaper which claimed that the German soldiers were fighting both the Bolsheviks and the Americans 'with equal fanaticism'. About this he wrote:

> This must have made our Allies laugh, considering the fact that they captured 40,000 prisoners in one day almost without a fight. Correspondents report that there is only one obstacle hampering the American advance: the roads are clogged with hordes of German prisoners. There is no need to guard them as they march towards the prisoner-of-war camps; and at the camps, the guards' job is not to stop them running away, but to make sure they do not trample each other to death in their rush to get inside . . . People abroad may ask: why, then, did the Germans defend Küstrin so stubbornly? Why are they fighting so furiously in the streets of Vienna? Why did they resist so desperately at Koenigsberg, which is hundreds of kilometres from the front on the Oder? To find the answer, one has to recall the terrible wounds that have been inflicted on Russia. But that is something many people do not wish to hear about, and others want to forget.

He linked this with one of his ritual attacks on 'the protectors of the hangmen'. At the time of the Dreyfus case, world opinion had been incensed by the injustice done to one innocent Jew. In Russia, the Nazis had killed millions of innocent Jews. Yet there were people in the West who had the audacity to criticize Soviet sources for publishing so-called 'exaggerated reports'; and he again vented his wrath on these 'foreign appeasers', as he called them. 'In the West, the Germans are saying "We do not want to play any more", and behaving towards the Americans as if they were a neutral Power.' But the Germans on the Weser were very different from those on the Oder, because in the East, where they had committed countless crimes, they would find no protectors. 'This is why we did not capture Koenigsberg by telephone, and had to use something other than cameras to take Vienna.' He ended on a conciliatory note, however, describing how shattered the Americans were when they saw the evidence of German bestiality. 'The day is near when we shall meet our friends. We shall shake them by the hand – the Americans, the British and the French – and we shall all say "Enough!"' The word 'enough', as Ehrenburg explains in his memoirs, was meant to refer to the appeasers, and to all those who wanted to protect the Nazis.

But this closing paragraph was not sufficient to forestall what was to happen a few days later. On 14 April *Pravda* published a lengthy article under the heading: 'Comrade Ehrenburg Oversimplifies'. It was signed by the new head of the Propaganda Department, G. F. Alexandrov. He was a much less influential person than Shcherbakov, who was by then fatally ill, and whom he had replaced. But in the circumstances, the name of the person signing the article was of little importance, since the brief had quite obviously been dictated by Stalin. By chance, Alexandrov had seen Ehrenburg at an official function the evening before, and had gone out of his way to be nice to him. Clearly, Alexandrov wanted to convey that he was not to blame for what would appear in *Pravda* the following morning. The whole episode was characteristic of the atmosphere at what Khrushchev was much later to describe as 'The Court of Joseph the First'. It must have belatedly occurred to Stalin that, for some time now, Ehrenburg had not been saying the right things. Or he may have decided that Ehrenburg had become too independent, and that, with peace almost at hand, it was time to rein him in. So now, in response to Ehrenburg's presumptuous article entitled 'Enough!', Stalin, through Alexandrov, was saying 'enough!' to its author.

Alexandrov's (or Stalin's) attack focused particularly on Ehrenburg's description of Germany as 'a gigantic gang'. He wrote:

> Comrade Ehrenburg asserts that all Germans are the same, and that they will all have to answer in equal measure for the crimes committed by the Nazis. But it is not difficult to prove that Comrade Ehrenburg's assertion does not correspond to the facts, since it has become especially clear in recent months that different Germans behave differently. Some German officers continue to fight for their cannibalistic regime, but others have thrown bombs at Hitler, or have tried to persuade the German troops to lay down their arms.

Alexandrov then enlarged on this theme, quoting extracts from German newspapers to support his argument that it was incorrect to represent the population of Germany as a single whole. He went on:

If one accepted Ehrenburg's view it would follow that the whole German population would have to share the fate of Hitler and his clique. In this instance, needless to say, Comrade Ehrenburg does not reflect Soviet public opinion. The Red Army has never aimed at exterminating the German people. That would be stupid and senseless. One can understand why the Nazis tell lies about our Army and our State, and scream their heads off about the Red Army allegedly trying to exterminate all Germans. But when such opinions are voiced by genuine anti-Fascists and active participants in the struggle against Nazi Germany, it is strange and impossible to comprehend. The Soviet people has never identified the people of Germany with the ruling criminal clique.

There followed a relevant quotation from Stalin, and another from the Yalta Declaration, to show that there was complete unanimity on this point within the Grand Alliance.

Alexandrov then criticized Ehrenburg's theory that the reason the Germans were surrendering in the West but continued to resist in the East was their fear of Soviet retribution. There was some truth in that, he said, but it was not the whole story. The main reason was that the Nazis were trying to provoke dissension between the Soviet Union and its Western Allies, in order to accomplish by military and political trickery what they had failed to achieve in battle. That was why Koenigsberg had not been captured by telephone and Soviet soldiers had had to use something more lethal than cameras to take Vienna. Ehrenburg's erroneous conclusions merely confused the issue.

It has to be said, however, that if Ehrenburg had tended to oversimplify the German problem, Alexandrov in turn certainly oversimplified Ehrenburg's views, and Ehrenburg felt very bitter about it. He had not made any assertion that all Germans were the same and would have to answer for Nazi misdeeds in equal measure; nor could one deduce from his articles that the whole of the German population would have to share the fate of the Hitler clique. But he *had* been saying the wrong things for some time, and quite apart from the way his writings had been exploited by the enemy, he had also acquired the reputation of a German-hater in the West; and for a number of reasons, this did not suit Stalin at that time. There was, of course, no appeal against Stalin's veto, and nothing more by Ehrenburg appeared in the Soviet Press until the war was over.

Since the war in fact ended only a few weeks later, the punishment was not harsh by Soviet standards. Indeed, it could even be argued that it was scarcely a punishment at all, since Ehrenburg's name reappeared in *Pravda* on 10 May 1945, under an article celebrating the first day of peace. Yet history had moved fast in the weeks preceding that long-awaited day, and to be forced to remain silent at such a time was a severe blow to someone who, throughout the terrible years of war, had strained every nerve to find words which might help to bring victory nearer. For months, Ehrenburg had been saying: 'We must get to Berlin!' Now, Soviet troops had finally reached Berlin, but he had not been allowed to go. Instead of watching the final collapse of Nazi Germany at close quarters, he had been forced by *Pravda*'s grand remonstrance to stand idly by. True, he received many letters expressing sympathy and admiration for all he had done, and *Red Star* was inundated with inquiries as to why there were no more contributions from Ehrenburg in the paper. But those in the Soviet Union who had always looked on him as an alien in their midst were jubilant, and the new editor of *Red Star*, whom Ehrenburg disliked intensely, was cuttingly rude to him after the appearance of Alexandrov's article in *Pravda*. It was left to Leonid Leonov, a writer no less eloquent than Ehrenburg, to thunder against alleged Nazi protectors and appeasers (especially the Vatican) in a manner acceptable to Stalin.

At last, however, the ban was lifted, and Ehrenburg was able to write his article hailing the dawn of a new day of peace. And on this occasion he did manage to say all the right things. He even inserted a couple of sentences to stress that there could be no question of enslaving the German people as a whole: they would be able to live in peace once they had cleansed themselves of the evil of Fascism. It was an adequate piece of writing. But it left an impression that Ehrenburg would have written something infinitely more impressive had he been allowed to write it in Berlin.

It must have been about the time that he wrote his article in celebration of peace restored that he also wrote a poem (not intended for publication) on the theme of victory. It was a poem impregnated with melancholy. He had waited for victory so long, like a man in love, and now, as victory advanced towards him, they did not recognize each other. In his memoirs, he says that when someone later asked him why he had written the poem, he replied that he honestly did not know. But this does not sound very convincing. It seems more likely that either he did not want to discuss his feelings with others, or that he preferred not to analyse them even to himself. He admits that during the weeks of enforced idleness following *Pravda*'s attack on him, he was much preoccupied with the future. He no longer believed that East-West harmony was possible, and he was also worried about what would happen in the Soviet Union itself. He had heard alarming reports of returning Soviet prisoners-of-war being treated as criminals by the Soviet authorities. Yet, in his memoirs, he says that on Victory Day he rejoiced just like everybody else, and thought of Stalin as the architect of victory, not as the man responsible for the Great Terror. It was a natural enough reaction. The day on which the war ended in Europe and the evil nightmare of Nazism finally faded was conducive to wishful thinking. So one must ask why he did not recognize victory as she came towards him. It is difficult to say. But perhaps it was because, having worshipped victory from afar and given her all he could, he now feared that they had both simply done their duty, and there was nothing left but anticlimax. And he could only have felt cruel disappointment at being ordered off-stage just before the grand finale took place.

CHAPTER XXVII

The optimistic vision of the future that Ehrenburg had briefly conjured up in 1944, when the Allied Armies of East and West were advancing simultaneously on Nazi Germany – the vision of East-West harmony and of a Europe in which a liberalized and universally respected Russia would be accepted as an equal – did not seem all that unrealistic at the time. There were people in the West, it is true, who had some insight into what was really going on behind the scenes and who doubted that such a relationship could be established; and there were others who, for ideological and other reasons, did not want to see it established. But ordinary people everywhere had been deeply moved by Russia's ordeal, and were full of admiration for her achievement. It was hard to imagine that the Soviet Union and the Western Powers would revert to mutual hostility after the war, or that inside Russia there could be a return to the terrible purge-trial atmosphere of the distant thirties. By the end of the war, Russia had achieved the supreme distinction: she had become a symbol of sacrifice, courage and endurance.

After the war, this vision slowly faded as the stark outlines of the postwar world took shape. Even so, Russia was treated by and large like a patient convalescing after a severe illness, whose irritating and wilful caprices had to be indulged and forgiven. The fount of goodwill in the West seemed inexhaustible. If hopes of lasting East-West friendship finally had to be abandoned, it was solely because Stalin deliberately chose to crush them. I remember a lecture given by the then diplomatic correspondent of the BBC, Thomas Barman, at the beginning of 1947. It consisted in part of a political fantasy, in which Barman suggested what the leader of an imaginary Parliamentary Opposition in Russia might have said to Stalin and his colleagues on the Government front bench in an imaginary foreign affairs debate in the Supreme Soviet: 'Less than two years ago, we towered above the rest of mankind. We had earned universal acclaim. But now, the world has turned away from us, in disappointment and frustration. How could you let it happen?'

Whereupon there would have been cries of 'Resign!'

To Stalin, however, Western acclaim was infinitely less important than the preservation of the kind of State he was determined to consolidate (at least this seems to me a safe assumption, even though the origins of the Cold War were complex). Furthermore, Stalin was convinced that, in order to preserve such a State, the Soviet Union must withdraw into isolation. As long as it stopped short of starting another war, a hostile West was preferable to a friendly one: Western hostility could be resisted and invoked as a pretext for doing whatever Stalin saw fit to do at home. Western friendliness, on the other hand, if allowed to gain ground in the minds of the Russian people, could only undermine the Soviet regime. But at the same time, contacts with those Westerners who had not lost their admiration for Russia in spite of Stalin's policies should be exploited.

Stalin must have felt that there was a place for Ehrenburg in this scheme of things. Ehrenburg knew how to talk to such people; he spoke the kind of language they understood. This meant that he must be allowed certain liberties, but it was a risk worth taking. Ehrenburg would probably know where to stop, and if, by some mischance, it turned out otherwise, there were always ways of stopping him. Moreover, Stalin needed a propagandist who could skilfully shift the blame for destroying the Grand Alliance in peacetime on to the West, and Ehrenburg seemed to be just the right man for the job. The attitude he had developed towards the West had happened to be inopportune in the spring of 1945, but it was exactly what Stalin needed in 1946. Ehrenburg was angry with the Western Powers: he felt they were taking Russia's sacrifices for granted, and he also felt strongly that Fascism was not dead, but that certain hostile elements in the West were intent on keeping it alive. All this provided scope for righteous indignation, and that was something of which Ehrenburg had always had an ample supply.

In short, he could be expected to co-operate. During the war he had abandoned his formerly ambiguous attitude, had ceased to be Paul, son of Saul, hesitating on his private road to Damascus, and had proclaimed his total commitment to the regime which had eventually led the country to victory. Yet now that the war was over, it was evident that the total co-operation demanded of him would bring him little joy. Once more, he would have to seek refuge in fighting what he regarded as injustice abroad, while manifestly evil things were being done at home. Some of these he managed to disregard. He does not seem to have been much disturbed, for example, by the crudely imperialist manner in which Stalin tried to annex part of Iran and a large slice of Turkish territory; although the argument, advanced on Stalin's orders by two learned Georgian professors, that the part of Turkey claimed by the Soviet Union had been the cradle of Georgian culture and must therefore be united with the Georgian Soviet Republic, could have come straight out of *Julio Jurenito*.

There was one thing, however, that Ehrenburg could not ignore, and that was the renewal of Stalin's campaign against literature and the arts, a campaign inaugurated by Andrei Zhdanov in a notorious speech attacking the poetess, Anna Akhmatova, and the satirist Mikhail Zoshchenko. It did not take long, in fact, before Stalin's plans became clear: literature was to be replaced by third-rate advertising copy, and the visual arts by what Ehrenburg later referred to as 'that cursed photography'. Meanwhile, Russia's cultural isolation was to be reinforced by a relentless drive against so-called 'kowtowing' to the West, coupled with chauvinistic praise for all things Russian, regardless of merit or historical truth. To a man of such wide culture as Ehrenburg, whose tastes ranged from Mexican art to François Villon, this was particularly repugnant. Collaboration in such circumstances could only lead to one result, servility, and Ehrenburg abased himself to accept an almost completely servile role. I say 'almost', because even in that fetid and stifling atmosphere, he did manage to keep a small particle of independence. This was, admittedly, microscopic by Western standards, and therefore went largely unnoticed in the West; but it was fairly conspicuous in Russia, even if it did not provide much comfort to anyone except Ehrenburg himself.

He did not sink into this morass all at once, but was drawn into it gradually. When the war ended, his position seemed weak, and he felt restless and uneasy. Help came from an unexpected quarter: from Alexandrov, the man who had previously rebuked him, at Stalin's behest, for prematurely 'oversimplifying' the German problem. Alexandrov was soon to be in trouble himself, but at that time he was still head of the Propaganda Department, Agitprop. He suggested one day that Ehrenburg should visit the Balkan countries, and write about his trip for *Izvestia*. Ehrenburg accepted, and seems to have vastly enjoyed the experience. As the renowned Soviet wartime propagandist, he was fêted wherever he went. Moreover, his travels in Bulgaria and, especially, in Yugoslavia brought out the latent Slavophile in him. This was a side of his character that Viktor Shklovsky had once noted reprovingly, but Ehrenburg himself was not in the least ashamed of it, particularly in 1945, the year which he regarded as marking a great Slav triumph over German hubris. From the Balkans he went on to Nuremburg, where he watched part of the trial of the former Nazi leaders. He had often dreamed of such a trial, but now, like many others, he merely wondered how the mediocrities in the dock could have come so near to deciding the fate of mankind. His final stop was Berlin. He had dreamed of that, too; or rather of getting there with the troops to witness the downfall of Hitler's thousand-year Reich. Now that Reich no longer existed. It was 'Germany – Year Zero', as the Italian film-maker Rossellini put it, and Ehrenburg found himself looking with fresh eyes at a city where he had spent two years of his life. He wrote:

> I arrived at dusk. I used to know Berlin well. Yet as I wandered through streets that were no longer streets, I failed to recognize the once familiar crossings, and kept losing my way among heaps of rubble. It is difficult to feel sorry for a city which had come to typify arrogance and vulgarity, and those who called themselves the master race deserve nothing but contempt. But I must say this: only a Fascist can delight in a spectacle of destruction. It is Fascism I want to see destroyed and reduced to ashes like Berlin. When it comes to that, stones do not matter: human attitudes do.

A few months later, Ehrenburg was invited to attend a conference arranged by the Association of American Newspaper Editors. At fifty-five, he was at last to see the country about which he had written so many different things at different times. In his early writing, he had anathematized it as the home of the villainous Mr Cool. Then, in a sudden reversal of mood, he had hailed it as the land whose technical achievements were pointing the way to the art of the future. In his later years, he learned something of the United States from certain American writers whom he greatly admired, and now, whenever he was asked what he thought of America, he usually began by paying tribute to Hemingway, Steinbeck, Caldwell or Faulkner.

On his American trip, Ehrenburg represented *Izvestia*, and travelled with two companions: Major-General Galaktionov, as a correspondent for *Pravda*, and the poet and playwright Konstantin Simonov, who went on behalf of *Red Star*. They flew to the United States in the private aircraft of General Bedell Smith, who had just been appointed American Ambassador to the Soviet Union, and were treated as guests of honour. The United States Government invited them to stay on after the editors' conference ended, and to visit any part of the country they cared to see. Ehrenburg chose the South.

Politically, it was a time of transition from the wartime East-West alliance to the Cold War. It was at that point still an undeclared war, but it was already very noticeable, as could be seen from the quarrel over Iran and the resulting acrimonious polemics in the United Nations Security Council (while Ehrenburg was there, the Soviet delegation under Mr Gromyko staged its first walk-out, refusing to take part in the debate), as well as from the tone of the Soviet Press and the attitude adopted by certain American newspapers. But the vision of East-West friendship was too attractive to be abandoned easily. The conference which Ehrenburg attended was addressed by a number of eminent statesmen, including the first UN Secretary-General, Trygve Lie. Later, after he had come to the conclusion that Stalin was playing a ruthless and dangerous game, Trygve Lie was to become the Soviet Government's *bête noire*. But at the time of Ehrenburg's visit, in April 1946, his speech to the assembled editors showed a deep aversion from Cold War attitudes. Trygve Lie said he was not seriously concerned about the dispute in the Security Council. What really worried him was the fact that Fascism and Nazism still represented a threat to peace, and that some countries were still ruled by people with Fascist and Nazi ideas. And this, coming as it did from the highest official of the world organization, must have been music to Ehrenburg's ears. He himself was the best-known member of the Soviet group at the conference, and was given a friendly reception. He was asked if he could do anything to make things easier for Western correspondents in Moscow: some had been refused entry visas, while those already on the spot were beginning to find conditions oppressive. He promised to raise the matter, and added good-humouredly: 'I don't myself issue visas. If I did, I'd probably hand them out very liberally – perhaps that's the reason why it is not my job to issue them.'

He stayed in the United States for two months, and attended innumerable functions, including a rally organized by the Jewish Council for Soviet War Relief, at which one of the Council's leading members, Rabbi Wise, praised the Soviet Union's record in the fight against discrimination (i.e. anti-Semitism). Ehrenburg made many speeches, mainly conciliatory in tone (although he frequently complained about what he described as anti-Soviet slanders in certain American papers), he travelled to Tennessee and Mississippi, and finally summed up his impressions in a 'farewell message' which he wrote for United Press. It appeared in the *New York Times*, under the heading: 'Ehrenburg Finds US Complex'. He had once been rebuked for 'oversimplifying' Germany; now he went out of his way to demonstrate that the American scene was anything but simple. 'This is a great and complex country', he wrote, and went on to thank the Americans for the friendly reception they had given him, for the 'tenderness' of his welcome (his translator must have been very anxious to stick literally to the Russian text), and for its 'cordial straightforwardness'. He praised much of what he had seen: 'the high standard of living, and the thousands of things which make life agreeable'. Unlike some foreign visitors, he did not fall into the error of unfavourably contrasting America's material wealth with a lack of spirituality. On the contrary, he specifically stressed 'the spiritual possibilities of the American people', whom he called 'a young nation with a great future'.

But he had also found plenty of painful contradictions. He had met idealists dreaming of a better world, but he had also met men who in all but name were 'slave-drivers – slave-drivers except for the whip'. In New York, he said, he had seen a box of cigars costing 200 dollars, whereas in Mississippi he had met a family of eight who had only 200 dollars a year to live on. (In a comment, the *New York Times* admitted the disparity, but added that Mississippi was a notoriously backward State, and that Ehrenburg was not giving a true picture of America since a casual reader might overlook the fact that he was talking only of Mississippi.) He expressed his admiration for the 'magnificent universities, the splendid laboratories and museums', but was puzzled by a Lions' Club luncheon 'where full-grown men – manufacturers of suspenders or electric cookers – pretended to be lions and roared on command'. To this, the *New York Times* added a further comment:

> On the whole, isn't it reassuring for a Soviet observer to find that American capitalists, as represented by their businessmen's luncheon clubs, are just a lot of fun-loving adolescents? Lions, Rotary and Kiwanis, together with the idealists Mr Ehrenburg found among us, ought to be a fair indication that the United States is not plotting to drop atomic bombs on the Soviet Union. Nor is there any overwhelming reason to believe that the rulers of the Soviet Union are spoiling for a fight.

The comment must have been intended to set Ehrenburg's mind at rest. His diatribes against 'anti-Soviet slanderers', whom he accused of preparing for a third world war, were clearly Moscow-inspired. But he also appeared to be genuinely shocked by the fact that people in the United States were openly discussing the possibility of a war with Russia. To Ehrenburg, as to many Europeans, it seemed monstrous that such sentiments could be aired only a year after the holocaust of the Second World War. 'I want to shout: "No, such a war is impossible!" ' as he put it in his farewell message. On another occasion, he observed that people in America were talking about another war not in the conditional but in the future tense. It is worth mentioning one typical episode. After Ehrenburg's departure, one of the American papers published an account of his visit to Tennessee by someone who had been present, in which the writer accused Ehrenburg of bad manners for refusing to inspect the Fontana Dam, on the grounds that he was more interested in talking to people (it was, surely, a perfectly legitimate wish, even though his refusal to visit the dam may have seemed discourteous). But a conversation he had with a farmer turned out to be distinctly unpleasant. The farmer told him that all his sons were in the Army: 'They helped to lick the Germans, and if we have to fight the Russians, we'll lick them too!' Although Ehrenburg brushed this aside with a joke, it must have sent a shiver down his spine. The *New York Times*, it was true, had said that the United States had no intention of dropping atomic bombs on the Soviet Union, which at that time had none. But why were Americans talking about a new war as if it were something quite ordinary, and not an apocalyptic event which must at all costs be avoided? Ehrenburg was not, of course, the only one to be shocked by all the talk about war. Unfortunately, the conviction that the United States might resort to war against Russia gained so much ground in Europe over the next two or three years that when Stalin launched his so-called Peace Movement the United States found itself at a serious disadvantage, and the Peace Movement, which was designed solely to serve Soviet interests, was at various times taken seriously by people of unquestionable integrity.

In due course, Ehrenburg published a lengthy series of articles about his American journey in *Izvestia*, and these broadly followed the same lines as his farewell message to the Americans. Once more, he went out of his way to stress that the United States was a complex phenomenon and must not be judged superficially (he seemed genuinely anxious to bring this home to his Russian readers). When the articles became known in the United States, however, they provoked a decidedly hostile reaction. There was no real justification for it, but by then the Cold War was well under way.

Indeed, there was evidence of fresh East-West tension wherever one turned, as Ehrenburg himself found out when he paid a brief visit to Canada. The first question put to him was: what did he think of the Soviet spy network, the first of the major postwar sensations of its kind, which had just been uncovered there? Ehrenburg gave a predictable answer: that the story had been blown up solely in order to poison East-West relations. All the same, he was profoundly depressed. For someone who had once hoped so ardently for East-West understanding, it was not pleasant to see an espionage scandal making nonsense of such hopes.

He had stopped briefly in Paris on his way to the United States, and on his way back to the Soviet Union he stopped there once more, finding it exhilarating to revisit a city which he had always looked on as a second home. In 1944, General de Gaulle had conferred on him the Cross of the Legion of Honour, and he was still officially treated as a distinguished guest – he was highly praised by the French Prime Minister, Georges Bidault, for example, when they appeared together at a public meeting. But in France, too, the atmosphere was changing. Some of the French newspapers attacked him, and he himself wrote a disparaging article about Western tactics at the Peace Conference which was then in session in Paris.

There seemed to be no escape from the growing threat of the Cold War, and in the following year, 1947, it acquired an officially-recognized status. One can argue about the exact date when this happened: whether it was when the Soviet Foreign Minister, Molotov, condemned the Marshall Plan, with its provisions to put Europe back on her feet with American help; or whether it was at the meeting of Communist Party leaders in Poland, at which Zhdanov, speaking on behalf of the Soviet Politburo, branded all Western policies as implacably hostile to the Soviet Union and announced the setting up of the Cominform. What really mattered was that the United States, as the most powerful nation in the West, now ranked as the Soviet Union's Enemy No. 1. So Ehrenburg assumed the role of a leading anti-American propagandist. Although he still occasionally mentioned such names as Hemingway, Steinbeck and Faulkner, he no longer shunned oversimplification, but began to recall everything he had always disliked about America. Indeed, he even reverted to the baleful image of Mr Cool, to whose inventory of destruction, he said, one sinister new element had now been added: the atomic bomb, which 'certain savages' on the other side of the Atlantic would like to use against the Old World.

At the same time he still clung to certain wartime memories, perhaps in order to preserve at least a vestige of integrity. For example, he occasionally produced a few appreciative words about Britain, which some people found surprising, since he had never been thought to have particularly warm feelings for that country. On the anniversary of VE Day in May 1947, he wrote an article which predictably exalted the Red Army and criticized the West, but it also contained this passage: 'When the German Fascists were bombing Coventry, the English showed great steadfastness, and I respect them for it. It was not just the Channel but the courage of her people that saved Britain.' An American correspondent, in a dispatch from Moscow, dismissed this as 'a patronizing pat on the back'. Personally, I believe that Ehrenburg was being sincere, and was trying to show that he still enjoyed a certain margin of liberty, even if a very restricted one. He recognized that Britain had suffered, had known hardship and privation, and was now in the throes of austerity. But America was different. Talking about a new war in the future tense, America was complacent, America was self-indulgent, and – the greatest sin of all – America was rich.

In 1947, he finished his first postwar novel *The Storm* – a vast panorama of Russia at war. It contained the admission (although he refrained from saying who was to blame) that, at the outset, the Soviet side had fought badly. There were references to a number of Soviet citizens who had failed to distinguish themselves when the supreme test came; and there was a detailed description of the massacre of Jews at Babi Yar, near Kiev. Part of the novel was set in France, and some Soviet critics, mindful of Stalin's campaign against kowtowing to the West, thought that Ehrenburg had made the French characters too attractive. It was doubtless for this reason that the members of the Stalin Prize Committee recommended that *The Storm* should be awarded the second prize rather than the first: their function was not to judge works on their literary merit but to anticipate Stalin's wishes. It turned out, however, that Stalin had not only read *The Storm*, but approved of it. 'Why not give it the first prize?', he said.[1]

So Ehrenburg was duly awarded first prize; clear proof that there was an important place for him in Stalin's future scheme of things.

---

[1] According to the writer Alexander Fadeyev, who was chairman of the Stalin Prize Committee, Stalin even spoke approvingly of the love affair between the novel's Soviet hero, Sergei, and his French girlfriend, Mado. Nevertheless, he shortly afterwards promulgated a decree forbidding Soviet citizens to marry foreigners, even from the socialist bloc countries; a good example, one might say, of *proïzvol*, or arbitrary rule, as practised by Stalin, although the English word 'arbitrary' only faintly reflects the force of the Russian. (E. de M.)

CHAPTER XXVIII

Ehrenburg managed to retain that place, in spite of the fact that he was a European at a time when a campaign was being waged against all forms of Western culture. He retained it even when Stalin's anti-Jewish campaign got under way, although at one point a certain Golovenchenko, a member of the Central Committee, exultantly but erroneously announced at a public meeting that he had been arrested.

The decision to launch a campaign against the Jews was carried out by stealth, however, and did not immediately become apparent. For example, when Solomon Mikhoels, the great Soviet Jewish actor and theatre director, who was also the chairman of the Jewish Anti-Fascist Committee, was killed in Minsk early in 1948, this did not at first appear to be a manifestation of official Soviet anti-Semitism. Officially, he was reported to have died in a car accident. It was only later that Mikhoels was posthumously branded as 'an enemy of the people', and it is now generally accepted that he was murdered by the Soviet secret police. Indeed, a Soviet newspaper admitted as much after Stalin's death, laying the blame for it on the head of the secret police, Beria; and Stalin's daughter, Svetlana Alliluyeva, provides further confirmation of it in her book *Only One Year*.

At the time, however, the announcement of Mikhoels's death brought so many glowing tributes to his memory in the Soviet Press from so many prominent Soviet intellectuals that no one could have suspected that the authorities wanted to get rid of him. It was not until eight months later that Soviet Jews were given a direct warning that the Government disapproved of certain tendencies that had been gaining ground among them. It came in the form of an article in *Pravda* on Israel and Soviet Jewry. The article was by Ehrenburg.

The fact that Israel had been created with Soviet support had led some Soviet Jews to assume that they could safely and openly sympathize with the new Jewish State. It was a naïve assumption. Stalin was not about to tolerate anything that smacked of divided loyalty. Even less was he going to allow Soviet Jews to emigrate to

Israel. Yet some of them considered this a practical possibility, and Golda Meir, who was the first Israeli Minister to the Soviet Union, raised the matter with a senior Soviet Foreign Ministry official almost as soon as she arrived. Mordecai Namir, who was counsellor and later chargé d'affaires at the Israeli Legation, relates in his book, *A Mission to Moscow*, how the famous Soviet Jewish film director, Mark Donskoy, seemed to be greatly attracted to Israel at the time, and tried to propagate the idea that it would be in the Soviet interest to permit such emigration, in order to prevent Israel from becoming populated exclusively by Jewish bourgeois elements. Ehrenburg's *Pravda* article was the first of a series of measures designed to combat such heresies – measures which steadily grew more severe.

The article appeared on 21 September 1948, just eleven days after Golda Meir had presented her credentials, and was a somewhat curious composition. Ostensibly, Ehrenburg was replying to a letter he claimed to have received from a German Jewish student who had spent the war in the French Resistance Movement, who was now living in Munich in the American zone of Germany, and who did not like the way people there were behaving towards the Jews. He wanted to know more about the Soviet attitude towards Israel, and whether Israel could solve the so-called 'Jewish Question'. The student may well not have existed. Ehrenburg's 'reply' was clearly based on an official brief, and was addressed both to Soviet Jews and to the Israeli Government; and it provided a good example of the kind of compromise that was now expected of him. It was not that he had been asked to propound anything that he found repugnant; he was supposed merely to say what broadly tallied with his own beliefs. In fact, he seized the chance to raise certain matters which the Soviet authorities would doubtless have preferred him to pass over in silence.

In the first part of the article he addressed himself to Soviet Jews and summarized the official Soviet attitude towards Israel. The Soviet Government had supported the creation of the new State, he said, because it always sided with the oppressed against the oppressors; in this case, the British and their 'Arab mercenaries'. But that did not alter the fact that Israel was a capitalist State, and there was no reason to assume that Israeli capitalists were any better than their counterparts anywhere else. The message Ehrenburg was conveying was thus transparently clear: Soviet Jews must regard Israel as a country with which they could not possibly have anything in common. Then he came to the second part of his argument, which was directed against Zionism. To settle in Israel might make sense for a disillusioned German Jew, who was shocked to see that there were still traces of Nazism in his own country, but it provided no solution for the bulk of Jewry. Jewish communities in various parts of the world differed from one another as much as they differed from other nations. Jewish solidarity, in so far as it existed, was a direct result of persecution, and was therefore an artificial phenomenon; if all people with red hair or turned-up noses had been systematically persecuted in the same way, they, too, would have developed a sense of solidarity. The 'Jewish Question' had been invented by anti-Semites.[1] It could not exist under socialism, and for that reason there was no need for the Jews of Eastern Europe to go to Israel in search of a solution. The primary task was to abolish obscurantist prejudices, whereupon the so-called 'Jewish Question' would automatically solve itself.

All this was plainly what the editor of *Pravda* and his superiors had instructed Ehrenburg to say. But it also happened to be part of his own basic philosophy; it was the view traditionally held by liberals and socialists, Jewish and non-Jewish alike, and indeed by all those who looked upon nationalism as something fundamentally bad. They argued that it was precisely because of their unique although tragic experience in the Diaspora that the Jews could rid themselves of the shackles of nationalism more easily than any other people; whereas Zionism, as a nationalist creed, was endeavouring to put the clock back, and was therefore by definition reactionary. As for anti-Semitism, it would gradually subside and eventually vanish altogether as mankind advanced towards the rule of reason. And it has to be said that to many of those who were not committed to Zionism, all this made perfectly good sense – until Hitler arrived on the scene. At which point even inveterate cosmopolitans and internationalists began to question their previous assumptions: if the twentieth century could throw up such a malevolent figure, by an accident of history which had cost 6,000,000 Jewish lives, could one still believe in progress and the eventual triumph of reason? A Jewish State might have some unpleasant nationalistic features, but it was preferable to Auschwitz. It is impossible to say whether Ehrenburg

[1] cf. Jean-Paul Sartre's *Portrait of the Anti-Semite*, Secker & Warburg/Lindsay Drummond, London, 1948, which incisively develops the same argument within an historical context.

himself ever had such thoughts, either during the Nazi era or in its immediate aftermath. Before then, he had certainly had no sympathy for Zionism. It is true that in 1911, at the age of twenty, he wrote a poem about the despised and rejected Jewish people, a people of outcasts who should return to Jerusalem, and if destined to perish, should die there, where they had once known happiness. But that had been a youthful cry of despair rather than a political programme. In *Julio Jurenito*, he had also produced some arguments which accorded with Zionist philosophy, when he claimed, for example, that full assimilation was impossible, and represented himself, Jurenito's only Jewish disciple, as the eternal outsider. But although he probably believed this to be at least partly true, it was also a pose. The fact is that he relished being an outsider, even an outcast, not because he was a Jew, but because he was Ilya Ehrenburg; and he certainly did not suggest Zionism as a remedy. In a later essay, he had likened the Jews to 'a spoonful of tar' in the broad mass of mankind; an additive that would be missed if it were not there. He had allowed one of his heroes, Lazik Roitshvantz, the prototype of the kindly, long-suffering but never-despairing Jewish scapegoat, to die in Palestine; but for Lazik, Palestine was not the promised land, and he died an unhappy man. Ehrenburg himself had been a cosmopolitan all his life, and in the autumn of 1948, when he wrote his 'reply' to the imaginary German Jewish student, it was natural enough for him to invoke his own traditionally cosmopolitan position.

This being so, one has to ask why Ehrenburg nevertheless still considered himself a Jew. He gave his answer to this question in the same article, although the Soviet authorities would probably have preferred him not to dwell on it. But having said all the things he had been instructed to say, he went on to speak in his own voice, and he spoke with passion. To explain why he regarded himself as a Jew, he quoted his friend, the left-wing Polish Jewish poet, Julian Tuwim, whom he much admired. Tuwim had asked himself a similar question, and had come up with the answer: 'Because of the blood.' This did not mean, however, that he was preaching racialism. As Tuwim put it: 'There are two kinds of blood: there is the blood that flows *through* one's veins, and there is the blood that flows *from* one's veins.' (He meant the blood of those who had fallen victim to anti-Semitic persecution.) He would not call it 'Jewish blood', said Tuwim; Jewish blood was just like any other kind of blood. Nevertheless, it was blood which had flowed *from* Jewish veins, and for that reason, Tuwim, who in the same breath proclaimed his love of Poland and of Polish culture, spoke of himself as a Jew. This also became Ehrenburg's credo. After the death of Stalin, when he could speak more freely, he formulated it clearly: 'As long as there is a single anti-Semite left in the world, I shall proudly call myself a Jew.' By that time, furthermore, he no longer disguised the fact that he was thinking specifically of Russia and not just of the world at large. In 1948, he avoided any such insinuation, but in quoting Tuwim, he also quoted one of Stalin's pronouncements, to the effect that anti-Semitism was a barbarous phenomenon. It was his way of jogging the Soviet leader's memory.

In spite of this, Ehrenburg's article, and his behaviour in the months that followed, gave rise to much controversy and criticism. Many Jews, especially in Israel, were angered and shocked when they saw what he had written in *Pravda*: this was not what they had expected of the man who, during the war, had spoken so movingly of the martyrdom of the Jewish people. Many looked upon the article as a servile exposition of the official line; it did indeed reflect the official line, and much of Ehrenburg's life during that period was one of almost, although not quite absolute, servility. On the other hand, the Russian Jewish writer, Grigory Svirsky, whose book, *Hostages*, is a major work on the plight of the Soviet Jews, took a different view. The *Pravda* article, he said, provided indisputable evidence that 'no matter how clouded the horizon, Ehrenburg always struggled against the muddy tide, and always did what he could'. Indeed, if one looks at it dispassionately, it is clear that Ehrenburg used the columns of *Pravda* not only to condemn anti-Semitism in general, but also to restate his own Jewishness; and this at a time when the horizon was becoming exceedingly clouded, and the tide muddier than ever. Some people still felt that he should have refused to write the article altogether, since he must have known what a deeply depressing effect it was bound to have on Soviet Jews. Presumably, he realized this only too well. Yet to encourage the euphoria which had spread among Soviet Jews after the creation of the State of Israel would have been an act of criminal folly. Soviet Jews had to be warned, even though many were impervious to such warnings.

Two weeks later, on 6 October 1948, Golda Meir and other members of the Israeli Legation went to the Moscow Synagogue to attend the Jewish New Year service. Thousands of Jews mobbed them outside the building, and later formed a procession to accompany them part of the way back to the Legation. It was a spontaneous demonstration by Soviet citizens of their attachment to a foreign non-Communist State; and *that* was something that Stalin must have considered impossible – before it actually happened.

But Ehrenburg's warning was also addressed to the Israeli Government, as a clear and unambiguous affirmation that there would be no Soviet support for Jewish emigration. Mordecai Namir took the point, and reported to his Government in appropriate terms. Some two months later, in late November 1948, he met Ehrenburg at a diplomatic reception. It was on the same occasion that the film director, Mark Donskoy, approached Ehrenburg and floated his idea that, if Soviet Jews were allowed to emigrate to Israel, they would provide a useful counterweight to the influence of the Jewish bourgeois elements in the population. Ehrenburg's reply to this followed roughly the same pattern as his *Pravda* article, although he expressed it even more forcefully. First of all, he stressed his own internationalist (i.e. anti-Zionist) position. He then told one of his favourite stories, an anecdote about the wise counsel given by the Sephardic Rabbi Shem-Tov to King Pedro the Cruel of Castile in the fourteenth century (his purpose may well have been to show that, although opposed to Zionism, he knew a great deal about Jewish history and remained interested in all things Jewish). Finally, he told Namir that, although he was not a diplomat, he would like to offer the Israeli Government some friendly advice: it should stop trying to tempt Soviet Jews with the lure of Zionism and leave them in peace. If it did not, it would eventually run into strong opposition from the Soviet authorities, and from Soviet Jews themselves. It was his way of saying that serious trouble lay ahead, and he repeated his warning before leaving the reception.

On the Government level, there was no immediate deterioration in Soviet-Israeli relations. But for Soviet Jews, trouble had already started. In November 1948, Stalin dissolved the Jewish Anti-Fascist Committee; in the following month, a number of its leading members were arrested, and the arrests continued into 1949.[1]

[1]The Jewish Anti-Fascist Committee had been created not long after the German attack on the Soviet Union in June 1941, with the purpose of rallying international Jewish support and aid, and Ehrenburg was one of its more prominent members, although his manifold other activities probably limited his role in its activities. However, he was certainly well acquainted with many of his fellow committee members. In his memoirs, there are numerous references to Mikhoels, and a lengthy appreciation of the life and work of Perets Markish.

Among those detained were the writers Bergelson, Fefer, Kvitko, and the outstanding Yiddish poet Perets Markish, whom Ehrenburg held in high esteem. Three and a half years later they were shot. To begin with, the arrests took place in great secrecy. But on 28 January 1949, the Soviet Press published an open attack on a group of theatrical and literary critics, and it was this that marked the start of Stalin's campaign against so-called 'cosmopolitanism'. It was, in fact, the first official anti-Jewish campaign in Soviet history, since it soon became clear that the term 'cosmopolitan' referred to any Soviet Jew who had retained or acquired a sense of kinship with Jews in the non-Communist world, and especially in Israel.[1]

Ehrenburg himself was not directly affected. He was by nature a true cosmopolitan, he had no ties with Israel, and although he had proudly emphasized his own Jewishness, he had done this mainly as a challenge to the anti-Semitic faction in the Soviet Establishment. Yet the campaign did not leave him entirely unscathed. First, there was his long-standing reputation as a cosmopolitan. Second, he had written a sympathetic account of the misfortunes of Lazik Roitshvanetz (even if this had never been published in the Soviet Union). Thirdly, during the war, his name had become a talisman to Jews all over the world. And finally, he had been a prominent member of the Jewish Anti-Fascist Committee, whose leaders were now under arrest. And so, from early 1949 onwards, when it became clear that the anti-Jewish campaign was to be pursued in earnest,

[1]The following passage from an authoritative work on the position of Jews in the Soviet Union indicates the scale of Stalin's anti-Jewish campaign: 'In November 1948, the Jewish Anti-Fascist Committee was dissolved and its newspaper *Einheit* closed down ... The really crushing blow was delivered in the same year. The MVD [Ministry of Internal Affairs] arrested all the leading Jewish personalities – writers, poets, artists, musicians and officials in the Government and the Party throughout the country. The entire élite was eliminated, leaving the Jewish minority leaderless and helpless. Within a few days 431 Jewish intellectuals were arrested and put in chains – 217 writers and poets, 108 actors, 87 artists and 19 musicians. The majority perished in concentration camps. Only a few returned alive ...' Joel Cang, *The Silent Millions, A History of the Jews in the Soviet Union*, Rapp & Whiting, London, 1969.

It is perhaps worth noting that while I was working as a foreign correspondent in Moscow in the early 1970s, two or three Soviet Jewish friends expressed their fears to me that the Government was about to make further mass arrests of Jews, for whom special camps were being prepared in Siberia and Soviet Central Asia. There was, of course, no official hint of any such move, and the rumours circulating were almost certainly false. But the fact that they could circulate at all showed that the fears engendered by Stalin's anti-Jewish campaign in the late forties, and the so-called 'Doctors' Plot' which preceded his death, were far from being laid to rest. (E. de M.)

Soviet editors thought it prudent not to publish his articles, and most of his acquaintances, apart from a handful of close friends, decided it would be wise to break off all personal contact. It was one of those precautionary moves they had become used to taking 'just in case'; a phrase which has had a deeply corrupting effect on Soviet society. Moreover, Ehrenburg soon learned that Soviet sub-editors had been instructed to delete all references to him in the Press. He said later that he expected the security police to come for him at any time. Then it came to his ears that Golovenchenko, of the Central Committee, had jubilantly informed a public meeting that he had been unmasked as an enemy of the people and was already under arrest.

According to Grigory Svirsky, Golovenchenko was a notorious Moscow Jew-baiter, who hated Ehrenburg and had long been hoping for his downfall. His jubilation was misplaced, but it was an ominous sign. Ehrenburg decided there was only one thing to do: to write personally to Stalin in order to clarify his position. He had earlier asked a senior Party official, Pospelov, to make inquiries on his behalf, but had received no answer. On receipt of Ehrenburg's letter, Stalin himself reacted immediately. He must have been infuriated to learn that an underling had dared to announce an arrest without first clearing the matter with him, and he instructed his deputy, Malenkov, to look into it. Malenkov telephoned Ehrenburg and asked, rather fatuously, where the story had originated. To which Ehrenburg sensibly replied: 'That's what I wanted to ask you!' The contents of their conversation immediately became known to all literary Moscow, and according to Svirsky, Golovenchenko was shortly afterwards taken off to hospital with a heart attack. Ehrenburg's telephone, which had been almost silent for weeks, now scarcely stopped ringing as Soviet editors fell over themselves to assure him they were printing all his articles they had previously been holding back, and to ask for more.

Ehrenburg was safe – for the time being. But as his memoirs make plain, during the following months he lived through a nightmare as bad as anything he had experienced before: as bad as when he had watched the Nazis entering Paris, or when he had been forced to attend the trial of his old friend, Bukharin. He had survived on earlier occasions because Stalin had found him useful. And he survived again now, as the anti-Jewish campaign exacted its toll, because Stalin once more needed his services. In April 1949, a Soviet-

sponsored World Peace Congress was to be held in Paris, and
Ehrenburg was to be one of the principal speakers.

His brief was to convince as many people in the West as possible
that Stalin's foreign policy was a policy of peace. But in the same way
as, seven months earlier, he had seized the opportunity offered to
him by *Pravda* for proclaiming that he was a Jew and would always
regard himself as a Jew, he now decided to refer obliquely to the
menacing developments he was witnessing inside the Soviet Union.
He prepared his speech for the Congress before leaving Moscow, and
deliberately included in it this passage: 'There is nothing more
repulsive than racial or national arrogance . . . Nations have always
learned, and will always learn, from one another . . . One can respect
national peculiarities and at the same time reject national isolation
. . .' No doubt as he wrote this, he fondly thought that he was
administering a thinly-disguised rebuke to the Soviet leadership for
its anti-Jewish campaign; but he had failed to take account of Stalin's
cunning. Before allowing Ehrenburg to leave for Paris, Stalin asked
to see the draft of his proposed speech, and when he read the passage
condemning racial arrogance, he did something totally unfore-
seeable: he marked the passage, and wrote in the margin: 'Bravo!'
Here was indeed a poisoned gift. It was praise, it was a promise of
further protection, and at the same time it was a sardonic reminder
that Ehrenburg could not escape his clutches. Of Ehrenburg's
supposedly shrewd gesture of defiance, nothing remained. But then,
Stalin was a past master at inflicting humiliation.

In his memoirs, Ehrenburg says that as a result of this episode, he
arrived in Paris in such a deep state of depression that he had only
one thought: how to find an excuse to be sent home, so that he would
not have to address the Peace Congress. His French Communist
friends, the poet Louis Aragon and his Russian-born wife Elsa
Triolet, had been alarmed by the news of the 'anti-cosmopolitan'
campaign, and kept asking him to explain what it was all about. 'I
could not tell them', Ehrenburg writes in his memoirs; by which he
plainly meant that he dared not tell them. He feared that if he
revealed the truth, it would be tantamount to sentencing himself to
permanent exile: he would have had to stay in France as an *émigré*,
and this was not at all what he wanted. In the long run, what helped
him was a vituperative article in a French newspaper, which
showered him with obloquy. This seems to have acted as a much-
needed tonic. In effect, he said 'Let's drink to our enemies!' and set

aside his earlier qualms about appearing before the Congress. At this point it has to be said that the Cold War was not always fought very skilfully or intelligently in the West. The Soviet Government was rightly condemned for a number of odious practices, but it was also not infrequently blamed for things it had not done. The more crude forms of anti-Soviet propaganda were largely counter-productive. They made people like Ehrenburg feel patriotic, and when, on top of this, there was widespread talk of a new world war, he found it easy to set his doubts aside.

So he duly made his speech to the Congress, including the passage condemning racial arrogance (he could hardly have omitted it, once it had received an enthusiastic imprimatur from Stalin in person!). Years later, after his memoirs had appeared with a description of this episode, some of his Jewish critics, especially those who had been close to the victims of the anti-Jewish campaign, expressed the view that a man of his experience ought to have anticipated Stalin's 'Bravo!' Others believed, however, that this was exactly what he *had* done: in other words, that he had inserted the crucial passage, not as an implied rebuke to Stalin, but in order to please him, and to mislead the outside world into thinking that there could not be any anti-Semitism in the Soviet Union. There is a sardonic endorsement of this view by Ester Markish, widow of the poet, Perets Markish, who was arrested in 1949 and executed in 1952, when she says in her book *Le Long Retour*: 'Inside the country, obscurantism was triumphant and all-powerful, but abroad – for export only – Ehrenburg the Jew was proclaiming the virtues of internationalism. How could one fail to say "Bravo"? Bravo indeed!'

One can understand her reaction. Nevertheless, I myself believe that Ehrenburg was being sincere. He had sought refuge in a very human delusion: he had imagined that if he stated publicly what was in theory one of the cardinal principles of the Soviet State – that anti-Semitism was an abhorrent phenomenon – he would automatically be registering a protest against the *de facto* repudiation of that principle. I also believe that he was genuinely horrified when he realized that, despite his velleities at rebellion, Stalin, by a mere stroke of the pen, had reduced him to the status of any other Soviet sycophant or lickspittle.

CHAPTER XXIX

Ehrenburg's behaviour during that period led to a number of charges being made against him. But the most serious charge of all only came to light much later, when Stalin was already dead. It stemmed from an encounter in 1950 between a foreign journalist, who had been imprisoned in Russia, and the Jewish writers Bergelson and Fefer, who were then also being held in prison.[1] In a conversation, they allegedly told him that Ehrenburg had testified against them and against other members of the Jewish Anti-Fascist Committee, and was therefore partly responsible for their present predicament. The journalist was eventually released, and published an account of his experiences in an Israeli newspaper. This was then picked up by *Le Monde*, which on 26 September 1957 also published Ehrenburg's reply.

The reply was phrased with considerable caution. Ehrenburg referred only to Beria's arbitrary actions, not to Stalin's; and he claimed that the tragic fate (i.e. presumably the execution rather than the initial arrest) of the Jewish writers, some of whom, he said, had been his intimate friends, had not become known until they were posthumously rehabilitated. But his main point was that a serious newspaper like *Le Monde* should not have repeated insinuations based on alleged statements by people who were no longer alive and could therefore neither confirm nor deny them. In an accompanying comment, *Le Monde* observed that it came down to a question of one man's word against another, and if one wanted to be impartial, one

[1]David Bergelson was a prominent writer and critic, author of a number of scholarly works, including *Three Centuries of Yiddish* (Vilna, 1926). Colonel Itzhak Fefer was best known as a Yiddish poet. He was for long an ardent admirer of Stalin, and in 1943 he accompanied Mikhoels on a mission to London and New York, seeking material aid for the Soviet war effort from British and American Jewry. Fefer and Bergelson were among a group of twenty-four prominent Soviet Jewish writers and poets arrested in late 1948. Fefer was the only one who broke down and 'confessed' during their trial, which followed several years in Soviet concentration camps. One member of the group went mad and died in an asylum. The others were all executed in early August 1952.

must attach equal importance to both.

The matter rested there. But a few years later the same accusation was made against Ehrenburg, this time in very different circumstances, and by a very different person: a Soviet woman writer called Galina Serebryakova, whose two husbands had both perished under Stalin, and who had herself spent twenty years in Siberia before being finally rehabilitated by Khrushchev. In December 1962 she was present at a meeting between Khrushchev and a group of Soviet writers and artists, at which Khrushchev, who was in a belligerent mood, argued fiercely about art and artistic freedom. Galina Serebryakova sided with the reactionaries. But she also made a personal attack on Ehrenburg, who was defending the liberal cause; and as often happens, especially in Russia, her attack had little or nothing to do with the subject under discussion. In short, she accused Ehrenburg of having been Stalin's accomplice, and of having betrayed certain of his Jewish colleagues; and she further claimed that confirmation of this could be obtained from Stalin's former private secretary, Poskrebyshev. At the time, most people assumed that Poskrebyshev was dead, but according to Serebryakova, he was still alive, and working on his memoirs in a sanatorium where she herself had spent a period of convalescence.

I had an occasion to discuss this episode with some of Ehrenburg's Soviet friends, who dismissed Serebryakova's allegation as malicious nonsense, one or two of them adding sadly that suffering does not always make people wise. The mention of Poskrebyshev's name certainly did not make the story any more credible, since Stalin's former secretary was anything but a trustworthy source. Nor could one unhesitatingly accept what Bergelson and Fefer were reported to have told their journalistic acquaintance in prison. Much more substantial proof would have been needed to back up a charge of betrayal, particularly as the Jewish Anti-Fascist Committee had not been a harmonious body. Some of its members met a tragic and inhuman fate, but this does not alter the fact that not all of them liked each other; and Ehrenburg is said to have disagreed with them about the role the Committee could or should play in peacetime. I also discussed the matter with some Soviet Jews who later emigrated to Israel, including Grigory Svirsky. Svirsky had not previously heard of Serebryakova's accusation, and was indignant when I told him about it. Ester Markish, too, told me she did not believe a word of it, although, as can be seen from her book, her judgement of Ehrenburg's behaviour under Stalin was otherwise extremely severe.

Many Soviet Jews, and in particular the friends and relatives of those arrested, were sharply critical of Ehrenburg. But on others, the fact that he remained in favour with the authorities during the anti-Jewish campaign paradoxically had a reassuring effect. The Israeli diplomat, Mordecai Namir (who incidentally took a charitable view of Ehrenburg's conduct) relates a conversation he had in the spring of 1949 with a Soviet Jewish intellectual who had a quiet job in a museum. He told Namir that he and his friends were at first deeply depressed by what was happening, but felt much better when they learned that Ehrenburg had gone to Paris to attend the Peace Congress: things could not be all that bad for Soviet Jews, they thought, as long as Ehrenburg was allowed to speak abroad. I myself found a similar reaction in a letter I had from a correspondent in Israel. He wrote:

> Whenever an article by Ehrenburg appeared during the anti-cosmo-politan campaign we felt that things could not be all that bad. Later, we read his novel, *The Ninth Wave*, with great delight, not because we couldn't see that it was muck (we saw that all right), but because it showed that Ehrenburg's books continued to be published. And when, in 1952, the worst year of all when people could hardly breathe, Ehrenburg was awarded the Stalin prize, that was a big boost to our morale.

Basically, of course, what made Ehrenburg suspect in the eyes of so many people was one simple but striking fact: the fact that he had survived. The question of *how* he managed to survive is obviously crucial. But it should not, in my view, be examined purely in the context of the anti-Jewish campaign. It is true that both Ehrenburg's Jewish friends and detractors seem to agree that Stalin's main motive in employing him was precisely the fact that he was a Jew; in other words, he was supposed to serve as a living refutation of any charges of anti-Semitism that might be levelled against the Soviet regime. Ester Markish takes the view in her book that Ehrenburg played a disgraceful role, by acting as a screen for Stalin's anti-Semitism. In short, the mere fact that he was allowed to travel abroad was a trick designed to pull wool over the eyes of Western observers and to conceal from them the true position of Jews in the Soviet Union.

To what extent were such strictures justified? It certainly cannot be denied that, whether he wished to or not, Ehrenburg did act as a screen. It could hardly have been otherwise. In those days, most Western Communists were almost totally subservient to Stalin, and whenever accusations of anti-Semitism were brought against the Soviet Government, they invariably answered in chorus: 'What about Ehrenburg?' So, in that sense, Ehrenburg did play a disgraceful role. It must be remembered, however, that at that time, most people in the Soviet Union, especially public figures such as officially recognized writers, were obliged to play a more or less disgraceful role in some form or another, until they in turn became victims of the regime; and not unnaturally, the overwhelming majority were not eager to accept that fate. Under Stalin, it would have been useless to protest against conditions at home in the hope that things could be changed by pressure from abroad.

Still, a dark cloud hangs over Ehrenburg's activities at that period. One may disregard the accusation, as many of his critics have done, that Ehrenburg betrayed other Jews, because it is unverified. One may feel, as I do, that his *Pravda* article on Zionism in September 1948 was a necessary warning to Soviet Jewry and should not be held against him. One may believe, as I do, that what he said about racial and national arrogance in his speech to the Peace Congress in Paris was a genuine cry from the heart, and not a smokescreen designed to mask the true nature of Stalin's policy. One may accept all this; but unfortunately, it does not mean that there was nothing blameworthy in Ehrenburg's behaviour at the time. I wish it were otherwise, but the facts speak differently.

To put it crudely: did he crawl and lie more than was absolutely necessary for a man in his position? In the opening chapter, I mentioned the press conference he gave in London in 1950, during which, in referring to the anti-cosmopolitan campaign in the Soviet Press, he made a remark that seemed almost inconceivably bold in the mouth of a Soviet citizen: 'I am not going to claim that no stupid articles ever appear in my country – it is more difficult to get rid of idiots than of capitalists.' It was also on that occasion that he was asked about the fate of the Soviet Jewish writers, Bergelson and Fefer (I am fairly certain that they were the only ones mentioned by name, not Markish). It was not a rhetorical question, nor was it raised simply to put Ehrenburg in an embarrassing situation. In those days, people really did want to know what was going on. It was almost impossible to obtain any reliable information from the Soviet Union. There had been rumours about the arrests of Jewish intellectuals, but no one could be certain whether this was true or not.

Ehrenburg's reply to the question was a lie. One can argue that he had no alternative, unless he was prepared immediately to ask for political asylum in Britain. Even if he had simply prevaricated, or changed the subject, as he did when asked an awkward question about the Korean War, it might have been forgivable. But in speaking of the Jewish writers, he did not merely prevaricate or dodge the issue, he produced a resounding lie with an air of utter conviction. He said he had not seen Bergelson or Fefer for two years (which meant, in effect, since the dissolution of the Jewish Anti-Fascist Committee). He also added that, in any case, he used to meet them only rarely, since neither of them belonged to his circle of close friends. And it was at that point that he produced an outright and unforgivable lie. If anything unpleasant had happend to them, he said, he would have known about it. He was talking in French, and I can still hear his words: 'Si quelquechose de mal [or de fâcheux – I don't remember exactly which] leur était arrivé, je l'aurais su.' This was not just a lie (he had indeed heard about the arrests, as his memoirs reveal), it was a lie so phrased as to carry the stamp of truth. It sounded so plausible, and, alas, so reassuring. Of course, people thought, if anything had happened to the Jewish writers, a person like Ehrenburg *must have known about it*, and since he had heard nothing, this must mean that Bergelson and Fefer, and presumably all the other Jewish intellectuals, were still at liberty: probably depressed, probably no longer able to write what they wanted, but at least not in gaol. After all, it might have been the case. The anti-cosmopolitan campaign, the dissolution of the Jewish Anti-Fascist Committee, the closure of the Yiddish theatre and the Yiddish publishing house in Moscow, all these were disagreeable developments, to be sure, but they did not necessarily imply that the cream of the Soviet Jewish intelligentsia had been sent to the concentration camps, where they were later shot. At a subsequent press conference in France, when asked about Bergelson, Fefer, Markish and others, Ehrenburg is supposed to have replied: 'I had nothing to do with them and I know nothing about them.' If accurately reported, this answer, too, was a crude and heartless lie (all it meant was: 'Leave me alone!'). It was therefore, in a sense, not as bad as the lie he told in London, which had been deliberately decked out to sound like the truth.

CHAPTER XXX

For Ehrenburg in the early fifties, there thus began a period of servility, punctuated by sporadic flashes of independence. It is true that these manifestations were so slight as to be imperceptible to the outside world. But they were noticed inside Russia: in a closed society people learn to be observant.

On his sixtieth birthday in January 1951, at a gathering arranged in his honour, Ehrenburg paid an emotional tribute to the *Vozhd*, the Supreme Leader, Stalin:

> From the bottom of my heart I want to thank the man who has helped me to write so much of what I have written, and who will help me in future, as he helps us all, to write those things of which I am still only dreaming. That man was with me at the front, and at the great meetings held in defence of peace. He was with me in the stillness of the night, as I sat poring over a sheet of paper in my room.

In delivering himself of this panegyric, he did not refer to Stalin by name, but he had named him on other occasions. 'If I now open my old books only rarely,' he said in the same speech, 'it is not because I am ashamed of them, or because I want to repudiate them; it is simply because I have no time. I want to write more.' It was a tortuous attempt to convey to those who were capable of grasping the point that he still felt affection for *Julio Jurenito*. Doubtless, as he composed his speech in the stillness of the night, he was keenly aware of Stalin's invisible presence. But in spite of the passage I have just quoted, it is doubtful whether he was thinking of him with gratitude. Rather, he must have been wondering how much he could still get away with, with Stalin looking over his shoulder.

His sixtieth birthday was celebrated in style. One of the less prominent critics did sound a jarring note, by referring to that period in the past when, as he put it, Ehrenburg had 'not yet managed to understand the true nature of Soviet society', and had 'failed to discern the radiant vistas that lay ahead'. But the same critic, presumably in order to show that these failings had now been overcome, also quoted from one of Ehrenburg's strictures on cosmopolitanism (an uncharacteristic one for him), in which he had described it as 'a world in which things lose their shape and colour and words become meaningless'. Meanwhile, various prominent figures in the Soviet literary Establishment paid tribute to the work he was doing for peace, and as a birthday present, the Writers' Union offered to republish a number of his books. For this he was paid handsomely, and built a *dacha*, or country cottage, out of the proceeds. But he also came up against one of those tragi-comic stumbling blocks which all Soviet writers encountered sooner or later, quite apart from the near-impossibility of getting anything worthwhile into print. For the new edition of his works, only those were selected which had originally been approved by Stalin. Yet even these were now found to contain passages which, it was feared, might displease Stalin in retrospect, and the publishers insisted on various deletions and amendments.[1] They discovered, for example, that in Ehrenburg's novel, *The Second Day*, which he had written after coming to terms with the Soviet regime, there was a mention of rape. It was only a passing mention, not a detailed description, but it had to go. They also discovered in the same book what they felt to be a superabundance of 'non-indigenous' (i.e. Jewish) names, and demanded that some of these be changed. Admittedly, these were merely pinpricks: far worse things were happening all over the Soviet Union. Besides, the Jewish characters in *The Second Day* were all purely subsidiary: it did not really matter whether they were Jewish or not. Understandably, however, Ehrenburg found such demands particularly humiliating, and did his best to resist them. As it happened, *The Second Day* was not republished until after Stalin's death, which may account for the fact that only one Jewish name had been altered: a certain 'Comrade Zak', who is mentioned just once, had been replaced by an indigenous-sounding 'Comrade Zaitsev'. Later, when yet another, much fuller, edition of Ehrenburg's works appeared (it even included an expurgated version of *Julio Jurenito*), 'Comrade Zak' was restored, at the author's insistence, to his rightful place.

In the early 1950s, out of a slavish devotion to the Stalin regime which to others seemed incomprehensible, Communist intellectuals in the West still either did not see, or wilfully refused to see, what was

---

[1] For a detailed account of some of Ehrenburg's battles with editors and publishers, and his appeals against censorship, see Appendices.

actually going on in the Soviet Union. But Ehrenburg was in a different position: he did know what was going on. As a leading member of the Soviet-inspired World Peace Movement, he could to some extent seek refuge in the magic word 'Peace'. But he was dismayed by other developments: by the expulsion of the Yugoslavs, who on Stalin's orders were now branded as 'traitors', and by the opprobrium heaped on men like Hemingway and Sinclair Lewis by second-rate Soviet propagandists, who regarded them as insufficiently pro-Soviet. Life was made somewhat more bearable by the fact that he was able to travel abroad, where he could talk to such people as the poet Louis Aragon, the scientist Frédéric Joliot-Curie, and other members of what a former French Communist, Dominique Desanti, who was then active in the Peace Movement, once called *La Très Haute Société Communiste* – or THSC for short. Life was also made easier for him by certain Cold War attitudes on the other side. Every time someone of note in the West spoke about a coming transition from a Cold to a Hot War, implying that this was inevitable or even desirable, it gave Ehrenburg another pretext for writing yet another stirring article about the Peace Movement. It must also have given him a kind of comfort to learn that the American authorities had refused to give the singer Paul Robeson a passport to travel abroad: at least here was proof that the Soviet Union was not alone in adopting such obstructionist practices. In short, every little bit helped. But unlike Western Communists, who voluntarily put on blinkers, Ehrenburg could not seek refuge in ignorance. To put on such blinkers, one must first be a believer. But although he was fully committed to the Soviet cause, Ehrenburg remained in many ways an inveterate sceptic. When the writer Alexander Fadeyev, the leading figure in the Soviet literary Establishment, went abroad and discussed the Soviet Government and its policies with *La Très Haute Société Communiste*, he always said 'we', even in private conversation. Ehrenburg, on the other hand, according to Dominique Desanti, always said 'they'. The use of this pronoun to describe those in power is common enough in most countries. But Soviet citizens are officially supposed to 'love' their government and to make a permanent show of their devotion. In other words, they are not supposed to refer to their rulers as 'they', and especially not when they are visiting a foreign country and mingling with members of the local Communist hierarchy.

But outside the exalted ranks of the THSC and the narrow circle of non-Communist intellectuals in the Peace Movement, Ehrenburg, on his visits to the West, now faced sharper hostility than he had ever encountered before, except during the period of the Nazi-Soviet Pact; and having remained a Westerner at heart, he found this hard to bear. As he puts it in his memoirs: 'It is difficult to explain why anti-Soviet journalists chose me as their favourite target. Perhaps they overrated my importance, or perhaps they were irritated by my knowledge of the West; at any rate, they wrote about me often and with malice.' Their attitude, however, was not difficult to explain. Like Ehrenburg, the Western Press was also engaged in a Cold War, and if it singled him out, it was because his name was already well-known to the public in the West; in addition to which there was a feeling that, precisely because he was basically a Westerner, he had no right to remain so firmly entrenched in the opposite camp. During his visits, various people who did not belong to the Peace Movement tried to establish contact with him, but they found his conversation disappointing. Admittedly, unlike other Soviet journalists on such occasions, he did not speak like a *Pravda* editorial, but he said virtually nothing of any consequence, and an informal meeting with him seemed merely to confirm that the Cold War had made all other topics of discussion impossible.

Waging a Cold War is not, of course, generally conducive to tolerance or objectivity, but I remember the *Manchester Guardian* publishing a tolerant and even sympathetic description of Ehrenburg's London press conference in the summer of 1950. The French authorities had refused him permission to enter France, and he was much incensed that, as an Officer of the Legion of Honour, he should be subjected to such shabby treatment. Unexpectedly, however, he was allowed to come to England, where he spoke at various meetings and press conferences. Being present at his London conference, I could not help admiring the cool way in which he fought a losing battle against a barrage of hostile questions. One of the very first to be raised concerned the fact that he was now a member of the Supreme Soviet. 'Which constituency do you represent?' asked the questioner. 'A harbour district in Riga,' replied Ehrenburg. In sweetly sardonic tones, the questioner then asked: 'Are you Latvian, Mr Ehrenburg?' 'No,' replied Ehrenburg quietly, 'I am Jewish' – thus neatly putting a stop to this line of inquiry, since any further attempt to throw doubts on his suitability to represent a Riga constituency would have smacked of anti-Semitism. The conference went on for two hours, and he remained outwardly unruffled throughout. It was only later that he revealed how much the effort had cost him.

In his memoirs, he describes how, when it was all over, he had to change his shirt. 'The hall was packed with journalists, and they behaved so provocatively that I kept breaking out in sweat. I had been to hundreds of press conferences, but I had never seen anything like this. I was constantly interrupted. One journalist rushed up to me and shouted: "Don't try to wriggle out of it! Give a straight answer! Yes or no?" ' I remember the incident he refers to, although my recollection of it is somewhat different from his. But as I said earlier, the assembled journalists, in spite of being addressed amicably as confrères, were in a pugnacious mood. Someone asked why the Soviet Union was imposing its policies by force on the countries of Eastern Europe? Ehrenburg countered by asking for a concrete example of such interference. Needless to say, there was no shortage of examples, but the questioner failed to produce one on the spur of the moment and began to look embarrassed. It was left to W. N. (Trilby) Ewer, the veteran diplomatic correspondent of the *Daily Herald* and the oldest journalist present, to retrieve the situation. Without leaving his seat or raising his voice, Ewer said in his quiet, authoritative voice: 'I don't see why we should give examples. Mr Ehrenburg has been asked a straight question. Can't he give a straight answer?' Looking back on that press conference as a whole, my own recollection of what happened is slightly less dramatic than Ehrenburg's. But his memoirs clearly show that he found it a considerable ordeal, and I can well imagine that, when he himself looked back on it ten years later, he had a vivid impression of hostile faces and cries of 'Answer! Yes or no?'

By that time, he had already begun writing a novel based on the Peace Movement and the Cold War. He called it *The Ninth Wave*, a title intended to represent a huge wave of popular protest against the atomic bomb. It turned out to be one of his worst books, but this was perhaps hardly surprising, since it was written in a period when what Stalin wanted was not literature, but a kind of crude advertising copy in praise of the regime. He subsequently refused to allow it to be included in his collected works, and said that he should never have written it. To go by his memoirs, what he particularly disliked about the book was not that it included a tendentious account of the political situation in Europe, and a not very convincing description of capitalist warmongers and venal journalists working for the CIA, but the way he had been forced to deal with the Soviet scene. If he ventured to portray a Soviet citizen in trouble, he had to make sure that character did not remain in trouble for long. If he mentioned injustice anywhere within the Soviet borders, he had to make justice triumph on the next page. Ehrenburg himself admitted later that he had had to 'sugar' certain chapters dealing with events in the Soviet Union, but that is an understatement. He drenched those particular sections in so much saccharine that he himself was finally sickened by it. He claims, however, that while he was working on the book, he consoled himself with the notion that he would be able to tell at least 'a part of the truth'.

Mark Twain once described truth as 'a precious commodity which must be used sparingly'. In the Soviet Union at that time, it was so strictly rationed that most people did not dare to use it at all. *The Ninth Wave* illustrates how Ehrenburg tried to deal with this dilemma. It contains three episodes that were intended to draw attention to certain unpalatable facts. They are, however, three very minor ones, since they take up altogether no more than the length of just over a page, in a book 870 pages long!

In one episode, a Soviet officer, who happens to be Jewish, who has fought all through the war, and who is now serving with the Soviet occupation forces in Germany, returns to his home city of Kiev on leave. He has lost his wife – she also fought in the war and was killed – and his mother and small daughter have been massacred by the Nazis at Babi Yar, near Kiev. He spends a few hours at Babi Yar thinking about them, then goes back into the city to look up a friend. As he approaches, a man with a moustache who is standing in the doorway asks him for a cigarette. When the officer tells him he has no cigarettes, the man with the moustache observes sourly: 'You never have anything to give to others. Why don't you push off to Palestine? You've got a State of your own now . . .'

Having just come from the place where his mother and daughter were slaughtered by the Germans, together with thousands of other Jews, the officer is rudely jolted by this remark. Years later, Ehrenburg described the scene as 'cruelly realistic'; but at the time he wrote it, he deliberately softened its impact. 'What does that fellow mean, daring to suggest that I should go to that American colony?' (i.e. Israel), the officer says to his friend indignantly. The friend tries to calm him down. The man with the moustache, he says, is a well-known blackguard, a former collaborator; fortunately, there are no more than a few hundred like him in the entire country. The friend's wife is so upset that, despite their cramped living quarters, she asks the officer to stay with them while he is in Kiev. This was Ehrenburg's way of putting things into proper perspective for the censor's benefit. He knew, however, that the ordinary reader could not fail to be struck by the observation of the man with the moustache. In effect, it meant: 'There are still Jew-baiters at large in the Soviet Union!' Furthermore, he was clearly implying that such people would not dare to behave so insolently if they had not been encouraged by the official anti-cosmopolitan campaign.

In another episode, a Soviet intellectual, a doctor by profession and a deputy of the Supreme Soviet, complains about the dullness of Soviet news presentation. It seems trifling, yet it is certainly an unorthodox comment, and most Soviet writers carefully avoided anything smacking remotely of unorthodoxy. 'They talk about interesting things [i.e. production successes – the word 'interesting' is again for the censor's benefit] but the way they present the information is such a bore!' the doctor grumbles – and many Soviet radio listeners must have silently assented. And in the third episode, Ehrenburg has a conversation between a visiting French writer and the young Russian woman who has been assigned to look after him. The writer is critical of the Soviet system, but has come to the Soviet Union to see things for himself. But whenever he asks a question, his woman guide invariably replies with a stock formula: 'As distinct from capitalist countries . . .', and ends by saying, 'Of course, you have nothing like this in France'; which not unnaturally gets on the Frenchman's nerves. Over the years, Ehrenburg must have listened to many such conversations, and found them deeply irritating. Already in the 1930s, he had attacked Intourist for giving foreign visitors a false picture of life in the Soviet Union. But at least at that time he had been able to publish a lengthy newspaper article, in which he did not mince his words. Now, he was reduced to inserting one brief episode in a very long novel, and even then he had to apply a liberal dose of saccharine to prevent the censor from cutting it out. In this instance, the pill is sweetened by the intelligent doctor, who says that the young woman is not very experienced and has not yet learned to distinguish between a good foreigner and a bad one; and since there are many 'bad' ones about, she must have thought it necessary to give only 'formal' answers. The Frenchman appears to be mollified by this explanation, especially as the doctor adds, 'We are not gods', and admits that even the Soviet Union has its shortcomings.

Ehrenburg made his point, but the reviewers criticized him for something else: for being soft on Britain! To some extent, this was true. The villains in *The Ninth Wave* are all either Americans, or Frenchmen who formerly collaborated with the Nazis, and who are now 'collaborating' with the United States. There is only a brief critical mention of the British Labour Government, which was then in power, and of the action of the British authorities in preventing people from attending the Congress of the Peace Movement in Sheffield. Ehrenburg had clearly not forgotten how, during the war, he had spoken in praise of British courage under the Nazi air raids. But there was something else which impressed him about Britain in 1950. Britain was poor; and in Ehrenburg's eyes, this was a virtue which placed her in a different category from America, and even created a certain spiritual affinity with Russia. Thus, in spite of the ordeal he had undergone at his London press conference, he manifestly tried to be fair in the article he wrote summing up his visit to Britain. To be sure, it contained a few obligatory barbs against the British Establishment, but he also had high praise for the stoical way the British were facing austerity and continued rationing, and for the absence of a large-scale black market. The calm with which Londoners were enduring the postwar shortages, he said, reminded him of their calm during the war. It was a generous encomium, and one that was widely at variance with official Soviet propaganda at that time, which in an excess of Cold War zeal repeatedly asserted that Britain had contributed virtually nothing to the defeat of Hitler (one Soviet magazine even tried to prove, ostensibly in all serious- ness, that the Battle of Britain had never taken place!). So Ehren- burg's tribute to Britain amounted to cocking a snook at the official line. Yet he seemed to be sure of his own position, and he returned a truculent answer to critics of *The Ninth Wave*: a writer, he said, was not a prisoner in the dock, and literary criticism should not be equated with the proceedings of a People's Court.

In 1951, while he was working on *The Ninth Wave*, he was invited to give a talk to students of the Moscow Institute of Literature, and *Literary Gazette* later published a summary of his remarks. He probably welcomed the invitation, since it gave him a chance to tell the students at least some of the things about which he really cared. He told them, for example, that there were basically only two kinds of books, irrespective of whether they were good or bad: those which the author had felt he must write (and in this context, rather surprisingly he cited his own novel, *The Storm*), and those written without any inner compulsion. The latter he dismissed in a couple of sentences: 'What can be more nauseating than childhood without pregnancy? One may be a poor writer, one may produce failures, but one must not become a supplier of ersatz art, one must not manufacture books that are not born out of an inner necessity.'

His intention was plain. He wanted the students to realize that practically all art produced in the Soviet Union at that time was ersatz art; and he ended his lecture with an anecdote about Henri Matisse. Matisse, he said, had once been shown an African sculpture of an enraged elephant, a magnificent example of African art, in spite of the fact that the elephant's tusks were not in the right position; after which he was shown another, more realistic statuette which also represented an elephant. The tusks were correctly placed – but it was not a work of art. This was typical of the kind of heretical attitude that Ehrenburg continued to adopt: a muted but unmistakable protest against crude realism, combined with a eulogy of Matisse, who, during the Stalin-Zhdanov crack-down on art, had been branded a 'formalist'. Ehrenburg wrote fairly frequently, in fact, about Western European culture (equally frequently, in his role as anti-American propagandist, contrasting it with American 'immaturity'), and whenever he did so, he usually referred to Matisse or Picasso. To speak in praise of Picasso was yet another minor heresy. From the Soviet viewpoint, Picasso was a welcome ally as a Communist and a prominent peace partisan, but he was unacceptable as an artist. As for Matisse, when Ehrenburg wrote about him on one occasion in *Literary Gazette*, the editor added a footnote, explicitly dissociating the paper from his views. But Ehrenburg was not deterred. In such matters, he clearly had a dispensation from a higher authority. Western diplomats called it *Narrenfreiheit*, or jester's licence, which was probably correct.

But the picture has to be kept in perspective. It was no doubt not easy, and even risky, to write about anti-Semitism in Kiev in *The Ninth Wave*, to ridicule the propaganda nonsense that was fed to foreign visitors, and to hint in a lecture to students that socialist realism might be the death of art; all this required more ingenuity and daring than the much greater liberties Ehrenburg was able to take some years later, after the death of Stalin. At the time, however, these brief flashes of defiance only served to illuminate a landscape of otherwise unredeemed servility. It is true that, in the political field, he did still try to demonstrate a brief spark of independence. It was the time of the Korean War, when the Chinese mounted their huge propaganda campaign against the alleged use of bacteriological weapons by the Americans. This was duly echoed by Soviet propaganda, and anybody of any consequence in the Soviet Union was expected to voice his boundless indignation at this monstrous new form of warfare. Ehrenburg differed from the rest only in that he referred to bacteriological weapons as perhaps not being 'the most terrible weapons in existence'; but he added that they were certainly 'the most repulsive'.

In essence, it was a fairly pathetic attempt to show that he was still not *quite* toeing the line; and as such, it was duly noted by the Soviet intelligentsia. But that was only because, in Stalin's time, almost every Soviet intellectual appeared to have a built-in microscope in his brain (and one which, incidentally, sometimes persuaded him that he was seeing things that were not really there). It was difficult to imagine, however, that Ehrenburg would ever again write anything of value. Once more, he seemed to be finished as a writer – and this time finished for good.

CHAPTER XXXI

Over the years, Ehrenburg had gone through a good many chameleon-like changes, including a phase of almost total submission to Stalin. But by the time his novel *The Thaw* appeared in 1954, Stalin was dead. It appeared initially in a Soviet literary magazine, and one of its more daring passages contained an oblique echo of the terrifying episode that had occurred shortly before the Soviet leader's death: an episode that later became known as the 'Doctors' Plot'. Nevertheless, the despot had not long departed, and Ehrenburg had to handle it with great discretion.

In the novel, a woman doctor called Vera Sherer is summoned to examine a sick child. She finds there is nothing wrong with it, but the over-anxious mother, still too frightened to rejoice, asks 'Are you quite sure?' To which the doctor curtly replies: 'If you have no confidence in me, why did you call me?' Then, realizing that this is not perhaps a very professional response, she apologizes: her nerves, she says, are in a bad state 'because of the things one has to listen to nowadays ... after that announcement'. The announcement in question is the one that was issued by the official Soviet news agency, TASS, on 13 January 1953, disclosing the arrest of a group of doctors, mainly Jews, on charges of having poisoned some of the Soviet leaders and of planning to poison others. As Russian readers would gather from her surname, Vera Sherer is Jewish, and the meaning of her abrupt remark is plain. She is hinting that, as a result of the TASS announcement, patients have become suspicious of *all* Jewish doctors, and do not hesitate to voice their distrust.

This was admittedly an oblique and tortuous way of raising a sensitive issue, but by referring to the so-called 'Doctors' Plot' at all, Ehrenburg was helping to destroy a taboo. It was true that after Stalin's death, the doctors had been rehabilitated and released from prison (except for some who seem to have died there); but having made public their rehabilitation, and condemned certain officials for what had happened, the Soviet authorities clearly did not want anyone to raise the monstrous business again. Ehrenburg was bold enough to do so, and many people were astonished at his temerity.

But there was another even more daring aspect to *The Thaw*, and here, Ehrenburg was treading on even more delicate ground. It has to be remembered that Khrushchev had not yet made his historic denunciation of Stalin and all the evils flowing from Stalinism. Yet one of the leading characters in the novel, a powerful bureaucrat called Zhuravlev, who is head of a large industrial enterprise in a provincial town, is given a symbolic role to play which is heavy with Stalinist undertones. Zhuravlev has a good war record, he works hard, and is generally regarded as an efficient manager. But his character has undergone an unpleasant transformation. From being cheerful and optimistic in his younger days, he has become hard and imperious, and when he laughs it is more like a harsh bark in which no one feels like joining. He was not afraid of death during the war, but now he is frightened of his superiors in Moscow. He also likes to surround himself with toadies and sycophants. A local artist paints his portrait, showing him seated behind an enormous desk, with all his decorations pinned to his jacket lapel, and staring at a model of a new machine tool. He is wholly engrossed in the enterprise he is running (he has a favourite saying: 'The factory and I are one'), and in order to increase production, he diverts certain funds allocated to housing to the construction of a new machine shop. From time to time, looking at the miserable communal huts in which the workers are forced to live, he feels briefly depressed and remorseful; but he persuades himself that, even in these ramshackle structures, the workers are better off than their fathers were in the old days.

In this way, Zhuravlev gradually loses all human attributes. His wife leaves him, and although this does not upset him particularly, he begins to be morbidly suspicious of everyone around him. People who formerly respected his efficiency, and especially his ability to keep a cool head in a crisis, now begin to refer to him as a blackguard, and one even remarks that, after talking to Zhuravlev, he feels as if he has been wallowing in mud. Finally, it is his disregard for human beings that proves to be his undoing. A storm destroys the wretched hovels in which the workers live, Zhuravlev is summoned to Moscow, and although he tells himself that he is not responsible for the weather and has always worked hard for the cause, he knows that his doom is sealed. Soon, reports reach the town that he has lost his job, and his favourite toady, preparing to fawn on Zhuravlev's successor, is soon making disparaging remarks about his former boss. In fact, everybody soon forgets about Zhuravlev. 'Where was he? What had become of him? There had been a storm which had caused a great deal of damage, and then it had moved away. Who remembers a storm once it has passed?'

But that leaves one crucial question: who *was* Zhuravlev? Was Ehrenburg trying to portray a basically decent man gone wrong under the corrupting influence of the Stalin era? Or was Zhuravlev meant to be, not just a minor Stalin (there were plenty of those about in the Soviet Union), but a symbol for Stalin himself? There are certain obvious parallels between the two men. Zhuravlev's wife leaves him, Stalin's wife committed suicide: neither could bear her husband's inhumanity. Zhuravlev likes to proclaim: 'The factory and I are one'; Stalin was the utterly ruthless personification of the maxim: '*L'État – c'est moi!*' People praise Zhuravlev for his ability to keep a cool head in a crisis; in 1954, Stalin was still officially acclaimed as the undisputed architect of the Soviet Union's wartime victory. (Ehrenburg must have remembered all too well how Stalin had lost his head in the first few weeks following the Nazi invasion, but he could hardly afford to remind his readers of that!)

Nevertheless, when *The Thaw* appeared in 1954, Soviet readers must have felt that it was still too dangerous to speculate openly about the possible symbolic significance of Zhuravlev's life, career and ultimate downfall, and public discussion therefore revolved mainly around another major theme of the novel: the abject state to which art and literature had been reduced under Stalin. This, at least, was a subject which was no longer taboo. In fact, since Stalin's death, there had been a number of signs of a mounting rebellion against the dead hand which he and his deputy, Zhdanov, had imposed on all creative art. An article in *Novy Mir* had caused a particular stir: it was by a writer called Vladimir Pomerantsev, and dealt with the question of 'sincerity' in Soviet literature. At a meeting in London, I myself had heard an eminent Soviet theatre director declare emphatically that no true work of art could be created to order, whether the order came from an individual or the State. Somewhat earlier, in October 1953, only seven months after Stalin's death (as it happened, this was also seven months before the appearance of *The Thaw*), Ehrenburg himself had sounded out the ground, in an article which appeared in the monthly journal *Znamya*. In this, he analysed at considerable length a question which, he said, had been put to him by one of his readers: why did Soviet novels no longer grip the reader, and why were the characters in those novels so unlike real people? Ehrenburg indulged in some convoluted prose to soften the impact of his conclusion, but the conclusion itself was unmistakable: writing was solely the business of the writer, and not of his political masters or those who were acting on their instructions. No one had ever told Chekhov what he should or should not write, nor could one imagine anyone 'ordering' Tolstoy to produce *Anna Karenina*. The time had come, said Ehrenburg, to resurrect certain words which had fallen into disuse – words like 'vocation' and 'inspiration' – and writers must also stop being afraid of literary critics. Ehrenburg did not actually use the word 'censor', but he strongly attacked the type of critic who, in effect, acted as a surrogate censor. Such people, he said, were so frightened of praising a book which had not been awarded a prize (i.e. had not received the stamp of official approval) that they listed all the things it did *not* contain, then blamed the author for omitting them. This produced the dreary result that writers often padded out their pages with indifferent stuff, simply in order to prevent the critics from saying, 'Why didn't the author deal with this or that . . . ?'

Unlike Pomerantsev, who had used some unfortunate similes and thereby incurred the wrath of the Establishment, Ehrenburg got his point across without earning any official rebuke; and having done so, in writing *The Thaw* he decided to go a good deal further. Now, he dispensed with convoluted prose to cushion the impact of what he was trying to say, and wrote a straightforward parable of two friends. As portrayed in the novel, both are talented artists. But one of them, a painter called Pukhov, lured on by the prospect of money and fame, has blindly followed Stalin's and Zhdanov's directives, and has abandoned art to produce vulgar and worthless kitsch instead. The other painter, Saburov, has meanwhile remained true to his vocation, even though this means poverty and hunger, without hope of acknowledgement or even of showing his work in public. There is an ironical complication, however, to this moral anti-Stalinist tale. Pukhov cultivates a cynical exterior, but like most would-be cynics in Ehrenburg's novels, he does not really succeed. He appreciates the money he is making, but is sickened by official praise, and when he sees his friend's work, it comes to him as a revelation. 'I know envy is an ugly word,' he says to Saburov, 'but I envy you.' And as he walks home, he is plunged into gloomy meditation. 'I shall never be able to paint like Saburov,' he thinks, 'not even if I go mad. I no longer have any feeling for art.' He has just finished a mural for an agricultural exhibition, and he reflects bitterly that 'even in an insane asylum, I would no doubt still go on painting chickens to order . . .' He reaches home, but although his room is well heated, he finds himself gripped by an icy chill.

Frost and ice outside, and in the hearts of men, is the leitmotiv of the novel. In the end, however, Ehrenburg leaves it to the repentant Pukhov to make the first gesture welcoming the thaw. Going for a walk in the park with his mistress, he sees the first snowdrops, and remembers how he used to enjoy splintering the frozen puddles when winter neared its end. He sees such a frozen puddle now, and rushes to trample on it, feeling an unspeakable delight as he breaks the ice. This is, of course, the ice of the Stalin era, and Pukhov's joyful gesture of liberation coincides with the news that, at last, two of Saburov's paintings are to be exhibited. As it turns out, the management of the exhibition has characteristically chosen two paintings that Saburov himself considers among his weakest and least successful. It is also a characteristic turn of the screw on Ehrenburg's part; a subtle way of suggesting that the thaw may prove to be a long drawn-out and difficult process. But at least it has begun.

But like his article in *Znamya* seven months earlier, *The Thaw* was a deliberately controversial piece of writing, its aim being to establish just how much the authorities were prepared to tolerate a year after Stalin's death. This was, of course, the question that every genuine writer or artist in the Soviet Union was asking himself. The situation was a fluid one. On one hand, the State no longer exercised a veto on literature and art, as it had done in Zhdanov's time, and it therefore implicitly granted a certain degree of creative freedom. On the other hand, the limits to that freedom were not defined, for the simple reason that different factions in the Soviet leadership and among the literary bureaucrats had differing ideas on where those limits should be drawn. So, before he started work, every genuine writer and every true artist had to ask himself: 'How far can I go?' The Soviet writer Leonid Leonov later provided a colourful illustration of the problem in a lecture he gave in London. 'Wily serpents hiss in one's ear: "Take the plunge and the angels of the Lord will look after thee!" ', said Leonov, in a rough paraphrase of a celebrated passage in the New Testament. At the time, however, many Soviet writers must have hesitated, wondering what protection they could expect from the angels of the Writers' Union if they dared to take the plunge.

In the end, it was Ehrenburg who took the plunge on their behalf. *The Thaw* seems to have been based on the following calculation: if it was praised (which was improbable) this would be an historic landmark; but even if it merely escaped complete annihilation by the official critics, it could still be regarded as a successful experiment, since it would show that *some* movement towards freedom in art and literature was possible; and what gave added weight to the experiment was the fact that the writer was himself a member of the literary Establishment. And this was important for a number of reasons, not least because, by the middle of that year (1954), the reactionaries had become extremely active. Alexander Tvardovsky, the liberal editor of *Novy Mir*, had been dismissed for publishing Pomerantsev's article on sincerity in literature, and Pomerantsev and several other 'rebels' were sharply taken to task in another literary monthly by the head of the Writers' Union, Alexei Surkov. *The Thaw* had to be handled more carefully, it is true, and the task of cutting it down to size, as it were, was entrusted to a rather more subtle literary panjandrum, the poet and novelist Konstantin Simonov. Like Surkov, he had acquired a bad name under the Stalin regime; but unlike Surkov, he did seem ready to admit that times were changing, although he chose to tread warily. By 1954, one could describe him as an enlightened reactionary, prepared to accept a cautious and very gradual measure of reform.

Simonov's review of *The Thaw* was a lengthy affair, and was published in *Literary Gazette* in two instalments. It was also, in many ways, a remarkable document, as typical of the period as the novel itself: in short, it showed how one could make a piece of writing look like a serious book review, containing a good deal that was true, and yet still ignore most of the points that mattered. Simonov was, of course, obliged to mention the title of the book but he completely ignored its significance. He also avoided any reference to Zhuravlev's importance as a symbol, and left it to the readers to draw their own conclusions. If it occurred to them that Zhuravlev bore a resemblance to Stalin, that was their business; an official critic was not supposed to encourage that kind of speculation. So Simonov dealt with Zhuravlev as if he were no more than a bad factory director, while heartily agreeing with the author that a man who cared nothing for the welfare of the workers should not have been given a responsible post in the first place. But while he agreed with

Ehrenburg on that point, he objected to the overall picture of Soviet life as depicted in the novel. For example, said Simonov, the decent characters in the book were the exceptions. Zhuravlev's wife was surprised when she met an upright and intelligent man; but why was she surprised? She herself was portrayed as a highly intelligent woman such as one 'rarely' met in Moscow; but why 'rarely'? Ehrenburg seemed to be suggesting that in the Soviet Union, the bad prospered while the good were few and far between; which was, indeed, exactly the point that Ehrenburg was making.

Simonov also noted that the book appeared to have been written in a hurry and its literary quality was uneven, which was undeniably true. *The Thaw* has no special literary value, and Ehrenburg must indeed have composed it in a hurry, if only because he felt there was no time to waste in launching his experiment. But Simonov's judgement was unduly harsh when he said that: 'In my opinion, this novel is much weaker than anything Ehrenburg has written in the past fifteen years.' *The Thaw* is not a major work of art, but from the purely literary point of view, it is still better than, for example, *The Ninth Wave*, the novel Ehrenburg had written to order shortly before Stalin's death.

Simonov then turned to the second theme in *The Thaw* – the state of the arts and the plight of the artist in the Soviet Union – and here, because it was no longer a prohibited subject, he could at least deal with the essential points. He began, however, by criticizing Ehrenburg's basic assumptions. According to Ehrenburg, there was only a stark choice between being a Saburov and starving for the sake of one's art, or a Pukhov who betrayed his vocation. But what was worse, Ehrenburg seemed to regard Pukhov simply as a victim of circumstances, as someone who secretly loved art, but had been compelled to betray it because he lacked the strength to withstand the temptations of hack work. This, said Simonov, was a travesty of the real situation, and he dismissed the novel as a regrettable failure.

In his concluding paragraphs, he did, however, acknowledge that this was 1954, and that Stalin had been dead for over a year. He admitted that the standards of Soviet art had not invariably been high, and that times were changing. As an example, he pointed to the case of Alexander Gerasimov, a consummate vulgarian who used to be Stalin's favourite painter, and who typified what Ehrenburg later described as 'that detestable photography'. Simonov, too, attacked the 'photographers', together with the 'naturalists', who refused to see that socialist realism could express itself in different styles, and who tried to strangle anything that was new. If only Ehrenburg had developed that theme, said Simonov, he would have received wide support. Instead, he had reserved his highest praise for Saburov, a formalist who was divorced from Soviet life; and in this way he had played into the hands of the 'naturalists', who would use his book as justification for their attitude. In short, it was clear that Simonov, the enlightened reactionary, felt that Ehrenburg was moving too fast and had gone too far.

* * *

Some years later, a reactionary Soviet woman critic in an attack on an exhibition arranged by a group of young Soviet artists, which she described as 'ideologically harmful', remarked sombrely that it had all started with Ehrenburg's *The Thaw*. And in that she was right. In spite of Pomerantsev's article and other early signs of rebellion, it was *The Thaw* that marked the beginning of the real battle between the Stalinists and the liberals; between those who had talent, and the mediocrities who were simply defending their own vested interests. The struggle that followed brought a succession of alternating victories and defeats, but on balance, there was for quite a time a slow but steady movement towards greater liberalism. Politically, the thaw gained ground in the early part of 1956, after Khrushchev's denunciation of Stalin at the Twentieth Party Congress, and as a result there was a leap forward in literature and art. After the Soviet intervention in Hungary later that same year, however, the bonds were once more tightened, and some official critics began to stress that the Party must reassert its guiding role in literature and the arts, especially in view of the deterioration in the international situation.

For his part, however, Ehrenburg seemed undismayed. In February 1957, in an article in *Literary Gazette*, he asserted that there was still not nearly enough freedom for art and creative writing, and, invoking the authority of the Twentieth Congress, he asked for more, 'in spite of the current anti-Soviet propaganda campaign abroad', as he put it (he meant the storm aroused by the Soviet intervention in Hungary). Moreover, he stressed that he was addressing both the Soviet public and his friends in the West. For the benefit of the former, he once again dismissed those critics who analysed each new book 'for the amount of sugar and acid' it

contained, to verify that 'the right proportions' had been maintained. After the Twentieth Congress, said Ehrenburg, this kind of
approach was an anachronism. To his friends in the West, especially
those who had been deeply disturbed by the Hungarian intervention,
he gave a reassuring pledge concerning Soviet literature and the arts.
'We are advancing steadily. There will be no going back.' The
publication of his article, he added, was the best proof of that.

It was a surprisingly confident statement, and one which suggested
that he had official backing. Two weeks later, however, the
authoritative Soviet Party journal, *Kommunist*, came out with an
editorial which suggested the opposite: that perhaps Ehrenburg had
been *too* confident. The editorial certainly had threatening over-
tones. It recalled the Zhdanov decrees, which had had such a
paralysing effect on all creative work in the late forties and early
fifties, and claimed that they were still basically valid. It also rebuked
certain publishers for having produced ideologically harmful books.
But *The Thaw* was not included in the list, and *Kommunist* admitted
that at one time things had been carried too far, that the cult of Stalin
had had an adverse affect on the situation, and that it had been
wrong to ban works by certain authors. In short, the article appeared
to suggest that, while the authorities were determined not to let
things get out of hand, they had no intention of going back to the bad
old days of the Stalin-Zhdanov era. On the other hand, in May 1957,
Khrushchev had several meetings with Soviet writers, and told them
that Party control over literature and art was essential and would
continue: what he had said about Stalin did not mean that they could
now do as they pleased. He also particularly criticized a new literary
almanac which had been started by a group of progressive writers, in
the mistaken belief that the thaw would soon be followed by spring;
but he also expressed the hope that those who had gone wrong
would soon see the error of their ways. It was a warning and an
admonition, but not a total clamp-down.

It was not until the following year that a vicious onslaught was
launched against Ehrenburg by a writer who, to judge by his
behaviour, would have welcomed such a clamp-down. The attack
came from a well-known Stalinist die-hard, Vsevolod Kochetov,
whose novel *The Brothers Yershov* was being serialized by a
Leningrad magazine; and as he was writing it, Kochetov may well
have imagined that, after Hungary, he would be able to settle
accounts with Ehrenburg once and for all. So, in his own novel, he

attacked not only *The Thaw*, but the thaw in general and in all its manifestations: political, literary, and even climatic. The thaw, said Kochetov, was 'a rotten, slushy season', the season when 'flu germs flourished, and he drew a parallel between it and the Hungarian uprising. He had to be rather more cautious in his attack on the political thaw, since this was generally identified with Khrushchev's de-Stalinization campaign, but he must have taken comfort from the fact that, in his meetings with Soviet writers, the latter had spoken of Stalin's achievements as well as Stalin's mistakes. As a form of reinsurance, no doubt, Kochetov did mention briefly the Party's efforts to liquidate the harmful consequences of the so-called 'Cult of Personality' (the official euphemism for Stalinism); but at the same time, he sneered at those who had kept silent for decades, and then became extremely vocal when they thought they could jump on the new bandwagon. They were, he said, like vermin which had been hiding in the cracks of walls during the long winter, and had crept out into the open 'at the first signs of the thaw'.

Finally, without actually naming either *The Thaw* or its author, but still making his meaning absolutely clear, Kochetov poured scorn on both. He, at least, was in no doubt that Stalin and Zhuravlev were intended to be one and the same person. A couple of years ago, he said, an author had written a story about the director of an industrial enterprise (i.e. Zhuravlev), who had been punished for producing steel instead of houses for the workers. Yet the director had been right, and the author, instead of denigrating him, ought really to have bowed before him in gratitude; because if the director (i.e. Stalin) had been less keen on constructing steel foundries, the author would probably have ended up in some ravine feeding the worms (a transparent allusion to the Babi Yar massacre).

By the time Kochetov's novel appeared between hard covers, however, the panic over Hungary had subsided. Kochetov and his fellow reactionaries were still riding high, but when a reviewer in *Pravda* came to deal with *The Brothers Yershov*, he tempered his praise with an expression of regret: Kochetov had attributed 'formalistic' tendencies to too many people, and had failed to take into account that a number of writers who had been guilty of 'formalism' in the past had since mended their ways. Ehrenburg survived the body blows dealt him by Kochetov, but the atmosphere remained heavy and menacing, and some people felt it safer to treat him as if he were still under a cloud. A Moscow publishing house had accepted a collection of his essays on French culture, including one in which he defended Picasso (to orthodox critics a 'formalist' and 'a corrupting influence'), but changed its mind about bringing it out; and when the campaign of persecution against Pasternak began, the same publishers demanded that Ehrenburg should delete a passing reference he had made to one of Pasternak's poems. Ehrenburg was furious, and appealed to a senior Party official who had helped him in the past. The text was allowed to stand unaltered.[1]

Pasternak's *Dr Zhivago* was beyond the range of the thaw, but the thaw continued in spite of that sordid affair. Indeed, in 1959, the year in which Harold Macmillan visited Moscow and Nikita Khrushchev travelled to the United States, it acquired an international currency, as statesmen, political commentators and others began to use it freely in their analyses of East-West relations, contrasting it with the deep freeze of the Cold War. Meanwhile, inside the Soviet Union, the battle for the cultural thaw continued.

There were, of course, many people who supported the liberal cause, including the poet and critic, Alexander Tvardovsky, long reinstated as editor of *Novy Mir*, who was fighting with particular vigour and encouraging results. Ehrenburg himself, apart from writing his memoirs, which were to play a major part in the struggle, never took his sights off the enemy. For example, he sharply rebuffed the woman critic who had suggested that *The Thaw* was the cause of all the trouble and charged Ehrenburg with being at least partly responsible for current ideological deviations. He did not consider *The Thaw* an ideological error, he said, and proudly recalled that he had written it two years before the Twentieth Party Congress. He added, furthermore, that he was only too glad to take full moral responsibility for the works of those artists who preferred to use their own eyes instead of relying on the lens of a camera. And he deplored the way some of the most talented Soviet artists had been treated: in one case, the artist's first exhibition took place only after his death; in another, the case of Ehrenburg's friend, Falk, only a few months before his death; while the works of the great Armenian painter, Partiros Saryan, had been shown to the public only after a lengthy hiatus, by which time Saryan was seventy-five. In numerous articles and interviews, Ehrenburg constantly insisted that the purpose of literature was not to describe industrial or agricultural production, but to portray human beings and to uphold human values. He was

[1]See Appendices.

saying, in effect, that literature must be literature, and not the crude advertising copy demanded by Stalin and Zhdanov.

In 1960, *Novy Mir*, under the editorship of Alexander Tvardovsky, began the publication in serial form of Ehrenburg's memoirs, which were to become a landmark in postwar Soviet literature. Two years later, in its November issue, the same review also published Solzhenitsyn's *One Day in the Life of Ivan Denisovich*. It looked as if the uncertainties of the thaw were over and spring had finally arrived. But as so often happens in the Soviet Union, such optimism was premature. Only a few months later, Khrushchev publicly denounced the publication of certain books which, he said, gave a 'wrong and one-sided picture of the phenomena connected with the "Cult of Personality"·', and of the changes that had occurred following his anti-Stalin speech at the Twentieth Party Congress; and he included *The Thaw* in that category.

In fact, Khrushchev was talking nonsense. *The Thaw* could not give any picture, either true or false, of the changes following the Twentieth Congress, for the simple reason that it had appeared two years before the Congress was held. By now, in any case, the political content of *The Thaw* had long been overtaken by events, and was largely forgotten. All that lingered in people's minds was the title – the *image* – of 'the thaw'. Khrushchev himself was, of course, well aware of this, and went on to explain why it was an image which he could not accept. 'The idea of the thaw', he said, 'is generally associated with a period of instability, of unfinished business, and with fluctuations of temperature when it is difficult to forecast what the weather will be like.' A literary image of this kind, he declared, did not reflect the real significance of the changes which had taken place in Soviet society since the death of Stalin. In retrospect, there was a certain justification for this view. Khrushchev plainly did not wish his rule to be permanently identified with the notion of the ice breaking up. A thaw is certainly preferable to an ice age, but it does imply instability and fluctuation; whereas he, like all statesmen, was anxious to be remembered as the creator of something stable and enduring.

Khrushchev's speech, made in March 1963, marked the climax of a reactionary offensive which had been launched some three months earlier, in which Ehrenburg was one of the main targets. Since 1956, he had been under fire from various quarters. There had been the scurrilous attack by Kochetov (from the official viewpoint, Kochetov was a useful dinosaur, although not all that influential); there had been poisoned darts from certain critics smarting under the vitriolic attacks they themselves had suffered at Ehrenburg's hands; and there had been a few outbursts from cranks who did not matter. But now shots were being aimed at him from high levels in the hierarchy, and in the end, a salvo was fired from the summit.

It all began in December 1962, at a time when hopes had been aroused by the publication of Solzhenitsyn's story of Ivan Denisovich in *Novy Mir*, and when there were other signs of what appeared to be a burgeoning spring. But on 1 December, Khrushchev visited (or was inveigled into visiting) an art exhibition in the Manège, opposite the Kremlin, an exhibition which included a number of experimental works by Soviet artists. He was outraged by what he saw, and did not mince his words: he described the paintings as 'shit'. Just over two weeks later, on 17 December, he and Leonid Ilyichev, the Party Secretary in charge of cultural affairs, summoned a number of Soviet writers and artists, including Ehrenburg, to a meeting in the Kremlin. Ehrenburg's contribution to the discussion was never published, but from a later statement by Ilyichev, it was possible to gather the drift of his argument. His main point was that there could be no arguing about tastes, that innovations always encountered resistance, and that Lenin, although he did not care for modern poetry, had never tried to impose his own preferences on others (such references to Lenin always infuriated the die-hards!). Ilyichev, for his part, poured scorn on modern art, but as far as is known (his speech was published only in an abridged form), he did not mention Ehrenburg by name.

But the controversy over Soviet art proved to be only a preliminary skirmish. The real storm broke over a passage in Ehrenburg's memoirs, as they appeared in *Novy Mir*, and it had nothing to do with the state of the arts. In one of the instalments, Ehrenburg said that he had lived through the years of the Great Terror of 1937 and 1938 'with clenched teeth', and had learned to remain silent without losing faith, even though he was filled with agonizing doubts about the intelligence of the country's leadership. But this clearly implied that he had never doubted the innocence of the victims, and he was swiftly taken to task by an orthodox critic called Yermilov. Writing in *Izvestia*, Yermilov observed sardonically that Ehrenburg must have had one great advantage over the vast majority of ordinary

Soviet citizens, who had not experienced any such doubts, but had been shocked and grieved that there should be so many enemies of the people in their midst. Since Ehrenburg appeared to have known so much, said Yermilov, why had he remained silent? There were others who had doubted 'the propriety of certain actions' (by the authorities) and had fought to put things right, but their weapon had not been silence. To this, at least, Ehrenburg had a ready reply: he had not been present at a single meeting, he said, at which anyone had raised a voice in protest against the arbitrary arrest and persecution of innocent people. In an editorial postscript, however, *Izvestia* took Yermilov's side.

It was a belated storm, and in many ways an artificial one. The section of Ehrenburg's memoirs containing the disputed passage had appeared in May 1962. By now, it was late January 1963: a long time for anyone to nurture feelings of indignation. So it looks very much as if, towards the end of 1962, when Khrushchev was in a truculent mood, someone had persuaded him that it was time to rap Ehrenburg over the knuckles. This was duly done, and it was plain that certain people greatly enjoyed his discomfiture. In early March 1963, there was another meeting between Party leaders and intellectuals, and this time, Ilyichev made an open attack on Ehrenburg. The latter, he said, had produced a so-called 'theory of silence', but he had not really practised it himself. 'You were not silent in those days, Ilya Grigorievich,' said Ilyichev bitingly. 'You produced your own eulogy!' And he went on to quote gleefully from Ehrenburg's speech at his sixtieth birthday celebration in 1951, thanking Stalin for all the help he had given him as a writer. There were, of course, a number of die-hards and unrepentant Stalinists present at the meeting, and it must have been music to their ears to hear this magisterial rebuke to the great liberal, the prophet of the thaw, the cultured Westerner and patron of modern art. But Ilyichev went further: he suggested that Ehrenburg's orthodox critics were, in fact, more worthy of respect than Ehrenburg himself. He did make one magnanimous concession. He was not blaming Ehrenburg for having eulogized Stalin in 1951, he said, because 'we all spoke and wrote like that at the time . . . But *we* believed,' he added, 'whereas *you*, as it now turns out, did *not* believe, but nevertheless said and wrote the same things . . .' At which point, according to *Pravda*, there was an outburst of applause. It was really a fantastic situation. People to whom lying had become second nature were pretending that they had always been truthful and sincere, while they accused of hypocrisy someone who, like them, had submitted to the dictator, but at least now had the courage to admit that he had done so knowingly.

Finally, the next day, Khrushchev made his own contribution to the anti-Ehrenburg campaign. *The Thaw*, he said, was a harmful work, and he compared Ehrenburg's attitude unfavourably with that of 'that outstanding writer and true patriot' Sholokhov (he must have known that the two were at daggers drawn).[1] He also contrasted Ehrenburg's approach with that of Galina Serebryakova who had slandered him only three months earlier: unlike Ehrenburg, said Khrushchev, she had been imprisoned for many years, yet she had never lost heart, and was now writing books that the people and the Party really needed.

Ehrenburg was crushed. True, he had gone through other bad moments in his long career: during the Great Terror when he had returned to the Soviet Union from Spain; when he was attacked by *Pravda* in the spring of 1945 and prevented from following the victorious Soviet troops into Berlin; and at the time of the notorious 'Doctors' Plot', just before Stalin's death. But he was now over seventy, and the exhausting struggles of the past had taken their toll. He did not even know whether the next volume of his memoirs would be published, or whether he would ever again be allowed to go abroad, on one of those privileged foreign assignments that had become part of his life. He must have wondered at that point whether his career as a writer and journalist had finally come to an end.

Yet, as had happened more than once in the past, things took a turn for the better. The regime needed him, and having dealt him a stinging rebuke, now decided to overlook his eccentricities. Within a few months, Ehrenburg was one of the main speakers at a European Writers' Forum in Leningrad, and his speech was later published in *Literary Gazette*. Moreover, while other Soviet participants in the Forum obediently toed the official line, Ehrenburg seemed as determined as ever to show that he had not abandoned his independent attitude towards art and literature. He also published an article on international affairs in *Pravda*. The next instalment of his memoirs did not appear in *Novy Mir* until the beginning of 1965 (by which time Khrushchev was no longer in power), but the

[1]Mikhail Alexandrovich Sholokhov. An exemplar of socialist realism, author of, *inter alia*, *Virgin Soil Upturned* and *Quiet Flows the Don*.

important point was that it *did* appear; and in due course, the memoirs were published in book form, under the title of *People, Years, Life*.

On balance, he had won. He had not written *The Thaw* in vain. He had acted as a pathfinder. Later, the emergence of Solzhenitsyn and other dissident writers brought a new dimension of unorthodoxy to overshadow the officially-approved Soviet literary scene. But as Nadezhda Mandelstam remarks in the second volume of her memoirs, *Hope Abandoned*, Ehrenburg was always the odd man out among Soviet writers, and he may well have been the one who first roused people into reading *samizdat*.[1] He sat on many rehabilitation committees, and played a leading part in securing the posthumous publication, or republication, of major works written by victims of the Stalin era. His greatest achievement during that period, however, was probably in the field of the visual arts. It was largely owing to him that the Soviet attitude towards art in general gradually changed, and this in spite of the fact that, to Khrushchev, modern art meant 'painting fir trees upside down' (he was apt to put it rather more coarsely when he was in a bad mood). Kochetov, in *The Brothers Yershov*, had warned the Soviet Establishment that if it allowed the (officially consecrated) doctrine of socialist realism to co-exist with what he ironically called 'socialist' impressionism, this would lead to 'socialist' formalism, then to 'socialist' abstractionism, and eventually to 'socialist' capitalism. Yet it was during the thaw that the impressionists were taken out of the basement storerooms of Soviet museums, and hung where the public could see them. Nor did the process stop there. It was one of Ehrenburg's moments of triumph when he opened the Picasso Exhibition in Moscow, and saw the long queues of people waiting to get in. Similar exhibitions followed, and if so many Picassos and Matisses can now be viewed at

[1]'He was always the odd man out among the Soviet writers, and the only one I maintained relations with all through the years. He was as helpless as everybody else, but at least he tried to do something for others. *People, Years, Life* is in effect the only one of his books to have played a positive part in this country. His readers – mostly members of the minor technical intelligentsia – first learned dozens of names quite new to them from this book. Once they had read it, their further evolution proceeded rapidly, but with the usual ingratitude of people, they were quick to disown the man who had first opened their eyes. All the same, there was a great crowd at his funeral, and I noticed that the faces were decent and human ones. It was an anti-Fascist crowd, and the police spies who had been sent to the funeral in force stood out very conspicuously. It was clear, in other words, that Ehrenburg had done his work well, difficult and thankless though it was. It may well have been he who first aroused people into reading samizdat. *Hope Abandoned. A Memoir*, trans. Max Hayward, Collins & Harvill Press, London, 1974.

the Hermitage in Leningrad and the Pushkin Museum in Moscow, much of the credit for that goes to Ehrenburg.

The thaw was indeed an era of hope: of prisoners returning from the camps and from exile, of increasing East-West contacts and of East-West *détente*. Ehrenburg, with his gift for prophecy, foresaw the coming of the thaw in the year after Stalin's death. But as he chose that title for his novel, he unwittingly picked on the right image in yet another respect. The thaw, as Khrushchev correctly observed, is a fitful season of instability and fluctuation; and so, in the political sense, it proved to be. During those hopeful, exhilarating, maddening and unpredictable years, no one knew which way the wind would blow next. Unfortunately, the thaw was not followed by spring.

CHAPTER XXXII

Ehrenburg's memoirs, which began appearing in the early 1960s and which he called *People, Years, Life*, were his last major work and his best since *Julio Jurenito*, written some forty years earlier. He described them as a 'confession' rather than a chronicle. By that, however, he did not mean anything resembling Jean-Jacques Rousseau's exercise in self-castigation, and he made it clear that he had no intention of dealing with various 'affairs of the heart'. All he meant was that he would try to tell the truth as he saw it: about the people he had known, the epoch through which he had lived, and the things life had done to him and to others while history was being made. To tell the *whole* truth, as he himself admits, proved impossible; and time and again in the memoirs, he apologizes for having to remain silent on certain vital topics. But even so, he does manage to say a great deal.

There are a number of reasons why the memoirs are a remarkable document. To begin with, Russia is a country that sets great store by poetry – it is something that is a part of people's lives. In his memoirs in the early sixties, Ehrenburg was the first to pay proper tribute to two of Russia's greatest poets, Osip Mandelstam and Marina Tsvetayeva, both of whom were victims of Stalin's Terror (Mandelstam died in one of the camps of the Gulag, and Tsvetayeva committed suicide). Some time later, a Soviet literary magazine published Tsvetayeva's memories of her childhood, and in her two-volume autobiography, *Hope Against Hope* and *Hope Abandoned*, Nadezhda Mandelstam produced an unforgettable portrait of the Stalin era, although this circulated only in a clandestine form in samizdat. But when Ehrenburg's memoirs began appearing in *Novy Mir*, his chapters on Mandelstam and Tsvetayeva blazed a new trail, and earned him much gratitude, admiration and affection.

But the memoirs revealed much else besides. Nowhere else in Soviet literature, for example, was there anything to approach Ehrenburg's appreciation of the Russian Menshevik leader, Yuli Martov, who at one time had worked together with Lenin; Martov who, in the early years after the Revolution, when Mensheviks could still take part in public life, had tried to speak on behalf of a peaceful opposition in Russia, and who had finally left the country in 1920. In a volume passed for publication one year *after* the death of Stalin, the *Great Soviet Encyclopaedia* refers to Martov as a renegade and a traitor, who in 1905 allegedly betrayed the interests of the workers, and in the First World War helped the bourgeoisie to deceive the people. Later, in a Soviet play called *Lenin in Geneva*, Martov was turned into a figure of fun, with Lenin indignantly turning his back on him. The latest edition of the *Encyclopaedia*, a rather more civilized compilation than the one started under Stalin, does contain a more sober and objective account of Martov's activities, but this appeared only in 1974. Ehrenburg had met Martov at the beginning of the First World War in Paris, and in his memoirs he describes him as a gentle and attractive person, a man of the utmost integrity, even though he struck him as bookish and remote from life. But Ehrenburg portrays him with so much warmth and affection that one can vividly picture the incurable Russian-Jewish idealist, in poor health, freezing for lack of a warm overcoat, and deeply depressed by the failure of the Second International to prevent the war.

It was also only in the memoirs that Soviet readers could find a record of the kind of conversation that Ehrenburg had had in 1924 with a Jewish watchmaker in Odessa, and which summed up in a few words what so many people had felt during that early period of Soviet history, after private enterprise had been restored on a limited scale under the New Economic Policy. 'I see from the papers', said the watchmaker, 'that they're once again hitting out at Curzon [in Soviet eyes at that time, Lord Curzon was Public Enemy No. 1] but I don't imagine they'll frighten Curzon. *I* am the one who is afraid. I am afraid of the tax inspector, I am afraid of the GPU,[1] and I am afraid of you. How do I know what sort of a person you are and why you want me to tell you so many things . . . ?'

Let me give a further example. No one but Ehrenburg could have revealed to the Soviet reading public how, in 1943–4, together with the writer Vasily Grossman (who fell into permanent disfavour after the Second World War), he had compiled a unique collection of documents relating to the persecution and extermination of Jews in the Nazi-occupied regions of the Soviet Union. He and Grossman

---

[1]The State Political Administration, one of the predecessors of the KGB.

called it *The Black Book*; it first appeared in a Soviet magazine, and after lengthy delays, it was actually published as a separate volume, only to be destroyed in the late forties, when Stalin disbanded the Soviet Jewish Anti-Fascist Committee, and launched the so-called anti-cosmopolitan campaign. Ehrenburg also disclosed that *The Black Book* figured in a number of cases brought before the Soviet courts, in which Jews were sentenced for crimes they had never committed. He discovered this in 1956, when a member of the State Prosecutor's Office, who had been instructed to rehabilitate the wrongly condemned victims, asked him what *The Black Book* stood for, since his name had been mentioned in that connection.

Until that time, it had not been exactly the custom to refer to declared opponents of the Soviet regime as men of integrity. In the sixties, Ehrenburg proved that it could indeed be done, although with one important proviso: that the people concerned had been dead long enough. Such revelations might still have been possible in the following decade, except that Ehrenburg's memoirs could not have appeared in the seventies for quite another reason: the manner in which he had dealt with the Stalin era. At the beginning of the seventies, it even looked for a time as if Leonid Brezhnev might be preparing a full-scale rehabilitation of Stalin. He did not go that far. But he did insist that sufficient exposure had by then been given to the 'Cult of Personality', and that it was time to put a stop to any further denunciations.

Ehrenburg, it is true, had not been the only one to deal with the iniquities of the Stalin cult while this was still permitted. Solzhenitsyn's *One Day in the Life of Ivan Denisovich* was, of course, in a class by itself. But there were a number of other remarkable literary documents, including one which concerned the fate of Mikhail Koltsov, who had been *Pravda* correspondent and Stalin's personal envoy in Spain during the civil war. In a volume of essays devoted to his life and work, Koltsov's brother described how, on his return to the Soviet Union, Koltsov was gripped by an invisible hand which led him step by step to his doom. Ehrenburg himself had done a good deal of careful investigation by the time he reached that point in his memoirs at which he had to deal with the Great Terror, and was able to produce many new and hitherto unpublished details. He revealed for the first time, for example, that the celebrated theatre director Vsevolod Meyerhold had not died in a labour camp, as was generally believed, but had been executed. Ehrenburg had managed to unearth an official admission that Meyerhold had died the day after being sentenced to a term of imprisonment 'without the right to send or receive letters'. This could mean only one thing: that he had been shot within twenty-four hours of sentence being passed.

In making their attacks on Ehrenburg in 1963, Khrushchev and Ilyichev had concentrated on something which plainly touched them on the raw: his so-called 'theory of silence', i.e. his claim that, during the Great Terror, many people, including himself, had not really believed in the guilt of the accused, but had kept silent, as he had done, because there was really no alternative. Critics who echoed the Establishment line also made two other points. Yermilov, who fired the first shot in the campaign, drew attention to Ehrenburg's heretical views on freedom, while others remarked that he seemed to ignore the division of the world into two 'contrasting and antagonistic systems'.

Yermilov specifically singled out a passage in the memoirs in which Ehrenburg confessed that he had been unable to support the Bolshevik Revolution at the outset because he had been brought up on nineteenth-century ideas of freedom. (It is worth noting, incidentally, that in the 1960s, nearly half a century after the event, it was perfectly permissible for a convert to admit that he had initially opposed the Revolution; but it was dangerously heretical to suggest, as Ehrenburg appeared to be doing, that he had done so because he felt the Revolution was incompatible with freedom.) In the early 1930s, Ehrenburg finally decided to make his peace with the Soviet Government, which amounted to a repudiation of freedom. No sooner was Stalin dead, however, than he set out on a deliberate quest to regain the freedom he had lost, and he seized on every possible pretext to make his meaning clear. In the memoirs, for example, he pointedly recalls the moment of his first arrival in Paris in 1909, when his concierge refused even to glance at his passport, telling him she was not in the least interested in such a document. And, as related in Chapter XX, he also quoted freely from Cervantes, particularly Don Quixote's remark to his faithful squire: 'Freedom, Sancho, is one of the most precious gifts bestowed by Heaven: none of the treasures hidden in the bowels of the earth or at the bottom of the sea can compare with it. Servitude, on the other hand, is the worst misfortune that can befall a man.' Ehrenburg cited this passage in describing a journey he had made through La Mancha, Don Quixote's home province, during the Spanish Civil War. No Soviet censor could reasonably object to Cervantes being quoted in this context; yet every intelligent reader knew that this was a *cri de coeur* on behalf of countless Soviet citizens, intellectuals and others alike.

As for the disastrous consequences of the loss of freedom, these are underlined in the memoirs time and time again. Ehrenburg warns his readers, and particularly the younger Soviet writers, that the questions he had raised as far back as the Writers' Congress of 1934 (where he had made a strong plea for creative freedom) are likely to remain still 'topical' for a very long time to come; and he adds that an author is always hounded if he dares to express a thought before it has become a truism. Yet it is not an author's business, he adds, simply to reproduce truisms.

To justify the absence of cultural freedom inside the Soviet Union, the Soviet Establishment continued to claim that the division of the world into two dissimilar and antagonistic blocs applied not only to politics and economics, but to culture as well. Yet this went entirely against everything that Ehrenburg, as a true cosmopolitan, had always stood for. For him, the opposite of literature was trash, the opposite of good taste was vulgarity, and culture remained culture, whatever the political background against which it manifested itself (although he did recognize that, in certain circumstances, politics could be the death of culture). In short, Ehrenburg saw himself not only as a Russian and a Jew but as a European, and he thought of the arts first and foremost in terms of one all-embracing European culture.

He was, of course, acutely aware that a large number of people, both in the Soviet Union and in the West, did not see it that way at all, and in the memoirs he gives some amusing examples of the ignorance, the prejudices and the misunderstandings which regularly bedevilled relations between East and West, ranging from the writer Alexei Tolstoy being mistaken in Paris for Leo Tolstoy ('The news of your death must have been a *canard*!') to a Russian *émigré* who, after spending only a few days in the French capital, was repelled by the 'lechery' of the inhabitants merely because he saw couples kissing in public places. Ehrenburg was also annoyed by the habit, prevalent among certain French intellectuals, of looking on every Russian as a spiritual masochist tormented by his *âme slave*.

It must be said that all this paled into insignificance compared with Stalin's postwar policy of isolating Russia from the outside world, a policy reinforced by his campaign against all those who allegedly kowtowed to the West. Yet even in that restrictive atmosphere, Ehrenburg found opportunities to make his point. When Western propagandists, who were often too lazy or too ill-informed to distinguish between true Russian culture and the abysmal mess Stalin had made of Soviet cultural life, attacked Russia as barbaric, Ehrenburg retorted sharply that world literature was as unthinkable without *War and Peace* as it was unthinkable without *Madame Bovary*. Ostensibly, he was defending the honour of Russia, and the censor could hardly object to that. But it was also his way of restating, in the midst of a Stalin-inspired orgy of chauvinism, that culture was one and indivisible.

Once Stalin had departed from the scene, however, Ehrenburg saw it as his mission to make the new generation understand that theirs was part of a much larger European cultural heritage. Young people had a right to know about the literary and artistic life of Paris, about the Rotonde where he had spent his formative years in the company of poets and artists like Apollinaire, Modigliani and Soutine, as well as about the Poets' Café in Moscow, the haunt of Mayakovsky and his friends in the early years after the Revolution. Those had been years of free experimentation in art and literature, under the enlightened patronage of Lunacharsky. There had been little to eat, but an abundance of creative enthusiasm. It could be cold and dreary outside, but inside, in the theatre, awaited a world of warmth and brilliance, with productions like Hoffmann's *Princess Brambilla* or Carlo Gozzi's *Princess Turandot*. A great deal of exhibitionist nonsense was talked among the Moscow intelligentsia, but some superb verse was written as well. The younger generation, it is true, were now beginning to hear about the Poets' Café from other sources: but only Ehrenburg could tell them about the Rotonde.

This was not a difficult task, although some of the official critics continued to complain about Ehrenburg's unorthodox views on art. But there were other matters which he considered vital, and to include those in his memoirs he had to fight a long and arduous battle with various editors and publishers. At times it was a concealed war of attrition, at others it flared into the open in lurid polemics. Ehrenburg stubbornly stuck to his guns, and eventually he won on most counts. He was not able to include everything he would have liked in the memoirs, but at least all six parts, ending with the death of Stalin, as he had originally planned, did appear in print.

In the early months of 1963, however, while the anti-Ehrenburg campaign was at its height, it looked as if the last two parts might not appear at all. Until then, the difficulties Ehrenburg had encountered had been relatively minor ones. In negotiating with Alexander Tvardovsky over the serial publication of the memoirs in *Novy Mir*, he was dealing with an editor who stood for everything that was progressive in Soviet literature. But if Tvardovsky was an inspired editor, as well as a fine poet and writer, he was treading an extremely difficult and delicate tightrope, and he plainly did not want to make his journal more vulnerable than it already was. Moreover, he did not always share Ehrenburg's views on a number of questions, so that when certain explosive issues cropped up, he insisted on cuts and alterations.[1] One such demand concerned a passage on the Nazi-Soviet Pact. I do not know what Ehrenburg wrote originally, but it can hardly have been more lapidary than the brief agreed version which finally appeared: 'On 1 September [1939] Molotov declared that this Pact served the interests of universal peace. Two days later Hitler started the Second World War.'

Such difficulties were, perhaps, only to be expected. But in 1963, when Yermilov's bitterly hostile article appeared, Ehrenburg's position became precarious, especially after his vigorous protest and Yermilov's arrogant reply, which was clearly written on instructions from above. The effect of all this, both on readers and publishers, was, however, immediate and unmistakable. Admirers sent messages to Ehrenburg exhorting him to stand firm. A sixteen-year-old girl wrote to assure him that if the publishers refused to handle his works, she and her friends would copy them out by hand – and for a time it even seemed as if Ehrenburg might have to avail himself of this touching offer and accept a restricted circulation in *samizdat*! By then, the first section of part five of his memoirs had appeared in *Novy Mir*, but it was suggested that no further instalments should appear. Ehrenburg at once pointed out, notably in a personal letter to Khrushchev,[2] that this would make a disastrous impression both at home and abroad. After much protestation on Ehrenburg's part, the remaining two instalments of part five did finally appear, but his personal position continued to deteriorate.

In the circumstances it seemed doubtful whether part six, which was to cover the most controversial events of the postwar period,

[1]See Appendices 7 and 8.

[2]See Appendix 5.

would ever see the light of day, or whether the publishing house which had brought out one volume of his memoirs would agree to go on with the planned publication of further volumes. The director of that enterprise happened to be a left-over from the Stalin era and acted in predictable fashion, i.e. on the principle that when a man was down it was both prudent and pleasurable to give him an extra kick or two. Consequently, before publishing the next volume, he demanded that Ehrenburg should completely alter certain chapters, even though these had already appeared in serial form in *Novy Mir* and were thus widely known to the public. Fortunately, if the bureaucrats were predictable in their behaviour, Khrushchev was not.

Soon after Khrushchev had fired his final broadside in the anti-Ehrenburg campaign, Ehrenburg wrote to him once more, saying that although he was no longer young, he had no wish to retire and felt that he could still be of value.[1] For about three months, nothing happened. Then, suddenly, Khrushchev asked Ehrenburg to come and see him. They had a long conversation, during which Ehrenburg is said to have spoken with great frankness, and to have told Khrushchev that the kind of control over the arts which was now being introduced would not work unless the authorities were prepared to put people in prison – a practice which Khrushchev surely would not wish to restore. Khrushchev appeared to be in a conciliatory mood. He assured Ehrenburg that he certainly did not want him to stop writing, and said that he should complete part six of his memoirs. Shortly after that, as related earlier, Ehrenburg was invited to address the European Writers' Congress in Leningrad, and it looked as if his troubles were over.

In fact, they were far from over. It is true that the die-hard publisher had had to swallow his Stalinist sentiments and accept Ehrenburg's text as it stood. But part six of the memoirs did not appear in *Novy Mir* until nearly eighteen months later, and then only after endless bargaining over cuts and changes with Tvardovsky, renewed threats of a halt to publication, counter-threats by Ehrenburg to withdraw the manuscript, renewed appeals to Khrushchev, and much acrimonious bickering. At the last minute, *Novy Mir* tried to suppress an entire chapter, which was no more controversial than many of those already published, but which must have frightened someone on the editorial board, perhaps because of

[1]See Appendix 9.

the politically uncertain situation following the downfall of Khrushchev (he had been stripped of all his posts in October 1964, and it was now 1965). After all these hesitations, the last instalment of the memoirs did finally appear in *Novy Mir*. But it took another year for the last volume to be published between separate covers, and a further six months before it was republished as part of Ehrenburg's collected works.

During all that long and exhausting struggle, Ehrenburg had known little peace, but the final result had been worth it. In book form, the memoirs were fuller and more detailed than the serial version, and that in itself was no mean achievement. But there was still one thing that Ehrenburg had not been able to achieve. In one of the very early chapters, describing his initiation into revolutionary activity and how he joined a militant Bolshevik organization while still at school, Ehrenburg mentions a certain Nikolai Ivanovich. He meant, of course, Bukharin. He would no doubt have liked to pay a glowing tribute to the man who had played such a decisive part in his youth, who had so warmly recommended *Julio Jurenito* to Soviet readers, and whom he had last seen in the court room where Bukharin was tried and sentenced to death. In the last resort, all he had managed to wrest from the censors were a few token concessions. But to a public accustomed to reading between the lines, token concessions matter. The question put to Ehrenburg at the Moscow readers' meeting proved that some people knew perfectly well what it was all about; and in that sense, one may say that Ehrenburg rehabilitated Bukharin, something Khrushchev failed to do.[1]

The published editions of the memoirs end with the death of Stalin. But Ehrenburg obviously still had much more to say, and before long he was writing again. Tvardovsky must have breathed a sigh of relief when part six was finished, but he was too good an editor not to express interest in part seven. Ehrenburg advised him to wait until it was completed. In the meantime, as he had often done on previous occasions, he sent a few excerpts to another magazine. This time it was *Nauka i Zhizn* (*Science and Life*) which published the new material, but not before making certain cuts. Ehrenburg was not consulted on the matter, and resented it bitterly. Less than two

---

[1] In the early 1960s, Khrushchev reportedly received Bukharin's widow in the Kremlin, and there was speculation that he might announce Bukharin's rehabilitation, but in the end nothing came of it. (E. de M.)

months later, he was dead.

'I wish I could be certain,' a young reader once wrote to him, 'that by the time I reach your age I shall have seen a quarter of what you have seen and acquired a tenth of your knowledge.' To Soviet young people, thirsting for knowledge and starved of contact with the outside world, Ehrenburg's memoirs did indeed come as a revelation. So the comment of one young reader can perhaps be seen as a fitting epitaph on this difficult and devious but in the end undaunted survivor of the worst years of Soviet rule.

POSTSCRIPT

Ehrenburg died on 31 August 1967, amid the new conformity of the Brezhnev era. He was buried in the Novodevichy Cemetery in Moscow, and thousands turned up for his funeral, including many leading figures of the Soviet literary Establishment. A double line of soldiers with arms linked formed a cordon in front of the cemetery gates; on two occasions, the crowd burst through. Ehrenburg would doubtless have been pleased by the turbulence of this farewell. In many ways, he ended his life as he had begun it: as a rebel.

I met him only once. It was at a Greek National Day reception at the Greek Embassy in Moscow in March 1965, and we exchanged small talk for some minutes. He was amiable yet distant, but what struck me was how frail he looked. His skin was like parchment, and his suit looked too big on him; but his glance was keen, mistrustful and searching (he had never sought contact with foreign correspondents in Moscow, and it was doubtless a little late in the day to start doing so!). By then, the worst of his battles with authority were over. He had weathered the storms of two years earlier, when he had been under attack from both Khrushchev and Ilyichev, but he had also had an exhausting tussle with the Sovietsky Pisatel (Soviet Writer) publishing house over the publication of the last volume of his memoirs, and he gave the impression of being physically and mentally drained by the experience.

At that time, his appearances in Moscow were becoming more and more infrequent. He preferred to spend his time at the *dacha* he had built in the pleasantly-named village of New Jerusalem, outside Moscow, where, like Candide, he cultivated his garden and delighted in growing exotic species (one of those who sent him some rare plants was the dowager Queen Elizabeth of Belgium).

After the French Revolution, when the terror imposed by the revolutionary tribunals had finally subsided, someone asked the Abbé Sieyès what he had done during that dangerous time. The Abbé replied simply: 'I survived.' Looking back on his life, Ehrenburg could say the same; indeed, he was *the* great survivor on the Soviet literary scene, which had so frequently been strewn with victims. In those last years of his life, however, he must sometimes have reflected on the cost. It is true that from the early thirties onwards, he had intellectually accepted the Soviet regime, even if emotionally he detested many of its manifestations; in that respect, he was a kind of Houdini in reverse, whose trick was to climb into his chains rather than out of them. But towards the end, the chains had clearly begun to chafe. He certainly felt, as he said in the final chapter of his memoirs, that, in the modern world, moral considerations lagged well behind the sheer acquisition of knowledge; and on more than one occasion, he emphasized that what Soviet society needed most urgently was a rehabilitation of conscience. All this was a far cry from the heedless exuberance of his bohemian youth, from the brilliant but destructive satire of *Julio Jurenito*, and from that period when he had worshipped the god of Constructivism, exalting the machine over the culture of the past. Now, with the mellowing of old age, he was plainly aware that, despite Khrushchev's denunciation of the Stalin tyranny, there had been no real change of heart among untold thousands of Soviet Party officials and bureaucrats, and that *Homo Sovieticus* was still blind to certain fundamental human aspirations. Hence, this belated call for a rehabilitation of conscience.

A vast project! But it was no doubt partly for this reason that he fought bitterly against the cuts which prudent and puritanical editors and publishers demanded in the memoirs (as if openly to mention Bukharin might capsize the Soviet ship of State!). For this reason, too, he joined in the protests against the Sinyavsky-Daniel trial.[1] And

[1]The Sinyavsky-Daniel trial, in February 1966, marked a watershed in relations between the Soviet authorities and those non-conformist spirits who, by questioning the basic tenets of the regime, or in some cases merely by insisting on the strict observance of what they called 'Leninist legality', came to be known as 'dissidents'. Andrei Sinyavsky, at that time a lecturer on Russian literature, was arrested on 8 September 1965; Yuli Daniel, a poet and translator, was arrested four days later. After the usual preliminary investigation, their case came before a Moscow court in February 1966, an occasion which I attended – or rather, did *not* attend, since foreign correspondents were not admitted to this so-called 'open' trial, and had to stand for long hours in the biting cold outside the courtroom. Both men had published satires on Soviet society under pseudonyms in the West; and both were thus charged with slandering the regime, Sinyavsky being sentenced to seven years' and Daniel to five years' hard labour. What the authorities had surely not foreseen was the great volume of protest to which this verdict gave rise, including a letter of 4 April 1966, signed by sixty-two members of the Soviet Writers' Union and addressed to the Praesidium of the Supreme Soviet, of which Ehrenburg was a co-signatory. (E. de M.)

in May 1967, only three months before his death, he showed his disapproval of the sycophantic posturings of the Writers' Union by setting off on a visit to Italy on the very eve of the Soviet Writers' Congress. The significance of this gesture was not lost on his old adversary, Mikhail Sholokhov, who told the Congress with heavy-handed sarcasm: 'Ilya Grigorievich should not have hurt us all like that!' and went on to blame Ehrenburg for showing a bad example to the young by 'his individualism and contempt for the norms of society'.

Ehrenburg, meanwhile, had made his point. The 'norms of society', as defined by someone like Sholokhov, were precisely those he had been struggling against for most of his creative career. On the younger generation, starved of contacts and avid for enlightenment on the world beyond the Soviet frontiers, he plainly had a major impact, and, I would like to think, a lasting one. Nor should one overlook his influence on the younger generation of Soviet writers, poets and artists. As Evgeny Evtushenko, during one of his poetry-reading tours, remarked to a friend of mine in London: 'Ilya Ehrenburg? He taught us all to survive.'

ERIK DE MAUNY

APPENDICES

APPENDIX 1
Introduction to *Julio Jurenito* by Nikolai Bukharin

Julio Jurenito is first and foremost an interesting book.

One might, of course, comment in 'serious' vein and at length on the author's 'individualistic anarchism', his nihilistic 'hooliganism', his hidden scepticism and so on. It is not difficult to see that the author is not a Communist, that he has no deep belief in the coming order of things, and no special desire to see that order introduced. All this would be perfectly true and correct.

But none of this prevents his book from being a most fascinating satire. Through his own brand of nihilism, and by his highly provocative attitude, he is able to reveal a number of comic and repulsive sides to life under all regimes. But he is particularly successful in those pages describing the ravages of capitalism and war, capitalist culture and its virtues, and the summits of its philosophy and religion. The author is a former Bolshevik, with an inside knowledge of the socialist parties, a man of broad vision, with a deep insight into the Western European way of life, a sharp eye and an acid tongue. He has written a lively, interesting, attractive and clever book.

They say that there can be no arguing about tastes – *de gustibus non est disputandum*. And yet – probably because people have forgotten all about Latin gerunds and gerundives – that is all they do: argue about taste. For our part, we hope the public will show good taste and will enjoy reading this remarkable novel, *Julio Jurenito*.

APPENDIX 2
Letter from Ilya Ehrenburg to Stalin on the Jewish Question in the USSR (1949)

Dear Joseph Vissarionovich,

I have decided to trouble you only because of a question which I cannot resolve myself and which seems to me extremely important.

Comrade Mints and Comrade Marinin today showed me the text of a letter to the editor of *Pravda* and suggested that I should sign it. I consider it my duty to share my doubts with you and to ask your advice.

It seems to me that the only radical solution to the Jewish Question in our socialist State is full assimilation, and that those of Jewish origin should merge with the peoples among whom they live. I fear that a collective statement by a number of people active in Soviet cultural life, whose only common link is their origin, may strengthen nationalistic tendencies. The text of the letter speaks of a 'Jewish people', and this may encourage nationalists and others who have not yet understood that there is no such thing as a Jewish nation.

I am particularly worried about the influence such a 'letter to the editor' may have on the broadening and strengthening of the world movement for peace. Whenever, in various commissions, and at press conferences, the question has been raised as to why there are no Jewish schools or newspapers in the Soviet Union, I have invariably replied that after the war there no longer remained any breeding-ground for the former 'Pales of Jewish Settlement', and that the new generation of Soviet citizens of Jewish descent had no wish to set themselves apart from the peoples among whom they live. The publication of this letter, signed by scientists, writers and composers, who speak of a so-called Soviet Jewish community, may fan the repellent anti-Soviet propaganda which is at present being spread by the Zionists, Bundists and other enemies of our Motherland.

In the eyes of French, Italian, English and other progressive forces, the term 'Jew' has no meaning as a representative of a nationality, but only a religious significance, and slanderers may use this 'letter to the editor' for their own base designs.

I am convinced that it is essential to fight energetically against all attempts to revive Jewish nationalism, which inevitably leads to betrayal. It seems to me that, for this, what is essential is to have, on one hand, explanatory articles (including some by people of Jewish origin), and on the other, an explanation by *Pravda* itself, expressing what is already so well-formulated in the text of the letter: i.e., that the overwhelming majority of Jewish-born workers are deeply devoted to the Soviet Motherland and to Russian culture. Such articles, it seems to me, would be a powerful deterrent to foreign slanderers, and would provide sound arguments for our friends who are fighting for peace.

You will understand, dear Joseph Vissarionovich, that I cannot resolve these questions by myself, and that is why I have been so bold as to write to you. The letter in question represents an important political step, and therefore I decided to ask you to designate someone to inform me of your opinion on the desirability of my signing such a document. If leading comrades convey to me that the publication of this document and my signature to it may be helpful in the defence of the Motherland, and for the Peace Movement, I shall at once sign it.

With deep respect,
Ilya Ehrenburg

APPENDIX 3

Letter from Ilya Ehrenburg to Alexei Adzhubei (Khrushchev's son-in-law, and at the time of this letter, editor of *Izvestia*)

Moscow, 18 March 1958

Dear Alexei Ivanovich,

I am writing to request that, with the help of your staff, you check the justification for the expulsion from the Komsomol of a young girl student of the Moscow Institute of Literature, G. A. Arbuzova.

I saw this girl for the first time yesterday, and what she told me seemed to me sufficiently important for me to write to you in person.

Among the main charges made against Arbuzova are the following two:

1. Eighteen months ago, Arbuzova edited a wall newspaper devoted to a critique of the Picasso Exhibition. Included in it were both positive and negative judgements on the works of this artist.

2. Arbuzova spoke with approval of my article, 'The Lessons of Stendhal', after it appeared in the review *Foreign Literature*.

I was one of the organizers of the Picasso Exhibition, and am thus one of those responsible for the so-called 'Arbuzova affair'. I realize that there can be widely differing opinions of my article, 'The Lessons of Stendhal', but none that I can see of a criminal nature. This article is included in a collection of my essays which the Sovietsky Pisatel publishing house is now bringing out. So you can understand, dear Alexei Ivanovich, in what a difficult moral situation I have been placed by the decision of the Komsomol Committee of the Literary Institute.

I know that your newspaper frequently talks of the need for an understanding approach to our young people, and I hope that, if members of your staff, after due inquiry, establish that Arbuzova was indeed expelled from the Komsomol for the reasons I have mentioned above, then you will find a means of coming to her defence.

With sincere respect,
Ilya Ehrenburg

APPENDIX 4

Extract from a letter from Ilya Ehrenburg to V. S. Lebedyev (literary adviser to Khrushchev)

Moscow, 20 January 1961

Dear Vladimir Semyonovich,

I have decided I must trouble you with the following question. In the February issue of the review *Novy Mir* there appears the concluding section to the second part of my book *People, Years, Life*. One chapter in this second part has run into difficulties. It concerns Pasternak. I consider him a major lyric poet, and in my reminiscences of the early years of the Revolution, I have written about him as a lyric poet. It seems to me that since a Commission was only recently set up to take care of Pasternak's literary legacy, a Commission of which I am a member, it is now up to us to publish a selection of his poems. After all that has happened concerning *Dr Zhivago*, a new edition of his poems will be more readily understandable to the reader who has read my chapter devoted to Pasternak as a poet. I do not like his novel *Dr Zhivago*, and have written to this effect. I have also described how this novel has been exploited in the West in the interests of the 'Cold War'. The publication of the above-mentioned chapter would, in my opinion, be politically expedient, rather than a 'transgression'. This viewpoint is also shared by A. T. Tvardovsky and the entire editorial board of *Novy Mir*. However, the editorial board is not itself able to surmount the difficulty which has arisen, and I have therefore decided to ask you, if you consider it feasible, to ask Nikita Sergeyevich Khrushchev for his opinion . . .

Yours respectfully,
Ilya Ehrenburg

APPENDIX 5
Letter from Ilya Ehrenburg to N. S. Khrushchev

Moscow, 13 February 1963

Dear Nikita Sergeyevich!

I am troubling you only because the question I am concerned with is not of a literary but a political nature, and demands a firm decision, but Leonid Fyodorovich Ilyichev, to whom I telephoned, was not able to see me.

The editor of *Novy Mir*, A. T. Tvardovsky, has informed me that he has been requested to drop from the February issue of the review the continuation of part five of my memoirs. When the preceding parts were being published, Glavlit and other organs informed the review that certain cuts and changes must be made. I met most of their demands and the memoirs continued to appear. But on this occasion, the instruction that a series of chapters must be removed from the February issue was not accompanied by any proposals for corrections or changes in the text.

I am addressing myself to you, Nikita Sergeyevich, not as an author struggling to get his work into print, but as a Soviet citizen who is worried about the possible political repercussions of the decision conveyed to me by A. T. Tvardovsky. I would not be troubling you but for the fact that the first instalment of part five appeared in the January issue of *Novy Mir*, with the words: 'To be continued'. But in our literary reviews, there has never been a single instance in which a work already in process of publication was broken off with the phrase: 'To be continued'.

I fear that this will not only surprise the readers, but will be used by anti-Soviet circles abroad, all the more since translations of my memoirs have appeared in many foreign countries. This places me, as a public figure, in a false situation.

In my view, if *Novy Mir* states in its February number that the publication of *People, Years, Life* will be continued in such-and-such a later issue, that may prevent the development of a regular anti-Soviet campaign. I am sure you will understand the motives which guide me.

With deep respect,
Ilya Ehrenburg

APPENDIX 6

Letter from Ilya Ehrenburg to L. F. Ilyichev,
Party Secretary for Cultural Affairs

Moscow, 8 September 1963

Dear Leonid Fyodorovich,

I am writing to you for the following reason. The third and fourth parts of my memoirs, *People, Years, Life* were due to appear last year as a separate volume from the publishers Sovietsky Pisatel, and the proofs had already been passed by Glavlit. At the beginning of August this year, the publishers proposed that I should make a major revision of these two parts, to meet certain criticisms.

During my meeting with N. S. Khrushchev, I told him about this, and added that, in my opinion, to revise a book which has already been published in a monthly journal, and in separate editions in a number of foreign countries, was not only unacceptable to me personally, but also politically harmful. Nikita Sergeyevich agreed with me. Subsequently, Comrade Lesyuchevsky sent me a letter reaffirming his earlier proposal. I sent Comrade Lesyuchevsky's letter to Comrade Khrushchev's Secretariat, but I fully understand that N. S. Khrushchev cannot concern himself with the publication of this or that particular volume. I hope that you can help me to resolve this question, which is important to me because I am now finishing the sixth and final part, about which I spoke with N. S. Khrushchev.

I have one further request. The second volume of my collected works has been submitted by Goslitizdat to Glavlit, but so far the latter has not yet replied.

Many thanks in advance. I have written rather than telephoned so as not to take up your time.

Sincerely yours,
Ilya Ehrenburg.

APPENDIX 7

Letter from A. T. Tvardovsky, editor of *Novy Mir*,
to Ilya Ehrenburg

Moscow, 24 June 1964

Dear Ilya Grigorievich,

I have once more read through – this time in proof form – part six of your memoirs.

As editor, I find I will have to delete from the text certain passages which we have already discussed at length, 'bargained over', and dealt with in correspondence. This is my final decision, and I am obliged to inform you that, unless these cuts are made, I cannot pass the proof for publication.

1. Your explanation as to why the chapter on Fadeyev is missing, which has placed our editorial board in a curious and equivocal position, about which I have already written to you (Chap. 13, page 5, the entire paragraph);

2. Your phrase 'I *naïvely* sought a defence' – this concerns your letter to the Central Committee (page 73, second half of proof);

3. The penultimate paragraph of Chap. 6, concerning the coming generation, which seems to me an attack on the all-round development of the individual under Communism;

4. The inclusion of the renegade Fast among the names of the most celebrated writers who have joined in the struggle for peace (Chap. 16, page 21);

5. The reference to a certain 'unidentifiable' Nikolai Ivanovich (i.e. Bukharin).

Please don't fail to let me know what you want to do about these points.

Respectfully,

A. Tvardovsky.

APPENDIX 8

Letter from Ilya Ehrenburg to A. T. Tvardovsky
(dictated by telephone)

Moscow, 25 June 1964

Dear Alexander Trifonovich,

I would be glad if you could let me know in what form you would find a reminiscence of Fadeyev acceptable. You cannot compel the reader to forget what I have already written and published in *Novy Mir*, with a promise of further recollections of Fadeyev to follow.

The word 'naïvely' on page 73 may be deleted.

In the penultimate paragraph of Chap. 6, so that the reference to the coming generation should not seem like an attack, as you have described it, I suggest an alternative reading: 'I do not want to think that people in the future will not possess the same cultivated sensibilities as distinguish any of the heroes of Shakespeare, Goethe or Leo Tolstoy from the copulation of apes.'

The name of Fast may be deleted.

I cannot agree that there should be no recalling of Nikolai Ivanovich, but if this very common name and patronymic strike you as politically inadmissible, then I am prepared to add those of Semyon Borisovich and Grigory Mikhailovich.

I am somewhat pained by the tone of your letter, which is at variance with the tone of our conversation in your office. I attribute this to your feeling out of sorts, and not to your personal attitude towards me.

Respectfully yours,
I. Ehrenburg

APPENDIX 9
Letter from Ilya Ehrenburg to N. S. Khrushchev

Moscow, 14 August 1964

Dear Nikita Sergeyevich!

A year ago you agreed to see me. I remember our conversation with a feeling of sincere gratitude. If I am troubling you once again, it is only because my present circumstances have become complicated and extremely unpleasant. We were able to talk together as man to man, and nobody else was present during our conversation. I trust that the present letter will be passed on to you.

I came away from our last meeting feeling encouraged. When we last talked together, we discussed the need for me to finish my volume of memoirs. This I have now done. A. T. Tvardovsky and the editorial board of *Novy Mir*, after receiving the manuscript, asked me to make a few changes, which I duly did. The editorial board announced publicly that publication would be completed in 1964.

The opening section of the sixth and final part of the memoirs was due to appear in the July issue of the review. Recently, the editorial board told me they had been obliged to omit part six, on instructions from above, and they were powerless to resolve the question. This part of my book covers the period from the end of the war to the end of 1953.

I consider (and so does the editorial board of *Novy Mir*) that in describing this period, I maintained the correct political proportions. At the end of the book, I write about the period following the death of Stalin, when our country entered a new phase. The book ends with some reflections on those very questions which we touched upon during our conversation. There are no political sensations in the book, nor anything that might be exploited by our adversaries.

I spent altogether five years labouring over these memoirs. So for me, they add up to a very important work. You will, I am sure, understand how painful it is for a writer, especially for one who is no longer young, to see his work suddenly cut short. There is the further point that the readers, both in our country and abroad, will not fail to realize that publication of the final section of the work has been forbidden. Personally, Nikita Sergeyevich, I find all this distressing. For more than thirty years, I regularly worked for the Soviet Press. This year is the first in the whole of that time during which not one newspaper has approached me with a request for any kind of article. Let me give just one minor example. A group of Moscow physics students asked me to talk to them about my meetings with Joliot-Curie and Einstein. At the last moment, the meeting was called off. I have even found it difficult to arrange meetings with my constituents. I am willing and able to continue my work as a writer and as a journalist, and to take part in the struggle for peace. But the banning of my memoirs sets me back to just where I was before our meeting.

We are neither of us any longer young, and I am sure that you will understand me, and issue an instruction authorizing the review to publish this work.

Respectfully,
Ilya Ehrenburg

APPENDIX 10

Fragmentary record of I. G. Ehrenburg's appearance at a readers' meeting at which his memoirs, *People, Years, Life*, were discussed[1]

On 9 April 1966, at Moscow District Library No. 66, there was a discussion of I. G. Ehrenburg's book *People, Years, Life*. In accordance with the agenda of the meeting, the readers spoke first, expressed their opinion of the book, and posed a number of questions, both verbally and in writing, after which Ehrenburg was given the floor. The following is a brief fragmentary record of his remarks.

I shall not reply to questions that are requests for information, if I may

[1]The above document, which has been described as Ehrenburg's literary testament, is taken from a German version of what took place at the meeting. Unfortunately, it has not been possible to trace the original Russian transcript of proceedings. The German version is somewhat crude and clumsy and contains several ambiguities. For example, the questioner named as Ter-Grigoriev is identified first as a doctor, then later as a general (unless, of course, there were two different people of the same name present). It is nevertheless a key document. Ehrenburg's meeting with his readers took place barely more than a year before his death, and his answers to their questions clearly reveal his sentiments in the final stage of his long career. (E. de M.)

so term them. For example, four questions have been asked concerning my relationship with Evtushenko. What do you expect of me? That I should unmask him? Or that I should fall down on my knees before him, as if before a new Blok on Russian soil? Nor will I answer political questions. As a non-Party man, I can permit myself to refrain from commenting on the Party Congress.

It has been said here that my book was not written for millions of readers, but for a very few, a selected few thousand. Time passes, and books that were written for thousands eventually become books for millions, while books written for millions (I do not mean the number of copies – that is determined, not by the readers, but by the authorities!) simply cease to be literature. Who today, for example, reads Demyan Bedny or Panferov? I am not ambitious and I do not regard it as an honour to be printed in millions of copies. I feel close to Stendhal, who wanted to be read in a hundred years, and he is read and will be read . . .

What is urgently required from us at this moment? *We must rehabilitate our conscience*! And that (since religion has been renounced) can only be achieved by art. Art, however, is not a comprehensively defined term: art is diverse, because people are diverse. One person perceives the world visually, another aurally, and so on . . . Art reaches one person through Picasso, another through Rembrandt, a third through Pushkin and Gogol, a fourth through Beethoven. Some are affected by the usual art forms, others by the unusual, the new . . . The important thing is that it should be genuine art and not its imitation, and one must be able to distinguish genuine art from imitation, as women can tell a natural wave from a permanent wave . . .

A person in whom there is only knowledge but not consciousness (and by consciousness I mean conscience) – that person is not yet a human being, but only a semi-finished product, even though he may be a talented physicist or who knows what. The evil of our world is that it has become a world of such semi-finished products . . . I have a little notebook from 1932 – the shorthand minutes of a Komsomol meeting at the Kuznetstroi (industrial complex), where a discussion took place on the theme of love. The question was asked: Should a Komsomol member, who works on a building site, marry? One young man got up and said: 'Of course he should! I used to waste hours and hours trying to talk the girls round, and now I get home and not a minute is lost . . . How much more time that gives me for work!' That is how it all started! And now we have this world of knowledge without consciousness, this world of semi-finished products who adapt not only their thoughts and social feelings but also their relations with other people to the most recent instruction or directive of such and such a date.

. . . I am accused of having made a hash of the end of my memoirs, which deals with Stalin. It has been asserted that it was my duty to unmask him to the very end, etc. Dr Ter-Grigoriev, who was born in 1931, said in his remarks: 'That is your duty as a man with a world-wide audience, if only because another person with a similarly wide audience has recently indulged in the unworthy exercise of juxtaposing the lawless, anti-democratic acts of our own period with the revolutionary legality of the first period of the Revolution.' I cannot agree. In a letter which I received, and which is circulating in Moscow, I am reproached with having called Stalin intelligent. But how can one regard as stupid a man who decisively outwitted all his, doubtless intelligent, colleagues? It was intelligence of a special kind, with cunning as its main ingredient. It was an amoral kind of intelligence, and that is what I wrote about. I do not think anything would be gained if I were to add a few abusive epithets concerning Stalin. I did what I am capable of doing, within the limits of my own understanding, and drew a psychological portrait with the greatest economy of means. But that is as far as my understanding of the matter goes. I admit this openly, as I have done before. The historical essence, after all, does not lie in Stalin's personality, but in what Togliatti once said: *How could Stalin come to power?* And how did he manage to remain in power for so many years? I do not understand that either. Millions believed in him without reservation, and went to their deaths with his name on their lips. How could that happen? I see a cock in a chalk circle or a rabbit facing the jaws of a giant snake – and I do not understand. References to the lack of culture and the backwardness of our people are not the answer. I find such explanations unconvincing. After all, we have seen analogies in another country, where these reasons did not exist. I long to have an answer to this *cardinal question*, the most important question of all if a repetition of a similar horror is to be avoided in the future. And I invite anyone who *does* have the answer to ring me up, and to come and see me, and then, *I* will not be the one to do the talking, but my visitor – and I will listen for hours on end if necessary.

I will now answer some of the questions that have been asked:

1) Has not the time come to name a certain friend in the Bolshevik underground organization in Moscow who led me into revolution-ary action?
2) Similarly, a question about a certain friend who, during our reunion in Vienna, served as the reason for my leaving the Party.

As to the first question: You insult me! I have never considered that the time was not opportune to mention one of my best friends, Nikolai Ivanovich Bukharin, by name. However, I do not decide what may be printed: I only write. It was not I who decided on certain omissions, but the publishing houses, and not only during the editing stage, but even while the type was being set! This was reflected particularly in the fifth part of my memoirs. It was printed at a time when my book did not please N. S. Khrushchev, and its fate was decided by people for whom

Khrushchev's every word was law, just as now it is the law for them to blacken Khrushchev's name.

As to the second question: Here matters are just the other way round. My publishers would be only too happy if I were to identify this person by name. However, I consider it tactless, and even immoral, to do so, since my remarks concerning that incident in Vienna could be interpreted as assertions prompted by the subsequent activities of this individual, and the fate that befell him.

. . . Will there be another edition of my memoirs? I have been promised that there might be one as early as this year, as part of volumes eight and nine of my collected works. And even without a preface! . . . However, I have become superstitious, and I am touching wood that nothing will go wrong.

Will it be possible to reinstate the cuts made in earlier editions, and if so, which ones? I do not know. I have added some material: 1) On Fadeyev (it has not been printed); 2) On Tynyanov (I realize that one must give more than I have given).

Now, concerning the articles written during the war: I do not regret them, nor do I underestimate them (which is what I have been accused of by the comrade here who saw active service throughout the war). This also goes for the article 'Kill the German!' The attack on that article was an attempt to play a political game with the Germans, and it was decided that I should be sacrificed, as a person whom they particularly hated. That this was both an unjustifiable and unjustified game very soon became clear: the sacrifice of Ehrenburg did not make the Fascist actions against the people of the Soviet Union any less cruel or less bestial.

General Ter-Grigoriev has quoted the biblical legend of the forty years during which the Jews wandered in the desert. But in my opinion he has not interpreted it correctly. The point is not that Moses, over a period of forty years, wanted to change the slave mentality of his people, but that forty years were required for those people who remembered the state of slavery to physically die out. That is how I understand the legend. And I think that the legacy of our terrible years can only be wiped out when the people who were educated by those years physically disappear from our society. I am not saying this only of people of my own age, but also of those who are some twenty years younger than myself. My hope rests with the young people who did not undergo such an education. I love them very much. Of course, they also do stupid things, but they have the spirit of criticism, the spirit of independent thought. They are not simply obedient to directives, but are seeking for themselves. And they will find! They will find, but only if they succeed in rehabilitating their conscience . . . And if we fail to restore conscience to its proper place in our lives, if we fail to rehabilitate conscience, then all this nonsense about the moon and the sputniks will be seen as a foolish circus trick in the final phase of the history of mankind.

APPENDIX 11

To the Secretariat of the Central Committee of the Communist Party of the Soviet Union

(?1966)

During the past year, *Literary Gazette* and various other literary reviews have been attacking me with accusations which can in no way be described as comradely criticism. Using quotations torn out of context, the critics accuse me of writing with ulterior political motives (see article by 'Literator' in *Literary Gazette*), of idealizing bourgeois society (see article by Comrade Starikov in the same review), and of adopting a position close to that of the Yugoslav and Polish revisionists (see article by Comrade Shcherbina in the review *Moskva*). Since *Literary Gazette* and the others are controlled by comrades who all follow a particular line in common and fully share the viewpoint of the writers of the articles directed against me, I am deprived of the possibility of replying to the above-mentioned charges. So tens of millions of readers are being given a distorted picture of my writings and of my political and moral position. I must also point out that certain of my articles quoted by the critics I gave to the publishers only after they had been shown to comrades of the Central Committee of the CPSU. Thus, for example, before publishing the article 'A Necessary Explanation', I asked leading comrades whether they considered its publication opportune and politically useful.

These criticisms have grown steadily sharper and, in my view, more and more inadmissible. In the review *Neva*, Comrade Arkhipov accuses me of practising a 'mystification' on Soviet readers, i.e. of a conscious intention to lead them astray. He bases his charge of 'mystifying' the readers on the fact that I have described how, in his last years, Babel was working on a novel, and that his manuscript has disappeared. In support of this, Comrade Arkhipov says that manuscripts by Yasensky and Vasiliev *have* been found. I do not know the circumstances in which Beria's people either preserved or destroyed manuscripts, but as for Babel working on a novel, I heard this more than once from his own lips. And I had further confirmation of it from those near to him. I have allowed myself to cite just one instance from Arkhipov's article, but both there and in a whole series of other articles, equally unfounded accusations occur. I have no right to waste the time of the Secretariat of the Central Committee, and I will refrain from giving further examples. Of course, I could appeal to the People's Court to defend me from these slanders. But the choice of such a course might be exploited by our enemies, so naturally I am not making any approach to the organs of Soviet justice.

Only one course remains open to me – to ask the Secretariat of the Central

Committee of the CPSU whether in such circumstances I can continue my literary work and pursue my public activities, when I am defamed not only as an artist but as a citizen.

BIBLIOGRAPHY

Works by Ilya Ehrenburg in Russian

Povest o Zhizni Nekoi Nadenki i o Veshchikh Znameniyakh Yavlenikh Yei. Portret Avtora i Illyustratsii Raboti Diego M. Rivera, (*The Tale of a Certain Nadenka and of the Prophetic Signs Revealed to her. With a Portrait of the Author and Illustrations by Diego M. Rivera*), Paris, 1916.

Molitva o Rossii, (*A Prayer for Russia*), Moscow, 1918.

Neobychainye pokhozhdeniya Khulio Khurenito i ego uchenikov – Mosye Delay, Karla Shmidta, Mistera Kulya, Aleksei Tishina, Erkolay Bambukhi, Ilyi Erenburga i negra Ayshi – v dni mira, voini i revolutsii, v Parizhe, v Meksike, v Rime, v Senegale, v Kineshme, v Moskve i v drugikh mestakh, a takzhe razlichnye suzhdeniya Uchitelya o trubkakh, o smerti, o lyubvi, o svobode, ob igre v shakhmati, o yevreiskom plemeni, o konstruktsii i o mnogom inom. (*The Extraordinary Adventures of Julio Jurenito and his disciples – Monsieur Delhaie, Karl Schmidt, Mr Cool, Alexei Tishin, Ercole Bambucci, Ilya Ehrenburg and Aysha the negro – in days of peace, war and revolution, in Paris, Mexico, Rome and Senegal, in Kineshma, Moscow and other places, as well as various reflections by the Master on pipe smoking, death, love, freedom, chess, the tribe of Judah, constructivism and many other matters*). Moscow-Berlin, 1922.

Opustoshayushchaya Lyubov, (*Stikhi*), (*Ravaging Love*, (*Poems*)), 1922.

Zarubezhnye Razdumya, (*Foreign Reflections*), Moscow, 1922.

A Vse-taki Ona Vertitsya, (*And Yet the World Goes Round*), Moscow-Berlin, 1922.

Zolotoe Serdtse: Misteriya. Veter: Tragediya. (*The Golden Heart: A Mystery. The Wind: A Tragedy*), Moscow-Berlin, 1922.

Portreti Russkikh Poetov, (*Portraits of Russian Poets*), Berlin, 1922.

Trest D.E. Istoriya Gibeli Evropi, (*The D.E. Trust. The Story of the Destruction of Europe*), Kharkov, 1923.

Portreti Sovremennikh Poetov, (*Portraits of Contemporary Poets*), Moscow, 1923.

Zhizn i Gibel Nikolaiya Kurbova. Roman, (*The Life and Downfall of Nikolai Kurbov. A Novel*), Berlin, 1923.

Zverinoe Teplo, (*Feral Warmth*), Moscow-Berlin, 1923.

Lik Voini, (*The Face of War*), Moscow, 1924.

Bubnovy Valet. Rasskazi, (The Jack of Diamonds. Short Stories),
Moscow-Leningrad, 1925.
Trinadtsat Trubok, (Thirteen Pipes), Kharkov, 1925.
Shest Povestey o Legkikh Kontsakh, (Six Tales with Happy Endings),
Moscow, 1925.
Lyubov Zhanni Ney. Roman, (The Love of Jeanne Ney. A Novel), Riga,
1925.
Nepravdopodobnaya Istoriya, (An Improbable Story), Berlin, 1925.
Leto 1925 goda, (Summer 1925), Moscow, 1926.
Rvach, (The Go-Getter), Odessa-Moscow, 1927.
V Protochnom Pereulke, (In Potochny Lane), Paris, 1927.
Sbornik Sochinenii v Vosmi Tomakh. (Collected Works in Eight
Volumes), Moscow-Leningrad, 1928.
Bely Ugol, ili Slezy Vertera. Esse, (White Coal, or the Tears of Werther.
An Essay), Leningrad, 1928.
Zagovor Ravnikh. Roman, (Conspiracy of Equals. A Novel), Berlin-Riga,
1928.
Lazik Roitshvanets, (Lazik Roitshvanets), Berlin, 1929.
Desyat L. S. Khronika Nashego Vremeni, (Ten Horse-Power. A Chronicle
of our Time), Berlin, 1929.
Yedini Front, (United Front), Berlin, 1930.
Anglia. Ocherki, (England. Sketches), Moscow, 1931.
Fabrika Snov. Khronika Nashego Vremeni, (The Dream Factory. A
Chronicle of our Time), Berlin, 1931.
Viza Vremeni, (The Visa of Time), Leningrad, 1933.
Moskva Slezam ne Verit, (Moscow Does Not Believe In Tears), Moscow,
1933.
Ispania, (Spain), Paris, 1933.
Den Vtoroi, (The Second Day), Moscow, 1934.
Zatyanuvshayasya Razvyazka. Esse, (A Delayed Solution. Essay),
Moscow, 1934.
Ne Perevodya Dikhaniya, (Without Pausing for Breath), Moscow, 1935.
Khronika Nashikh Dnyei, (Chronicle of Our Days), Moscow, 1935.
Granitsi Nochyu. Sbornik Zhurnalisticheskikh Statyei, (The Frontiers of
Night. Collected Newspaper Articles), Moscow, 1936.
Kniga dlya Vzroslikh. Roman, (A Book for Grown-Ups), Moscow, 1936.
Vne Peremiriya. Sbornik Rasskazov, (Beyond the Armistice. Collected
Stories), Moscow, 1937.
Ispanski zakal. Fevral-Yul 1937. Korrespondentsi Kotorye Bili
Napechatani v Gazete 'Izvestia', (The Spanish Temperament.
February–July 1937. Dispatches Published in Izvestia), Moscow, 1938.
Chetire Trubki, (Four Pipes), Moscow, 1936.
Vernost. Ispania, Parizh. Stikhi, (Fidelity. Spain, Paris. Poems), Moscow,
1941.

Za Zhizn. Stati i Esse, (To Life. Articles and an Essay), Moscow, 1942.
Ozhestocheniye, (Bitterness), Moscow, 1942.
Voina, (The War), June 1941–April 1942; April 1942–March 1943; April 1943–March 1944. Three volumes. Moscow, 1942–4.
Svoboda. Poemi, (Freedom. Poems), Moscow, 1943.
Rasskazi Etikh Let, (Stories of Those Years), Moscow, 1944.
Dorogi Evropi, (The Roads of Europe), Moscow, 1946.
Derevo. Stikhi 1938–1945, (The Village. Poems 1938–1945), Moscow, 1946.
Padenie Parizha, (The Fall of Paris), Moscow, 1947.
Lev na Ploshchadi. Komedia. Za mir, za Demokratiyu! Pyesi, (The Lion on the Square. A Comedy. For Peace and Democracy! Plays), Moscow, 1949.
Burya, (The Storm), Moscow, 1948.
Za Mir, (For Peace), Moscow, 1950.
Nadezhda Mira, (The Hope of Peace), Moscow, 1950.
Za Mir, (For Peace), Moscow, 1952.
Sochineniya v Pyati Tomakh: 1) Padenie Parizha; 2) Burya; 3) Devyaty Val; 4) Povesti, Rasskazi i Stikhotvoreniya; 5) Ocherki i Stati, (Selected Works in Five Volumes: 1) The Fall of Paris; 2) The Storm; 3) The Ninth Wave; 4) Tales, Short Stories and Poems; 5) Sketches and Articles), Moscow, 1952–4.
Lyudi Khotyat Zhit, (People Want to Live), Moscow, 1953.
Ottepel, (The Thaw), Moscow, 1954.
Soviest Narodov. Esse i Rechi, (The Conscience of Peoples. Essays and Speeches), Moscow, 1956.
Frantsuzskii Tetradi. Zametki i Perevodi, (French Notebooks. Notes and Translations), Moscow, 1958.
Frédéric Joliot Curie, (Frédéric Joliot Curie), Moscow, 1958.
Perechitivaya Chekhova, (On Re-reading Chekhov), Moscow, 1960.
Putevye Zapisi. Yaponskie Zametki. Razmyshlenya v Gretsii. Indiiskie Vpetchatlenya, (Travel Notes. Japanese Jottings. Reflections in Greece. Indian Impressions), Moscow, 1960.
Lyudi, Godi, Zhizn, (People, Years, Life), Moscow, 1961.
Ya Zhivu. Stikhi, (I Live. Poems), Tel Aviv, 1971.
Letopis Muzhestva. Publitsisticheskie Stati Voennikh Let, (Annals of Courage. Newspaper Articles of the War Years), Moscow, 1974.
V Odnoi Gazete. Reportazhi i Stati 1941–1945 goda. (In One Newspaper. Dispatches and Articles 1941–1945), Moscow, 1979.

Works by Ilya Ehrenburg in English Translation

The Love of Jeanne Ney, trans. Helen Chrouschoff Matheson, Peter Davies, London, 1929.

A Street in Moscow, trans. Sonya Volochova, Grayson & Grayson, London, 1933.

Out of Chaos, trans. Alexander Bakshy, H. Holt & Co, New York, 1934.

A Soviet Writer Looks at Vienna, trans. Ivor Montague, Martin Lawrence, London, 1934.

Russia at War, trans. Gerard Shelley, Hamish Hamilton, London, 1943.

The Fall of Paris, trans. Gerard Shelley, Hutchinson & Co. London, 1945.

The Russians Reply to Lady Gibb, Ilya Ehrenburg and his readers, *Soviet War News*, London, 1945.

We Come as Judges, Soviet War News, London, 1945.

The Storm, trans. Eric Hartley and Tatiana Shebunina, Hutchinson International Authors, London, 1949.

Peace is Everybody's Business, Two Speeches in London, July 1950, *Soviet News*, London, 1950.

The Ninth Wave, trans. Tatiana Shebunina and Joseph Castle, Lawrence & Wishart, London, 1955.

The Thaw, trans. Manya Harari, Harvill, London, 1955.

Julio Jurenito, trans. Anna Bostock and Yvonne Kapp, MacGibbon & Kee, London, 1961.

People and Life. Memoirs of 1891–1917, trans. Anna Bostock and Yvonne Kapp, MacGibbon & Kee, London, 1961.
(NB: This is the first volume of Ehrenburg's six-part memoirs, *People, Years, Life*. The general title given to the memoirs in English is slightly different: *Men, Years – Life*. To avoid confusion, I have in each case cited the original Russian title.)

The Spring, trans. Humphrey Higgins, MacGibbon & Kee, London, 1961.

Chekhov, Stendhal and Other Essays, trans. Anna Bostock and Yvonne Kapp, MacGibbon & Kee, London, 1962.

First Years of Revolution, (vol. II of *People, Years, Life*), MacGibbon & Kee, London, 1962.

Truce. 1921–1933, (vol. III of *People, Years, Life*), trans. Tatiana Shebunina, MacGibbon & Kee, London, 1963.

Eve of War. 1933–1941, (vol. IV of *People, Years, Life*), MacGibbon & Kee, London, 1963.

The War. 1941–1945, (vol. V of *People, Years, Life*), MacGibbon & Kee, London, 1964.

The Stormy Life of Lazik Roitshvantz, trans. Alec Brown, Elek Books, London, 1965.

Post-War Years. 1945–1954, (vol. VI of *People, Years, Life*), trans. Tatiana Shebunina and Yvonne Kapp, MacGibbon & Kee, London, 1966.

The Life of the Automobile, trans. Joachim Neugroschel, Urizen Books, New York, 1976.

Miscellaneous

Veshch, (*Object*), ed. E. Lisitsky and I. Ehrenburg, Berlin, 1922.
Muy i Oni, (*Us and Them*), D. Savich and I. Ehrenburg, France, 1931.
Ilya Ehrenburg. Kritikobiograficheskii Ocherk, (*Ilya Ehrenburg. A Critical Biography*), T. Trifonov, Moscow, 1952.
Vospominania ob Ilye Ehrenburge: Sbornik, (*Reminiscences of Ilya Ehrenburg*), comp. G. Belaya and L. Lazarev, Moscow, 1975.
Die satirischen Werke von Ilya Ehrenburg, Rahel-Roni Hammermann, Vienna, 1978.
Aesthetische Theorie und Künstlerische Praxis bei Ilya Ehrenburg 1921–32. Studien zum Verhältnis von Kunst und Revolution, Holger Siegel, Tübingen, 1979.
Chornaya Kniga, (*The Black Book*), ed. Vasili Grossman, Jerusalem, 1980.

A NOTE ON TRANSLITERATION

In transliterating Russian names and words, I have tried to steer a middle course between the scholarly systems used by the British Academy and the American Library of Congress, with their plethora of diacritical markings, and a simplified system which is admittedly inconsistent. For example, I have generally avoided rendering the Russian soft sign ('ь') to indicate palatalized consonants except where absolutely necessary, and I have commonly used 'y' and 'ye' rather than 'ii' or 'ie' for masculine adjectival endings. But I have preferred to keep 'ego' for genitive endings, even although the 'g' is pronounced 'v'. In the case of some common Christian names, I have stuck to the English form, e.g. Alexander rather than Aleksandr.

(E. de M.)

INDEX

abstract art, 29, 43
Adzhubei, Alexei, letter to, 7, 283
Akhmatova, Anna, 218
Aksakov, Sergei Timofeyevich,
132
Albania, 173
Alexandrov, Georgi Fyodorovich,
218; attack on Ehrenburg,
212–13
Alicante, 173
Alliluyeva, Svetlana, 226
Alsace, 150
America: Ehrenburg's prejudice
against, 68, 114, 219, 224;
praised in *And Yet the World
Goes Round*, 84; first visit to
(1945), 219–23; and talk of
possible war with Russia, 222;
Ehrenburg's propaganda against,
223–4
Amsterdam, 30
anarchists, 156–7, 159–61
And Yet the World Goes Round
(Ehrenburg), 83–6, 88
anti-cosmopolitanism, 6, 12, 232,
238, 239, 270, 272. *See also*
anti-Semitism
anti-Semitism, 6, 7, 12, 121, 123,
126, 128, 185, 190, 220,
226–40, 269–70
Antonov-Ovseyenko, Vladimir
Alexeyevich, 161, 163
Apollinaire, Guillaume, 29, 273
appeasement, 169–70, 174–8, 187
Aragon, Louis, 234, 243
Arbuzova, G. A., 283
art, modern: Ehrenburg's study of,

83–6, 88–9; Communist
disapproval of, 88, 99, 101;
campaign against, 139, 144,
153, 200, 218, 249, 253, 259,
262; changing attitude to, 266–9
Artsybashev, Mikhail Petrovich,
100
Association of American
Newspaper Editors, 219–20
Association of Foreign Students, 10
atomic bomb, 61, 224, 245
Attlee, Clement, 10
'Au-dessus de la Mêlée'
(Ehrenburg), 72
Austin, Paul, 28, 143
Austria, 150

Babel, Isaac Emmanuilovich,
152–3, 166, 292
Babeuf, Gracchus, 10
Babi Yar, 224
Bakunin, Mikhail, 156, 160, 161
Balmont, Konstantin Dmitrievich,
72, 85
Barcelona, 159, 160, 163, 169,
173
Barman, Thomas, 216
Bartenstein, 207
Bata, Tomas, 131
Baudouin, Paul, 185
Bedny, Demyan, 289
Belgium, 2, 52, 54, 173
Benedictine Order, 4, 26, 28
Bergelson, David, execution of,
232, 236, 237, 239, 240
Bergery, Gaston, 170
Beria, Lavrenti Pavlovich, 226,
236

300

INDEX